The Law and Teacher Employment

Gloria Jean Thomas
University of North Dakota, Grand Forks, North Dakota

David J. Sperry
University of Utah, Salt Lake City, Utah

F. Del Wasden
Brigham Young University, Provo, Utah

West Publishing Company
St. Paul New York Los Angeles San Francisco

Copyeditor Joan Torkildson
Test & Cover Design Rokusek Design
Compositor Parkwood Composition

Printed in the United States of America
98 97 96 95 94 93 92 91 8 7 6 5 4 3 2 1 0
Library of Congress Cataloging-in-Publication Data

Thomas. Gloria Jean.
The law and teacher employment / Gloria Jean Thomas, David J. Sperry, F. Del Wasden.
p. cm.
Includes index.
ISBN 0-314-82749-8
1. Teachers—Legal status, laws, etc.—United States. I. Sperry, David J., 1944–
II. Del Wasden, F. III. Title.
KF4175.T48 1991
344.73′ 078—dc20
[347.30478]

91.8466
CIP

Contents

Preface

This text was prepared as a primer for those interested in the basic legal principles governing teacher-employer relations in American public education. As such, the book is designed to be used as a text in teacher preparation programs, as an in-service resource for new school board members, and as a reference manual for those involved in the legal dimensions of the public schools, including teachers, administrators, teacher union/association leaders, school board members, and attorneys representing school districts.

The material addresses the major issues in teacher-employer relations and is organized and presented in ten chapters. Each chapter is developed in the following manner:

1. an introduction to the historical background of the legal issues within the chapter topic
2. a list of legal principles
3. a discussion of the case law governing decisions about each principle
4. a summary of the issue, including trends in the development of the topic
5. questions relating to the topic with responses based on the case law discussion

Unique to the format of this book is the list of key legal principles located near the beginning of each chapter. These principle statements are outlined and appear in a box. Each principle is subsequently examined and expanded upon in the chapter discussion. These summarized statements of the law will provide a concise overview of the law to individuals encountering school law for the first time and will help experienced educators, school board members, and attorneys refresh their memory of the law. In this sense, the book serves as a multiple-use reference manual. The questions and responses section adds to the versatility of the book in providing a good review for the classroom student of concepts discussed in the individual chapters as well as serving as a reference section for individuals seeking a brief summary or responses to commonly asked questions.

The authors would like to acknowledge the following individuals who reviewed the manuscript while it was being prepared.

Professor Joseph C. Beckham
College of Education
Florida State University

Frederick K. Grittner
Supreme Court Administrator and Clerk of the Appellate Courts
Minnesota Supreme Court

Professor Clifford Hooker
Educational Policy and Administration
University of Minnesota

Dr. Burton M. Nygren
Superintendent of Schools
Mounds View Public Schools
St. Paul, Minnesota

Carol O'Toole
Attorney At Law
Minneapolis, Minnesota

Wendy Rossi
Language Arts Resource Teacher
St. Paul Public Schools

Dean John Sikula
Graduate School of Education
California State University

We appreciate the contributions they made to the development of this book.

1 Contracts

Contracts between teachers and their employers have long been used to define the legal rights and responsibilities of both parties. The first contracts between village schoolmasters or schoolmarms and town councils may have been oral agreements, but written employment contracts were soon preferred. Whether they were written or oral, early contractual provisions often consisted of long lists of expected duties for the teacher in return for a salary (sometimes just room and board) from the school board. A typical contract at the turn of the century might consist of the following provisions for the teacher, while the board's responsibilities would be to enforce these duties and then pay the teacher:

> I promise to take a vital interest in all phases of Sunday-school work, donating of my time, service, and money without stint for the benefit and uplift of the community.
>
> I promise to abstain from dancing, immodest dressing, and any other conduct unbecoming a teacher and a lady.
>
> I promise not to go out with any young men except insofar as it may be necessary to stimulate Sunday-school work.
>
> I promise not to fall in love, to become engaged or secretly married.
>
> I promise to remain in the dormitory or on the school grounds when not actively engaged in school or church work elsewhere.
>
> I promise not to encourage or tolerate the least familiarity on the part of any of my boy pupils (North Carolina, 1930).

A balance between teacher and board duties was not attained until after World War II. The struggle by teachers to reduce the hold the board had over their private as well as professional lives resulted in tenure laws, the growth of teachers' associations, and the demand for collective bargaining of teaching contracts. Instead of the individual teacher having to negotiate a contract with the school board, experienced professional negotiators in many districts now meet with representatives of the school board to write a contract that delineates rights as well as responsibilities of both parties. Individual teacher contracts are written that comply with the provisions of the master contract with the teachers' association.

The courts have been involved in interpreting teachers' contracts from the earliest history of schools, although the caseload has increased as the formality and scope of contracts have increased. General contract law has been well defined by statute and by the courts, and its legal applications are similar throughout all jurisdictions. Guidelines from general contract law apply to teachers' contracts, and teachers and school boards must negotiate contracts that comply with the established principles of contract law.

Legal Principles

Principle I *Contractual Relationship*

The relationship of a public schoolteacher with an employing school board is created by contract and governed by general principles of contract law as well as by statutes and case law pertaining to contracts and teacher-employer relations.

Principle II *Power to Contract*

The power to contract with a teacher is vested exclusively in the school board and cannot be delegated to any other body or official.

Principle III *Competent Parties*

Because the making of a valid contract requires competent parties, both the teacher and the employing school board must have the authority to bind themselves to a formal, legal relationship. A teacher and the school board must follow the procedures for creating a binding contract.

Principle IV *Mutual Assent*

Because a contract is designed to protect the interests of both parties, a teaching contract must be based on the mutual assent of the teacher and the school board as to the terms, conditions, and obligations of the contract.

Principle V *Consideration*

A contract requires that the parties agree to give valid and adequate consideration, something of value, in return for a promise or act of value. In a legally enforceable teaching contract, a teacher agrees to perform teaching duties and services in return for salary and benefits from the school board.

Principle VI *Clear Meaning*

A contract must be clear and definite so that neither teacher nor school board must guess at its meaning or intention. Most terms of a teaching contract are expressly written to state the obligations of both parties. However, general policies and regulations as well as state statutes may be incorporated into the contract by implication.

(continued on next page)

Legal Principles (continued)

Principle VII *Legal Subject and Form*

All subject matter of a teaching contract must be lawful, and the contract must be in the form required by law.

Principle VIII *Breach of Contract*

Once a teacher and a school board agree to the terms of a contract, they are obligated to perform the commitments made to each other in the document. Failure to fulfill the obligations is a breach of contract, and the wronged party is usually entitled to recover damages.

Principle IX *Termination of Contract*

The freedom to contract implies the freedom to rescind the contract at any time the parties mutually desire to end their contractual relationship. Termination of a teaching contract may also result from acts of God, illness, death, statutory prohibition, or other occurrences beyond the control of the teacher or the school board.

Discussion

The relationship of a public schoolteacher with an employing school board is created by contract and governed by general principles of contract law as well as by statutes and case law pertaining to contracts and teacher-employer relations. **Principle I**

The formality of general contract law has evolved from simple oral agreements ratified by a handshake to the elaborate, written agreements couched in legal jargon that sometimes frustrate the parties whose signatures are to indicate approval of the contractual provisions. However, every contract, regardless of its complexity, must contain five essential elements:

1. The parties to the contract must be competent.
2. The contract must be based upon the mutual assent of the contracting parties.
3. The contract must include valid and adequate consideration.
4. The contract must be sufficiently clear and definite.
5. The subject matter of the contract must be lawful and in a form required by law.

These elements are mandatory for the making of any valid and legally enforceable contract, including teacher contracts. While observing these general principles, a teacher's contract must also adhere to all applicable federal and state statutes, such as those defining contract law, civil rights laws, and tenure statutes. Because the courts have always been active in contract law, teaching contracts must also comply with case law applicable to contracts generally and to teaching contracts specifically.

In signing a teaching contract, a public schoolteacher and the employing school board create a legal relationship (*Kirk v. Miller,* 1974). The parameters of the relationship are governed by contract law, whose principles have been more precisely established by tradition and now by statute than many other areas of legal question. The courts become involved when the teacher and school board do not agree on the basic definition or application of the principles of contract law. In 1984 the South Dakota Supreme Court ruled that a teacher did not have a valid contract when only he had signed it and the school board had not:

> It is well settled that when by statute the mode and manner in which contracts of a school district may be entered into are limited and any other manner of entering into a contract is expressly or impliedly forbidden, a contract not made in compliance therewith is invalid (*Minor v. Sully Buttes School District No. 58–2,* 1984).

As shown in *Minor,* a contract is not legally enforceable until it is ratified or signed by both parties. Similarly, a letter of intent, a promise of a job from a principal, a notice of employment, an application, or an invitation to apply for a position does not constitute an enforceable contract. For example, in 1986 a survey was circulated to see if the teachers in a Louisiana school planned to continue to teach the following year. A teacher who returned the survey with an affirmative response did not have her contract renewed, and she filed suit. The court, in overruling her claim, differentiated between a contract and an invitation:

> An offer has been defined as a proposal to enter into a contract, but all proposals are not offers since the proposal must meet certain conditions. One condition is a declaration by the offeror of his intention. The second requirement is that the proposal must be precise in that it firmly reflects the intent of the offeror to enter into a contract and must contain certain language distinguishing it from mere proposals or invitations to negotiate. It must also be precise and complete so that the essential requirements of the contract are entered into with the indication that acceptance by the offeree will suffice to form the contract (*Knipmeyer v. Diocese of Alexandria,* 1986).

In addition to disputes over the definition of a contract, many court cases arise when the provisions of a contract have conflicted with statutes. Claims that a contract must be honored even though it violates a statute will not be upheld. The general principles of contract law must be applied within the constraints of other applicable statutes and case law, and a contract that violates statutes is void and cannot be ratified (*Perry v. Milwaukee Board of School Directors,* 1986).

In agreeing to provisions in a contract, a teacher cannot sign away statutory rights or agree to violate the law. A contract may supplement rights under statute and define the exercise of rights within the contractual relationship, but no element of preemption or recision of rights may be present (*Chambers v. Central School District School Board of Greene County,* 1987).

Therefore, the elements of contract law cannot be considered separately from other statutes that define teacher-employer relations. Contract law has evolved from the unwritten elements of the common law, and those elements must be observed in every contract. However, statutes governing such topics as tenure, dismissal, reduction in force, promotion, salary schedules, and assignment must be observed in the writing of contracts. Before signing a contract, a teacher should become knowledgeable about the basic elements of contract law to be sure the contract is legally valid. School boards must also ensure that all teaching contracts adhere to general contract law as well as to all other statutes that involve the employment relationship between a teacher and a local board.

The power to contract with a teacher is vested exclusively in the school board and cannot be delegated to any other body or official. **Principle II**

Contract law is precise in establishing who is qualified to enter into contracts. The subject matter of the contract will determine whose signatures will make it legally enforceable, and the signature of any other party will not be valid and will void the contract. In most states, the power to contract with teachers is vested in local school boards by the state legislature, and that power may be exercised only by a school board acting as a body, not as individuals. The Kansas Supreme Court explained in 1964 that a school district may exercise only such powers as the state has delegated to it:

> A school district is an arm of the state existing only as a creature of the legislature to operate as a political subdivision of the state. A school district has only such power and authority as is granted by the legislature and its power to contract, including contracts for employment, is only such as is conferred either expressly or by necessary implication (*Wichita Public Schools Employees Union, Local No. 513 v. Smith,* 1964).

The authority to contract with teachers may not be delegated to any other agency, board, or official. The local school board, therefore, becomes the employer, not the board president, the board secretary, the superintendent, the district personnel director, the building principal, or the search committee. An obvious practical problem arises when the school board, as the employer of teachers, must recruit teachers. With few exceptions, a school board cannot as a body undertake the travel, evaluation of applications, and interview processes necessary to recruit and screen all potential professional employees for their district. As long as only the mechanics of the employment process are delegated to the board president, superintendent, personnel director, principal, or search committee, leaving the actual contracting to the school board, the board has not allowed others to usurp its vested power as the employing body. The courts have become involved in many cases when school boards have wrongfully delegated their contractual power or individual officials have unlawfully assumed the board's authority to contract with teachers. Teachers have also brought suit when they have assumed that the person with whom they had had contact about employment in a school district had the power to contract, not realizing that only the school board could ratify employment decisions.

Two Colorado cases demonstrate the legal problems that arise for teachers and school boards when the laws concerning power to contract are violated. In 1967 a school board authorized the superintendent to employ a principal-teacher for the high school, and the president and secretary of the board signed a blank contract form. The superintendent found a person who wanted the job and filled in the blanks on the contract, including period of employment and salary. The teacher signed the contract and claimed he put it on the superintendent's desk the next day. (Later in court the superintendent alleged he never found it.) Ten days later, on the day before classes were to begin, the principal was discharged on the grounds that he failed to be present for a registration day. He sued the district, alleging a breach of contract even though the board had never officially acted to approve a contract with him. The Colorado Supreme Court ruled that a valid contract had never existed between the board and the principal and that the principal was not entitled to any relief:

> The power to employ teachers and fix their wages is not a mere ministerial or administrative matter, where little or no judgment or discretion is involved, but on the contrary is a legislative or judicial power involving the exercise of considerable discretion. Hence, under the general rule, such power cannot be delegated. The power to employ teachers has been conferred by the legislature exclusively on the school board, and therefore it cannot be delegated (*Big Sandy School District No. 100-J v. Carroll,* 1967).

Whether the superintendent was acting as the employer or merely as the designated messenger of the board in carrying out the board's employment decisions was the issue in the second Colorado case in 1968. A teacher received a letter from the school superintendent advising her that the school board had asked him to notify her that that day was to be her last day of teaching. A hearing, which the teacher elected not to attend, was held one month later, and the board voted to dismiss her. The state supreme court ruled that the superintendent had acted under the direction of the school board and the subsequent hearing afforded the teacher the opportunity to be heard; therefore, there was no breach of contract (*Snider v. Kit Carson School District R-1,* 1968).

School boards must be careful to follow legal procedures in authorizing superintendents or others to recruit teachers. Teachers must also be aware that superintendents or others who may recruit them to positions in their districts are not the employers and that school boards may not always accept their recommendations for hiring teachers. A Minnesota teacher who moved to South Dakota to be a band director did not have a contract when he began teaching because the board had not met to act on his contract. In the two weeks before the board met, the teacher had problems with the band, and the board refused to approve the contract even though the teacher had signed it (*Minor v. Sully Buttes School District No. 58-2,* 1984). In 1985 a teacher from Georgia moved to Massachusetts to teach band after he answered an advertisement and was interviewed by the school music directors. Before the end of the first month, he was fired, and he took his case to court. Because the music directors had never submitted his name to the school committee, which had sole authority to employ teachers, the court ruled the teacher had never had a valid contract (*McAndrew v. School Committee of Cambridge,* 1985).

To make any changes valid, additions, deletions, and amendments to contracts must be approved by both parties before they sign a contract. An Arkansas high school principal signed and returned his contract after adding the provision that he receive rent-free housing, which had been included in his past contracts with that district. At the next meeting the school board voted not to renew his contract. He sued for breach of contract, but the court ruled that no contract had been created because a majority of board members had not signed it (*Morton v. Hampton School District No. 1,* 1985).

The power to contract implies the power to end a contract as long as legal procedures are observed so that no breach of contract may be claimed. As the employer of teachers, a school board also has the exclusive power to terminate a teacher's employment, and that power may not be delegated. A school board in Montana authorized the superintendent to request a teacher's immediate resignation or to begin dismissal proceedings if she refused to resign after she had pleaded guilty to a misdemeanor theft charge. She submitted a letter of resignation on the day the request for resignation was delivered to her by letter from the superintendent, but she later filed suit, claiming the superintendent could not terminate her employment. The court ruled that the superintendent was merely carrying out ministerial acts and that the board had already voted to dismiss her (*Booth v. Argenbright,* 1987).

Although school boards have broad powers vested in them related to the employment of teachers, they may not take action beyond the powers legally conferred upon them. A contract made by a board acting beyond its power is an *ultra vires* contract, and the courts will hold it invalid and unenforceable (*Vail v. Board of Education of Paris Union School District No. 95,* 1983). Those who sign contracts with boards found to have used *ultra vires* authority are generally unable to recover damages.

School boards are the lawful employers of teachers, regardless of who may recruit teachers, conduct interviews, or make tentative offers of employment. Those duties may be delegated to other school committees or officials, but the power to contract is vested exclusively in the school board. Teachers must recognize that the school board is the employer and that all contracts, before being valid, must be signed by the board. School boards must be careful not to attempt to delegate their employment power to superintendents, search committees, or other bodies or individuals involved in the recruitment and selection of teachers. The courts will recognize only employment contracts ratified by the school board as the agency upon which the state has conferred the power to contract.

Principle III

Because the making of a valid contract requires competent parties, both the teacher and the employing school board must have the authority to bind themselves to a formal, legal relationship. A teacher and the school board must follow the procedures for creating a binding contract.

The first element of a valid contract is that both parties must be competent. Competency defined in legal terms means that both parties to a contract must have the authority to bind themselves to a formal, legal relationship. To be a competent party in the contracting process for teachers and school boards, a teacher must meet the minimum requirements set by state statute, such as being of legal age, having requisite mental capacity, being a United States citizen, and holding a certificate of health. The most important prerequisite to legal competency for a teacher is the holding of a teaching certificate that verifies the teacher is licensed to teach in the state. A school board is considered a competent party when it has been legally selected and exercises its legitimate power, vested in it by the state legislature, to be the contracting agent with teachers. When one or both parties are found incompetent, a contract is void.

Most of the court cases regarding competent parties involve questions of certification. As early as 1890, the North Dakota Supreme Court stated that "every contract relating to the employment of a teacher who does not hold a lawful certificate of qualification is void by express terms of the statute" (*Goose River Bank v. Willow Lake School Township,* 1890). In 1987 a tenured teacher who had a continuing contract as an administrator desired to become a principal when he was defeated for reelection as superintendent. The court ruled he was not entitled to a principal's contract because he did not hold a principal's certificate and his continuing contract did not obligate the board to appoint him to a position for which he was unqualified (*Greene v. School Board of Hamilton County,* 1987). When teachers sign contracts without holding the required certification, the board is not bound to grant them salary or any other benefits that are part of a valid contract.

An additional requirement for competency for both parties is to follow the procedures for creating a binding contract. Failure by either party to follow procedures will often void a contract. The importance of adhering to procedures under contract law was seen in an Ohio case in 1894 when a teacher's contract was ruled invalid because the board of education did not follow the required roll call procedure in voting on whether or not to offer the teacher a position (*Board of Education of New Concord School District v. Best,* 1894).

In recent years the procedures to be followed by both parties have become more exacting. A Florida teacher was notified that his continuing contract was null and void because he had failed to maintain a valid teaching certificate. The court upheld the school board's policy stipulating that teachers had to earn additional credits to keep their certificates current (*Gamble v. Mills,* 1986). In 1988 a teacher forgot to turn in her contract on the date it was due and put it in the school board's mailbox at 7:30 the next morning. The board, after a hearing, voted to terminate her contract because she had failed to adhere to the requirement that contracts be returned on or before their due date. The Nebraska Supreme Court ruled for the board (*Niedbalski v. Board of Education of School District No. 24 of Platte Center,* 1988).

A case where the legal competency of both parties was questioned arose in 1986. The school board hired a teacher for an elementary art position, but her contract was terminated on grounds that she was not a competent party because she did not have a license to teach. A year later, after she had completed her certification, the superintendent again recommended her for the position, and the board voted 3–2 to hire her. The acting chairman of the board notified her to sign an employment contract. However, because in the past no teaching contract had been approved by a vote of fewer than four members, the issue came up at the next board meeting when all board members were present. At this second meeting, the board voted 4–3 against hiring her. She challenged the board in court, claiming the second vote was a violation of procedure. The Indiana appellate court ruled that the state code did not require a majority vote of the full governing body to approve a teacher's contract but just a majority vote of a quorum. Therefore, her contract was ruled valid (*Board of School Trustees of South Vermillion Board Corporation v. Benetti,* 1986).

The competency of the contracting parties will be the first consideration when a contract is challenged in court. Teachers must be sure that they have valid certificates for teaching in the state, including all endorsements or credits needed to teach assigned subject matter. Teaching certificates must be kept current. Policies and procedures established by state statute, board policy, and collective bargaining agreement must also be followed for a teacher to enter into a binding relationship with the school board. School boards must also ensure their competency as the employing party by following all procedures, including giving proper notice, complying with open meeting laws, and adhering to fair voting processes. Procedural irregularities commonly void teaching contracts, and the courts will use contract laws and written policies to determine whether or not a contract is legally enforceable by virtue of having been signed by competent parties.

Principle IV

Because a contract is designed to protect the interests of both parties, a teaching contract must be based on the mutual assent of the teacher and the school board as to the terms, conditions, and obligations of the contract.

Because a contract is an agreement, both contracting parties must consent to the terms, conditions, and obligations of the contract before it can become final and legally valid. To determine the conditions of a contract, a formal offer is made by one party and a formal acceptance is given by the other. However, if the offeree wants to bargain further with the offeror about the terms of the contract, the original offer is nullified and the counteroffer can be extended and either accepted or rejected. This negotiating back and forth until agreement is reached is called the "meeting of the minds," or reaching mutual assent by the parties. When both parties mutually agree to the conditions of an offer, those terms and obligations become the binding contract and all previous offers or versions of the contract are void.

When a school district offers a contract to a teacher, the teacher must agree to the conditions of the contract as written. Any changes in the contract constitute a counteroffer, which must be negotiated with the board before any signing of the contract occurs. As with all contracts, there must be mutual assent between teacher and school board on the conditions of the contract before it will be valid. When teacher and school board disagree on the terms of a contract, the courts may be asked to determine whether or not the parties ever reached a meeting of the minds before the contract was signed. Lack of mutual assent will nullify the contract.

A teacher who was selected as principal of a summer school program received notice that her appointment was subject to full funding of the program and to the approval of the board of education. Before the board met, however, the criteria for summer school positions were revised, and the board decided that the teacher was no longer qualified for the position. After she was notified that she could not be approved for the principalship, she went to court, claiming that a contract was created when the summer school program received full funding. The court determined that no valid offer and acceptance had been made because the board had not approved the contract. The lack of mutual assent invalidated the contract (*Board of Education of District of Columbia v. Wilson,* 1972).

Teachers who attempt to make changes in contracts before signing them will not prevail in court because the changes nullify the original contract, and further negotiating between teacher and school board is needed before a contract can exist. A principal who added rent-free housing to his contract before he signed and returned it was released from service at the next board meeting. The court upheld the board action (*Morton v. Hampton School District No. 1,* 1985).

The requirement that teaching certificates be kept up to date has led to contract disputes when school boards have insisted on teachers earning additional credits and teachers have refused to do so. In February 1960 a teacher who had had no formal education since 1934 was informed that her contract would be nullified unless she earned six credit hours by March 1961. She refused to get the additional professional training and so was terminated. The court upheld her dismissal (*Last v. Board of Education of Community Unit School District No. 321,* 1962). Another teacher did not have enough credits to renew her certificate when it expired. When her contract was issued in March, it contained a clause that her teaching certificate had to be current by the middle of July or the contract would become null and void. She signed the standard contract but refused to sign the condition, and the contract was revoked. The court ruled that her refusing to sign the condition, which was reasonable, meant she had failed to execute the contract and she had no right to continued employment (*Nelson v. Doland Board of Education of Doland School District No. 56–2,* 1986).

In another 1986 case, the contract for a teacher who had worked only under one-year contracts included a provision that she would be carefully evaluated during the next year. At the end of the year, the principal, who conducted the evaluations, recommended that her contract not be renewed. She went to court, claiming breach of contract because the evaluations had not followed the standard district procedures and she and the principal had never agreed upon alternative procedures. However, the court ruled for the district because the teacher had signed her contract, indicating assent to the conditions, and had also signed all the evaluations (*Borman v. Gorham-Fayette Board of Education,* 1986).

A signature on a contract indicates that mutual assent has been reached by the contracting parties, and claims after the fact about any of the terms or conditions of the contract will almost always fail in court. A North Carolina court explained the legal view of mutual assent in 1985:

> In order to be binding, an offer to enter into a contract in the future must specify all the essential terms and leave nothing to be agreed upon as a result of future negotiations. To constitute a valid contract, the parties must assent to the same thing, their minds must meet as to all essential terms (*Braun v. Glade Valley School, Inc.,* 1985).

Teachers must understand the importance of coming to a meeting of the minds with the school board on the terms of their contracts. Signing a contract but expecting to make changes later will generally lead to disappointment because the signatures indicate agreement with the contract as written. Teachers and school boards must negotiate the terms and conditions of teaching contracts before any signatures are put on a contract so that mutual assent to all provisions of the contract is reached, and the contract is a valid testament to that assent.

Principle V

A contract requires that the parties agree to give valid and adequate consideration, something of value, in return for a promise or act of value. In a legally enforceable teaching contract, a teacher agrees to perform teaching duties and services in return for salary and benefits from the school board.

Legal consideration in contract law means that something of value must be given by one party in return for a promise or act of value from the second party. The values of the consideration need not be equal but must be adequate and not too illusory or indefinite. Some legally recognized value must be promised and exchanged before a contract will be enforceable. In teaching contracts, the consideration is the teacher's performance of instructional duties in return for a salary from the school board. The courts do not often become involved in questions of adequacy of the consideration but will rule in cases when the existence of consideration in a contract is the issue. Lack of consideration often differentiates offers and invitations of employment from contracts.

Intentions do not provide evidence of consideration in court. In 1940 an Ohio school board passed a resolution extending the superintendent's contract for twenty-three months, but the resolution did not fix any compensation for the extended time. The new school board refused to recognize the extension of the superintendent's contract, and he turned to the courts. However, the court noted that no enforceable contract existed:

> No inference as to the amount of compensation can be drawn from the language used by the [school board] in the resolution ... As an appointment without compensation ... would not be binding upon the [superintendent], neither would it be binding upon the [school board]. There would be no consideration for the promise and, therefore, no binding contract (*State ex rel. Melvin v. Board of Education of City of St. Bernard,* 1940).

Several teachers brought legal action to recover damages for breach of contract when they were notified that they had been selected to teach summer school and then all summer school classes were canceled. They had received letters from the assistant superintendent informing them that their appointments were contingent on budget approval and summer school enrollment and asking that they sign and return a portion of the letters indicating their acceptance of the appointments. The teachers claimed the letters were offers of employment, which, when accepted by their signing and returning the sections, became contracts. The court ruled that no enforceable contracts existed because no consideration had been given. The letters of appointment had contained no information about compensation:

> The general rule is that price is an essential ingredient of every contract for . . . the rendering of service. Accordingly, an agreement must be definite as to compensation. . . . Since the terms of the summer school employment including the compensation to be paid, were not stated or agreed upon, that promise was too uncertain to form a basis of a contract (*Ayer v. Board of Education of Central School District No. 1,* 1972).

When tenure statutes do not specify that teachers on continuing contracts have to sign new contracts, teachers must be aware that provisions of preceding contracts, including salary and benefits, may also continue because compensation must be specified for contracts to be valid. In 1974 tenured teachers in New York refused to sign new contracts, and the court said the school board was justified in paying them on the basis of the preceding year's salary and benefit schedule (*Davis v. Board of Education of Aurora Public School District No. 131,* 1974). Most collective bargaining procedures provide for updating of salary schedules even when tenured teachers do not have to sign yearly contracts.

Most compensation cases involve collective bargaining agreements, not contracts with individual teachers. The days of each teacher negotiating a salary package with the school board are past. Nevertheless, teachers should be aware that their contracts, before they are valid, must include provisions about compensation. Vague references to "adequate pay for services rendered" and other nonspecific clauses will probably not be upheld in court. School boards must write contracts that are definite as to consideration so that teaching contracts will be legally enforceable.

Principle VI

A contract must be clear and definite so that neither teacher nor school board must guess at its meaning or intention. Most terms of a teaching contract are expressly written to state the obligations of both parties. However, general policies and regulations as well as state statutes may be incorporated into the contract by implication.

The majority of contract cases arise from differing interpretations of the provisions in teacher contracts. Almost any contract can be challenged in court because of its being unclear or indefinite, and teachers and school boards have called on the courts to interpret many teacher contracts. The role of a court is not to rewrite contracts to make them legally tenable; therefore, when a contract is not clear and its conditions and terms are not specific or definite, the courts will declare the contract void.

The United States has come to insist on written contracts in almost all situations because oral contracts are so difficult to support in court. In 1891 a teacher entered into an oral contract with a school trustee, who promised to pay her "good wages." Later she claimed that although she was ready and willing, the trustee refused to allow her to teach. When the teacher took her case to court, she learned that no valid contract existed:

> It is necessary . . . that contracts made with teachers should be certain and definite in their terms . . . in order that when the time comes for the teacher to enter upon duty there may be no misunderstanding as to what his rights are. Any other rule would put in peril the school interests. . . . Until there is a definite contract, it can hardly be said that a teacher has been employed, and the public interest demands that there should be a definite agreement before the time arrives for the schools to open; otherwise the school corporation may be at the mercy of the teacher, or else there be no school (*Fairplay School Township v. O'Neal,* 1891).

To avoid such claims, the most common type of contract between teachers and school boards is now an express contract. Such a contract not only is written but also explicitly includes the mutual obligations of both teacher and school board. The legal duties and responsibilities are written in such definite terms that few claims of vagueness or misunderstanding of contractual conditions are possible.

The insistence upon clarity and specificity does not require a teaching contract to include every duty and responsibility of a teacher. The nature of the teaching profession results in even the most express contract including reference to some implied duties. Federal and state laws and local rules and regulations are incorporated by reference in most contracts, not by listing every law and policy to which the teacher is subject. A teaching contract often refers to the responsibility teachers have for knowing and applying all policies and procedures in the teachers' handbook as well as the provisions of the district master contract. These implied duties are as much a part of the contract as express duties, and the courts will uphold them as long as the terms can be interpreted clearly in the educational context.

However, implied provisions are often challenged in court. In 1933 an Oregon teacher challenged his dismissal for not performing implied contractual duties. He had not followed a state board of education mandate that called for "teachers in the public schools [to] inculcate in the minds of their pupils correct principles of morality and a proper regard for the laws of society." The court upheld his dismissal (*Bump v. Union High School District No. 3,* 1933). Many termination cases involving teachers are based on the implied clauses of teacher contracts. When the courts are able to determine that the implied duties are reasonable and closely related to the responsibilities of professional educators, the provisions are upheld. However, if teachers are left to guess at the meaning of the implied sections of a contract, the contract will be ruled invalid.

The courts have given some guidelines for determining when a contractual duty is too vague to withstand judicial scrutiny. In 1986 a Colorado appellate court stated that "words used in a contract are to be given their plain and generally accepted meaning" (*Bevsek v. Huerfano School District RE-1,* 1986). An Illinois appellate court added that "a contract must be definite and certain in its conditions and courts will not supply missing terms so as to infuse a contract with the requisite certainty" (*McCutcheon v. Chicago Principals Association,* 1987).

Nevertheless, many cases have arisen with definitions of contractual terms as the issue. In South Carolina a school director was dismissed after continuing conflict with the faculty and turmoil in the school environment caused by his admitted callous insensitivity to basic human concerns and inexcusably abrasive and juvenile behavior in dealing with colleagues and students. Because of its charge to provide high-quality education, the school board determined that they would be in violation of public policy if they did not dismiss the director. The court upheld the board's action even though the director claimed the complaints about his actions were vague:

> Absent contractual language to the contrary it may be assumed that when words or phrases utilized in a teaching contract incorporate terms given specific meaning by statute, it was intended to give the statutory meaning to the contractual terms (*Kizer v. Dorchester County Vocational Education Board of Trustees,* 1986).

A tenured teacher who did not maintain a valid regular teacher's certificate claimed that the rule applied only to those seeking initial contracts, not those on continuing contracts. The court upheld the termination of his contract:

> The meaning of the contract is clear and unambiguous and requires no judicial interpretation. . . . Generally, words in a contract should be given their natural meaning or the meaning most commonly understood in relation to the subject matter and circumstances, with a reasonable construction preferred to one that is unreasonable (*Gamble v. Mills,* 1986).

In 1987 a Montana superintendent filed suit when his contract was not renewed after one year of employment. He claimed his contract was "open-ended," not for a definite term, even though the contract stated he was "employed to act as superintendent . . . for a period of no less than one year." Dismissing the complaint, the court said the contract was for one year:

> Where the language of a written contract is clear and unambiguous there is nothing for the court to construe; the duty of the court is simply to apply the language as written to the facts of the case, and decide the case accordingly (*Nordlund v. School District No. 14,* 1987).

An Illinois appellate court in 1989 was faced with a case involving a contract that stated: "These positions will be filled at the Board's discretion." In ruling that the application of the clause was "far from simple understanding," the court discussed the requirement that the terms of a contract be clear:

> A contract term is ambiguous when it is reasonably capable of having been understood in more senses than one because the language or expression are not definite or due to the term having a double or multiple meaning. However, the mere fact that the parties take a divergent view of the meaning of the contract language does not render the agreement ambiguous (*Lewis v. Board of Education of North Clay Community Unit School District No. 25, Clay County,* 1989).

However, some contracts have been nullified by the courts because of vague or confusing terms or conditions. The time provisions in a teacher's contract in Arkansas were ruled ambiguous because four different timelines were used: 9 academic months, 200 days, 10 calendar months, and from August 2, 1982, through May 31, 1983. That none of these time periods exactly overlapped any other caused the court to rule in favor of a teacher whose pay had been docked for not being present on the last day of school (*Maddox v. St. Paul School District,* 1985).

Teachers are subject to all rules and regulations of the school board, regardless of when the board passed them. Policies that exist prior to the signing of a teacher's contract are a valid part of the contract, and teachers are also responsible for abiding by all regulations passed after the contract is in effect. Reference to these policies is usually part of the express contract. In 1963 a teacher refused to sever his financial interests in a liquor store in spite of board policies mandating that such ties conflicted with a teacher's duties. The court ruled against his claim that nothing in his contract forbade his connection with the store:

> The general rule is that regulations and operational policies adopted by a school board prior to making a contract with a teacher form a part of the contract, and the teacher's employment is subject thereto. . . . It also seems to be the law that a regulation adopted after a teaching contract is made becomes a part of it and the employment is subject thereto (*Romeike v. Houston Independent School District,* 1963; also *Myrtle Springs Reverted Independent School District v. Hogan,* 1985).

In summary, a teacher is responsible for all express and implied provisions of the teaching contract. School boards should strive for clarity when writing contracts and use terms common to education so that teachers, administrators, and board members have no difficulty interpreting them. The courts will not guess at the meaning of terms and generally will not substitute their interpretation for the understanding of educators. If terms are so ambiguous that teachers cannot reasonably understand them, the courts will rule a contract null and void. All school districts must carefully follow their own rules and regulations because the courts will not favor the school board that violates its own policies.

All subject matter of a teaching contract must be lawful, and the contract must be in the form required by law. **Principle VII**

The freedom to make contracts encourages people to bargain and to negotiate agreements without supervision of legislative or judicial rule. However, this right to enter into contracts cannot be extended to include subjects that are illegal or that violate the rights of either party or third parties. While underworld or underground contracts that deal with illegal subjects certainly exist, the courts are never asked to enforce them. The courts do become involved when claims are made that contracts violate statutes, policies, or regulations or that rights are in jeopardy if a contract is observed. Any such contract is legally unenforceable, and the courts will declare it void.

Few cases have come before the courts where claims have been made that teaching contracts are invalid because of illegal subject matter, although some cases have arisen because contracts were in violation of statutes or individual rights. In 1890 the courts ruled that warrants (scrip used in place of cash to pay teachers) were invalid if the teacher who received them did not hold a lawful certificate of qualifications. The stores, shops, and banks that accepted such warrants were unable to redeem them with the school district, and the court upheld this policy (*Goose River Bank v. Willow Lake School Township,* 1890).

One major issue dealing with legality of contracts at present involves supplementary contracts offered to teachers to cover their extra duty responsibilities (*Hachiya v. Board of Education, Unified School District No. 307, Saline County, Kansas,* 1988; *Slockett v. Iowa Valley Community School District,* 1984; *Smith v. Board of Education of Urbana School District No. 116 of Champaign County, Illinois,* 1983; *Swager v. Board of Education, Unified School District No. 412, Sheridan County, Kansas,* 1984; *Unified School District No. 241, Wallace County, v. Swanson,* 1986). The courts are upholding such contracts as long as they do not violate the teachers' regular contracts or tenure statutes. In 1987 a Washington school district argued that teachers had waived their right to contest supplemental contracts because they had agreed to the contracts in the collective bargaining agreement. The courts disagreed, ruling that the school district may not offer a contract that contains a condition that the employee waive his or her continuing contract rights. Even if a teacher signed such a waiver, it would not be valid or enforceable (*Kelso Education Association v. Kelso School District No. 453,* 1987). All issues surrounding supplemental contracts have not yet been fully considered by the courts. However, supplemental contracts generally may not interfere with other existing contractual rights.

The proper form for contracts once was a greater issue than it is today because the written contract is now the standard. However, oral agreements are still recognized by some courts. A paraprofessional, who claimed her oral contract with the principal to hire her as a teacher was breached, did not have a valid claim, according to the courts, because the state's three-year statute of limitations for oral contracts was in effect (*Crutchfield v. Pulaski County Special School District,* 1986). The ruling may have been different had the complaint been timely.

More cases concerning the written form of contracts are being heard as details concerning teaching contracts are challenged in court. In 1982 the contract between a school board and an assistant principal was the subject of a court case because it had not been written on a form approved by the state board of education, as stipulated by statute. The court ruled that the statute was directory only, not mandatory, making the assistant principal's contract valid (*Board of Education of Alamogordo Public Schools District No. 1 v. Jennings,* 1982). In a 1988 case, the question of the validity of typewriting over printing on a contract arose. The Nebraska Supreme Court clarified how priority issues have traditionally been resolved:

> Typewriting is writing within the contemplation of the statute providing that when an instrument consists partly of written and partly of printed form, the writing controls the printed form where the two are inconsistent (*Niedbalski v. Board of Education of School District No. 24 of Platte Center,* 1988).

Although few cases have arisen over the legality of subject matter in teaching contracts, school boards and teachers should remain aware that the courts will hold any contract that involves illegal subjects or that violates statutes or policies invalid and unenforceable. Almost all teachers' contracts are written, and that aspect of contract form is seldom questioned. Yet, in a society when every procedure and detail will be scrutinized when a contract is challenged in court, school boards must ensure that contracts adhere to every regulation and statute governing legal form. Teachers and boards must recognize that any contract found in violation of mandatory rules on form and procedure will be nullified by the courts.

Principle VIII

Once a teacher and a school board agree to the terms of a contract, they are obligated to perform the commitments made to each other in the document. Failure to fulfill the obligations is a breach of contract, and the wronged party is usually entitled to recover damages.

The signing of a contract obligates the signers to perform the duties and responsibilities stated in the contract. A contract is not a casual promise to do something as long as the terms of the contract are convenient or enjoyable for the contracting parties. The parties to a contract are legally bound to meet the terms and conditions of the contract. When a party fails to meet contractual obligations, the party is "in breach" of the contract. The wronged party is usually able to recover damages when a contract has been breached. Damages are assessed to make the injured party "whole," or in the position the party would be if the breach had not occurred. In teacher-employer relations, either the teacher or the school board could breach the contract and be held liable to the other party for damages. The courts have been asked to rule in many cases on whether or not a teaching contract has been breached and, if so, what damages are due.

One of the earliest education cases was heard in 1938 by the United States Supreme Court and established standards for breach of contract cases. Roots of the case began in 1927 when the Indiana legislature passed a tenure act that applied to all public schoolteachers. Several years later the legislature passed an act repealing the tenure statute. When a tenured teacher's contract was canceled, she claimed the state could not breach her contract by subsequent legislation. The United States Supreme Court ruled in the teacher's favor and in so doing gave tenure statutes more legal weight because the repeal of a tenure law could no longer affect the contract status of those teachers who had already earned tenure under the law (*State of Indiana ex rel. Anderson v. Brand,* 1938).

Similar cases have defined the scope of tenure laws in regard to teaching contracts. In 1978 a tenured teacher's eleven-month contract was changed to ten months by the school board, which claimed the privilege of altering contracts that exceeded Minnesota's minimum requirement for the length of a teaching contract. However, the state's supreme court ruled that when the eleventh month was not designated an extra duty, the protection of the state's continuing contract statute enveloped the entire period of the contract. Hence, the teacher's eleven-month contract was protected by tenure (*Rochester Education Association v. Independent School District No. 535,* 1978).

A tenured teacher in Texas was employed for 20 extra days each year as part of her contract although local funds paid for the extra days. When the local funding ended, the school board cut her extra 20 days, and she sued for breach of contract. The court ruled that the 20 days were part of her continuing contract and could not be modified unilaterally without a hearing:

> Even if the District should decide to do away with [continuing] contracts in the future, an existing continuing contract continues for future school years without the necessity for annual nomination or reappointment (*James v. Hitchcock Independent School District,* 1987).

Breach of contract cases have been brought for other issues besides the definition and application of tenure laws. Many clauses in statutes and contracts have been used to attempt to validate claims of breach of contract or to support the defending party's action that led to the claim. In 1945 a music teacher signed a contract with the provision that she would not teach anywhere else in Texas during the contract period. When she left and took a job in another Texas district, the court ruled that she breached the contract (*Mission Independent School District v. Diserens,* 1945). An Arkansas teacher was ruled in breach of contract when she took a leave of absence without following the procedures in the school board regulations (*Special School District of Ft. Smith v. Lynch,* 1967).

Claims of breach of contract are also brought by teachers against school boards on grounds of specific contractual provisions. In 1974 a school board voted to dismiss a tenured teacher who was also the principal, citing the statute that said a contract could be terminated when changes in local conditions warranted the elimination of a contract position. However, the court found that local conditions had not changed, and the teacher had merely been replaced by another teacher. The school district was found in breach of contract (*Kenaston v. School Administrative District No. 40,* 1974). A nonpermanent teacher's contract was not renewed at the end of the year, and she claimed the school board had breached her contract when she had not received her evaluation until January 12 because the statute specified that evaluations were to be received by January 1. The court ruled that the school board had substantially complied with the statute and so had not breached the contract (*Moran v. Board of School Trustees of Mt. Pleasant Township Community Schools, Delaware County,* 1986). Therefore, the courts will uphold breach of contract claims when the complaining party is able to show that the conditions of the contract have been substantially violated, but not every alleged mistreatment is a breach of contract.

When a contract has been breached, the issue of damages must be settled. Before tenure laws were passed, school boards were able to terminate a teacher's contract for arbitrary reasons, and teachers had no claim to their positions or their salaries. Now a school board's obligations are specified in both statutes and contracts. Usually a teaching contract also includes provisions defining the obligations of a teacher who breaches the contract. For example, teachers failing to appear to teach their classes, leaving without notice during the school year, or moving to another district for better jobs damage school districts by leaving them without needed teachers. Today both school boards and teachers are more aware of their legal responsibilities under contract because the courts will award damages to the injured party.

In 1966 a teacher was allowed to collect the value of her living quarters, which had been supplied rent free under her contract, as well as back pay when the court ruled that she had been wrongfully discharged (*Wyatt v. School District No. 104, Fergus County,* 1966). A teacher who was hired for three years as teacher and football coach was fired from the coaching position in the middle of the first year and informed that his salary for the next year would be $2,000 less. The court ruled that the teacher's salary had to be restored because, although extra duty assignments could be changed in the middle of the contract, the salary could not be reduced (*George v. School District No. 8R of Umatilla County,* 1971).

Teachers, too, must often pay specified damages when they breach a contract. A North Dakota teacher asked to be released from her contract six days before school started because her husband was moving from the area and she would not be able to meet her contract obligations. Because her request was within two weeks of the beginning of the school year, she was required to pay damages of 4 percent of her salary under the contract. Even though the school board found a replacement teacher, the court upheld the fixed-damages provision of the contract because of the difficulty of ascertaining damages in some situations:

> Thus, when we consider the damages caused by a teacher's breach of an employment contract, we cannot ignore the interruption to the school system and the resultant debilitating effect such interruption has upon the learning process of students in the school system. The possibility that the replacement teacher who was obtained may be less experienced or less qualified and, thus, a less effective instructor must also be considered in the assessment of damages. . . . Even if known, it would be extremely difficult to evaluate these damages on a monetary basis. . . . Such damages are not legally compensable but constitute a public injury which the school district was entitled to consider (*Bowbells Public School District No. 14 v. Walker,* 1975).

Because most tenure statutes, collective bargaining agreements, and teaching contracts include provisions for determining amount of damages and for hearing cases of breach of contract by administrative boards, the courts will not hear a case when the complaining party has not complied with specified administrative procedures (*Morgan v. Huntsville City Board of Education,* 1987). A teacher or school board who claims breach of contract must first comply with all administrative rules before turning to the courts.

Therefore, neither teacher nor school board may take their contractual obligations lightly. The terms and conditions of a contract must be fulfilled by both parties, and breaching the contract can lead to liability for damages. Contracts have become much more specific than in the past regarding recovery of damages for breach of contract, and the courts will generally support such provisions. Although violation of nonmandatory procedures may not be upheld as breach of contract, school boards and teachers should recognize the legal ramifications of failing to comply with the provisions of a teaching contract. With courts frequently awarding punitive as well as actual damages, neither a teacher nor a school board can afford to be found in breach of contract.

Principle IX

The freedom to contract implies the freedom to rescind the contract at any time the parties mutually desire to end their contractual relationship. Termination of a teaching contract may also result from acts of God, illness, death, statutory prohibition, or other occurrences beyond the control of the teacher or the school board.

The parties who agree to a contract may mutually agree to terminate a contract, but the key concept is that both parties must freely agree to end their legal relationship and then follow the procedures for rescinding their earlier agreement. Duress, coercion, or fraud by one party to force the other party to end their contract would be ruled a breach of contract. Most teachers' contracts include provisions whereby the contract may be terminated, and following those provisions prevents any claims of breach. The courts become involved when the procedures for legally terminating a contract are not followed or when the teacher or school board claims that fraud or coercion resulted in a wrongful termination.

In 1978 the Kansas Supreme Court ruled that a teacher's contract had been terminated by mutual agreement after the teacher submitted a letter of resignation and the school board voted to accept it. Although the teacher later wanted to withdraw the resignation, sufficient evidence indicated that both the teacher and the school board intended by mutual agreement to end the contract (*Brinson v. School District No. 431,* 1978). A teacher in an Oregon case also wanted to withdraw her resignation, which she had submitted without giving sixty-day notice as required by contract because she did not want to be transferred to another school. The school board accepted her letter, though, and the court upheld the board's action by explaining the concept of mutual release from a contract:

> A teacher contract can be terminated by mutual agreement ... in which the minds of the parties must meet on an identical proposition which they both understand alike and to which they both assent in the same sense (*Pierce v. Douglas School District No. 4,* 1984.)

Mutual agreement to rescind a contract is the most common method for concluding a teacher-employer relationship before the contract expires. However, other events or circumstances may force termination of a contract. An act of God that could not be reasonably foreseen at the time the contract was executed would excuse its performance. An example of such an act would be the destruction of a school by a flood, fire, tornado, or other natural disaster. Any event that causes fulfillment of a contract to be impossible will excuse performance as long as fraud, irresponsible behavior, or illegal actions have not caused the impossibility. To be recognized by the courts, these emergency conditions for recision of a contract must be based on the fact that performance of the contract is prohibited by law or prevented by circumstances beyond the control of either the teacher or the school board. Death or an illness that renders a teacher permanently unable to fulfill the contract would terminate a teaching contract. For example, in 1976 a music teacher was excused from his contractual obligations because of his deteriorating eyesight (*Oneal v. Colton Consolidated School District No. 306,* 1976).

All contracts that are freely entered by mutual agreement may also be freely terminated. As long as the teacher and the school board adhere strictly to provisions in a contract allowing for its termination, neither party may bring action against the other for breach of contract. Undisputed evidence that a contract is impossible to fulfill due to acts of God or other events unforeseen and uncontrollable by either party will also terminate the contract. Teachers and school boards need to understand and follow all provisions for legal termination of a contract so that mutual agreement leaves no room for claims of breach and expensive damage claims.

Summary

Teaching contracts specify the terms under which teachers and their employing school districts are mutually bound into legal relationships. Where school boards were once able to make heavy demands upon a teacher's personal as well as professional life, tenure laws and the strength of teachers' associations have resulted in contracts that balance the duties and rights of both parties.

General contract law applies to teachers' contracts, which must also comply with applicable statutes and judicial decisions. A basic contract must have competent parties, be based on mutual assent, include valid consideration, be clear and definite, and involve legal subject matter in legal form. A contract that violates any of these elements is invalid and unenforceable.

The power to contract with teachers is vested in local school boards by the state legislature, and that power may not be delegated to any other body or official, including the superintendent or individual members of the school board. School boards may delegate the mechanical or ministerial duties involved in recruitment and selection of teachers to superintendents, personnel directors, principals, or search committees, but the responsibility of contracting is held exclusively by the school board.

The courts will continue to be asked to rule on contract cases because of the complex nature of contract law. As the language used in contracts becomes more complicated and less understandable to many teachers and individual school board members, misunderstandings will arise. The demand for more specific contract provisions, especially in the area of supplemental duties, may lead to more litigation as teachers and school boards struggle to determine how to write a specific contract for a professional position. Contracts that are overly vague and those that are overly specific both can be challenged in court by one party or the other claiming the contract has been breached. The inclusion of orderly termination procedures and provisions for mutual release from a contract should be part of every contract to prevent some claims of wrongful discharge and breach of contract.

Questions and Responses

1. What are the mandatory elements of a legal contract?

To be valid and legally enforceable, every contract must include these five elements:

a. The parties to the contract must be competent.
b. The contract must be based upon a mutual assent of the contracting parties.
c. The contract must include valid and adequate consideration.
d. The contract must be sufficiently clear and definite.
e. The subject matter of the contract must be lawful and in a form required by law.

2. What is meant by "competent parties"?

In the legal sense, competent parties to a contract indicate that both parties are able to bind themselves to a legal relationship. In a teacher's employment contract, the teacher must show such proofs of competency as being of legal age, holding United States citizenship, having a certificate of health, and, most important, holding the proper certification for the state, subject matter, and grade level applicable to the contract. The school board, if properly selected, is the competent party by virtue of holding the vested power to contract with teachers.

3. What is "consideration" in a contract?

Consideration is the thing of value given by one party to a contract in exchange for a promise or act of value from the other party. In a teaching contract, the teacher promises to perform instructional duties in exchange for a salary and benefits from the school district. The consideration does not have to be of equal value, but it must be valid and adequate.

4. When must an employment contract be in written form?

Under common law, oral contracts are recognized, but the complexity of contract law mandates that most contracts be written. In the United States, most employment contracts must be written, including those between teachers and school boards. However, the mandatory form of contracts varies from state to state, and some teaching contracts rely on oral agreements. The courts will uphold contracts, written or not, as long as statutes and case law are followed. Written contracts are easier to defend in court.

5. When a contract consists of both typeset and typewritten or handwritten sections, which sections will take precedence?

Common law and statutes indicate that typewritten or handwritten portions of contracts will take precedence over the printed sections because the typewritten or handwritten sections usually indicate new terms of agreement between the contracting parties. However, the sections would have to be explicit in indicating that both parties have agreed to changes from the printed sections, and other changes may never be added after signatures have been affixed.

6. Who has the power to make a contract with teachers?

State legislatures in most states have vested the power to contract with teachers exclusively with local school boards. The local board may take recommendations from local committees, agencies, or officials, but all contracting must be done by the board acting as a body of the whole, not as individuals. The board president or secretary acting alone has no power to contract.

7. When may a superintendent, a principal, or a search committee offer a job to a prospective teacher?

A superintendent, principal, personnel director, search committee, or board president may be delegated certain mechanical or ministerial duties in the recruitment and selection of teachers, but contracting may be done only by the school board. At times, a job offer may be extended to a prospective teacher by another official, but the teacher must realize that such an offer is only an invitation, not a contract for a position. Until the board acts on the recommendations of other bodies or officials, no contract has been made, and the teacher has no entitlement to position or salary.

8. When may a teaching contract be terminated?

As with all contracts, a teaching contract may be terminated when the contracting parties agree by mutual assent to end their legal relationship. This action is not the same as a breach of contract when one party violates the provisions of the contract, making the contract void. Coercion, duress, or fraud may not be used by one party to force the other party to agree to terminate a contract. The impossibility of fulfilling a contract because of acts of God, changes in statutory provisions, illness, death, and other unforeseen emergencies may also terminate a contract.

9. What is meant by "breach of contract"?

When one party fails to abide by or to fulfill the provisions of a contract, that party is said to be "in breach" of the contract. The injured party is usually eligible for damages when the contract has been breached so that the party will be in the same position he or she would have been had the contract not been breached.

10. What are implied provisions in a teaching contract?

Contracts consist of express and implied sections. The express parts are those specified and written in the contract. Implied provisions are those that indicate obligations without specifying each one. For example, a teaching contract may state that a teacher is responsible for complying with all state statutes, board policies, and procedures in the teachers' handbook. These provisions are seldom written into the contract, but reference is made to them so that teachers know they must understand and follow them. Usually teachers will also be held responsible for following board policies that are passed after the contract is ratified. Fewer implied provisions are being found in teaching contracts as teachers' associations press for explicit duties and responsibilities to be part of all contracts. However, professional positions include many duties and rights that cannot be enumerated in any contract, and most teachers are expected to abide by such expectations.

Case References

Ayer v. Board of Education of Central School District No. 1, 330 N.Y.S.2d 465 (1972).
Bevsek v. Huerfano School District RE-1, 728 P.2d 325 (Colo. App. 1986).
Big Sandy School District No. 100-J v. Carroll, 433 P.2d 325 (Colo. 1967).
Board of Education of New Concord School District v. Best, 39 N.E. 694 (Ohio 1894).
Board of Education of Alamogordo Public Schools District No. 1 v. Jennings, 651 P.2d 1037 (N.M. App. 1982).
Board of Education of District of Columbia v. Wilson, 290 A.2d 400 (D.C. App. 1972).
Board of School Trustees of South Vermillion School Corporation v. Benetti, 492 N.E.2d 1098 (Ind. App. 1 Dist. 1986).
Booth v. Argenbright, 731 P.2d 1318 (Mont. 1987).
Borman v. Gorham-Fayette Board of Education, 502 N.E.2d 1031 (Ohio 1986).
Bowbells Public School District No. 14 v. Walker, 231 N.W.2d 173 (N.D. 1975).
Braun v. Glade Valley School, Inc., 334 S.E.2d 404 (N.C. App. 1985).
Brinson v. School District No. 431, 576 P.2d 602 (Kan. 1978).
Bump v. Union High School District No. 3, 24 P.2d 330 (Or. 1933).
Chambers v. Central School District School Board of Greene County, 514 N.E.2d 1294 (Ind. App. 1 Dist. 1987).
Crutchfield v. Pulaski County Special School District, 647 F.Supp. 884 (E.D. Ark. 1986).
Davis v. Board of Education of Aurora Public School District No. 131, 312 N.E.2d 335 (Ill. App. 1974).
Fairplay School Township v. O'Neal, 26 N.E. 686 (Ind. 1891).
Gamble v. Mills, 483 So.2d 826 (Fla. App. 4 Dist. 1986).
George v. School District No. 8R of Umatilla County, 490 P.2d 1009 (Or. App. 1971).
Goose River Bank v. Willow Lake School Township, 44 N.W. 1002 (N.D. 1890).
Greene v. School Board of Hamilton County, 501 So.2d 50 (Fla. App. 1 Dist. 1987).
Hachiya v. Board of Education, Unified School District No. 307, Saline County, Kansas, 750 P.2d 383 (Kan. 1988).
James v. Hitchcock Independent School District, 742 S.W.2d 701 (Tex. App.-Houston [1st Dist.] 1987).
Kelso Education Association v. Kelso School District No. 453, 740 P.2d 889 (Wash. App. 1987).
Kenaston v. School Administrative District No. 40, 317 A.2d 7 (Me. 1974).
Kirk v. Miller, 522 P.2d 843 (Wash. 1974).
Kizer v. Dorchester County Vocational Education Board of Trustees, 340 S.E.2d 144 (S.C. 1986).
Knipmeyer v. Diocese of Alexandria, 492 So.2d 550 (La. App. 3 Cir. 1986).
Last v. Board of Education of Community Unit School District No. 321, 185 N.E.2d 282 (Ill. App. 1962).
Lewis v. Board of Education of North Clay Community Unit School District No. 25, Clay County, 537 N.E.2d 435 (Ill.App. 5 Dist. 1989).
Maddox v. St. Paul School District, 697 S.W.2d 130 (Ark. App. 1985).
McAndrew v. School Committee of Cambridge, 480 N.E.2d 327 (Mass. App. 1985).
McCutcheon v. Chicago Principals Association, 513 N.E.2d 55 (Ill. App. 1 Dist. 1987).
Minor v. Sully Buttes School District No. 58-2, 345 N.W.2d 48 (S.D. 1984).
Mission Independent School District v. Diserens, 188 S.W.2d 568 (Tex. 1945).
Moran v. Board of School Trustees of Mt. Pleasant Township Community Schools, Delaware County, 501 N.E.2d 472 (Ind. App. 2 Dist. 1986).
Morgan v. Huntsville City Board of Education, 510 So.2d 260 (Ala. Civ. App. 1987).
Morton v. Hampton School District No. 1, 700 S.W.2d 373 (Ark. App. 1985).

Myrtle Springs Reverted Independent School District v. Hogan, 705 S.W.2d 707 (Tex. App. 6 Dist. 1985), cert. denied, 480 U.S. 906 (1987).
Nelson v. Doland Board of Education of Doland School District No. 56-2, 380 N.W.2d 665 (S.D. 1986).
Niedbalski v. Board of Education of School District No. 24 of Platte Center, 418 N.W.2d 565 (Neb. 1988).
Nordlund v. School District No. 14, 738 P.2d 1299 (Mont. 1987).
Oneal v. Colton Consolidated School District No. 306, 557 P.2d 11 (Wash. App. 1976).
Perry v. Milwaukee Board of School Directors, 388 N.W.2d 638 (Wis. App. 1986).
Pierce v. Douglas School District No. 4, 686 P.2d 332 (Or. 1984).
Rochester Education Association v. Independent School District No. 535, 271 N.W.2d 311 (Minn. 1978).
Romeike v. Houston Independent School District, 368 S.W.2d 895 (Tex. Civ. App. 1963).
Slockett v. Iowa Valley Community School District, 359 N.W.2d 446 (Iowa 1984).
Smith v. Board of Education of Urbana School District No. 116 of Champaign County, Illinois, 708 F.2d 258 (7th Cir., 1983).
Snider v. Kit Carson School District R-1, 442 P.2d 429 (Colo. 1968).
Special School District of Ft. Smith v. Lynch, 413 S.W.2d 880 (Ark. 1967).
State ex rel. Melvin v. Board of Education of City of St. Bernard, 34 N.E.2d 285 (Ohio App. 1940).
State of Indiana ex rel. Anderson v. Brand, 303 U.S. 95 (1938).
Swager v. Board of Education, Unified School District No. 412, Sheridan County, Kansas, 688 P.2d 270 (Kan. App. 1984).
Unified School District No. 241, Wallace County v. Swanson, 717 P.2d 526 (Kan. App. 1986).
Vail v. Board of Education of Paris Union School District No. 95, 706 F.2d 1435 (7th Cir., 1983); aff'd., 466 U.S. 377 (1984).
Wichita Public Schools Employees Union, Local No. 513 v. Smith, 397 P.2d 357 (Kan. 1964).
Wyatt v. School District No. 104, Fergus County, 417 P.2d 221 (Mont. 1966).

2 Assignments and Reassignments

In the early history of public schools in America, assignment of teachers was a simple matter: each one-room school had one teacher. Reassignment was also simple because few options existed. A teacher who desired a transfer left one school and moved on to the next town. When the village council desired to make a reassignment, the teacher was asked to leave and a new teacher was hired. As schools grew and school districts were organized, the right to assign and reassign teachers remained under the authority of local school boards. Although some guidelines for assignment and transfer of teachers may be issued at the state level, teaching assignments are the prerogative of local boards. Teacher organizations often attempt to include teacher assignment and reassignment as negotiating items in collective bargaining contracts, but the courts have generally ruled that these responsibilities are nondelegable. Ideally, all teacher assignments and reassignments are made with the best interests of students and the school in mind.

The majority of court cases pertinent to teacher assignment predate World War II. Since that time, case precedent, contract law, and certification requirements have established the rights of school boards and teachers in assignments. The availability of more qualified teachers has led to fewer arbitrary assignments on the part of boards, making board decisions less open to challenge. Hence, teacher assignment is an area of less conflict and litigation than teacher transfer or reassignment.

Abuses in the exercise of power to reassign teachers have led to court action. Unreasonable teacher transfers often contributed to the passage of employment tenure laws, and courts have been called upon to interpret sections of tenure laws pertinent to reassignment. Procedures to be followed by school boards in reassigning teachers have become part of many collective bargaining contracts, opening yet another area where the courts have become involved in teacher employment decisions. In the absence of law or a legally binding agreement, school boards may exercise almost unquestioned power to make reasonable transfers, but when statutes or contracts stipulate procedures, boards are obligated to follow them.

Because legislative enactments, state board mandates, and case law regarding the assignment and reassignment of teachers are specific to each state, the decisions of the courts may not be generalized to other jurisdictions. State high courts or appeals courts interpret state tenure and employment laws pertinent to assignment and reassignment, and the decisions may be only generally applicable in other states.

Legal Principles

Principle I *Right of Boards*

The assigning of a public school teacher to a specific school and classroom is normally a discretionary right of the board of education of the employing school district. A public school teacher has no legal right or privilege to demand a specific building or classroom assignment unless allowed by statute or contract.

Principle II *No Demotion*

The transferring of a public school teacher from one school or assignment to another is normally a discretionary right of the board of education of the employing school district. However, the board has a legal obligation to see that no element of demotion takes place unless a lawful demotion is being carried out.

Principle III *In Good Faith*

A board of education must make an assignment or reassignment of a public school teacher to a school and classroom in good faith and in a reasonable manner; that is, an assignment must be made in the best interest of the school system and not for any nonvalid or discriminatory reason. A reassignment should never be made to force a teacher to resign.

Principle IV *Legal Certification*

A public school teacher may not be assigned or reassigned to a position for which he or she is not legally qualified. A teacher may refuse any assignment or reassignment for which he or she is not legally qualified without violating a teaching contract because a valid contract demands competent parties.

Principle V *Grounds for Dismissal*

The refusal of a teacher to accept an assignment or a reassignment for which he or she is legally qualified and which the board of education has the power to make may constitute proper grounds for dismissal.

Discussion

Principle I

The assigning of a public school teacher to a specific school and classroom is normally a discretionary right of the board of education of the employing school district. A public school teacher has no legal right or privilege to demand a specific building or classroom assignment unless allowed by statute or contract.

In any school district, some buildings, classrooms, grade levels, or subjects may be viewed as more desirable than others as teaching assignments. An unofficial hierarchy or seniority system sometimes evolves in school districts, resulting in some teachers viewing specific assignments as their right or privilege. Because few school districts recognize these informal seniority systems, teacher assignments do not have to be made in compliance with such systems.

The authority to assign teachers to schools, classrooms, grade levels, and curricular subjects almost always devolves on the local school board from powers vested in the state legislature or state board of education. Local school boards must follow certification requirements, avoid discriminatory assignment practices, and adhere to tenure laws, but the courts have consistently declared that assignment responsibility belongs to local boards. Courts of appeal in California stated this view in 1929 and again in 1967:

> The right to determine the nature and location of the teacher's assignment to services is exclusively vested in the school board acting in a quasi-judicial capacity, with which province the courts have no right to interfere (*Dutart v. Woodward,* 1929).

> Subject only to the requirement of reasonableness, a school district is entitled to assign teachers anywhere within their certificate, according to the needs of the district. . . . The welfare of school districts demands that they have broad discretion to assign their teachers in the best interests of the school system. Consequently, the courts should not lightly undertake to interfere with the exercise of this discretion, where it is not in conflict with statutory law (*Adelt v. Richmond School District,* 1967).

However, when state statutes, tenure laws, or contractual provisions establish guidelines for making teacher assignments, local school boards must adhere to them as they exercise their authority to make teacher assignments. In 1985 a school board in Pennsylvania reassigned a junior high principal to a position as assistant senior high principal when one junior high was closed. Because the public school code mandated that realignment of staff be based solely on seniority, the court ruled that the board had been wrong in failing to appoint the junior high principal to the senior high principalship when he had more seniority than the person named to the position (*Gibbons v. New Castle Area School District,* 1985). Similarly, in 1986 a West Virginia school board ignored a statute requiring consideration of seniority when filling vacancies. While upholding the board of education's discretion in matters relating to hiring and assigning of school personnel, the court reminded the board that "this discretion must be exercised reasonably, in the best interest of the schools, and in a manner which is not arbitrary and capricious" (*Dillon v. Board of Education of County of Wyoming,* 1986).

Some teacher organizations have questioned the right of local boards to make teacher assignments. In 1986 a teacher association filed a grievance when the school board did not appoint the more senior of two qualified counselors to a counseling position. The appellate court of Illinois cited a long list of precedent cases to show that the power to make discretionary appointments to teaching positions was vested exclusively in the school board and was not delegable (*Board of Education of Rockford School District No. 205 v. Rockford Education Association,* 1986).

Although school boards have lost discretionary rights in some areas of teacher employment because of legislative enactments and collective bargaining, the right of initial assignment or appointment to positions usually still rests with local boards. Good faith efforts by school boards in making teacher assignments generally result in teachers accepting their assignments as being in the best interests of students and the district.

Principle II

The transferring of a public school teacher from one school or assignment to another is normally a discretionary right of the board of education of the employing school district. However, the board has a legal obligation to see that no element of demotion takes place unless a lawful demotion is being carried out.

As part of their employment authority and responsibility, school boards generally have the power to reassign or transfer teachers between positions, schools, grade levels, divisions, or classes. Statutory limitations, especially as established by tenure laws, set guidelines in many states for the transfer of teachers, but school boards almost always retain the discretionary right to reassign teachers as long as the transfers are reasonable and within certification stipulations.

The right of school boards to reassign teachers was established in nineteenth century court cases. In 1880 an Illinois appeals court stated that the school board could require teachers to teach in any department where the best interests of the school would be served and that reassignment was as much a part of the contract and as binding on the teacher as if it had been written into the contract before the teacher signed it (*Jacksonville v. Akers,* 1880). In 1890 the California Supreme Court handed down a decision that became precedent for many succeeding reassignment cases:

> We do not wish to be understood as holding that the board of education has not the power to transfer a teacher from one school to another of the same grade. The statute does not guaranty [*sic*] to a teacher the right to continue in any particular school, but to continue, as such teacher, in a certain grade; and the transfer of teachers from one school to another may be necessary for the good of the schools, and should not be prohibited (*Kennedy v. Board of Education,* 1890).

Court cases involving teacher transfers most often arise when teachers view reassignments as illegal demotions because of real or perceived loss of status, salary, or professional responsibility. The burden of proof is usually on the teacher to show that the board lacked authority to make a reassignment or that a reassignment was actually a demotion. If the teacher can show that a demotion, not a transfer, occurred, the courts must then determine if adequate due process was afforded the teacher, especially if tenure statutes apply.

The question of demotion because of a perceived reduction in rank or grade arose in *Rosenthal v. Orleans Parish School Board* (1968). A biology teacher was transferred from the high school for exceptional students to another high school in the district because of discrepancies between her grading policies and those of other teachers at the school. She sought protection under Louisiana's tenure laws, claiming the transfer placed her in a position of lower rank and dignity. The court ruled that the students, not the faculty, were exceptional at the first school and that because both teaching positions paid the same salary and had the same rank and dignity, no demotion had occurred. In the ruling, the court defined a four-part test to determine whether or not a reassignment is actually a demotion:

1. A reduction in salary is involved.
2. The new position requires the teaching of subjects for which the teacher is not qualified.
3. The teacher must undergo additional training to obtain certification for the new position.
4. The transfer follows a dismissal without formal notice or hearing, leaving a blot on the teacher's record (*Rosenthal v. Orleans Parish School Board,* 1968).

Even when some loss of status results from a reassignment, the courts do not always rule such a reassignment illegal. When the dean of students at a California high school was reassigned to a classroom position, he claimed it was an illegal reassignment. The court ruled that he had no tenure as an administrator and had merely served in such a position at the pleasure of the appointing board:

> His demotion involves a reduction in compensation and some loss of professional standing. But those consequences follow in every case of the discharge of any employee-at-will. We are not persuaded that public school administrators hold some kind of special status that entitles them, as a matter of constitutional right, to more formality in their transfer than the law affords to employees in general (*Hentschke v. Sink,* 1973).

In 1977 another California court similarly upheld the reassignment of a counselor to a classroom position even though it involved a reduction in salary (*Thompson v. Modesto City High School District,* 1977). In a 1982 case, an Alabama high school teacher, who had coached for ten years, resigned his coaching duties and was transferred the following year to an elementary school because of a surplus of high school physical education teachers. The court ruled the transfer was not for political or personal reasons and that the teacher had suffered no loss of status (*Hood v. Alabama State Tenure Commission,* 1982). In 1983, the California courts held that the school board's authority to make transfers extended to the assignment of administrative personnel:

> A school district's right to reassign its administrative or supervisory personnel to different positions is extremely broad and subject to only two limitations: that the reassignment be reasonable and that the reassigned position be within

> the scope of the certificate under which tenure was acquired or the work assigned be of a rank and grade equivalent to the position in which tenure was acquired (*LaBelle v. San Francisco Unified School District,* 1983).

In another 1983 case, the Montana Supreme Court ruled that an administrator reassigned to a teaching position because of her position having been eliminated as part of a budget reduction was entitled to her salary for the last year she served as Coordinator of Intermediate Education. However, the reassignment was held to be valid because the board had the authority to reassign personnel for financial reasons (*Sorlie v. School District No. 2,* 1983). The status of a Pennsylvania teacher who had held supervisory positions without the requisite certification became the focus of the courts when she claimed her reassignment to a classroom position was a demotion. When the court affirmed her demotion as valid, she was not eligible for back pay (*School District of Philadelphia v. Brockington,* 1986).

The right to decide upon teacher transfers has been sought by teachers' bargaining agents during negotiations. However, in 1982 an appellate court of New York ruled that public policy prevented a school district from bargaining away its responsibility to transfer or reassign teachers:

> The authority to assign and reassign teachers is essential to maintaining adequate standards in the classroom and is a nondelegable responsibility imposed upon the school superintendent subject to the approval of the board of education (*Sweet Home Central School District v. Sweet Home Education Association,* 1982).

In summary, transfer and reassignment are often viewed as punitive or negative actions, but teachers and administrators should perceive transfers made in good faith to be in the best interest of the school system. The West Virginia Supreme Court of Appeals expressed this view in 1970:

> It is conceivable that many teachers are transferred by county boards of education, not because of inefficiency, misconduct or unfitness, but rather because of the mere fact that they are competent, efficient teachers, and that, therefore, a proper administration of the county public school system dictates the basis of transfers to places and positions where the teachers' special qualifications will better promote the entire public school program of the county (*State ex rel. Withers v. Board of Education of Mason County,* 1970).

Teachers, administrators, and school boards must realize that the laws pertinent to transfer and reassignment are specific to each state. Teachers usually have no right to request a transfer or to refuse a reassignment because the authority to make reassignments rests with the school board. Generally, no element of demotion may be part of a reassignment. Because salary reductions and lowering of grade and rank are defined differently by each state, familiarity with state laws is necessary in determining the validity and legality of teacher transfers and reassignments.

Principle III

A board of education must make an assignment or reassignment of a public school teacher to a school and classroom in good faith and in a reasonable manner; that is, an assignment must be made in the best interest of the school system and not for any nonvalid or discriminatory reason. A reassignment should never be made to force a teacher to resign.

The interests of the school district and its students must be the paramount concern of a school board when making teacher assignments and reassignments. Abuses of discretionary authority to make teacher reassignments led to clauses in tenure acts and collective bargaining agreements to protect teachers from unreasonable transfers, particularly those made in an attempt to force a teacher to resign. Claims often arise concerning assignments and transfers that violate constitutional rights, and the courts will overrule any assignment that can be shown to have been made for illegal, arbitrary, or discriminatory reasons.

In 1929 a teacher filed suit after she was assigned to teach students in a tuberculosis sanatorium. The court agreed that the school board's action was not reasonable:

> There is no doubt that within the limitations prescribed by law and reason the school board possesses the exclusive province of assigning teachers to their specific work. But the board has no arbitrary authority to assign a teacher to a school where the sanitary conditions would endanger her health or life, nor to a school wherein the pupils are afflicted with a contagious disease.... The action of the board in classifying and assigning a teacher to a specific work must be performed in good faith and in accordance with the law (*Dutart v. Woodward,* 1929).

The courts have become involved more often in reassignments alleged to have been made in bad faith than in initial assignment cases. In *State ex rel. Ging v. Board of Education of City of Duluth* (1942), the Supreme Court of Minnesota handed down a decision which is often cited by other state courts in teacher reassignment cases. The court upheld the right of school boards to make reassignments as long as they are in the best interests of the school district:

> If for any reason sufficient classes are not available for all tenure teachers, the board and superintendent should and do have the power, in good faith, to shift and rearrange the teaching force without reference to prescriptive rights of any single teacher to a particular classroom, building or division of the school system.... But though the power so to transfer teachers unquestionably exists, it must be exercised in good faith and for the best interest of the school district and must be based upon actually existing school conditions ... and not for the purpose of compelling a teacher's resignation (*State ex rel. Ging v. Board of Education of City of Duluth,* 1942).

As *Ging* implies, the courts will review cases carefully when claims arise that a transfer was made to force a teacher to resign. Due process guidelines are established by many states to void such transfers, and the courts uphold these procedures (*State of New Mexico ex rel. State Board of Education v. Montoya,* 1963; *Board of Education, Tucson High School District No. 1 v. Williams,* 1965; *State ex rel. Pemberton v. Wilson,* 1972).

The courts have also become involved when violations of tenure laws and collective bargaining agreements have been alleged. Generally, tenure laws and negotiated agreements may not supersede the school board's right to make transfers but may establish procedures which the board is obligated to follow. In 1935 a California court summarized the obligations of school boards to make teacher assignments and transfers in accord with state tenure statutes:

> There is nothing in the tenure law which interferes with the general power and right of a board of education to assign teachers to particular classes and to particular schools in accordance with its judgment and desire reasonably exercised. A teacher, in acquiring a permanent status, does not thereby acquire a vested right to teach any certain class or in any certain school. While a board would have no right to evade the plain meaning of the tenure act by assigning a teacher to a class of work for which he was not qualified, for the purpose of compelling his resignation, it has the power to reasonably change assignments with respect to a permanent teacher so long as the work assigned is of a rank and grade equivalent to that by which the permanent status was acquired and so long as the assignment is one for which the teacher in question is qualified (*Mitchell v. Board of Trustees of Visalia Union High School District,* 1935).

In 1985 a tenured teacher in Illinois was able to show that the school board acted in bad faith in reassigning her to a half-time position. The court ruled that a reassignment that subverts the state tenure law cannot be tolerated even if under the guise of discretionary authority and duty (*Pennell v. Board of Education of Equality Community Unit School District No. 4, Gallatin County,* 1985).

The courts will also intervene when individual rights are violated by teaching assignments. In 1967 a teacher who was transferred to a home teaching position from teaching high school senior government classes because he wore a beard was ordered reinstated. The wearing of a beard was ruled a liberty right of which a teacher could not be deprived (*Finot v. Pasadena City Board of Education*, 1967). Another California teacher was transferred for speaking against school policies. The courts ruled that the exercise of First Amendment rights cannot be the reason for a transfer:

> We concede that the superintendent obviously has and must have very broad discretion in transferring teachers from one school to another, i.e., when it in fact "is in the best interests of the district". . . . and his discretion ordinarily will not be reviewed or interfered with by the trial court. It is *only* when it is asserted that the motivation for transfer is based on a teacher's exercise of constitutionally protected rights that the trial court will conduct an independent review of the record to determine whether the assertion is true (*Adcock v. Board of Education of San Diego Unified School District,* 1973).

In Kentucky the supreme court overruled the transfer of several teachers that resulted from their actions in supporting a school board candidate whom the superintendent opposed. Even though the board claimed the transfers were "for the betterment of the schools," the court said they were punitive actions in "a vendetta against the teachers and employees" (*Calhoun v. Cassady,* 1976).

The United States Court of Appeals, Ninth Circuit, ruled that the transfer of an Arizona teacher was invalid because it was based on her exercise of First Amendment rights. The counselor, who had special training in the counseling of Mexican-American children, had complained that Spanish-speaking students were being discriminated against because they were tested in English. She was transferred to an upper-class Anglo school and told that her former position was abolished because of lack of funds; actually, a part-time counselor had been hired for the position (*Bernasconi v. Tempe Elementary School District No. 3,* 1977).

Assignment or reassignment of teachers based on any discriminatory criteria or for any allegedly discriminatory purpose may be a violation of teachers' civil rights. After the United States Supreme Court determined that school faculties had to be desegregated (*Rogers v. Paul,* 1965; *Bradley v. School Board of City of Richmond,* 1965), the integration of faculty became a major component of government-ordered desegregation actions. Many school boards were faced with having to adhere to court-ordered guidelines or to establish their own standards for making teacher assignments without perpetuating or creating single-race faculties. In 1968 a federal appeals court struck down a school board practice in Chicago that encouraged teacher assignment on the basis of race, i.e., black teachers to predominately black schools and white teachers to predominately white schools (*United States v. School District 151 of Cook County,* 1968).

In 1970 the United States Court of Appeals, Fifth Circuit, provided guidelines to assist school districts under desegregation orders in assigning staff so that "in no case will the racial composition of a staff indicate that a school is intended for Negro students or white students" (*Singleton v. Jackson Municipal Separate School District,* 1970). Many subsequent cases involving the desegregation of faculty referred to the *Singleton* tests for assignment and reassignment of teachers (*McPherson v. School District No. 186,* 1976; *Alvarado v. El Paso Independent School District,* 1976). In a Michigan case, a school board argued that "the assignment of Black teachers to Black schools was to bring about a better kind of communication pattern." The federal court disagreed with this rationale:

> The efficacy of assigning Black teachers disproportionately to a particular school for purposes of their relationship with Black students assumes the continued existence of racially identifiable schools. It is an indicium of intent to maintain the facility as a racially identifiable school, and the practice itself helps make a given school racially identifiable (*N.A.A.C.P. v. Lansing Board of Education,* 1976).

In 1978 the Fifth Circuit Court ruled that a lower court had been in error when it had not insisted on immediate compliance with the *Singleton* requirement that the faculty of each school in a district reflect the systemwide racial ratio of faculty members. The Circuit Court reminded the school district that the United States Supreme Court had rejected "with all deliberate speed" guidelines for desegregation in 1969 (*Alexander v. Holmes County Board of Education,* 1969), and that although *Singleton* guidelines did not require the permanent use of mathematical ratios, such ratios are effective as "a starting point in eliminating vestiges of segregation in both student and faculty assignments." *Singleton* "contemplates an initial reassignment so that the racial ratio at every school reflects the systemwide ratio, followed by the utilization of a non-discriminatory hiring, firing, and assignment policy thereafter" (*United States v. DeSoto Parish School Board,* 1978).

In 1979 the United States Supreme Court struck down the 1951 Dayton Board of Education policy of "dynamic gradualism." Under this policy, black teachers were being assigned to white or mixed race schools when the surrounding communities were judged ready to accept black teachers. The court ruled that purposeful discrimination was still being practiced when the majority of all black teachers were assigned to schools that were 90 percent or more black and only 9 percent of white teachers were assigned to such schools (*Dayton Board of Education v. Brinkman,* 1979).

Continuance of racially identifiable schools in a Mississippi school district led the Fifth Circuit Court to mandate that the desegregation of faculty did not have to await the nondiscriminatory hiring of new teachers. The court stated that the interests of students were most important when teacher reassignments were made:

> The plan for the reassignment of teachers should attempt to distribute the task of teaching at schools considered less desirable between more experienced and newly hired teachers so that students who are perhaps under the greatest learning disability and in need of the best teachers are not relegated to the tutelage of novices (*United States v. Lawrence County School District,* 1986).

Teacher reassignments resulting from desegregation actions led some teachers to file suit, claiming that transfers and reassignments had violated their individual constitutional rights. For example, in 1979, 25,000 teachers of the Los Angeles City Unified School District filed a class action suit, arguing that the desegregation plan from the United States Office of Civil Rights violated their equal protection rights under the Fourteenth Amendment because it took race into account in the mandatory reassignment of teachers. The court upheld the desegregation plan whereby the faculty composition of each school in the district had to reflect the racial and ethnic minority/majority ratio in the district (*Zaslawsky v. Board of Education of Los Angeles City Unified School District,* 1979).

As a result of efforts to desegregate the nation's schools, claims of reverse discrimination in teacher assignment and reassignment have been made. In 1984 a white female teacher was reassigned so that the faculty ratio of two schools would be within guidelines set by the Office of Civil Rights. She claimed reverse discrimination, but an appellate court of California ruled for the district:

> Ethnicity may . . . be taken into account in the assignment of teachers. . . . To maintain a racial balance, the district must employ some means to ascertain the districtwide ethnic composition and then allocate its faculty to obtain an ethnic balance. To do less would deprive students of the opportunity to be educated in a system reflecting the society in which they are to live (*Bolin v. San Bernardino City Unified School District,* 1984).

In 1989 a federal district court in Texas ruled on a case of alleged reverse discrimination in coaching assignments in a school district no longer under court-ordered desegregation mandates. The case arose after a newspaper reported that there were no black high school varsity coaches although 80 percent of the team members were black. Shortly after the story was published, two assistant varsity football coaches—one white and one Hispanic—were transferred to the sophomore football staff and replaced with two black coaches. Because the school district had been declared unitary in 1984, the district was not under any court order to establish racial quotas for teaching assignments and, indeed, was to make personnel decisions on objective, nonracial standards. The court ruled that the coaches were victims of illegal discrimination (*Covington v. Beaumont Independent School District,* 1989).

The United States Office of Civil Rights continues to establish rules for faculty desegregation in school districts where racial separation still exists. However, as school districts are declared unitary, strict mathematical ratios for faculty are inappropriate standards for assigning and reassigning teachers. School districts should adopt fair hiring, assignment, and transfer policies to maintain balance in the racial composition of their teaching staffs.

To conclude, a school board must always have the welfare of the district and students in mind when assigning and reassigning teachers but must not overstep the limits of authority by violating teacher rights, tenure laws, or collective bargaining agreements. When an assignment is legal, reasonable, and in the best interests of students and the school district, the courts will generally not interfere with the authority of local boards to make assignments and reassignments of teachers.

Principle IV

A public school teacher may not be assigned or reassigned to a position for which he or she is not legally qualified. A teacher may refuse any assignment or reassignment for which he or she is not legally qualified without violating a teaching contract because a valid contract demands competent parties.

Certification from the state is the legal evidence of a teacher's qualifications. Certification standards and procedures differ from state to state, but generally a teacher may not legally be assigned to teach a subject or grade level without proper certification. If a school board does assign or transfer a teacher to a subject or grade level outside the area of the teacher's certification, the board is violating contract law. A fundamental requirement for a valid contract is competent parties; a teacher assigned to an area for which no certificate is held is not a competent party. Because a school board cannot lawfully make such an assignment, teachers may refuse a teaching assignment for which they do not have certification without jeopardizing their contracts or tenure positions.

Early contract law was not as specific as it is today; therefore, the courts often defined the first contractual relationships between teachers and school boards. In 1925 a teacher was contracted to teach grades 1 through 8 in a "common school." She consented to teach grade 9 only until the lower grades had full attendance. When the teaching load made instructing the ninth grade impossible for the teacher, the board suggested that one of the young female pupils teach the lower grades to allow the teacher time with the ninth grade; the teacher was to pay the student teacher $20 of her own salary. The teacher refused the board's suggestion and was forced to resign. The court ruled in favor of the teacher for reimbursement of salary because the board had broken the contract (*School District No. 21 v. Hudson,* 1925).

In a 1926 case, a teacher was licensed to teach domestic science, history, civics, zoology, and education but, after signing her contract, was requested to teach high school English and German, neither of which she was qualified to teach. She took a state examination in an attempt to earn certification in these subjects but failed it. The board then discharged her, and she sued to recover payment for the unexpired term of her contract. The court ruled in favor of the teacher:

> If it should be declared to be the law that a trustee, after entering into such a contract with a teacher, could demand of such teacher that she teach some particular subject, not covered by the license of such teacher, and that a failure of such teacher to procure a license covering the subject so demanded of her to be taught constitutes a breach of her contract, then is the way open to any trustee to render of no effect any contract he may have made with any teacher (*Jefferson School Township of Miami County v. Graves,* 1926).

In a similar case, a teacher who held a college provisional certificate to teach certain subjects was appointed to a teacher-librarian position. The board knew she was not certified as a librarian but applied for and received an emergency certificate for her. A year later, she was dismissed for failure to hold a teacher-librarian certificate. The court upheld the teacher's right to employment (*In re Womar,* 1940).

Usually the courts strictly observe the specifications on a teacher's certificate when an assignment issue arises, not a teacher's claim of experience and training or lack of the same. However, the courts ruled differently in a 1943 case. A tenured teacher who had taught only upper grades and band was reassigned just two weeks before the beginning of the school year to a one-room school with seven lower-grade students and, of course, no band. Even though his teaching certificate was for grades 1 through 9, he successfully established that he had no training or experience below fifth grade. The court agreed with the teacher:

> Neither the superintendent nor the board of trustees possessed any statutory right to assign the [teacher] to a position for which he was not qualified.... [The teacher] was within his rights in declining the new offer so made him (*Smith v. School District No. 18, Pondera County,* 1943).

In 1983 a teacher who suspected that she would be reassigned to a subject she did not want to teach withdrew her certificate in that subject area. When she was assigned to teach social studies as well as her physical education and health classes, she said she did not feel qualified to teach social studies and had voluntarily withdrawn her certification. The board refused to change her assignment, and she did not teach her sociology classes for 39 consecutive days. After receiving a warning, she was dismissed on grounds of insubordination and excessive absences. The court ruled that in the state certification statute, "position" was not synonymous with "field of study." Thus, the teacher could be assigned to the social studies classes even though she did not feel qualified to teach sociology. The court also said her action in withdrawing her certificate without the knowledge of her employers constituted a breach of contract (*McLaughlin v. Board of Education,* 1983).

In summary, the courts usually consider only legal certification, not training or experience unrepresented by the certificate, when legal contract disputes arise. Although teachers do not have to accept assignments for which they are not legally qualified, they should be sure they understand how certification and tenure statutes of their state define "qualification." The courts will consider only strict legal definition, not expectation, seniority, desire, or experience of the teacher. School boards must be certain that teachers' certificates cover all grade levels and subjects to which they are assigned. To protect themselves should the question of certification arise, teachers should never accept assignments that they are not legally qualified to fulfill and should be certain their teaching certificates are current.

Principle V

The refusal of a teacher to accept an assignment or a reassignment for which he or she is legally qualified and which the board of education has the power to make may constitute proper grounds for dismissal.

Because the school board has the authority to make assignments and teachers have no right to reject assignments within their certification areas, a teacher who refuses an assignment or transfer may be dismissed, regardless of tenure. The grounds for dismissal may be insubordination, willful violation of contract, or persistent negligence, as demonstrated by the Pennsylvania Superior Court in 1942:

> The School Code ... reserved to the board the power to assign [the teacher] to duties for which he was properly qualified under his teacher's certificate.... A refusal to accept an assignment which a board has the power to make may be classed as "persisent and wilful [*sic*] violation of the school laws of this Commonwealth on the part of the professional employee," and a direct violation of his contract, and also amounts to "persistent negligence"; and for such conduct a teacher may be dismissed and his contract terminated (*Commonwealth ex rel. Wesenberg v. School District of City of Bethlehem,* 1942).

Early cases show how definitions and expectations of teaching positions have evolved. In 1910 a teacher went on a leave of absence from June to August; on her return she was reassigned to a different grade at a different school for a lower salary. She refused the transfer and demanded restoration of her salary. The court ruled that the transfer was legal because it was to the same statutory grade level and that she had refused a lawful assignment (*Loehr v. Board of Education,* 1910). In 1931 a teacher reassigned to full-time teaching duties instead of part-time vice-principal duties received a decrease in salary and then was dismissed for refusing the lower salary. The court ruled that the board had the right to restructure teacher duties and salary (*Fidler v. Board of Trustees of Roseville Union High School,* 1931).

In a 1943 case, a teacher who was reassigned to the fourth and fifth grades insisted her contract was for only the seventh grade and reported there, supplanting the teacher who was assigned to the seventh grade. In upholding the teacher's dismissal for neglect of duty, the court said that the board had discretionary power to assign, reassign, and transfer teachers (*Consolidated School District No. 4, Bryan County v. Millis,* 1943). Other teachers have also claimed that years of experience qualified them to teach only certain grades or subjects. Upon reassignment, they have not appeared to teach their classes, claiming breach of contract on the part of the district. The courts have upheld their subsequent dismissals (*Harrisburg R-VIII School District v. O'Brian,* 1976; *Collins v. Wakonda Independent School District No. 1,* 1977).

In a 1954 case, an Idaho teacher was informed, three days before school was to start, of her transfer to a school 22 miles away. She claimed breach of contract, but the court said the board had conformed to the contract and that her refusal to accept the transfer constituted legal grounds for discharge:

> The contract gave [the teacher] no right to choose the school in which she would teach. That was expressly left to the judgment, discretion and direction of the governing officers of the district (*Bullock v. Joint Class "A" School District No. 241,* 1954).

A Utah teacher was transferred after he refused to attend a school workshop that was using materials purchased with federal moneys because he was personally averse to the use of federal funds in public schools. When he sued the district because of the transfer, the court upheld the board's decision, although the court stated it did not understand why the teacher was transferred and not dismissed for insubordination (*Brough v. Board of Education of Millard County School District,* 1970).

In 1983 a teacher who had continual conflict with a new principal was recommended for reassignment the following year to a position at equal rank, pay, status, and even an equal distance from her home. She failed to report for work and was dismissed for willful neglect of duty. Noting the reasonableness of the transfer, the court held in favor of the board:

> A school board has not only a right, but a duty, to transfer teachers in the best interests of the pupils and the system.... [The teacher's] mere expectancy of continued employment does not restrict the School Board's power to transfer teachers (*Slaughter v. East Baton Rouge Parish School Board,* 1983).

A Texas case began in 1983 when a football coach was relieved of his coaching duties after he tackled an eighth grade player for poor performance during practice. After a hearing, the coach was temporarily reassigned to the transportation department because no teaching vacancies were available. Alleging discriminatory actions by the school district, the teacher filed a complaint with the Equal Employment Opportunity Commission, which dismissed his complaint. The next year, he was reassigned to a middle school science position; he held certification in science and had had previous teaching experience in that subject. Continuing to claim that he was a victim of racial discrimination and that he was not qualified to teach science, the teacher was eventually terminated for irremediable deficiencies in his teaching, poor attitude, lack of cooperation, and unwillingness to acknowledge a need for improvement (*Dooley v. Fort Worth Independent School District,* 1987).

Teachers should recognize that their contracts obligate them to accept reasonable assignments from their employing school boards. To do otherwise may lead to dismissal for insubordination or breach of contract. Because they do not usually acquire tenure for a particular school, grade, or subject, teachers legally must accept any position for which they are qualified according to their state certification, as long as the assignment was made in good faith by the board.

Summary

Although the specificity of contract law and emergence of collective bargaining agreements have modified employment procedures, school boards generally retain authority and responsibility for assigning and reassigning teachers. Teachers usually have no legal right to expect assignment to a preferred position or to continue in a current position. However, a reassignment may not be a disguise for a demotion nor a ploy to force a teacher to resign. Except when violations of constitutional rights, state statutes, or collective bargaining agreements are alleged, the courts continually refuse to interfere with the decisions of school boards regarding assignment and transfer of faculty.

Teacher assignments and reassignments must not be made on any racially discriminatory basis because the courts require desegregation of faculty as part of general school desegregation orders. Failure to desegregate faculties or continuation of *de facto* segregation by racially distinguishable staffs has led to a large number of court cases involving teacher assignment and reassignment. Once balance is achieved and nondiscriminatory hiring, assigning, dismissing, and transferring procedures are established, the courts will support school board employment decisions.

School boards must use their discretionary power to make teacher assignments and reassignments in good faith and for no arbitrary, illegal, or invalid reason. Teachers must recognize that the school board has the right as the employer to make assignments and reassignments in the best interests of the district and its students. Teachers may legally refuse assignments or transfers that are outside their certification areas, but the courts usually do not accept a teacher's claims of training and experience that are not legally represented by the certificate. Therefore, school boards and teachers must abide by the specification of certificates in making and accepting teaching assignments and reassignments.

Questions and Responses

1. Who has the authority to assign, transfer, or reassign teachers?
The local school board almost always retains the responsibility and authority to make assignments and reassignments of school personnel. Administrators and representatives from teachers' organizations may serve an advisory function in the process but usually have no role in finalizing assignment and reassignment decisions. State laws and state board of education guidelines for assigning and transferring teachers vary widely from state to state. Generally, however, school boards have the authority

to make assignments and reassignments that are reasonable, in good faith, and in the best interests of the school system.

2. How may a collective bargaining agreement affect teacher assignment and reassignment?

School board assignment and transfer decisions usually are not negotiable. However, when collective bargaining agreements outline procedures for making assignments and reassignments, a school board is then obligated to follow them, although final decision-making authority is retained by the board. Failure to abide by such procedures would be a breach of the negotiated contract. Teachers' associations are gaining more and more influence over the reassignment process through negotiated agreements that become part of the master contract.

3. What criteria do courts use in determining whether or not an assignment or reassignment is legal?

An assignment or transfer decision must be made in good faith, be reasonable, be in the best interests of the school system, and not be in violation of any statute or individual constitutional right. Also, the assignment or transfer must be within the bounds of a teacher's certificate.

4. When is a transfer considered a demotion?

The courts would probably view a transfer as a demotion if any one of the following criteria applied to the reassignment:

a. A reduction in salary was involved.
b. The new position required the teaching of subjects for which the teacher was not qualified.
c. The teacher had to undergo additional training to obtain certification for the new position.
d. The transfer followed a dismissal without formal charges or hearing, leaving a blot on the teacher's record.

5. When is a tenured teacher subject to reassignment?

Tenure laws that address the subject of reassignment may establish guidelines for the transfer of teachers according to seniority or other tenure-related criteria. If a state's tenure statute details the procedures for making transfers, the local school board is obligated to follow them. However, the school board retains the authority to make reassignment decisions, and the courts have upheld decisions made on reasonable, valid criteria in spite of tenured teachers' claims of violation of their tenure rights. Tenure laws usually do not protect a specific position, school, subject area, or grade for a teacher but merely a position in a district. Therefore, reassignments may be made legally without violating tenure statutes.

6. What rules and procedures govern a school board's decisions pertinent to achieving a racially balanced faculty?

The United States Supreme Court has ruled that assignment of faculty and staff to schools on the basis of race is unconstitutional if such assignments lead to all black teachers at predominately black schools and all white teachers at predominately white schools. A school district under desegregation orders must include the desegregation of faculty as part of its plan. Many courts have used the guidelines established by the United States Court of Appeals, Fifth Circuit, in *Singleton v. Jackson Municipal Separate School District* (1970) to mandate or enforce desegregation orders for school districts. As a minimum requirement, desegregation of faculty usually involves the reassignment of teachers so that a school cannot be identified as "black" or "white" by the racial composition of its teachers. Once a racially balanced staff is achieved and fair hiring, firing, and reassigning policies are established, desegregation orders usually call for an end to mathematical ratios, and the authority to make decisions regarding assignment and reassignment of teachers returns to the local school board.

7. When may a teacher refuse to accept a reassignment?

A teacher may refuse a transfer if it violates individual constitutional rights or it is a subterfuge to get the teacher to resign. A teacher may also refuse a reassignment to a subject area that is not part of the teacher's certification because such a reassignment would be a violation of contract law. Contracts require competent parties, and lack of proper certification would make the teacher incapable of signing a valid contract. Also, a teacher may refuse a transfer that is an illegal demotion.

8. May a teacher request assignment or transfer to a school located nearer his or her home for economic and convenience reasons?

A teacher has no legal right to expect or demand an assignment or reassignment to any particular building, classroom, grade level, or subject. If the school district allows such requests, teachers must realize that the requests remain subject to the discretion of the board and that assignments and transfers are made in the best interests of the school district and students.

9. When may a school board reassign an administrator to a classroom teaching position?

Generally, administrators may be reassigned to any teaching position for which they hold certification when the transfer is in the best interests of the school system. The reassignment may not be a form of demotion unless such reassignment adheres to guidelines for a legal demotion action. In some states, administrator to classroom teacher transfers are considered demotions because of the perceived drop in rank and status. A decrease in salary or responsibility is evidence of a demotion in many states, and reassignments that involve such decreases would not be upheld in court.

10. Will a claim of lack of experience or qualification protect a teacher from a transfer?

A school board has the right to reassign a teacher to any position for which the teacher is legally qualified and which does not violate any statute or constitutional right. A teacher may not hide behind a claim of inexperience, lack of training, or lack of qualifications if the teacher certificate belies such a claim. The courts will usually evaluate the certificate in a strict legal sense, and other claims will not be upheld.

Case References

Adcock v. Board of Education of San Diego Unified School District, 513 P.2d 900 (Cal. 1973).
Adelt v. Richmond School District, 58 Cal.Rptr. 151 (Cal.App. 1967).
Alexander v. Holmes County Board of Education, 396 U.S. 19 (1969).
Alvarado v. El Paso Independent School District, 426 F.Supp. 575 (W.D. Tex. 1976).
Bernasconi v. Tempe Elementary School District No. 3, 548 F.2d 857 (9th Cir., 1977), cert. denied, 434 U.S. 825 (1977).
Board of Education of Rockford School District No. 205 v. Rockford Education Association, 501 N.E.2d 338 (Ill.App. 2 Dist. 1986).
Board of Education, Tucson High School District No. 1 v. Williams, 403 P.2d 324 (Ariz. App. 1965).
Bolin v. San Bernardino City Unified School District, 202 Cal.Rptr. 416 (Cal. App. 1984).
Bradley v. School Board of City of Richmond, 382 U.S. 103 (1965).
Brough v. Board of Education of Millard County School District, 463 P.2d 567 (Utah 1970).
Bullock v. Joint Class "A" School District No. 241, 272 P.2d 292 (Idaho 1954).
Calhoun v. Cassady, 534 S.W.2d 806 (Ky. 1976).
Collins v. Wakonda Independent School District No. 1, 252 N.W.2d 646 (S.D. 1977).
Commonwealth ex rel. Wesenberg v. School District of City of Bethlehem, 24 A.2d 673 (Pa. Super. 1942).
Consolidated School District No. 4, Bryan County v. Millis, 139 P.2d 183 (Okl. 1943).
Covington v. Beaumont Independent School District, 714 F.Supp. 1402 (E.D.Tex. 1989).
Dayton Board of Education v. Brinkman, 443 U.S. 526 (1979).
Dillon v. Board of Education of County of Wyoming, 351 S.E.2d 58 (W.Va. 1986).
Dooley v. Fort Worth Independent School District, 686 F.Supp. 1194 (N.D.Tex. 1987).
Dutart v. Woodward, 279 P. 493 (Cal.App. 1929).
Fidler v. Board of Trustees of Roseville Union High School, 296 P. 912 (Cal. App. 1931).
Finot v. Pasadena City Board of Education, 58 Cal.Rptr. 520 (Cal.App. 1967).
Gibbons v. New Castle Area School District, 500 A.2d 922 (Pa.Cmwlth. 1985).
Harrisburg R-VIII School District v. O'Brian, 540 S.W.2d 945 (Mo. App. 1976).
Hentschke v. Sink, 109 Cal.Rptr. 549 (Cal.App. 1973).
Hood v. Alabama State Tenure Commission, 418 So.2d 131 (Ala.Civ.App. 1982).
In re Womer, 11 A.2d 146 (Pa. 1940).
Jacksonville v. Akers, 11 Ill.App. 393 (1880).
Jefferson School Township of Miami County v. Graves, 150 N.E. 61 (Ind. App. 1926).
Kennedy v. Board of Education, 22 P. 1042 (Cal. 1890).
LaBelle v. San Francisco Unified School District, 189 Cal.Rptr. 530 (Cal.App. 1983).
Loehr v. Board of Education, 108 P. 325 (Cal.App. 1910).
McLaughlin v. Board of Education, 659 S.W.2d 249 (Mo.App. 1983).
McPherson v. School District No. 186, 426 F.Supp. 173 (S.D. Ill. 1976).
Mitchell v. Board of Trustees of Visalia Union High School District, 42 P.2d 397 (Cal. App. 1935).
N.A.A.C.P. v. Lansing Board of Education, 429 F.Supp. 583 (W.D. Mich. 1976).
Pennell v. Board of Education of Equality Community Unit School District No. 4, Gallatin County, 484 N.E.2d 445 (Ill.App. 5 Dist. 1985).
Rogers v. Paul, 382 U.S. 198 (1965).
Rosenthal v. Orleans Parish School Board, 214 So.2d 203 (La. App. 1968).
School District No. 21 v. Hudson, 277 S.W. 18 (Ark. 1925).
School District of Philadelphia v. Brockington, 511 A.2d 944 (Pa.Cmwlth. 1986).
Singleton v. Jackson Municipal Separate School District, 419 F.2d 1211 (5th Cir., 1970), cert. denied, 402 U.S. 944 (1971).

Slaughter v. East Baton Rouge Parish School Board, 432 So.2d 905 (La.App. 1983).
Smith v. School District No. 18, Pondera County, 139 P.2d 518 (Mont. 1943).
Sorlie v. School District No. 2, 667 P.2d 400 (Mont. 1983).
State ex rel. Ging v. Board of Education of City of Duluth, 7 N.W.2d 544 (Minn. 1942).
State ex rel. Pemberton v. Wilson, 481 S.W.2d 760 (Tenn. 1972).
State ex rel. Withers v. Board of Education of Mason County, 172 S.E.2d 796 (W.Va. 1970).
State of New Mexico ex rel. State Board of Education v. Montoya, 386 P.2d 252 (N.M. 1963).
Sweet Home Central School District v. Sweet Home Education Association, 455 N.Y.S.2d 685 (N.Y.A.D. 1982).
Thompson v. Modesto City High School District, 566 P.2d 237 (Cal. 1977).
United States v. DeSoto Parish School Board, 574 F.2d 804 (5th Cir., 1978).
United States v. Lawrence County School District, 799 F.2d 1031 (5th Cir., 1986).
United States v. School District 151 of Cook County, Illinois, 404 F.2d 1125 (7th Cir., 1968).
Zaslawsky v. Board of Education of Los Angeles City Unified School District, 610 F.2d 661 (9th Cir., 1979).

3 Extra Duties

Teaching in America's public schools has always encompassed many more duties than those associated with classroom responsibilities. Early pioneer teachers not only had to teach the rudiments of reading, writing, and arithmetic but also were required to start the fire, keep the woodbox stocked, take out the ashes, and provide all maintenance needed by the one-room, one-teacher schoolhouses. Later, student out-of-class activities and clubs were organized and supervised by teachers who had special interests or abilities in music, athletics, debate, drama, and journalism. In isolated communities of early America, the school provided the only opportunity for teachers to practice their special interests, and students benefited from teachers' desires to organize bands, sports teams, plays, and newspapers.

As schools and curricula became more established, the "extracurriculum" came to be an accepted and expected part of the educational experience afforded by the schools. For some subjects, such as music or physical education, extra activities have become an integrated part of the curriculum, and those teachers know that organizing and supervising performance groups or interscholastic teams will almost always be part of their responsibilities. When any activity is deemed necessary to student development, school boards or administrators assign a teacher as the organization or activity adviser. Student activities at night, on weekends, and away from school usually require the presence of teachers if the activity is school sponsored or sanctioned. As the extracurriculum has proliferated, a teacher's extra duty assignments have increased in number and responsibility but often without commensurate monetary compensation.

A teacher's administrative duties have also changed since the one-teacher schools where the teacher was room monitor, furnace cleaner, attendance officer, lunchroom supervisor, and transportation coordinator. Most schools have regular duty rosters that assign teachers to certain places and times to monitor student behavior before and after school, during breaks between classes, in cafeterias and gymnasiums, and on playgrounds. The reporting of grades and tardies, of efforts to comply with state and federal regulations, and of money collections for school lunch, yearbooks, and field trips is among the administrative tasks that require much time on the part of every teacher. Even custodial, bus driving, and secretarial tasks are not unknown to teachers.

As they have viewed extra duties as more demanding, less related to their personal and professional areas of expertise, and less compensated, teachers have questioned whether these tasks may legally be required of them. Disputes involving extra assignments have resulted in court action. "Implied duty" clauses in teacher contracts are usually upheld in court as a legitimate exercise of a school board's discretionary authority. When litigation involving these clauses has arisen, the courts have usually upheld teacher extracurricular assignments shown to be closely related to the entire educational program for which the teacher must share responsibility. Only when the extra duty has been seen as completely unrelated to the professional responsibilities of the teacher, demeaning, or unreasonably demanding have the courts ruled against such an assignment.

However, many school districts are now issuing contracts that stipulate a teacher's extra duty assignments, and others are issuing two contracts: one for the primary teaching assignment and one for extra duties. The question of whether or not a teacher must accept a contract for extra duties as a condition for continued employment has recently come before the courts. Extra duties have also become part of negotiated agreements and a major source of dispute in contract negotiations. When either teachers or administrators are accused of violating contract provisions pertaining to extra duties, the courts have sometimes been asked to settle the dispute.

Some extra duty assignments include supplemental pay because of their time demands, perceived importance, or ability to attract outside funding. The courts have become involved again when teachers dispute over who is entitled to such paying positions. Charges of wrongful transfer and dismissal have sometimes resulted from the loss of an extra duty assignment. The courts have relied on contractual stipulations and collective bargaining agreements when making rulings on assignments that involve supplemental pay. Usually no teacher is entitled to an extra duty assignment unless the contract includes it.

As extra duty assignments become more numerous and teachers view some as infringing on their professional and personal time and others as special privileges, more of these assignments will likely become the subject of court action. Interpreting contract language in respect to extra duties will be the major task of the courts in these cases.

Legal Principles

Principle I *Legal Obligation*

Where contract agreements contain no provision regarding the assignment of extra duties, past practice and some legal decisions suggest that a teacher has an obligation to accept such assignments as long as the amount of time required is not unreasonable and the assignments are reasonably related to the teacher's area of expertise.

(continued on next page)

Legal Principles (continued)

Principle II *Categories of Duties*

Courts tend to divide extra duties into two categories: (1) activities foreign to a teacher's area of instructional expertise and (2) activities closely related to teaching and classroom activities.

Principle III *Unrelated Duties*

As a general rule, extra duties that are foreign to teaching may not be required of a teacher unless specifically stipulated in the employment contract. Some courts look upon the assignment of unrelated extra duties as beyond the scope of a teacher's contract and free teachers from any legal obligation to accept such assignments.

Principle IV *No Entitlement*

Except as stipulated by contract or statute, a teacher has no entitlement to an extra duty assignment. Supplemental income, status, or privileges may accompany assignment to certain extra duties because of board policy, community values, or outside funding. However, extra assignments are generally only adjuncts to the regular teaching contract.

Principle V *Refusal of Supplemental Contract*

When a supplemental contract is issued to a teacher in addition to a master teaching contract, the teacher may have the right to refuse the supplemental contract without affecting the conditions of the primary contract.

Discussion

Principle I

Where contract agreements contain no provision regarding the assignment of extra duties, past practice and some legal decisions suggest that a teacher has an obligation to accept such assignments as long as the amount of time required is not unreasonable and the assignments are reasonably related to the teacher's area of expertise.

Tradition suggests that teachers are obligated to fulfill all responsibilities that are reasonably associated with the educational program of the school. Keeping the fire going was once such a duty; serving as class adviser or organization sponsor is now a common extra duty that complements classroom experiences. The courts generally support the assignment of extra duties to teachers when the duties are reasonable and especially when they are related to a teacher's overall administrative responsibilities or to his or her area of expertise or professional interest.

The great expansion in extracurricular activities for students in the 1950s resulted in the first significant court cases where teachers questioned their extra duty assignments, especially those receiving no extra compensation. In 1951 New York teachers went to court in an attempt to have board of education resolutions regarding extra assignments annulled. The resolutions stated that every teacher was required to give service outside of regular classroom instruction and that the principal would be responsible for making reasonable assignments. In refuting the teachers' claims, the court defined the importance of extra duties in statements that would be quoted in succeeding court cases:

> The broad grant of authority to fix "duties" of teachers is not restricted to classroom instruction. Any teaching duty within the scope of the license held by a teacher may properly be imposed. The day in which the concept was held that teaching duty was limited to classroom instruction has long since passed .... Of course, it is recognized that any bylaw of a board outlining teachers' duties must stand the test of reasonableness. Any teacher may be expected to take over a study hall; a teacher engaged in instruction in a given area may be expected to devote part of his day to student meetings where supervision of such teacher is, in the opinion of the board, educationally desirable .... It does not follow that because an activity is conducted after regular class hours, it is not part of the regular curriculum (*Parrish v. Moss,* 1951).

The court in *Parrish* stated that a teacher could not expect additional compensation for out-of-classroom services, but teachers continued to press the case for supplemental salary for extra duty assignments. In 1955 a California English teacher claimed that supervising athletic events was not part of his contract and was unprofessional in nature, unreasonable, and foreign to his field of instruction. His suit said that teachers' assigned duties in a single teaching day should not require more than eight hours of performance and that they should not be assigned duties on days when they received no pay, e.g., Saturdays and holidays. The school board's right to assign teachers to assist in the supervision of school activities was upheld as the court addressed the issue of extra compensation.

> [The teacher] is not paid on a basis of so much per hour worked. Teachers are engaged in a professional employment. Their salaries and hours of employment are fixed with due regard to their professional status and are not fixed upon the same basis as those of day laborers. The worth of a teacher is not measured in terms of a specific sum of money per hour. A teacher expects to and does perform a service. If that service from time to time requires additional hours of work, a teacher expects to and does perform it ... without thought of measuring his or her compensation in terms of a given sum of money per hour. A teacher's duties and obligations to students and the community are not satisfied by closing the classroom door at the conclusion of a class. The direction and supervision of extra-curricular activities are an important part of his duties. All of his duties are taken into consideration in his contract for employment at the annual salary. All of this is, of course, subject to the test of reasonableness .... Supervising the students and being present to protect their welfare at school athletic and social activities, conducted under the name and auspices of the school, is within the scope of the contract and such assignments are proper so long as they are distributed impartially, they are reasonable in number and

> hours of duty and each teacher has his share of such duty (*McGrath v. Burkhard*, 1955).

The decisions in *Parrish* and *McGrath* established several standards that courts have used in subsequent cases involving teachers' extra duty assignments. Usually an extra assignment is legally defensible if the following criteria are met:

1. The duty is reasonable in number and hours of duty.
2. The duty is related to teacher interest, ability, and certification.
3. The duty is part of a program to benefit student development.
4. The duty is professional in nature.
5. All assignments are distributed impartially and equitably.

Twenty years after these cases, teachers in Illinois complained against nonteaching duties and cited the section of the state school code that allowed for the use of noncertified personnel to supervise some school activities. Because the supervision of games, pep rallies, and music programs on Saturdays and evenings was compensated at a lower rate than contract pay, the teachers believed noncertified personnel should be employed for these supervisory tasks. Citing *Parrish* and *McGrath*, the court upheld the use of teachers in nonclassroom duties:

> The assignments objected to do not appear to have been onerous in nature or unreasonably time consuming. They are not demeaning to the professional stature of the teacher and there is no evidence that such assignments were made in a discriminatory manner .... We are of the opinion that the assignments objected to are reasonably related to the teaching duties of the [teachers] and are not required to be set forth in writing (*District 300 Education Association v. Board of Education of Dundee Community Unit School District No. 300*, 1975).

In 1976 nearly 30 teachers (including 21 athletic coaches) in a New Jersey school district refused to perform their customary extracurricular assignments but continued teaching their classroom subjects. The district had never included extra duty assignments in its master contract but had relied on informal methods of assigning and accepting assignments. Demanding extra compensation for extra work, the teachers resigned from their extracurricular assignments as the school year began. However, citing standards from previous cases, the court disagreed that extra duty assignments were optional in the educational program:

> Extracurricular activities are a fundamental part of a child's education, making the supervision of such activities an integral part of a teacher's duty toward his or her students .... Realistically, the term "extracurricular" activity is a misnomer; it is not an "extra" in the life of a student, nor has it traditionally been considered an "extra" for teachers. Such activities are an essential part of a child's overall education. Learning and self-realization cannot take place in a vacuum; rather, they are fostered in an atmosphere of social interaction and furthered by the development of a healthy group orientation. Teachers, there-

> fore, in order to properly fulfill the responsibility they have undertaken to their profession, to their students, and to the community, must necessarily perform those activities deemed necessary and assigned to them by the board of education . . . .
>
> Of course, the touchstone for the exercise of such power is reasonableness. Assignments must be nondiscriminatory, related to a teacher's interests and expertise, and not require excessive hours. They need not, however, be compensated (*Board of Education of City of Asbury Park v. Asbury Park Education Association,* 1976).

Disputes continue to arise over duties much more closely related to actual classroom teaching than advising a student organization or attending an athletic contest. In nearly all cases where classroom administrative tasks have been challenged, the rights of school boards to assign such tasks have been upheld.

In 1963 a temporary teacher in Pennsylvania was discharged for not attending the school open house for parents, even after she had been told three times that attendance was mandatory. Her dismissal was upheld in court (*Johnson v. United School District Joint School Board,* 1963). A West Virginia teacher's dismissal for failing to attend parent-teacher conferences was overturned by the courts because he had taught 23 years without missing the conferences. However, his 20-day suspension without pay was upheld (*Fox v. Board of Education of Doddridge County,* 1977). The dismissal of a counselor for refusing to take his turn supervising a section of the campus before school in the mornings was upheld (*Jones v. Alabama State Tenure Commission,* 1981). New Jersey teachers assigned to supervise in-school suspension and to check the lavatories filed a grievance in 1982, demanding extra compensation or elimination of the duties. The court ruled that the assignments were managerial prerogatives and not open to challenge (*Board of Education of Vocational School in County of Camden v. Cam/Voc Teachers Association,* 1982). An Illinois court ruled that a school board could require a teacher to turn in single typed copies of his final exams without impairing the teacher's professional standing (*Thomas v. Board of Education of Community Unit School District No. 1,* 1983). A Colorado teacher refused to perform hall duty because "[it] was 'morally and ethically unacceptable' and would 'compromise [his] efforts to teach [his] classes in a democratic way' because it was 'a negation of his classroom teaching that students are responsible for their own behavior.' " His dismissal for insubordination was upheld by the state court of appeals (*Lockhart v. Board of Education of Arapahoe County School District No. 6,* 1986). In 1989 a Kansas teacher, backed by the local teachers' association, claimed that noon hallway and playground duties were extra duties and could not be assigned to teachers unless supplemental contracts were issued. The courts ruled that these duties were inextricably related to the educational process and could be assigned to teachers involuntarily as part of their primary contracts (*NEA-Goodland v. Board of Education, Unified School District, No. 352, Sherman County,* 1989). Therefore, assignments closely related to teaching duties are usually found to be reasonable requirements for teachers to fulfill, and court challenges seldom succeed.

The courts continue to support the assignment of extra duties to teachers as long as the criteria for reasonableness are met. What may be reasonable in one district may not be in another, as the courts have declared. The circumstances of the school, the abilities and interests of the faculty, the needs of the students, and the resources of the district may determine what assignments are reasonable and what duties may be compensated. A teacher in a small, rural school may expect to be assigned to a wider variety of extra duties than a teacher in a large, urban school. Because more teacher duties are becoming part of contracts and negotiated agreements, school officials making extra assignments and teachers receiving nonteaching assignments should be aware of contract stipulations and that the courts generally uphold extracurricular assignments that are a valid part of a teacher's responsibilities.

Courts tend to divide extra duties into two categories: (1) activities foreign to a teacher's area of instructional expertise and (2) activities closely related to teaching and classroom activities.

Principle II

In early schools a teacher's extracurricular responsibilities were often only vaguely related to professional teaching duties. As schools grew, noncertificated personnel were usually hired to perform custodial, maintenance, bus driving, and secretarial duties. Cases have come before the courts when teachers have been assigned to duties perceived as unrelated to their classroom responsibilities, and the courts have had to determine when extra assignments are so unrelated to a teacher's professional expertise as to be legally untenable.

In the 1951 case of *Parrish v. Moss,* the New York Supreme Court specifically designated tasks that could reasonably be expected of teachers and those so unrelated to teaching that they should not be assigned to certificated personnel:

> Teachers in the fields of English and Social Studies and undoubtedly in other areas may be expected to coach plays; physical training teachers may be required to coach both intramural and inter-school athletic teams; teachers may be assigned to supervise educational trips which are properly part of the school curriculum. The band instructor may be required to accompany the band if it leaves the building . . . . The duty assigned must be within the scope of teachers' duties. Teachers may not be required, for instance, to perform janitor service, police service (traffic duty), school bus driving service, etc. These are not "teaching duties." The board may not impose upon a teacher a duty foreign to the field of instruction for which he is licensed or employed. A board may not, for instance, require a *mathematics* teacher to coach intramural teams (*Parrish v. Moss,* 1951).

Implied duty clauses cannot be so broadly construed as to include duties unrelated to a teacher's major responsibilities. Yet, the circumstances of each particular case will be considered by the courts. In 1983 an elementary school principal was assigned additional duties of attendance officer and coordinator of the district outdoor education program when declining enrollments resulted in budget cutbacks. The principal willingly accepted the latter duty but objected to the former, stating it "violates . . . reasonable expectations, and is bizarre, oppressive, unreasonable, arbitrary, and unconscionable." In ruling against the principal, the Iowa Supreme Court relied on the state statute that stated: "The principal shall perform such other duties as may be assigned by the superintendent." The court then further defined "other duties":

> We think, however, that the power to assign "other duties" is not unlimited. A principal could hardly be required to act as building custodian or bus driver. But short of such extreme examples, who is to draw a line between "other duties" which may be assigned and which may not be assigned? We hold that the decision should be in the discretion of the school authorities, with intervention by the courts only in instances which transcend the bounds of discretion (*Gere v. Council Bluffs Community School District,* 1983).

Therefore, the courts have often divided extra duty, nonteaching assignments into two categories when ruling on the reasonableness of such assignments. Depending on state statute and teacher contracts, the duties closely related to actual teaching responsibilities are usually upheld by the courts. Tasks that more reasonably should be performed by noncertificated personnel are more difficult for the board to justify as teacher assignments. School boards and administrators should carefully assign to teachers those tasks that are related to teaching responsibilities and not expect them to assume other, less related tasks.

Principle III

As a general rule, extra duties that are foreign to teaching may not be required of a teacher unless specifically stipulated in the employment contract. Some courts look upon the assignment of unrelated extra duties as beyond the scope of a teacher's contract and free teachers from any legal obligation to accept such assignments.

The assignment of extra duties that are foreign to a teacher's professional responsibilities usually will not be supported by the courts. In small school districts, in districts with strained budgets, or when teachers have special interests or abilities, unrelated extra assignments may be made with the teacher's consent. Teachers may perform bus driving, registration, secretarial, or maintenance duties as special, one-time assignments, in lieu of other duties, to receive supplemental pay, or to facilitate the operation of the school. However, should conflicts over such duties arise, the courts usually state that the duties cannot be required unless explicitly written into the teacher's contract.

In 1951 an English teacher successfully challenged in court his assignment to take tickets at a high school football game. The Pennsylvania county court upheld the assigning of extra duties to teachers only when the duties were directly related to furthering student knowledge:

> Modern day schools are more and more offering to their students opportunities to participate in extra-curricular activities, most, if not all, of which broaden the experience and knowledge of the pupils participating therein. The assignment of teachers to supervise such activities is well within the powers of the school boards.

> However, we cannot see how an assignment to collect tickets at a football game can be considered in such a category. Were the [teacher] assigned to sit with the students in a cheering section to help to inculcate in them the attributes of loyalty and good sportsmanship, we might regard such an assignment as having some direct relation to the education of his pupils but the assignment to sit beside a gate and collect tickets bears no such relation. It is a task which any adult could perform and can be motivated by the desire of the school board to cut down the expenses of the game. We feel that such an assignment is not within the field which a teacher must perform and to require him to do so is a demotion in type of position (*Coronway v. Lansdowne School District No. 785,* 1951).

In another Pennsylvania case, a history teacher went to court when he was dismissed for refusing to be the sponsor for the boys' bowling club. The club met at a privately operated bowling alley, and the school bore none of the costs of bowling. No intra- or intermural bowling competitions were held. The sponsor was present merely to maintain discipline; no coaching or teaching was required. The court upheld the state superintendent's recommendation for reinstatement of the teacher, stating that the voluntary association of boys interested in bowling did not seem related to the school program:

> Schools have no duty to supervise students in their play after school and off school premises when such play is not genuinely connected with the school program. If the rule were otherwise, a professional employee could be required to act as lifeguard over a group of students desiring merely to disport themselves on the beach, or he could be required to sit idly by in a private home or other place while students play chess, bridge, or construct models of aircraft, merely to see to it that participants behave themselves .... There are circumstances under which school supervision off the school premises after hours is indicated and proper, and there are circumstances under which it is improper....
>
> School teachers must realize that they are subject to assignment by the school board to any activity directly related to the school program; classroom duties in school hours do not constitute *all* their duties. On the other hand, school boards must realize that their power of assignment of school teachers to extracurricular duties is not without limitation and restriction; ... the activity to which a school teacher is assigned must be related to the school program and the assignment must be fairly and reasonably made (*Pease v. Millcreek Township School District,* 1963).

Incidental duties must be related to the educational program of the school before the courts will uphold them. Because many extra duties cannot be shown to be professional in nature or related to a teacher's professional responsibilities, school boards and administrators need to evaluate the extra duty assignments of teachers for a valid relationship. The courts rely on the explicit and implied duties contained in contracts and collective bargaining agreements when ruling on whether or not an extra assignment is reasonable, and teachers should realize that contractual definitions, not individual assignment preferences, will be used in court.

Principle IV

Except as stipulated by contract or statute, a teacher has no entitlement to an extra duty assignment. Supplemental income, status, or privileges may accompany assignment to certain extra duties because of board policy, community values, or outside funding. However, extra assignments are generally only adjuncts to the regular teaching contract.

Many extra duty assignments are perceived as onerous impositions on a teacher's professional and personal time. However, some assignments are viewed as rewards, opportunities to supplement income, positions of prestige, or professional privileges. The loss of such assignments leads to court cases when teachers believe they are entitled to the salary or benefits that accompany duties beyond their teaching responsibilities. In most cases, teachers possess no tenure and no entitlement to extra assignments unless they are included in teaching contracts.

The majority of the cases where teachers have gone to court to keep their extra assignments have involved athletic coaches. The supplemental salary and the status of coaching some sports teams become more important to some teachers than their regular teaching assignments. In 1938 a teacher of history, civics, and physical education was also the football and basketball coach. When he was relieved of his football coaching duties, he refused to continue coaching basketball and was dismissed for refusing to perform regularly assigned duties. He then contended that he was hired to teach and that "teach" did not include coach. The court disagreed:

> "Teach" as thus used has a comprehensive as well as a restricted meaning. The School Code restricts its meaning to instruction within the qualifications expressed in the teacher's certificate; but in a broad sense, it refers to general instruction within the field certified .... There can be no doubt that a comprehensive definition of "teaching" physical education embraces all fields of athletics, including coaching football and basketball (*Appeal of Ganaposki,* 1938).

In recent years as society has attached more and more importance to school athletics, teacher-coaches have struggled to remain in their coaching positions. Many have resorted to litigation, but coaching is almost always an adjunct position with no privileges of job security except as accompany tenured classroom positions. Generally, the courts maintain that a coach has no entitlement to the extracurricular duty of coaching or to its supplemental income (*Lexington County School District One Board of Trustees v. Bost,* 1984; *Grounds v. Tolar Independent School District,* 1986). In 1983 two Illinois football and baseball coaches were removed from their coaching positions "for the good of the school's athletic program." They sued for reinstatement and damages, claiming the Fourteenth Amendment guaranteed them a hearing before dismissal, but the court upheld the district:

> The Fourteenth Amendment due process clause does not guarantee a football or baseball coach a job at a public high school even if his teams always win and his players idolize him. The ultimate decision who is the best man to coach

a state high school athletic team rests with state school officials, not with the federal courts (*Smith v. Board of Education of Urbana School District No. 116,* 1983).

A California teacher sued for $1,500,000 in damages when his year-to-year contract as head baseball coach was not renewed. The United States Court of Appeals, Ninth Circuit, ruled that the coach had never been promised the head coaching job for life even though they could "understand his pain at not being renewed, at not having the continued opportunity to do what he loves to do" (*Lagos v. Modesto City Schools District,* 1988).

However, an extra duty contract or applicable due process must not be violated by the removal of a teacher from coaching duties, as shown in a 1985 case. West Virginia state code requires teachers to enter into separate teaching and extracurricular activities contracts. A football coach's dismissal from coaching duties without notice (he heard of the action by reading the local newspaper) was ruled an illegal action because it violated his due process. The court ordered the district to reinstate him as football coach with back pay (*Smith v. Board of Education of County of Logan,* 1985). In a North Dakota case, a one-seventh reduction in a teacher's base teaching salary when he was removed as athletic director was ruled a severe enough reduction to require nonrenewal due process (*Coles v. Glenburn Public School District No. 26,* 1989). When all due process was observed in the release of a Wyoming teacher from his high school basketball coaching contract, the court ruled that his reputation had not been stigmatized and that the termination was valid (*Diehl v. Albany County School District No. 1,* 1988).

Other types of extra assignments also lead to litigation, especially when supplemental salary is involved. The issue of supplemental pay arose in 1982 when an orchestra teacher's additional salary was cut from $2,500 to $1,000 without notice. The supplemental salary was for conducting special rehearsals with orchestras and soloists and taking students to solo and orchestra competitions. After his salary decrease, the teacher refused to provide the rehearsals or to accompany the orchestra to a major competition, and he was dismissed for insubordination. However, the court ruled that he had to be reinstated because his insubordination was remediable and could not justify dismissal. The question was raised of whether the Saturday competition was part of teaching or nonteaching duties, but the case was resolved on other grounds (*Board of Education of Berwyn School District No. 100, Cook County v. Metskas,* 1982).

In 1984 two vocational agriculture teachers claimed they were demoted when the summer Future Farmers and Young Farmers of America programs were eliminated, causing a loss of supplemental income. The court ruled that a district had a right to abolish extra duties and that the decrease in supplemental salary was not a demotion (*Wagner v. West Perry School District,* 1984).

Disputes have arisen when supplemental pay has accompanied some extra duty assignments but not others. Because nearly every teacher is assigned to some extra responsibilities that require additional hours and effort, some teachers claim unfair treatment when coaches, band and choir directors, publications advisers, and vocational teachers receive supplemental salary. In 1984 the Ohio courts heard a case after a grievance filed by a group of teachers failed. The teachers alleged they performed extra services without extra pay while other teachers were compensated. The collective bargaining agreement did not require supplemental contracts for extra-curricular duties such as class sponsor or organization adviser, but additional compensation contracts were awarded for coaching, guidance, and other duties. The plaintiffs in the suit claimed violations of the equal protection and due process clauses of the Fourteenth Amendment. The court ruled that supplemental contracts were not needed unless compensation to base salary was authorized by the board. Board policy stated clearly that teachers could be required to perform duties other than teaching without additional compensation. The fact that the board had chosen to compensate some extra duties but not others was ruled a board prerogative (*Ballard v. Board of Education of Goshen Local School District,* 1984).

Therefore, contracts and board policy govern the area of extra duty assignments, both those awarding extra compensation to teachers and those just expected of teachers. The entire issue of the sometimes disparate compensation for extra duty assignments was encapsulated in a concurring opinion in *Ballard v. Board of Education* (1984):

> At first blush it seems somewhat incongruous that a math teacher, skilled in the profession, should be expected to supervise construction of a float for homecoming, after school hours, without compensation. Should the same math teacher also serve as an athletic coach, after school hours, it is quite customary to compensate the teacher via a supplemental contract. Such is true even though the float construction and the athletic contest are both extracurricular activities. I perceive that the obvious disparity in treatment is simply a mirror image of the views held not only by the various boards of education, but also by the public. Athletics and athletes apparently are more important than speech contests and orators as shown by the fact we pay rookie football players a million dollars a year to play professional football immediately after attending college and receiving a minimal education (*Ballard v. Board of Education of Goshen Local School District,* 1984).

In summary, few teachers can claim entitlement to an extracurricular duty unless it is part of the teaching or supplemental contract. Generally, no tenure privileges accompany extra duty assignments, even coaching, and dismissals and transfers of teachers from extracurricular duties usually do not have to follow strict due process. Teachers and administrators need to know what is included in the master and supplemental contracts regarding extra assignments, both those seen as inconvenient nuisance duties and those seen as rewarding, lucrative privileges. The importance of supplemental pay is beginning to change traditional contracting and collective bargaining practices and may ultimately change the way extra assignments are made and accepted.

Principle V

When a supplemental contract is issued to a teacher in addition to a master teaching contract, the teacher may have the right to refuse the supplemental contract without affecting the conditions of the primary contract.

Historically, a teacher's contract covered all curricular and extracurricular assignments, express and implied. As court cases involving extra duties arose, the need for clarification of the contract became apparent in many states. Many school districts, pressured by teachers' associations to differentiate extra duties from curricular duties, began to issue supplemental contracts for extra duties, particularly for those duties that awarded additional salary or stipends. A new issue arose when tenured teachers began to refuse to sign supplemental contracts for extra duties that carried no tenure provisions. The courts in a few states have been asked to resolve the question of a teacher's right to a primary teaching contract without acceptance of supplemental contracts.

In the 1980s, a series of cases in Kansas addressed the conflict that occurs between school boards and teachers when a teacher refuses to sign a supplemental contract. In the first case, a math teacher, who was also head basketball coach and assistant football coach, was informed that if he did not resign as basketball coach, he would be removed from the position. Accordingly, the teacher wrote a letter of resignation as basketball coach. The school board then wrote to him, acknowledging his resignation from his employment contract for the next year. When the teacher requested a hearing on his nonrenewal, the board refused, stating that his basketball coaching duties were an "integral and substantial part" of his continuing contract; therefore, his resignation from the position was a voluntary rejection of his entire contract. Although the contract itself was one instrument, the court construed it to consist of one primary contract for teaching math and two supplementary contracts for coaching duties. Citing evidence that school districts could and often did unilaterally remove teachers from coaching positions while retaining them as teachers, the court ruled that a teacher could also reject extra duties as a coach while retaining primary duties as a teacher (*Swager v. Board of Education, Unified School District No. 412, Sheridan County, Kansas,* 1984).

In a second case, another Kansas teacher wrote a letter of resignation as basketball coach and was reissued a contract for teaching history, drivers' education, and physical education, as well as supplementary duties as track coach and laundry supervisor but with the basketball position eliminated. When no applications for basketball coach were received, the superintendent assigned the position back to the teacher, who declined it. The school district brought a court action against the teacher on grounds of insubordination and breach of contract, but the appellate court, overturning the trial court decision, ruled in favor of the teacher (*Unified School District No. 241, Wallace County v. Swanson,* 1986).

In 1988 the Kansas Supreme Court heard another case dealing with tenured teachers' refusals to accept supplemental contracts. The teachers in this case were assigned extra duties as coaches, and, because their positions were in junior high schools where athletic practice was scheduled during the school day, their coaching duties fell during a regular class period. When they resigned their junior high coaching positions, they were then offered six-sevenths of a contract for the next year. (The school day was divided into seven periods.) The court cited previous state cases in ruling in favor of the teachers:

> The concern that a teacher must be free from coercion and intimidation in his or her decision to undertake supplementary duties such as coaching prevents

> such duties, even when conducted during the school day . . . from being treated as a part of the teacher's primary contract of employment (*Hachiya v. Board of Education, Unified School District No. 307, Saline County,* 1988).

How other states will regard these Kansas decisions has not been determined. States that issue both primary and supplementary contracts will need to provide guidelines for school boards and teachers so that contract law, tenure statutes, and dismissal procedures are observed. School districts may face the problem of having to hire additional persons to staff extracurricular positions if tenured teachers are able to refuse supplemental contracts but retain their primary teaching positions.

Summary

Extra duties have always been and will continue to be an important part of the teacher's responsibilities. The tasks may seem only peripherally related to a teacher's classroom duties, but the courts will usually uphold any assignment that is reasonable, related to student development, and not totally foreign to a teacher's expertise and interests. With the trend toward more explicit master contracts, supplemental duty contracts, and collective bargaining agreements, extra duties are becoming more definite as to scope and compensation. In some districts, teachers cannot be held responsible for any but contracted assignments. Usually, however, implied duties can be shown to be so crucial to the educational process that teachers can reasonably be expected to be assigned to them without additional compensation. At the same time, no firm trend is seen toward including extra duty assignments in tenure clauses, and most extracurricular activities will remain adjuncts to regular classroom assignments.

With more conditions involving extracurricular duties being written into master and supplemental contracts, school boards, administrators, and teachers need to be aware of those governing clauses when making, accepting, and terminating extra duty assignments. Teachers may not always be obligated to fulfill nor entitled to keep certain assignments. At the same time, a teacher's continuing primary position may not always depend on his or her acceptance of a supplemental contract, although this issue is too new to have arisen in many states. With courts relying on the language of contracts when disputes arise, extra duties must be assigned in accordance with reasonable guidelines for a teacher's professionalism, certification, and time and compensation schedules.

Questions and Responses

1. What are extra duties to which a teacher can be assigned?
In addition to normal classroom teaching responsibilities, a teacher almost always is assigned extra duties related to the extracurriculum of the school or to the efficient administrative operation of the school. Some of these duties are so closely related to classroom responsibilities that no real distinction is possible, e.g., supervising the playgrounds during recess. Others are related to the broad philosophy of student

development, e.g., serving as an adviser to a student club. Common examples of extracurricular duties include coaching athletic teams, serving as a class or organization adviser, accompanying school organizations on school-sponsored trips, conducting extra practices or rehearsals for student musicians, orators, and actors, and attending games, socials, concerts, and other school-sponsored events. Examples of traditional administrative duties include monitoring halls between classes, supervising campus areas before and after school, collecting lunch money, and reporting attendance.

2. Why are teachers assigned extra duties beyond classroom responsibilities?
Most educators agree that not all learning takes place inside the classroom; hence, the extracurriculum was developed. School administrators, boards, and teachers themselves usually recognize that the most natural instructors for the extracurriculum are teachers who share student interests so that students may benefit from teachers' expertise and interests. Therefore, most state education policies as well as local board policies provide for the assignment of extra duties to teachers, either by explicit statute or by implied duty clauses. Teachers are assigned extra duties for traditional, philosophical, legal, and practical reasons: teachers have always fulfilled duties outside the definition of classroom teaching; teachers are the natural leaders and instructors for subjects that are adjuncts to classroom teachings; most state codes provide for teachers to fulfill implied or explicit extra duties; and most school districts could not afford their extracurricular program were teachers not assigned to carry it out.

3. When is a teacher legally obligated to accept and fulfill extra duties?
Most state education codes indicate that teachers may be assigned other duties by their school boards or administrators. These implied duty clauses have usually been upheld by the courts when extra duty assignments have been questioned. Increasingly, teaching contracts and collective bargaining agreements include both implicit and explicit clauses that govern the assignment of extra duties, binding teachers to fulfill these extra obligations. Court precedent suggests that teachers can be expected to accept extra duties and that the assignments will be upheld by the courts if the following criteria are met:

a. The assignment is reasonable in number and hours of duty.
b. The assignment is related to teacher interest, ability, and certification.
c. The assignment is part of a program to benefit student development.
d. The assignment is professional in nature.
e. All extra duty assignments are distributed impartially and equitably.

However, when supplemental contracts are issued, teachers may not always have to sign supplemental contracts to retain their primary positions.

4. When may a teacher refuse an extra duty assignment?
Legal precedent for teachers to refuse extra duties is not prevalent, but some cases suggest that a teacher may refuse an assignment that is completely foreign to his or her professional assignment, especially when the assignment's contribution to student development cannot be shown. The courts will not uphold an extra duty that is unreasonable, arbitrary, discriminatory, or violative of a teacher's protected rights. Usually the burden of proof will be on the teacher to show that an extracurricular

assignment is unreasonable or in conflict with a teaching contract. In some states, a tenured teacher may be able to refuse to sign a supplemental contract without affecting employment in a regular teaching assignment.

5. What tenure rights or expectations of employment accompany extra duty assignments?

Unless stipulated by contract, no teacher is entitled to an extra duty assignment. Extra duties are almost always adjuncts to the regular teaching contract, even if formalized by a supplemental contract. The responsibilities, privileges, and compensation that sometimes accompany extra duty assignments are not guaranteed and usually may be terminated without formal due process. Many teachers, especially athletic coaches, have claimed that their professional tenure status included their coaching or other extracurricular contracts, but such claims have usually been found groundless in court.

6. How do the courts generally view implied extra duties of teachers?

Precedent suggests that courts divide extra duties of teachers into two categories: those closely related to classroom teaching responsibilities and those foreign to a teacher's major contract responsibilities. Because of implied duty clauses, the first will almost always be upheld in court if the assignment meets the criteria for reasonableness. The second category will probably not be supported by the courts unless the contract specifically includes such duties. For example, attending sports events, serving as organization sponsor, and supervising playgrounds can be implied as closely related to the educational process and professional responsibilities of the teacher. Assignments for driving buses, performing janitorial duties, assisting with secretarial, bookkeeping, or registration duties, or servicing the physical plant will probably not be viewed as acceptable extra duties for a teacher.

7. Why do some extra duties merit supplemental salary and others receive no extra compensation?

State statute or local board policy will usually determine if and when extra duty assignments will be compensated. The criteria for such decisions vary with the state or district but may include the number of hours of service, the values placed upon the activity by the community, the ability of the activity to produce revenue or attract outside funding, or government regulation. Suits by teachers claiming discrimination because class sponsors and hall monitors are not compensated for their hours and efforts while coaches and guidance counselors receive extra pay have usually been dismissed. School board prerogative usually reflects the values of society, and society rewards some duties more than others even if all are valuable to students and the community.

8. When may a teacher be expected to perform extra duties outside of school hours?

Many school activities take place outside of school hours, and nearly all events sponsored or sanctioned by the school require the presence of a teacher as an adviser. Teachers do not work at hourly rates; as professionals, they may expect to work in evenings, on weekends, and at almost any hour outside of school time. Whenever the class, organization, or group to which the teacher is assigned as an adviser is involved in activities, the teacher will be expected to be present. The courts will uphold such assignments as long as the time spent on extra duties is reasonable and does not violate contracts.

Case References

Appeal of Ganaposki, 2 A.2d 742 (Pa. 1938).

Ballard v. Board of Education of Goshen Local School District, 469 N.E.2d 951 (Ohio App. 1984).

Board of Education of Berwyn School District No. 100, Cook County v. Metskas, 436 N.E.2d 587 (Ill.App. 1982).

Board of Education of City of Asbury Park v. Asbury Park Education Association, 368 A.2d 396 (N.J. 1976).

Board of Education of Vocational School in County of Camden v. Cam/Voc Teachers Association, 443 A.2d 756 (N.J.Super.A.D. 1982).

Coles v. Glenburn Public School District No. 26, 436 N.W.2d 262 (N.D. 1989).

Coronway v. Lansdowne School District No. 785 (Ct.Com.Pl. of Delaware County, Pa. 1951).

Diehl v. Albany County School District No. 1, 694 F.Supp. 1534 (D.Wyo. 1988).

District 300 Education Association v. Board of Education of Dundee Community Unit School District No. 300, 334 N.E.2d 165 (Ill.App. 1975).

Fox v. Board of Education of Doddridge County, 236 S.E.2d 243 (W.Va. 1977).

Gere v. Council Bluffs Community School District, 334 N.W.2d 307 (Iowa 1983).

Grounds v. Tolar Independent School District, 707 S.W.2d 889 (Tex. 1986).

Hachiya v. Board of Education, Unified School District No. 307, Saline County, 750 P.2d 383 (Kan. 1988).

Johnson v. United School District Joint School Board, 191 A.2d 897 (Pa.Super. 1963).

Jones v. Alabama State Tenure Commission, 408 So.2d 145 (Ala.Civ.App. 1981).

Lagos v. Modesto City Schools District, 843 F.2d 347 (9th Cir. 1988).

Lexington County School District One Board of Trustees v. Bost, 316 S.E.2d 677 (S.C. 1984).

Lockhart v. Board of Education of Arapahoe County School District No. 6, 735 P.2d 913 (Colo. App. 1986).

McGrath v. Burkhard, 280 P.2d 864 (Cal.App. 1955).

NEA-Goodland v. Board of Education, Unified School District No. 352, Sherman County, 775 P.2d 675 (Kan.App. 1989).

Parrish v. Moss, 106 N.Y.S.2d 577 (1951).

Pease v. Millcreek Township School District, 195 A.2d 104 (Pa. 1963).

Smith v. Board of Education of County of Logan, 341 S.E.2d 685 (W.Va. 1985).

Smith v. Board of Education of Urbana School District No. 116, 708 F.2d 258 (7th Cir., 1983).

Swager v. Board of Education, Unified School District No. 412, Sheridan County, Kansas, 688 P.2d 270 (Kan.App. 1984).

Thomas v. Board of Education of Community Unit School District No. 1, 453 N.E.2d 150 (Ill.App. 5 Dist. 1983).

Unified School District No. 241, Wallace County v. Swanson, 717 P.2d 526 (Kan.App. 1986).

Wagner v. West Perry School District, 480 A.2d 1336 (Pa.Cmwlth. 1984).

4 Demotions

The early history of public schools is replete with examples of school board and administrative demotions of teachers. Some teachers were guilty of inappropriate behavior or inability to fulfill the requirements of their positions, and their demotions served the best interest of students and the schools. Other demotions were made arbitrarily and capriciously, protecting the spoils system rather than the rights of teachers or the educational welfare of students. Tenure laws in many states were passed to limit demotions of teachers to those justifiable on statutory grounds. Procedural guidelines were included in the laws to safeguard rights of teachers and the interests of the school system.

Cases involving the alleged demotion of teachers continue to come before the courts. The most common claim is that a reassignment or transfer is actually a demotion. If shown to be a demotion, a transfer may be ruled illegal, or stricter due process may have to be followed than would be required for a reassignment of duties. However, not every unwanted or unpleasant transfer can be ruled a demotion, and not every demotion is unlawful or unmerited. As true of most employment issues in education, demotion decisions are the prerogative of the school board acting in accordance with state law and negotiated agreements.

State laws concerning teacher reassignment, demotion, and transfer vary widely, and state appeals courts have been called upon to interpret their state tenure laws and other statutes pertinent to teacher demotion. A few cases have reached the federal appellate level and have become precedent for the states in those jurisdictions. Historic teacher demotion cases generally cannot be used to substantiate present claims without reference to the state law in effect at the time the precedent case was decided because changes in financial exigency, reduction in force, and collective bargaining laws as well as desegregation orders have brought about legislative changes in teacher transfer and demotion policies. States have the authority to establish school systems and the rules and procedures by which schools are governed, including employment policies. The courts are reluctant to interfere with those rights.

Legal Principles

Principle I *Legal Definition*

A legally recognized demotion of a public school teacher requires a reduction in either position or salary.

Principle II *Reduction in Position*

A demotion of a public school teacher based upon a reduction in position requires showing that the new position is less important, dignified, or prestigious, or contains less authority or responsibility.

Principle III *Due Process*

As a general rule, a public school teacher may not be demoted in either salary or position without prior consent or until after a hearing has been held and the findings uphold the allegations upon which the demotion is based.

Principle IV *Valid Causes*

Valid causes for the demotion of a public school teacher usually include the same general conditions that justify dismissal, such as incompetency, insubordination or unprofessional conduct.

Principle V *Financial Exigency*

A school district may lawfully demote a public school teacher for the purpose of efficient management of available resources or financial exigency. Usually such demotions must be administered across entire levels of teaching positions, not individual positions.

Principle VI *Desegregation Orders*

School districts under federal desegregation orders may lawfully demote a teacher in accordance with court-ordered integration plans. As a general rule, once a school district is desegregated, such guidelines allowing demotions for reasons of achieving racial balance are no longer in effect. Thereafter, fair employment practices in hiring, assigning, demoting, and dismissing teachers are to maintain racial equality of school teaching staffs.

Discussion

Principle I

A legally recognized demotion of a public school teacher requires a reduction in either position or salary.

Even though many reassignments are viewed by teachers as demotions because some teaching positions are less desirable than others or involve moving from a familiar to an unfamiliar teaching setting, most transfers made in good faith by school boards cannot be shown to be demotions. Generally, the courts have held that individual salary reduction or removal from a more responsible to a less responsible position constitutes a *prima facie* demotion and that one or both of these elements must be present before a claim of demotion can be upheld.

However, the various state codes contain different tests for legal demotion. Some states recognize only salary reduction as indicative of demotion. In others, salary decreases do not merit due process; only a reassignment that falls outside a teacher's area of certification is considered a demotion. In some states, loss of prestige in the eyes of fellow teachers or the community is recognized by the courts as evidence of a demotion. The statutory definition of "demotion" is used by the courts in teacher demotion cases. Unofficial seniority systems, teacher preference, or other in-school traditions are not used to determine if an illegal demotion has occurred.

Early court cases involving demotion necessitated the defining of terms in newly enacted tenure laws. For example, in 1903 a New York appellate court interpreted "reassignment" in the 1898 tenure law as meaning removal from office and appointment to a lower position. The reassignment of a teacher from one grade level to another with a reduction in salary was termed a violation of the tenure law, although a lateral transfer from one school to another with no change in grade level would have been upheld (*People ex rel. Callahan v. Board of Education of City of New York,* 1903).

State statutes now define "demotion" more clearly, but the courts continue to be asked to interpret these laws. For example, in 1947 the Pennsylvania state law defined demotion of a teacher as "removal from one position and an appointment to a lower position." When a teacher was reassigned to the junior high when a combined junior/senior high school was divided, he claimed he had been demoted. Ruling that the school board had never appointed the teacher to a higher status, the court said that he had not been demoted (*Appeal of School District of Pittsburgh,* 1947).

Michigan law defines demotion as "to reduce compensation or to transfer to a position carrying a lower salary." Thus, a principal's reassignment to a visiting teacher position with no reduction in salary was not ruled a demotion. Because he was tenured as a teacher, not as a principal, he was subject to reassignment at the discretion of the superintendent and board (*Street v. Board of Education of School District of City of Ferndale, Oakland County,* 1960). In 1983 this same Michigan statute became the focus of litigation when an elementary school principal claimed he had been demoted after being denied salary increases for two successive years while other administrators did receive increases. Because the board had not reduced his salary, the court ruled that his situation was not a demotion:

> The school board clearly did not reduce [his] compensation. . . . The board also did not transfer [the principal] to a position carrying a lower salary. . . . We realize that the teachers' tenure act, as we interpret it, provides unorganized teachers and school administrators with precious little protection from arbitrary compensation decisions by school boards. When the tenure act was first adopted, the Legislature may not have anticipated that the denial of a salary increase may

have the impact of a salary decrease in a time of rampant inflation (*LeGalley v. Bronson Community Schools,* 1983).

A Pennsylvania school counselor reassigned to an eighth grade English teaching position claimed she was demoted, but she failed to show the reassignment was arbitrary, discriminatory, or founded upon improper consideration. Even though the teaching contract was for nine months and the counseling contract was for nine and one-half months, the court ruled that the evidence did not support her claim of loss of salary or reduction in position (*Commonwealth Department of Education v. Kauffman,* 1975). In 1982 a high school counselor transferred to an elementary teaching position with no loss of salary claimed demotion because the teaching position usually carried a lower salary and status. However, Missouri tenure laws recognized only transfer with loss of compensation as a demotion (*Glanville v. Hickory County Reorganized School District No. 1,* 1982).

In a 1984 Louisiana case, the definition of "salary" was expanded to include on-campus housing, one free meal per day, and other related benefits. The state board had terminated these benefits for the administrators of the Louisiana School for the Visually Impaired, and the assistant superintendent claimed he had been demoted. The courts ruled that the reduction in salary constituted a demotion because the emoluments of office had to be included in salary and ordered the administrator entitled to receive additional monthly salary equal to the value of his former salary benefits (*Pizzolato v. State Board of Elementary and Secondary Education,* 1984).

Thus, a claim of demotion must be accompanied by evidence of reduction in either position or salary or both, depending on state statute, before it will be sustained in court. A demotion must match the state's legal criteria before the court can declare that a demotion has occurred. Teachers who claim demotion because of reassignment must be certain that they have been demoted in their state's legal sense and recognize the wide diversity in the legal definition of "demotion."

A demotion of a public school teacher based upon a reduction in position requires showing that the new position is less important, dignified, or prestigious, or contains less authority or responsibility. **Principle II**

A reduction in salary is a concrete criterion by which to judge whether or not a demotion has occurred. Loss of status or reduction in position as evidence of a legal demotion is much less easily defined, and a teacher's perception of lower status may not stand in a court that must depend on legal definitions. Some state statutes are specific and others only general when addressing demotion based on these criteria; hence, trends from state court decisions are difficult to generalize to other states.

An important demotion case was heard in the Pennsylvania Supreme Court in 1959 shortly after the state legislature had abolished all legal distinctions between elementary and secondary schools. A teacher reassigned from the ninth grade to the sixth grade with no change in salary claimed she was demoted. The court, ruling no demotion had occurred, made this often-quoted statement:

> There is no less importance, dignity, responsibility, authority, prestige or compensation in the elementary grades than in secondary. Here the young student still pliant, still susceptible, still in the formative stage, receives his earlier impressions, his inspiration, his direction. Here personality traits are brought out and developed, tastes are instilled, habit patterns are established, character is formed. This is perhaps the most important period of life; the most crucial. The period which may determine a child's ultimate moral, ethical and intellectual stature. To be charged with the responsibility for children in this critical time of their lives is no demotion (*Appeal of Santee,* 1959).

Along with transfers from secondary to elementary positions, changes in teaching assignments and even extracurricular duties have been challenged as reductions in position. In 1967 a high school coach claimed he was demoted when he was relieved of football coaching duties and named as basketball coach. The court ruled that only a transfer, not a demotion, had occurred, regardless of the coach's perception of status and recognition (*Greene v. County Board of Education of Calhoun County,* 1967).

Reassignments of administrative duties are often alleged to be demotions on the basis of reduction of position. When the position of Supervisor of Instruction and Materials Director was abolished in a Tennessee school district, the administrator was reassigned to an assistant high school principal position with full salary. The court overruled her claim of demotion because the board's action had not been arbitrary or capricious and every effort had been made to resolve the problem equitably for the administrator (*Mitchell v. Garrett,* 1974).

A Kentucky high school principal claimed he was demoted when he was transferred to a middle school principalship because the new position involved one week less work and the supervision of fewer teachers. The court ruled there was no material difference in the two positions, although procedural violations voided the transfer (*Stafford v. Board of Education of Casey County,* 1982). In 1983 a principal who was reassigned to a classroom position claimed deprivation of his property rights under the Fourteenth Amendment. However, the court ruled that because he had not signed a contract for the next year, he could not lose property rights. His transfer had involved no loss of status so it was not considered a demotion (*Lyznicki v. Board of Education, School District 167, Cook County, Illinois,* 1983).

However, case law in some states indicates that the courts are defining reduction in position more broadly than in the past, especially in regard to administrative positions. The Pennsylvania Supreme Court said in 1975 that any alleged demotion should be eligible for a hearing:

> A demotion is, by its nature, relative. A change in the title of one's job may have no bearing on one's authority, prestige, or responsibility in any given organizational structure. It may be very difficult for persons outside the system to assess the "pecking order" accurately. For this reason, in cases where a demotion in type of position is alleged, the reviewing body requires a complete record in which testimony as to the relative standing of the old and new positions in the hierarchy is developed. We therefore hold that a professional employee who claims that he or she has been demoted . . . is entitled to a hearing . . . to

determine initially whether or not a demotion has, in fact, occurred (*Commonwealth, Department of Education v. Charleroi Area School District,* 1975).

In Massachusetts an assistant high school principal was transferred without his consent and without due process to the assistant principalship of a middle school. The appeals court upheld the trial judge's opinion that the principal had been demoted because fellow professionals would perceive the transfer to be a demotion (*Powers v. Freetown-Lakeville Regional School District Committee,* 1984).

Although sufficient substantive evidence of loss of importance, dignity, or prestige or reduction of authority or responsibility because of a change in position continues to be difficult to amass for legal purposes, some courts may be interpreting such clauses in demotion statutes more liberally than they have formerly. More courts are calling reassignment from administrative to teaching positions demotions whether or not salary reduction accompanies the transfer. Revisions of tenure laws and collective bargaining agreements are providing more definite guidelines for determining when reduction in position constitutes legal demotion as opposed to reassignment. However, state laws still vary widely in the use of reduction of status without salary loss as a determinant of demotion. Teachers should understand that legal interpretation will be used by the courts, not unofficial seniority traditions that develop in many school districts.

Principle III

As a general rule, a public school teacher may not be demoted in either salary or position without prior consent or until after a hearing has been held and the findings uphold the allegations upon which the demotion is based.

Many state statutes establish procedural guidelines to be followed for all transfers and demotions. Notice of the action and an opportunity for a hearing before an impartial tribunal usually comprise the minimal due process required when prior consent to a transfer is not given and a reassignment is claimed to be a demotion. Of course, a teacher may voluntarily accept a demotion, particularly when the alternative is dismissal. The courts become involved when a teacher claims a transfer is a demotion while the school board considers it merely a reassignment. If a demotion cannot be effected until after notice and hearing, school boards must be sure all procedures are properly observed when making every demotion and transfer. Failure to follow procedures established by statute or collective bargaining agreements will usually nullify a reassignment or demotion. Similarly, where appeal procedures are mandated by law, a teacher's failure to abide by them will usually be grounds for denying any relief to which the teacher may be entitled (*Clark v. Mt. Greylock Regional School District,* 1975; *Kaufman v. School Committee of Boston,* 1984). Many court cases on teacher demotion involve alleged violations of procedural guidelines.

One of the main tasks of the courts in demotion cases is to define the terms in the statutes to see whether or not specific procedures apply. In *State ex rel. McNeal v. Avoyelles Parish School Board* (1942), the Supreme Court of Louisiana set an important precedent when it defined "removal from office" in the tenure statute as including demotion, thus necessitating due process in demotion cases. In this case, a principal was demoted to a teaching position and his salary reduced with neither a written notice of charges nor a hearing. The court ruled that he was entitled to reinstatement and back salary.

Sometimes when proper procedures are not strictly observed, the teacher may win a technical victory in court but be given no relief. In 1955 a principal of a grammar school was transferred to a teaching position in the new consolidated school when her school was closed. Although she had a right to a notice and hearing because of the demotion, the court ruled that she had no entitlement to the position of principal at the new school; therefore, the court could offer her no effective relief (*Jantzen v. School Committee of Chelmsford,* 1955).

In a similar case, the principal of a junior/senior high school was retained as principal of the junior high school when the school was divided. He claimed that this assignment was a demotion because it reduced his rank, position, status, and prestige in violation of the state tenure law, and he demanded to be named principal of the high school. Even though the court agreed that he had been demoted, it ruled that the school board could not be forced to appoint him to a position of higher rank, status, and prestige (*Verret v. Calcasieu Parish School Board,* 1958).

In 1973 the courts in Pennsylvania handed down a decision regarding due process in demotion that is often quoted by other courts. In this case, an assistant principal was reassigned to a classroom position after receiving an unsatisfactory evaluation. He then demanded a hearing on grounds that the transfer was a demotion. The school board did not follow the procedures for demotion as outlined in the state school code: the list of charges was drawn up after the teacher requested a hearing; the board did not see the list of charges until the hearing; the demotion was effected before the hearing; the superintendent and principal made the demotion without authority because only the school board could demote a teacher. The court ruled that because the disregard of procedures had violated the assistant principal's rights and nullified the demotion, he was to be reinstated:

> Where a school board undertakes to terminate a contract, dismiss or demote a professional employe [*sic*], the procedure set forth in the School Code must be strictly followed, and failure on the part of the Board to comply therewith renders an attempted demotion abortive (*Board of School Directors of the Abington School District v. Pittenger,* 1973).

The same decision was reached in 1976 when an elementary school principal was reassigned to a teaching position after his adminisrative position was abolished. Because he had suffered not only a decrease in salary but also a reduction in duties and responsibilities, the action was termed a nonconsensual demotion. Because no hearing had been held before the demotion went into effect, the court ordered him reinstated with back pay (*Black v. Wyalusing Area School District,* 1976); *Barton v. Governing Board of Middletown Unified School District of Lake County,* 1976; *Glennon v. School Committee of Boston,* 1978).

When school boards follow procedural guidelines strictly, claims of violation of due process are difficult to substantiate, as shown by several Pennsylvania cases. In 1982 two middle school vice-principals' positions were abolished because of a drop in enrollment and a realignment of administrative staff occasioned by economic conditions in the district. Although they claimed due process violations, they failed to show that the board's action was arbitrary or founded on improper consideration, and the court upheld the demotions. (*Chester Upland School District v. Brown,* 1982).

When 240 professional employees were demoted because of the serious financial condition of their Philadelphia district, they claimed their individual rights were violated because of lack of hearings. Prior to the alleged demotions, the school district had conducted a mass hearing where the financial situation had been shown and budgetary cut procedures had been explained. The Supreme Court of Pennsylvania ruled that individual hearings prior to demotion were not necessary because if any demotion were later shown to be unjust, the case would be eligible for judicial review and that employee would be entitled to full back pay (*School District of Philadelphia v. Twer,* 1982).

In Philadelphia a superintendent temporarily assigned all administrators who held teaching certificates in secondary or special education to teaching positions for the duration of a teachers' strike. Any administrator who refused the temporary assignment risked demotion, suspension, or discharge. The administrators claimed they were demoted in violation of the state's tenure laws and so were subject to due process. The court disagreed and said the order had been justified (*Philadelphia Association of School Administrators v. School District of Philadelphia,* 1984).

In another Pennsylvania case, two vocational agriculture teachers claimed they were demoted without hearings when the school board discontinued summer Future Farmers of America and Young Farmers programs. The court ruled that extracurricular activities were not part of professional duties. Hence, the teachers' loss of supplemental pay did not constitute a demotion, and the collective bargaining clause requiring pre-demotion hearings did not apply (*Wagner v. West Perry School District,* 1984).

In 1987 a language arts coordinator for a Georgia school district was notified that she had been reassigned to a classroom teaching position. The teacher requested a full hearing, but the district claimed the change was a transfer, not a demotion, and so did not adhere to strict due process. However, the court ruled that a $3,232.80 decrease in pay and a decrease in working hours constituted a demotion, entitling the teacher to a full hearing (*Ellis-Adams v. Whitfield County Board of Education,* 1987). In a similar Missouri case, two principals were reassigned to classroom positions for the following year. They requested hearings before the school board where they could present and cross-examine witnesses. At the board meeting, these procedures were not followed because the superintendent claimed the changes in assignments were transfers, not demotions. The court disagreed, and the principals had to be reinstated until such time as the board complied with the state procedures law (*DeSoto County School Board v. Garrett,* 1987).

In summary, school districts must follow strict procedural guidelines established by state statutes, tenure laws, and collective bargaining agreements before demoting a teacher. The Pennsylvania Supreme Court noted some guidelines that school boards would be well advised to follow in determining when due process must be observed:

> When a professional employee claims that he has been demoted it is the school board's duty to grant him a hearing. At that hearing two questions are before the school board: (1) whether or not the professional employee has been de-

moted either in type of position or salary, and (2) in the event the professional employee has been demoted, the reason for such demotion must be made clear and apparent (*Smith v. School District of Township of Darby,* 1957).

Because of increasing awareness of their due process rights, more teachers are claiming that disagreeable reassignments are demotions requiring due process. The courts have held consistently that due process must be followed in cases of demotion and that violation of applicable due process will void a demotion. School boards should follow all procedures established for reassigning and demoting teachers, and teachers should adhere to all procedures for challenging such actions.

Principle IV

Valid causes for the demotion of a public school teacher usually include the same general conditions that justify dismissal, such as incompetency, insubordination or unprofessional conduct.

The demotion of a teacher is commonly associated with disciplinary action against that individual. Because demotions were once arbitrary decisions or were based on discriminatory, capricious bases, demotion is now addressed by state employment statutes, tenure laws, and collective bargaining contracts. Laws and contracts protect the teacher from unjustified demotions but do not prohibit the use of demotion as a disciplinary measure. Because demotion, removal from position, and dismissal are closely related, valid grounds for these punitive actions are usually similar in the statutes. Incompetency, insubordination, unprofessional conduct, neglect of duty, and just cause are among the most common conditions that justify a teacher's demotion. The courts will uphold a school board's decision to demote a teacher as long as the board shows that its action was reasonable, followed due process, was in the interest of the school, and was a valid disciplinary measure.

For example, in 1944 a teacher's salary was reduced when she refused to comply with a local board of education rule requiring teachers to attain additional college credits. The California Supreme Court ruled that the board's requirement and salary schedule were reasonable and that the teacher's demotion was legal (*Rible v. Hughes,* 1944).

Forty years ago, two related cases in Pennsylvania established precedent for demotion issues. In the first case, Dugan was a Supervising Principal of a school district with only an elementary school. She was certified by the state of Pennsylvania to serve in that position in any public school district of similar size in the state. After a high school was added to the district, she continued as Supervising Principal for 12 years and then was reassigned to the principalship of only the elementary school on grounds of incompetency for the district position because of lack of education and certification. The state supreme court ruled that her certification, which was unlimited and unconditional, did qualify her for the Supervising Principal position. Because her demotion in salary and position had been based on invalid grounds, the court ordered her returned to her former position (*Appeal of Dugan,* 1948).

In the four years that Dugan's case was in court, Ritzie served as Supervising Principal. When Dugan won her appeal and was reinstated, the school board created a new position, Principal of Elementary Schools, for Ritzie. Two years later, the school board abolished Ritzie's nonmandated position, and he was offered a teaching contract at a lower salary. He claimed that he was demoted. The state supreme court ruled that because Ritzie had claim only to a position as a professional employee, he was not entitled to the higher position or the higher salary. The court stated that Ritzie was "not demoted but merely returned to his former position of professional employee" (*Appeal of Ritzie,* 1953).

In 1971 a Tennessee high school principal charged with incompetence and neglect of duty was reassigned to an elementary principal position because the board believed he would be better able to handle the discipline of younger and fewer students. Overruling the teacher's claim of demotion, the court stated that the transfer was legal in spite of some minor procedural errors (*Potts v. Gibson,* 1971).

In a 1974 case heard before the United States Court of Appeals, Sixth Circuit, two principals who had encouraged participation in an illegal teachers' strike were ruled legally demoted to classroom teaching positions. The court overruled claims that their First Amendment rights of free speech had been violated (*Bates v. Dause,* 1974).

In 1982 an elementary school principal had serious problems with parents and staff after dictating that a new reading program be used. The superintendent finally ordered her and the other elementary school principal to exchange positions. On the first day of her transfer, the entire teaching staff at the new school walked out in protest over her reassignment to their school. At the close of extensive hearings, the school board voted to demote her to a classroom teaching position. The court sustained her demotion, ruling that she had had a thorough, impartial hearing and that the evidence was ample to show her inability in leadership functions. (*Lomas v. Board of School Directors of Northwestern Lehigh School District,* 1982).

As these cases illustrate, defining such grounds for demotion as "incompetency" and "unprofessional conduct" is difficult, but the courts generally uphold the judgment of the school board unless the demotion can be shown to have been arbitrary or a violation of individual constitutional rights. Teachers and administrators need to understand that statutory grounds for dismissal can usually be used for demotion as well as for dismissal or suspension.

Principle V

A school district may lawfully demote a public school teacher for the purpose of efficient management of available resources or financial exigency. Usually such demotions must be administered across entire levels of teaching positions, not individual positions.

Budget cuts, lack of anticipated revenue, and declining enrollments are becoming common conditions that necessitate teacher demotions. Realignment of staff helps alleviate financial crises, and the resulting salary revisions have generally been sustained by the courts when such actions are shown not to be arbitrary, discriminatory, or lacking due process. Sometimes collective bargaining agreements and tenure laws establish procedures for the revising of teacher salaries across an entire district or for a complete level or class of positions. Generally, financial exigency cannot be the rationale for the reduction of an individual teacher's salary.

As early as 1939 the Pennsylvania Supreme Court ruled that the state tenure law forbidding reduction in salary did not affect the general adjustment of the entire salary schedule when there was no consequent individual discrimination. All teachers' salaries could be reduced without any demotions effected because rank and grade were not changed (*Smith v. School District of Philadelphia,* 1939).

The interpretation of vague statutory terms can determine the success of a teacher's claim of invalid demotion. In 1940 the principal of a grammar school was demoted to a teaching position at half her salary when her school was closed for economic reasons. The Massachusetts tenure law stated that a teacher's salary could not be reduced except by a general salary revision affecting all teachers of the same salary grade equally, and so she sued for her full salary. However, the state supreme court ruled against her:

> The fact that the [principal] was chosen as a grammar school principal, and was paid the same salary as other such principals, does not show that she was in the "same salary grade" as the others after her school was closed and theirs were left open. She was not entitled to be classed with them as to salary after that marked change in situation occurred. After that change, she was the only person in her "salary grade," and the section [of the statute] cited afforded her no protection (*Downey v. School Committee of Lowell,* 1940).

In a similar Massachusetts case in 1973, the position of Director of Elementary Art was abolished, and the director was transferred to a teaching position at a lower salary. The court ruled that because she had been the only person in her salary grade, her reassignment did not violate the statute prohibiting reduction of a teacher's salary except by a general salary revision affecting all teachers of the same grade (*Kaplan v. School Committee of Melrose,* 1973).

The economic problems faced by some of the nation's largest school district have led to mass demotions of personnel. In 1973 the Los Angeles Unified School District sent notices of impending demotion and reassignment because of limited funds to 1,700 supervisors and administrators. A second notice of discontinuance of position and reassignment to teaching positions was sent to 777 employees. Finally, 178 administrators were actually demoted, and 24 of them were later reinstated in advisory positions. The courts ruled that all district administrators held tenure as teachers, not as administrators, and overruled the claims that the notices had been arbitrarily given because no specific reasons for demotion had been stated. Because they had no tenure as administrators, their administrative positions were not protected under the Fourteenth Amendment liberty and property interest clauses. Therefore, the mass demotions demanded by fiscal exigency had been lawfully accomplished (*Council of Directors and Supervisors of the Los Angeles City Schools v. Los Angeles Unified School District,* 1973).

In another mass demotion case, 30 guidance counselors in a Florida district were reassigned to classroom positions after a district decision to decrease the number of counselors because of financial constraints. The counselors alleged that the district had a *de facto* tenure system for counselors and that teaching was a completely different occupation from counseling. The court disagreed, and the demotions were upheld (*Mohr v. Dade County School Board,* 1973).

The principals and assistant principals in a Louisiana school district brought suit to have their salaries restored when all were reduced, but the court ruled that tenure laws prohibiting demotion had not been violated. The entire category of salaries had been reduced, but no one had been assigned to a position of lower rank:

> The authority to reduce salaries is not of itself inconsistent with the teacher tenure law's protection against a teacher's being improperly disciplined, removed or demoted. . . . Demotion . . . must therefore be understood as a change from a *position* of higher salary to a *position* of lower salary. Just as a general raise in salaries does not amount to a promotion of all principals, a general decrease in salaries is not a demotion (*Mouras v. Jefferson Parish School Board,* 1974).

Regardless of financial exigency, school boards must follow established guidelines before the courts will uphold a demotion. In the same Louisiana school district a year later, four assistant principals were demoted for budgetary reasons. However, the school board did not comply with procedural guidelines as stipulated by Louisiana's tenure law, and the court ruled that the plaintiffs were entitled to reinstatement (*Palone v. Jefferson Parish School Board,* 1975).

In 1982 two vocational agriculture teachers claimed they were demoted when the district's revised salary schedules meant they received lower supplemental income for their summer work than they would have received under the old schedule. The appeals court ruled that the action was not a demotion on the grounds that no material change had occurred in job assignment, duties, title, or position. The action had affected a whole class of teachers, not one individual (*Mitchell v. Caddo Parish School Board,* 1982).

Under Missouri law, restrictions on the power of school boards to demote teachers do not apply when demotions arise from the need to reduce numbers of employees for budgetary reasons. In 1984 St. Louis teachers whose jobs were eliminated were given the opportunity to take jobs at lower positions if they were qualified and if they had greater seniority than the incumbents of those positions. These demotions were ruled legal by the courts (*St. Louis Teachers Union Local 420 v. Board of Education of the City of St. Louis,* 1984).

Dropping enrollments in school districts and specific courses of study have also led to legal demotions of teachers, particularly when a decrease in number of students has led to budget problems. In 1982 a secondary school teacher was demoted from full-time to a 40 percent course load with a reduction in salary because no students had enrolled in one program for which she had primary responsibility. She claimed that less senior and nontenured teachers at the elementary level were not demoted although they held positions for which she was qualified. The school board stated that it chose not to demote the other teachers in positions where the demoted teacher had no experience because of reluctance to disrupt the established program at the elementary level. The court upheld the teacher's demotion because she was unable to show that the board's action was arbitrary or taken upon improper consideration (*Green v. Jenkintown School District,* 1982). In a 1984 case, the Pennsylvania appellate court ruled that an elementary school principal's alleged demotion to a sixth grade teaching position because of declining student enrollment was realignment of staff, not a demotion (*Fry v. Commonwealth,* 1984).

When school boards observe procedural guidelines, demotion for verifiable financial reasons will be upheld by the courts. Teachers and administrators whose positions are abolished because of financial exigency or whose salary schedules are revised because of budget cuts should become familiar with their state's tenure laws so as to recognize when their resultant reassignments or reductions in salary are legal demotions and when their rights have been violated.

Principle VI

School districts under federal desegregation orders may lawfully demote a teacher in accordance with court-ordered integration plans. As a general rule, once a school district is desegregated, such guidelines allowing demotions for reasons of achieving racial balance are no longer in effect. Thereafter, fair employment practices in hiring, assigning, demoting, and dismissing teachers are to maintain racial equality of school teaching staffs.

In the 1960s and 1970s when federal courts ordered many school districts to end their segregated systems once and for all, demotions of teachers and administrators became a major issue. To desegregate their schools, school boards demoted some teachers as staffs were combined and realigned to achieve racial balance. Many of those teachers and administrators so demoted claimed violation of tenure laws, but the courts generally ruled that the greater problem of persistent school segregation took precedence over tenure law stipulations.

Singleton v. Jackson Municipal Separate School District (1970), heard by the United States Court of Appeals, Fifth Circuit, became one definitive case on demotion of teachers in school desegregation cases:

> Staff members who work directly with children, and professional staff who work on the administrative level will be hired, assigned, promoted, paid, demoted, dismissed, and otherwise treated without regard to race, color, or national origin *Singleton v. Jackson Municipal Separate School District,* 1970).

To protect those demoted because of desegregation actions, the Fifth Circuit Court also stipulated that school boards establish nondiscriminatory procedures for determining who was to be demoted and that those who were demoted were to be given priority consideration for new positions equal to those lost because of desegregation actions. The *Singleton* guidelines defined demotion:

> "Demotion" . . . includes any reassignment (1) under which the staff member receives less pay or has less responsibility than under the assignment he held previously, (2) which requires a lesser degree of skill than did the assignment he held previously, or (3) under which the staff member is asked to teach a subject or grade other than one for which he is certified or for which he has had substantial experience within a reasonably current period. In general and

> depending upon the subject matter involved, five years is such a reasonable period (*Singleton v. Jackson Municipal Separate School District,* 1970).

Many subsequent school desegregation cases reference the *Singleton* guidelines. In 1971 a black high school principal who had been unlawfully demoted to an elementary principal position with a substantial decrease in pay was ruled entitled to back pay. His demotion had been a result of the desegregation of the school system, but according to *Singleton* he should not have lost salary (*Horton v. Lawrence County Board of Education,* 1971).

In 1977 the Fifth Circuit Court ruled that a teacher must show that *Singleton* guidelines apply to the case at hand and that each case "must turn on its own unique facts" (*Lee v. Pickens County School System,* 1977), thereby moving away from strict adherence to *Singleton.* As court-mandated desegregation has become less frequent, the need for exact application of the *Singleton* guidelines has decreased. When school districts become unified and establish nondiscriminatory policies for hiring, reassigning, demoting, and dismissing, *Singleton* can no longer be used to allege illegal demotions. Several cases heard in the 1980s show that teachers' claims of racially discriminatory demotion cannot be based on court-mandated desegregation orders of the 1960s and 1970s.

In 1980 a school counselor claimed she was demoted in violation of the *Singleton* guidelines. However, she could not show that a reduction in personnel because of desegregation resulted in her demotion. The school district had been ruled unified in 1970, and her position at that time had been unaffected by desegregation orders. Therefore, she could not claim protection from demotion under *Singleton* in 1980 (*Jones v. Birdsong,* 1980).

In *MacDonald v. Ferguson Reorganized School District R-2* (1981), a "reduction in responsibility" was claimed by two black principals who were transferred to assistant principal positions in the unified school when the district was under desegregation orders in the 1970s. The courts ruled that because the principals had much more responsibility in the larger desegregated schools, no demotions had occurred.

In 1983 the court ruled that a desegregation-related demotion could not be shown because too much time had elapsed between the time the district had been under court desegregation orders and the filing of the complaint. A football coach, who was demoted to assistant football coach and then passed over when head coaching vacancies occurred, waited too long to claim protection under *Singleton,* and the district's actions could no longer be questioned under those demotion guidelines (*Pegues v. Morehouse Parish School Board,* 1983).

In 1987 a Mississippi school district was charged with illegally demoting black teachers on the basis of race. However, the federal court declared that even though the district was still under court-ordered desegregation rules, there was no evidence of improper demotion, as defined in *Singleton* (*Montgomery v. Starkville Municipal Separate School District,* 1987).

Because most school districts are now faced with maintaining a racially balanced staff through fair employment practices, the need for the *Singleton* guidelines has diminished. However, a new issue surfaces when a school district's hiring, assigning, demoting, and dismissing policies result in alleged cases of reverse discrimination. In 1984 a school district's affirmative action program resulted in a white counselor being demoted to classroom teacher even though four black counselors with less seniority were retained. He claimed reverse discrimination. Citing the history of civil rights and affirmative action cases from higher courts, this federal court ruled against the counselor:

> "American history is a thunderous pronouncement that race consciousness must end. Racial preferences are morally wrong, and it is inevitable that the waters of anger and despair will rise up in the victims of affirmative action . . . The practical result of this case is that [the counselor] will leave the federal courthouse without an ounce of relief" (*Marsh v. Board of Education of City of Flint,* 1984).

Therefore, the trend evident in court decisions involving demotion continues to be an effort to realize racially balanced professional staffs in the public schools. Although few school districts remain under court-mandated and supervised desegregation orders, all school districts must act affirmatively to maintain racial equality. Teachers who are demoted should look to recent cases for guidance on challenging demotions. Claims of discrimination and reverse discrimination will continue until racial balance is established and accepted in the school systems of the country.

Summary

The issue of teacher demotion continues to come before the courts when the validity of the action is questioned. Many tenure laws and collective bargaining agreements now define demotion, and the courts will depend on those legal definitions to determine if a legal demotion has been effected. Demotion remains a valid disciplinary measure for individuals and a justifiable measure in times of financial exigency in school districts. However, due process guidelines must be observed whether the demotion involves one individual, an entire level of teaching positions, or all teachers in a district. Failure to abide by established due process usually results in nullification of a demotion. Although demotion was ruled a justifiable means to bring about racial equality in the staffs of school districts under desegregation orders, teachers in desegregated districts are no longer able to use those demotion guidelines as a basis for new claims of discriminatory demotion. Teachers must show that a school district's current employment practices are discriminatory or that a demotion violated fair employment policies before the courts will rule in their favor on such demotion cases.

Many demotion cases involve administrator to classroom teacher transfers. Some state laws recognize such a transfer, especially when accompanied by a reduction in salary, as a *prima facie* demotion. Although more courts are ruling these reassignments to be demotions, teachers and administrators must be familiar with their particular state's laws before claiming demotion or challenging their transfers in court. When school boards act in good faith, follow due process, and abide by state statutes, the courts will seldom overturn the demotion of a teacher or administrator.

Questions and Responses

1. What criteria are used by the courts to determine if a reassignment is a demotion?

State laws vary widely in their definition of "demotion." Generally, courts rule that a transfer or reassignment is a demotion when a substantial reduction in salary or position is involved. However, not all states recognize these criteria as evidence for demotion; therefore, teachers and administrators must become familiar with their particular state's criteria for teacher demotion. Courts will not base their decisions on a teacher's personal preferences for a position or on a district's informal seniority system; they will use only legal definitions based on statutes, board policies, or collective bargaining agreements.

2. Are all demotions of teachers illegal?

Many state tenure laws were passed to control arbitrary and capricious demotions of teachers. However, demotions are not automatically invalid or illegal. Demotions may be effected as valid disciplinary sanctions for individual teachers, as methods to control budgetary crises in school districts, and as measures to implement court-mandated school desegregation orders.

3. What is "reduction in position"?

Demotions based on reduction in position, loss of status, loss of prestige, or reduction in duties and responsibilities are more difficult to define than demotions based on reduction in salary. Formerly the courts interpreted such standards strictly, and few demotions were shown to have been effected based on this criterion. However, the courts now recognize more reassignments as demotions, especially those involving administrators transferred to classroom positions. State laws have diverse standards for demotion based on this criterion, and the courts usually uphold the judgment of school boards when reduction in position is used as the basis for transfers and demotions unless the school boards' decisions can be shown to have been arbitrary or in violation of individual rights.

4. What due process must be followed by school boards in demotion cases?

Tenure laws and collective bargaining agreements usually define the procedures to be followed in demotion of teachers. A minimum of notice of charges and a hearing on those charges before an impartial tribunal must usually be afforded the teacher who is being demoted or whose reassignment is alleged to be a demotion. School boards are obligated to follow the guidelines established by statute or negotiated agreement regarding demotion.

5. What are valid reasons for the demotion of a teacher?

A teacher may usually be demoted on the same grounds as he or she may be suspended or discharged. These vary according to state law but generally include such reasons as incompetency, neglect of duty, insubordination, unprofessional conduct, and other just cause. Financial exigency and desegregation of schools may also necessitate the demotion of a teacher, and such reasons for demotions will be recognized as valid by the courts.

6. When can financial exigency justify the demotion of teachers?
School boards may usually justify demotions of all teachers in a specific level or all teachers in a district on grounds of financial emergency as long as such an emergency can be shown. Salary schedules may be revised downward for teachers and administrators as long as the schedules apply across the board to all teachers in given classifications. Due process guidelines must be followed; financial exigency gives the school district no excuse to ignore established procedures for demotion. Usually an individual teacher may not be demoted for reasons of financial exigency unless that teacher is the only one in a particular teaching classification.

7. How are the courts ruling on claims of discriminatory demotions in school districts once under court-mandated desegregation orders?
School districts that have not been declared unitary for a sufficient amount of time to show that the teaching staff is racially balanced may still be challenged under the *Singleton* guidelines for determining demotions. *Singleton* stated that if a reassignment results in a teacher receiving less pay, having less responsibility, having a position requiring a lesser degree of skill, or being required to teach a subject or grade for which he or she is not certified or in which he or she has not had recent experience, the teacher was illegally demoted. However, if a school district is unified, *Singleton* guidelines usually can no longer be applied. A unified school district has been found to have implemented fair employment policies, and claims of discriminatory demotions must challenge those policies or claim a violation of those policies rather than the policies that accompanied desegregation orders.

8. When may administrators claim that they have been demoted when they are reassigned to classroom teaching positions?
Because most administrators hold tenure as teachers, not as administrators, the courts in most states have traditionally upheld the transfer of administrators to classroom positions. However, as the differences between administrative and teaching positions are becoming more defined by statute, policy, and contract, some courts are beginning to rule that such transfers are demotions, not realignment of staff. An administrator would have to know what the statutes and courts in a particular state say about administrative transfers to teaching positions before knowing if such reassignments would be upheld or overturned as demotions.

Case References

Appeal of Dugan, 59 A.2d 888 (Pa. 1948).
Appeal of School District of Pittsburgh, 52 A.2d 17 (Pa. 1947).
Appeal of Ritzie, 94 A.2d 729 (Pa. 1953).
Appeal of Santee, 156 A.2d 830 (Pa. 1959).
Barton v. Governing Board of Middletown Unified School District of Lake County, 131 Cal.Rptr. 455 (Cal.App. 1976).
Bates v. Dause, 502 F.2d 865 (6th Cir., 1974).
Black v.Wyalusing Area School District, 365 A.2d 1352 (Pa. Cmwlth. 1976).
Board of School Directors of the Abington School District v. Pittenger, 305 A.2d 382 (Pa.Cmwlth. 1973).

Chester Upland School District v. Brown, 447 A.2d 1068 (Pa.Cmwlth. 1982).

Clark v. Mt. Greylock Regional School District, 336 N.E.2d 750 (Mass.App. 1975).

Commonwealth, Department of Education v. Charleroi Area School District, 347 A.2d 736 (Pa.Cmwlth. 1975).

Commonwealth Department of Education v. Kauffman, 343 A.2d 391 (Pa.Cmwlth. 1975).

Council of Directors and Supervisors of the Los Angeles City Schools v. Los Angeles Unified School District, 110 Cal.Rptr. 624 (Cal.App. 1973).

DeSoto County School Board v. Garrett, 508 So.2d 1091 (Miss. 1987).

Downey v. School Committee of Lowell, 25 N.E.2d 738 (Mass. 1940).

Ellis-Adams v. Whitfield County Board of Education, 356 S.E.2d 219 (Ga.App. 1987).

Fry v. Commonwealth, 485 A.2d 508 (Pa.Cmwlth. 1984).

Glanville v. Hickory County Reorganized School District No. 1, 637 S.W.2d 328 (Mo.App. 1982).

Glennon v. School Committee of Boston, 378 N.E.2d 1372 (Mass. 1978).

Green v. Jenkintown School District, 441 A.2d 816 (Pa.Cmwlth. 1982).

Greene v. County Board of Education of Calhoun County, 197 So.2d 771 (Ala. 1967).

Horton v. Lawrence County Board of Education, 449 F.2d 793 (5th Cir., 1971).

Jantzen v. School Committee of Chelmsford, 124 N.E.2d 534 (Mass. 1955).

Jones v. Birdsong, 530 F.Supp. 221 (N.D.Miss. 1980).

Kaplan v. School Committee of Melrose, 294 N.E.2d 209 (Mass. 1973).

Kaufman v. School Committee of Boston, 463 N.E.2d 1195 (Mass.App. 1984).

Lee v. Pickens County School System, 563 F.2d 143 (5th Cir., 1977).

LeGalley v. Bronson Community Schools, 339 N.W.2d 223 (Mich.App. 1983).

Lomas v. Board of School Directors of Northwestern Lehigh School District, 444 A.2d 1319 (Pa.Cmwlth. 1982).

Lyznicki v. Board of Education, School District 167, Cook County, Illinois, 707 F.2d 949 (7th Cir., 1983).

MacDonald v. Ferguson Reorganized School District R-2, 530 F.Supp. 469 (E.D.Mo. 1981).

Marsh v. Board of Education of City of Flint, 581 F.Supp. 614 (E.D.Mich. 1984).

Mitchell v. Caddo Parish School Board, 415 So.2d 227 (La.App., 1982).

Mitchell v. Garrett, 510 S.W.2d 894 (Tenn. 1974).

Mohr v. Dade County School Board, 287 So.2d 337 (Fla.App. 1973).

Montgomery v. Starkville Municipal Separate School District, 665 F.Supp. 487 (N.D.Miss. 1987).

Mouras v. Jefferson Parish School Board, 300 So.2d 540 (La.App. 1974).

Palone v. Jefferson Parish School Board, 306 So.2d 679 (La. 1975).

People ex rel. Callahan v. Board of Education of City of New York, 66 N.E. 674 (N.Y. 1903).

Pegues v. Morehouse Parish School Board, 706 F.2d 735 (5th Cir., 1983).

Philadelphia Association of School Administrators v. School District of Philadelphia, 471 A.2d 581 (Pa.Cmwlth. 1984).

Pizzolato v. State Board of Elementary and Secondary Education, 452 So.2d 264 (La.App. 1984).

Potts v. Gibson, 469 S.W.2d 130 (Tenn. 1971).

Powers v. Freetown-Lakeville Regional School District Committee, 467 N.E.2d 203 (Mass. 1984).

Rible v. Hughes, 150 P.2d 455 (Cal. 1944).

St. Louis Teachers Union Local 420 v. Board of Education of the City of St. Louis, 666 S.W.2d 25 (Mo.App. 1984).

School District of Philadelphia v. Twer, 447 A.2d 222 (Pa. 1982).

Singleton v. Jackson Municipal Separate School District, 419 F.2d 1211 (5th Cir., 1970), cert. denied, 402 U.S. 944 (1971).

Smith v. School District of Philadelphia, 5 A.2d 535 (Pa. 1939).

Smith v. School District of Township of Darby, 130 A.2d 661 (Pa. 1957).

Stafford v. Board of Education of Casey County, 642 S.W.2d 596 (Ky.App. 1982).

State ex rel. McNeal v. Avoyelles Parish School Board, 7 So.2d 165 (La. 1942).
Street v. Board of Education of School District of City of Ferndale, Oakland County, 104 N.W.2d 748 (Mich. 1960).
Verret v. Calcasieu Parish School Board, 103 So.2d 560 (La.App. 1958).
Wagner v. West Perry School District, 480 A.2d 1336 (Pa.Cmwlth. 1984).

5 Discharge

Throughout the history of public schools, teachers have been discharged from their positions for innumerable reasons, some valid and some arbitrary or capricious. Prior to the enactment of tenure statutes, teachers had almost no protection from unreasonable discharge. Although many teachers attempted to claim they had been wrongfully dismissed, the courts generally upheld the rights of school boards as employers to discharge their employees at will. After World War II, tenure laws, court decisions, and collective bargaining agreements prevented teachers from losing their jobs for nonvalid reasons and gave them recourse when they suspected they had been discharged in violation of their rights to employment.

Many terms have been used to indicate the permanent or temporary severance of the employment relationship between teachers and school boards. Tenure statutes, school board policies, court rulings, teacher handbooks, collective bargaining contracts, and other employment documents are not consistent in their use of the terms, causing confusion that has, in itself, resulted in some court cases. In this work "discharge" is a generic term encompassing every type of separation of the teacher-school board employment relationship except separation by mutual agreement or that initiated by the teacher. Several types of teacher discharge have been defined by statute and the courts:

Dismissal: The permanent discharge of a nontenured teacher during a contract period or of a tenured teacher at any time is called "dismissal," although "termination" is also sometimes used.

Suspension: The temporary discharge of a teacher is called "suspension" because the teacher may return to employment once the reason for the suspension is resolved. However, a suspension may be a preliminary step to one of the other types of discharge.

Nonrenewal: Failure to renew an employment contract after it expires applies only to contracts of nontenured teachers.

Reduction in Force: Often called "furlough" and sometimes "suspension," a reduction in force (RIF) action is taken when a school district must discharge teachers because of financial limitations, declining enrollments, or reorganization of the curriculum or school structure.

Key to any discussion of teacher discharge is the concept of tenure. "Tenure" implies a teacher's right to employment and refers to a status conferred upon teachers who satisfactorily complete a probationary period and become eligible for guaranteed employment in a school district until they retire, leave the district or the profession, or are discharged for cause. Tenure benefits both the teacher and the employing school district. The teacher has a guaranteed position with accompanying salary and benefits, and the school board is able to attract and retain good teachers by protecting them from arbitrary employment decisions. Ultimately, society benefits from having dedicated teachers employed in the nation's schools. A Georgia appellate court explained this benefit in 1986:

> Teachers and principals are ... considered professionals whose services are affected with the public interest. It follows that state and local authorities have a legitimate interest in securing the employ only of those fit to serve the public interest (*Terry v. Houston County Board of Education,* 1986).

The criteria for attaining tenure and the rights that accrue to tenured teachers are defined by statute and vary from state to state. The majority of states have tenure or continuing contract statutes, and many school districts in states with no tenure laws have policies that provide for continuing employment status for teachers who meet specified criteria. Among the provisions of most tenure laws are the allowable reasons for discharge of tenured teachers and the procedures that school boards must follow to discharge a teacher on a continuing contract. Collective bargaining agreements must be made within the framework of tenure laws, and no statutory tenure rights are negotiable, although nonmandatory procedures may be part of contracts between teachers' associations and school boards. Even though critics of tenure claim that the discharge of tenured teachers has become nearly impossible, regardless of valid reasons for termination, the purpose for tenure laws remains as justifiable today as when the laws were first proposed:

> The Teacher Tenure Act was designed to accomplish a laudable purpose. If sanely and impartially administered the beneficent results to inevitably follow will vindicate the persistent efforts of its champions in procuring its adoption. It was intended ... to protect the worthy instructors of the youth of a [district] from enforced yielding to the political preferences of those theretofore having the power to grant or withhold employment to them; and to vouchsafe to such teachers employment, after a long term of satisfactory service to the public, regardless of the vicissitudes of politics or the likes or dislikes of those charged with the administration of school affairs (*Andrews v. Union Parish School Board,* 1938).

When the courts become involved in a case of teacher discharge, they must first determine the rights of the teacher under tenure laws and other statutes governing the various forms of discharge. Since the advent of tenure laws, the courts must balance the guaranteed employment rights of teachers with the rights of school boards as employers. Abuses of tenure have led to valid criticism, but arbitrary discharges of teachers are fewer when professional educators are able to turn to the courts to uphold their rights to employment.

Legal Principles

Principle I *Due Process*

The discharge of a public school teacher from employment must adhere to strict procedural rules. Application of the rules depends upon whether the teacher is tenured or nontenured and on the type of discharge: dismissal, suspension, nonrenewal, or reduction in force.

Principle II *Nonrenewal*

The nonrenewal of a nontenured teacher's contract usually requires little, if any, procedural due process.

Principle III *Statutory Reasons*

Generally, a public school teacher may be suspended or dismissed only for reasons defined by statute. Common reasons for which suspensions or dismissals are allowed include incompetency, insubordination, immorality, and just cause. The suspension or dismissal of a tenured teacher at any time or of a nontenured teacher during a contract period must follow strict due process.

Principle IV *Suspension*

A public school teacher may be suspended temporarily as a disciplinary action or as a prelude to other possible disciplinary actions.

Principle V *Incompetency*

A public school teacher may be suspended or dismissed for incompetency or the inability to perform professional duties effectively and to the satisfaction of students, parents, and supervisors. Because a teacher is presumed to be competent after completing professional training and meeting certification requirements, incompetency is usually difficult to use as justification for suspension or dismissal.

Principle VI *Insubordination*

A public school teacher may be suspended or dismissed for insubordination, neglect of duty, or the willful refusal to obey reasonable orders from the employing school board or supervisor. A teacher is expected to follow all valid policies, regulations, and contract provisions applicable to the teacher's professional position.

(continued on next page)

Legal Principles (continued)

Principle VII *Immorality*

A public school teacher may be suspended or dismissed for immorality, immoral conduct, or moral turpitude, all of which encompass actions inconsistent with the standards of good conscience as applied to a professional teaching position.

Principle VIII *Good Cause*

A public school teacher may be suspended or dismissed for good cause, which may include any possible wrong. Although "good cause" by itself is a vague term, it is often included in lists of statutory reasons for discharge to allow a school district some flexibility in resolving unforeseen problems that could lead to a teacher's valid suspension or dismissal.

Principle IX *Reduction in Force*

A public school teacher may be discharged when a school district faces financial exigency, declining enrollments, or district reorganization and must reduce its teaching staff. When reduction in force is a temporary measure, the most senior tenured teachers generally must be furloughed last and called back to open positions first.

Principle X *Recovery of Damages*

A public school teacher who is wrongfully discharged may seek reinstatement as well as recovery of damages, including lost salary, benefits, legal fees, and punitive damages.

Discussion

Principle I

The discharge of a public school teacher from employment must adhere to strict procedural rules. Application of the rules depends upon whether the teacher is tenured or nontenured and on the type of discharge: dismissal, suspension, nonrenewal, or reduction in force.

Although school boards were once able to discharge a teacher on any whim or excuse, they must now follow rules of procedure outlined in tenure laws, school board policies, and collective bargaining contracts. Not all procedural rules apply to all teacher discharge situations, and a school board is obligated first to determine the applicable rules for dismissals, suspensions, nonrenewals, or reduction in force. In addition to the type of dismissal, school boards must consider the tenure status of the teacher. The extent of procedural rules safeguarding teacher rights depends almost entirely on whether or not the teacher is tenured.

Before a teacher's right to employment will be supported by the courts, that right must be protected under an appropriate constitutional provision. Traditionally, no such protection was available for a teacher's position. However, the passage of tenure laws gave teachers entitlement to their positions, and such entitlement becomes a property interest protected by the Fourteenth Amendment: "No State shall . . . deprive any person of life, liberty, or property, without due process of law." When a teacher is entitled to a professional position because of having met all requirements for attaining tenure, he or she cannot lose that property interest without strict adherence to due process of law.

When a teacher discharge case comes before a court, the court must determine the extent of the teacher's threatened property interest. As the United States Supreme Court ruled in 1972, a property interest must be supported by more than a desire for employment or even a succession of renewed contracts:

> To have a property interest in a benefit, a person clearly must have more than an abstract need or desire for it. He must have more than a unilateral expectation of it. He must, instead, have a legitimate claim of entitlement to it. It is a purpose of the ancient institution of property to protect those claims upon which people rely in their daily lives, reliance that must not be arbitrarily undermined (*Board of Regents of State Colleges v. Roth,* 1972).

When any teacher, tenured or nontenured, is discharged at midyear, property interests are potentially offended because of existing contract provisions. Therefore, a teacher discharged during the school year must be accorded appropriate due process. At the end of a contract period, only tenured teachers generally have a claim to property rights and due process protection. However, a nontenured as well as a tenured teacher may demand due process if a discharge infringes on liberty interests. The United States Supreme Court has never precisely defined "liberty interest" but has given the term broad meaning:

> While this Court has not attempted to define with exactness the liberty thus guaranteed, the term has received much consideration and some of the included things have been definitely stated. Without doubt, it denotes not merely freedom from bodily restraint but also the right of the individual to contract, to engage in any of the common occupations of life, to acquire useful knowledge, to marry, establish a home and bring up children, to worship God according to the dictates of his own conscience, and generally to enjoy those privileges long recognized at common law as essential to the orderly pursuit of happiness by free men. . . . The established doctrine is that this liberty may not be interfered with, under the guise of protecting the public interest, by legislative action which is arbitrary or without reasonable relation to some purpose within the competency of the State to effect (*Meyer v. Nebraska,* 1923).

In teacher discharge cases, liberty issues arise if the discharge stigmatizes the teacher, jeopardizes a teacher's opportunities for future employment, or diminishes the teacher's name, honor, integrity, or reputation. Dismissals during the course of the year for any cause are much more damaging to the reputation of teachers than year-end discharges. Therefore, midyear dismissals of both tenured and probationary teachers affect liberty interests as well as property interests (*Cooley v. Board of*

Education of Forrest City School District, 1972; *Wertz v. Southern Cloud Unified School District No. 334,* 1975).

Once protected property or liberty interests are identified, the question arises of what process is due before that interest may be denied. The courts have defined two types of due process: substantive and procedural. Only procedural aspects of due process were recognized by the United States Supreme Court until 1923 when the Court ruled that due process of law possesses substantive protections as well (*Adkins v. Children's Hospital of the District of Columbia,* 1923). Other courts defined the concept:

> Due process, when applied to substantive rights, is interpreted to mean that the state is without right to deprive a person of life, liberty or property by an act that has no reasonable relation to any proper governmental purpose, or which is so far beyond the necessity of the case as to be an arbitrary exercise of governmental powers (*Valley National Bank of Phoenix v. Glover,* 1945).

Substantive due process has come to mean that a state must have a valid objective before depriving a person of Fourteenth Amendment rights, rights that include not only life, liberty, and property but have been extended to cover basic liberties not enumerated in the Constitution and all of the rights encompassed in the Bill of Rights. Tenured teachers are eligible for substantive due process under the Fourteenth Amendment.

Procedural due process means that a person may be deprived of life, liberty, or property only if prescribed procedures are followed. Three indispensable elements of procedural due process have been identified:

1. notice that a person is about to lose life, liberty, or property
2. an opportunity for a hearing
3. a hearing conducted fairly before an impartial tribunal.

Relevant laws, policies, and contracts may mandate additional procedures that must be observed during teacher discharge cases. The opportunity to be represented by an attorney, the right to confront and to cross-examine witnesses, the entitlement to an official record of the hearing, and the right to appeal the decision are common elements of due process invoked during teacher discharge cases. In 1988 an Arkansas federal court ruled that a tenured teacher who was dismissed for allegedly making sexual advances toward female students had been denied due process. The teacher was not given notice of the names of his accusers or the specific nature of the charges against him, nor was he allowed to cross-examine his accusers at the school board hearing, all of which violated the state law governing teacher dismissal (*Casada v. Booneville School District No. 65,* 1988). The United States Court of Appeals, Tenth Circuit, ruled that a statute requiring tenured teachers to pay half the cost of their hearings violated their due process rights (*Rankin v. Independent School District No. I-3, Noble County, Oklahoma,* 1989).

In summary, the discharge of a teacher from a position involves the balancing of the teacher's rights to employment under the Fourteenth Amendment against the school board's rights as the employer. Tenured teachers have entitlement to property rights that may not be taken away without due process of law. Both tenured and nontenured teachers have liberty interests of which they may not be deprived without strict adherence to both substantive and procedural due process. Teachers and school boards need to understand that minimal procedural due process in discharge cases includes notice and a hearing before an impartial tribunal but may involve other rules depending on the type of discharge being effected. Because due process must be followed exactly in teacher discharge cases, teachers and employers must understand and adhere to the provisions of tenure or continuing contract statutes, school board policies, and negotiated agreements.

Principle II

The nonrenewal of a nontenured teacher's contract usually requires little, if any, procedural due process.

Historically, nontenured teachers have had no rights to procedural due process—not even advance notice or reasons for the decision—when their contracts have not been renewed. Under contract law, once the terms of the employment contract have been completed by both parties, neither party has any obligation to nor claim on the other. However, recent statutes and policies sometimes require that probationary teachers be given reasons for nonrenewal and timely notice that their contracts will not be renewed so that they have an opportunity to seek other positions. The courts are often faced with allegations that nontenured teachers are actually eligible for due process. These allegations are often based on claims that the teachers' exercise of constitutional rights led to their not being rehired.

The two court cases that set the legal precedent for teacher contract nonrenewal cases involved junior professors in higher education, not public school teachers. The United States Supreme Court in *Board of Regents of State Colleges v. Roth* (1972) and *Perry v. Sindermann* (1972) explained clearly that nontenured teachers have no property rights or liberty interests under the Fourteenth Amendment.

In the first case, a teacher hired for a fixed term of one academic year was informed in February that he would not be rehired for the next academic year. He claimed his rights to procedural due process were violated when he was given no opportunity for a hearing. The United States Supreme Court, however, upheld his nonrenewal, stating he had neither property nor liberty interests in reemployment:

> The requirements of procedural due process apply only to the deprivation of interests encompassed by the Fourteenth Amendment's protection of liberty and property. When protected interests are implicated, the right to some kind of prior hearing is paramount. But the range of interests protected by procedural due process is not infinite. . . . [T]he terms of the [teacher's] appointment secured absolutely no interest in re-employment for the next year. They supported absolutely no possible claim of entitlement to re-employment. . . . In these circumstances, the [teacher] surely had an abstract concern in being rehired, but he did not have a *property* interest sufficient to require the University authorities to give him a hearing when they declined to renew his contract of employment (*Board of Regents of State Colleges v. Roth,* 1972).

Simultaneous to the *Roth* decision, the United States Supreme Court handed down a ruling in *Perry v. Sindermann* (1972), which involved a similar situation. An instructor in the state college system of Texas did not have his contract renewed, and he was allowed no opportunity for a hearing to challenge the charges of insubordination levied against him. However, this instructor had been employed on a series of one-year contracts for 10 years, leading him to have "a legitimate entitlement to job tenure," even though the college had no official tenure system. The Supreme Court ruled that the *de facto* tenure system implied in the faculty handbook at the college gave him the "equivalent of tenure." Therefore, he was eligible for a hearing before nonrenewal.

Most cases where nonrenewal of a teacher's contract is challenged refer to the *Roth* and *Perry* decisions. In 1973 a nontenured teacher who was not rehired because of her refusal to coordinate her teaching with that of other teachers claimed she should have been afforded a hearing because nonrenewal made her less attractive to other employers. The United States Court of Appeals, Seventh Circuit, ruled that no stigma on her name was created and no liberty interest was hurt because notice of the teacher's nonrenewal was not posted or publicized (*Shirck v. Thomas,* 1973). An Oregon teacher claimed she was deprived of liberty and property interests when her contract was not renewed after she had been employed for 14 years under annual contracts. The state supreme court ruled that the charges against her were not considered to "result in such an injury to reputation or employment opportunity as to constitute a deprivation of liberty requiring a predetermination hearing" (*Hawkins v. Linn County School District No. 14,* 1973). A group of teachers learned from the United States Court of Appeals, Sixth Circuit, that nontenured teachers have no "expectancy of continued employment" in a state with a tenure law (*Ryan v. Aurora City Board of Education,* 1976). An Arkansas probationary teacher tried to argue that she was eligible for more due process under state law because she had been terminated at her hearing before the school board although the written notice from the superintendent had been for nonrenewal. The United States Court of Appeals, Eighth Circuit, stated that a defect in the written notice did not violate a probationary teacher's due process rights (*Thompkins v. Stuttgart School District No. 22,* 1988). However, when a school board could not legally offer a teacher-coach a two-year contract but assured him that he would have a second year of continued employment, the United States Court of Appeals, Seventh Circuit, ruled he had a legitimate expectation of employment. The school board could not fire him nor decrease his salary in the middle of the first year, although it could remove him from his coaching position (*Vail v. Board of Education of Paris Union School District No. 95,* 1983).

No teacher, tenured or nontenured, may be punished for exercising constitutionally protected rights. The United States Supreme Court clearly stated this view in 1968 when it said "a teacher's exercise of his right to speak on issues of public importance may not furnish the basis for his dismissal from public employment" (*Pickering v. Board of Education,* 1968). Therefore, nontenured teachers may not have their contracts nonrenewed at the end of the contract period because they have exercised their constitutional rights. In many districts, school boards are under no compulsion to give such teachers reasons for the nonrenewal of contracts. If the school board does give reasons and those reasons include the exercise of a constitutional right or if the teacher is able to show that nonrenewal stemmed from the exercise of protected rights, the teacher may be eligible for reinstatement. The United States Supreme Court explained that interference with constitutional rights of nontenured teachers is impermissible:

> For at least a quarter-century, the Court has made clear that even though a person has no "right" to a valuable governmental benefit and even though the government may deny him the benefit for any number of reasons, there are some reasons upon which the government may not rely. It may not deny a benefit to a person on a basis that infringes his constitutionally protected interests—especially his interest in freedom of speech. For if the government could deny a benefit to a person because of his constitutionally protected speech or associations, his exercise of those freedoms would in effect be penalized and inhibited (*Perry v. Sindermann,* 1972).

However, claims of violation of First Amendment rights cannot shield a nontenured teacher from nonreemployment when other substantial reasons for nonrenewal exist. In 1973 a teacher who was not given a hearing on her nonreemployment claimed her First and Fourteenth Amendment rights were violated. The school board claimed she was ineffective as a teacher, used profanity in class, was inefficient and incompetent in fulfilling daily duties, and was unable to relate to ninth grade students. The United States Court of Appeals, Fifth Circuit, impressed with the woman's ability to act as her own defense during the trial, nevertheless stated that she had not suffered any loss of liberty rights:

> The record in this case ... describes the difficulties of an intelligent woman in her first year of teaching, whose ideas differed from those of her superiors in the school organization. We should have hoped that the principal of the school and school board officials and [the teacher], a highly capable woman, could have found some amicable way to communicate and to work out their differences. But whatever may be said of this unhappy breakdown in communication and its cause, the County Board of Education did not violate the [teacher's] constitutional rights (*Robinson v. Jefferson County Board of Education,* 1973).

The distribution of leaflets about the Woodstock rock music festival led to the nonrenewal of three Illinois teachers' contracts. The teachers claimed violation of First Amendment rights, but the United States Court of Appeals, Seventh Circuit, said that vulgar words and pictures in the leaflet were not protected speech:

> We do not believe that however much the reach of the First Amendment has been extended and however eager today's courts have been to protect the many varieties of claims to civil rights, the ... school board had to put up with the described conduct of [the teachers] (*Brubaker v. Board of Education, School District 149, Cook County, Illinois,* 1974).

In 1977 a United States Supreme Court ruling settled many of the legal issues in nonrenewal of contracts. The teacher in this case was not rehired and requested a statement of reasons. Because one of the enumerated reasons was the teacher's phone call to a radio station during which he criticized the school administration, he claimed his First Amendment rights had been violated. The court, admitting that the teacher had engaged in protected speech, upheld his nonrenewal because his unprotected conduct would have led to his not being rehired even if he had not called the radio station (*Mt. Healthy City School District Board of Education v. Doyle,* 1977).

The *Pickering* and *Mt. Healthy* decisions have been cited in numerous cases of alleged wrongful discharge of teachers when such actions have been based on the exercise of constitutional rights. For example, in 1978 a first-year teacher who spoke out about teacher salaries and was a leader in the teachers' association did not have her contract renewed. Because her nonrenewal was based completely on her exercise of free speech rights, the United States Court of Appeals, Eighth Circuit, overruled the school board (*Greminger v. Seaborne,* 1978).

Despite the United States Supreme Court's rulings in *Roth* and *Sindermann,* some courts have ruled or interpreted state statutes to mean that school boards must give nontenured teachers advance notice that they will not be rehired when their contracts expire. For example, a Kentucky court ruled that a teacher was entitled to timely notice and a statement of reasons for nonrenewal but disagreed that the reasons given her were unconstitutionally vague (*Sparks v. Board of Education of Ashland Independent School District,* 1977). In 1986 a federal court ruled that a nontenured teacher was entitled to none of the protections under due process and could be dismissed for any reason or no reason at all. However, the teacher was entitled to timely notice of nonrenewal (*Burk v. Unified School District No. 329, Wabaunsee County, Kansas,* 1986). In 1973 a federal district court in Minnesota summarized the reasons for a hearing to be held on nonrenewal:

1. Where the contract nonrenewal is related to the teacher's exercise of freedom of speech under the First Amendment.
2. Where the teacher is confronted with a charge that might seriously damage his or her standing and associations in the community.
3. Where the failure to re-employ the teacher imposes a stigma or other disability on him or her which forecloses future freedom to take advantage of other employment opportunities.
4. Where the teacher, by virtue of existing state policies, the contract terms, or similar understandings, has a reasonable expectancy of reemployment.
5. Where the adverse reports on which action is taken are prepared by the school's superiors or [teacher's] compatriots and are fabricated, without any foundation or basis in fact whatsoever or are maliciously designed so as to use the freedom of the probationary period for reasons of personal calumny, hatred, vindication or dislike thus using the probationary period as a sword rather than a shield (*Ferris v. Special School District No. 1,* 1973).

Nontenured teachers must realize that they are eligible for few procedural safeguards if they are not offered a contract for the next year. In some states, they may be entitled to advance notice and sometimes a list of reasons for nonrenewal, but hearings or opportunities to refute the reasons are seldom provided. School boards must recognize, however, that the constitutional rights of nontenured teachers must be observed, and the exercise of these rights can never lead to the nonreemployment of a teacher.

Principle III

> **Generally, a public school teacher may be suspended or dismissed only for reasons defined by statute. Common reasons for which suspensions or dismissals are allowed include incompetency, insubordination, immorality, and just cause. The suspension or dismissal of a tenured teacher at any time or of a nontenured teacher during a contract period must follow strict due process.**

In the days before tenure statutes provided job security for teachers and before court rulings granted them constitutional rights, teachers could often expect to be dismissed for any reason or no reason. Gradually, to protect good teachers from arbitrary dismissal and to provide the schools with a corps of qualified, dedicated teachers, state legislatures passed laws enumerating the reasons that could lawfully be used to dismiss or suspend teachers. Even though some statutory reasons have been challenged in court as vague, most have been upheld because they protect the right of school boards to dismiss teachers for cause while outlining reasons for dismissal that are understood by most professional educators:

> Legal cause [for teacher dismissal is] one which specifically relates to and affects the administration of the office ... something of a substantial nature directly affecting the rights and interests of the public ... one touching ... his performance of his duties, showing he is not a fit or proper person to hold the office (*State ex rel. Richardson v. Board of Regents of University of Nevada,* 1953).

Although not an exhaustive list, some often-mentioned statutory reasons for teacher dismissal or suspension include incompetency, neglect of duty, immorality, insubordination, unprofessional conduct, and other just cause. In states with laws listing the valid grounds for teacher dismissal or suspension, a teacher cannot be dismissed unless it can be shown that the teacher's action violated state law. The legal grounds for dismissal are usually the same for suspension and may also apply to demotion and other disciplinary sanctions.

However, no dismissal or suspension may be effected without observance of applicable due process. The rudimentary requirements of procedural due process—adequate notice and an opportunity for a fair hearing before an impartial tribunal—are usually expanded to include many other procedural safeguards. Statutes governing tenure and dismissal and collective bargaining agreements generally outline required due process. The courts are often asked to rule when violations of procedures are alleged.

In one early case, a Pennsylvania teacher was ordered reinstated when the court determined that the school board had violated the provisions of the state tenure act. The teacher should have been given a written statement of charges and written notice of the time and place of her hearing before she was dismissed. Additionally, the school board had failed to take a roll call vote on the dismissal, as was required by law (*In re Swink,* 1938). In 1956 the Connecticut Supreme Court ruled that the dismissal of a teacher required a fair hearing where the teacher would have an opportunity to cross-examine witnesses (*Conley v. Board of Education of City of New Britain,* 1956). The case often used to define procedural due process required for teacher dismissal cases was not an education case but one that formulated procedural standards for the termination of welfare rights. The courts refer to *Goldberg v. Kelly* (1970) in which the United States Supreme Court listed the following requirements of due process:

1. the opportunity to be heard at a meaningful time and in a meaningful manner
2. timely and adequate notice detailing the reasons for the proposed termination
3. the opportunity to confront and cross-examine witnesses
4. the opportunity to present arguments and evidence orally and in writing
5. the right to have legal counsel present at the hearing
6. a determination resting solely on the legal rules and evidence presented at the hearing, not hearsay
7. a statement by the decision maker of the reasons for the determination and of the evidence used to reach the decision
8. an impartial decision maker.

The question of impartiality arose in 1974 when a teacher and the school board held a private conference concerning the teacher's actions, after which a public hearing was granted. The school board then voted to terminate the teacher's contract. The teacher said the hearing on the dismissal should have been before a different body to ensure impartiality, but the United States Court of Appeals, Eighth Circuit, disagreed (*Swab v. Cedar Rapids Community School District,* 1974). Whether or not a hearing was held before an impartial decision maker was ruled an issue important enough to preclude a summary judgment in favor of the school board in a 1987 case. A teacher-coach was suspended without pay for beating a student, but the teacher produced evidence that board members harbored malice toward him and could not satisfy due process requirements of impartiality. Also, the fact that the son of one board member had been hired to replace the teacher "does not favor neutrality or fairness," according to a West Virginia federal court (*Cook v. Board of Education for County of Logan,* 1987).

The dismissal of a teacher during a contract period also necessitates strict adherence to due process because of the teacher's property rights in the contract. In 1963 a Washington court ruled that the school board had to provide notice of cause and an opportunity for a hearing on a dismissal during a contract period or the dismissal would not be valid (*Foster v. Carson School District No. 301, Skamania County,* 1963). A teacher who was dismissed in 1969 for wearing a beard was ordered reinstated by a federal court, which called procedural due process requirements to the attention of the school board:

> Two substantial deficiencies were present in the procedure [followed] in suspending and dismissing the [teacher]. First, [he] was not told what the charges against him were and that his refusal to remove his beard would result in his

> dismissal. [The teacher] was forced to guess as to the charges against him and as to what action, if any, the school committee might take. On the latter point, at least, [the teacher] may have guessed wrong.... Prior to [the teacher's] dismissal there was no written or announced policy ... that male teachers should not wear beards in the classroom.
>
> The particular circumstances of a dismissal of a public school teacher provide compelling reasons for application of a doctrine of procedural due process. ... The American public school system, which has a basic responsibility for instilling in its students an appreciation of our democratic system, is a peculiarly appropriate place for the use of fundamentally fair procedures (*Lucia v. Duggan,* 1969).

Some states do not allow the dismissal or suspension of a teacher for actions termed "remediable" until the teacher has been given an opportunity to correct deficient behavior. If the teacher does not improve or correct the deficiency in a reasonable amount of time, the school district may then dismiss the teacher. However, some actions are irremediable and may lead to immediate dismissal. When the teacher and the school board disagree on whether or not an action is remediable, the courts may be asked to rule on the dismissal issue.

Problems related to classroom management and teaching methods are often ruled remediable by the courts. Teachers dismissed for inability to maintain discipline (*Grissom v. Board of Education of Buckley-Loda Community School District No. 8,* 1979), excessive absenteeism (*Szabo v. Board of Education of Community Consolidated School District 54,* 1983), and ineffective teaching techniques (*Hanlon v. Board of Education of Parkway School District,* 1985) were ordered reinstated because these actions were deemed remediable. In 1986 a teacher's dismissal for excessive use of corporal punishment was overturned by the court on the grounds that putting a first grader in a closet and on three occasions swatting him in front of the class with his blue jeans lowered were remediable behaviors (*Swayne v. Board of Education of Rock Island School District No. 41,* 1986).

On the other hand, the courts have upheld the dismissal of some teachers for irremediable behavior. Having sexual relations with students is usually ruled irremediable (*Weissman v. Board of Education of Jefferson County School District No. R-1,* 1976). A teacher who challenged her dismissal was not able to show that her general incompetence as a teacher was remediable when she was accused of ruining pupils' attitudes toward school, being unable to develop teacher-pupil rapport, giving irregular homework assignments, grabbing students by the hair, arms, and shoulders, harassing and shouting at pupils, leaving the class unattended, and keeping pupils from recess and physical education class because schoolwork was not complete (*Gilliland v. Board of Education of Pleasant View Consolidated School District No. 622 of Tazewell County,* 1977). Conviction of a crime (*Chicago Board of Education v. Payne,* 1981), lying to school officials about reasons for absence (*Bethel Park School District v. Krall,* 1982), pinching the buttocks of second grade female students (*Board of Education of Argo-Summit School District No. 104, Cook County v. Hunt,* 1985), and striking a student in the genitals (*Mott v. Endicott School District No. 308,* 1986) were all deemed irremediable behavior on the part of teachers, and the courts upheld their dismissals.

The need for scrupulous observance of procedural due process in all dismissal cases involving teachers, even when the teacher's behavior seems irremediable or shocking to the conscience, has been seen in many cases when the failure of the school board to follow procedure has resulted in the courts ordering reinstatement. In 1984 a tenured teacher who was an assistant superintendent was dismissed for immorality and other just cause after being accused of sexually harassing several female employees. However, the school board did not follow the required process of waiting for a recommendation of dismissal from the superintendent before voting to terminate the teacher's contract. The court ruled for the teacher's reinstatement and recovery of damages, quoting a 1905 case:

> Statutory boards and officers must act within the scope of their authority and in obedience to the dictates of the statute under which they exercise authority, and when a statutory method is prescribed they [have] no discretion to say when the statute may be strictly complied with, and when it may not be followed. Such boards and officers can only discharge the full measure of their duties by doing that which the statute commands, and doing it in the manner prescribed (*Myers v. Greater Clark County School Corporation,* 1984, quoting *Silver, Burdett and Company v. Indiana State Board of Education,* 1904).

Therefore, school administrators and local boards should realize that the dismissal of a teacher must be based on statutory grounds and all actions that could lead to suspension or dismissal must fall within the purview of listed reasons for dismissal. An opportunity for remediation must be allowed unless a student or the school has been irreparably damaged or the harm cannot be reversed. Most importantly, teachers and school boards must recognize, understand, and follow all statutes and negotiated requirements for due process. Failure to follow due process may violate a teacher's right to employment, and the courts will often rule that a teacher must be reinstated, regardless of the grounds for dismissal or suspension.

Principle IV

A public school teacher may be suspended temporarily as a disciplinary action or as a prelude to other possible disciplinary actions.

The definition and application of suspension as a form of teacher discharge depend on state statute and school board policy. Teachers, administrators, school board members, legislatures, and the courts sometimes use the word indiscriminately to mean discharge, dismissal, termination, furlough, or unrequested leave of absence. The term indicates the temporary removal of a teacher from professional duties until the problem or situation causing the suspension is resolved. Suspensions may be either with or without pay, depending on statute, policy, and reason for suspension. Teachers take their cases to court when they believe they have been wrongfully suspended or their rights to due process have been violated.

Suspension is often used as a short-term form of discharge to discipline teachers for unacceptable behavior that is not serious enough to merit dismissal, although the statutory grounds for suspension are often the same as for dismissal. As due process for dismissal becomes more exacting, requiring more steps and more elapsed time between the alleged action and the actual dismissal vote by the school board, an interim measure is sometimes needed to remove the teacher from classroom duties before he or she can be formally dismissed. Teachers accused of actions that are grounds for dismissal are often suspended to protect students, the school, and themselves while due process is guaranteed.

Teachers are sometimes suspended for reasons not related to discipline. Temporary financial crises may result in suspension of teachers, and emergencies such as the destruction of a school may require suspending teachers. Occasionally, teachers are suspended when their physical or mental condition results in their temporarily being unable to perform classroom duties. Illness and injury are usually handled through leave of absence policies, but suspension allows school officials the flexibility they need to handle unforeseen situations not covered by other laws or policies.

As a disciplinary action, suspension can remove a teacher from school for any length of time as long as statutes and policies are observed. In 1986 a teacher who exposed himself to several fourth and fifth grade students over several years during the girls' private music lessons was suspended for the remainder of the school year. The school board vote was 4–3 with the minority preferring dismissal of the teacher (*Miller v. Grand Haven Board of Education,* 1986). A teacher who pleaded guilty to criminal negligent homicide after striking a teenager on a bicycle with his car was suspended for two years without pay (*Ellis v. Ambach,* 1986). The courts upheld these board decisions.

However, due process must be observed in suspending teachers. A superintendent suspended a teacher for three days without pay as punishment for hitting a student on the shoulder. The court overruled the suspension because only the school board had power to suspend; the superintendent could only recommend suspension (*Northeast Community Education Association v. Northeast Community School District,* 1987).

The use of suspension as a preliminary action to further disciplinary sanctions is a common practice, particularly when school board action cannot be immediate. A teacher who refused to let supervisory personnel into his classroom was suspended until a hearing before the school board. His dismissal for incompetence and willful neglect of duty was upheld by the courts (*Tichenor v. Orleans Parish School Board,* 1962). In 1969 a teacher was suspended after he refused to agree not to use an article from *Atlantic Monthly* as a supplementary reading. When the school board next met, he was dismissed (*Keefe v. Geanakos,* 1969). Another teacher was suspended for seven days for writing a vulgar word on the blackboard during the course of a discussion on taboo words, and then the school board voted to dismiss him (*Mailloux v. Kiley,* 1971). The United States Court of Appeals, First Circuit, later overturned the teacher dismissals in *Keefe* and *Mailloux* on the grounds of violation of academic freedom.

Suspension is also used when other administrative proceedings or civil or criminal court action is pending. A teacher turned to the courts to fight her dismissal for unknowingly showing obscene cartoons to her class. The court ruled that she should be reinstated, but the year she had been out of the classroom was ruled a valid 9-month suspension without pay (*DeVito v. Board of Education,* 1984). In 1983 a junior high teacher indicted for possession with intent to distribute cocaine was suspended pending the outcome of criminal proceedings. Although the teacher claimed he should not be disciplined until the criminal trial was concluded, the court upheld his suspension:

> Teachers ... are in a position of special public trust. As role models for our children they have an "extensive and peculiar opportunity to impress [their] attitude and views" upon their pupils. . . . More particularly, they also have special obligations to their pupils as to drugs. ... We think it within the discretion of the school committee to consider the indictment for possession of cocaine with intent to distribute to be an "indictment for misconduct ... in office" (*Dupree v. School Committee of Boston,* 1983).

Suspensions for medical reasons have not been challenged in court as often as those for disciplinary reasons. However, in 1980 a school counselor who could not concentrate on his work because of marital and family problems took extended sick leave and sought professional psychiatric help. The school district insisted that the suspension from duty was to continue until the psychiatrist certified that the counselor was capable of returning to school, and then he was to return for a 30-day probationary period prior to being returned to regular full-time status. The psychiatrist refused to give the certificate to the counselor when he desired to return to school, and the school district initiated termination proceedings without waiting for 30 days. The court upheld the long-term suspension and stated that a mental or physical disability may be cause for termination (*Smith v. Board of Education of Fort Madison Community School District,* 1980).

As a disciplinary sanction or as an interim measure, suspension can be used effectively to remove a teacher from the classroom and to observe due process. Because suspension is considered a serious sanction even if it only temporarily infringes on a teacher's employment rights, school boards and administrators must follow statutory provisions or board policies governing suspension, including all those applicable to dismissal if the ultimate result of teacher suspension may be dismissal. Teachers and school boards need to understand the local use of suspension and not confuse short-term discharge with other types of dismissal or termination.

Principle V

A public school teacher may be suspended or dismissed for incompetency or the inability to perform professional duties effectively and to the satisfaction of students, parents, and supervisors. Because a teacher is presumed to be competent after completing professional training and meeting certification requirements, incompetency is usually difficult to use as justification for suspension or dismissal.

Charges of incompetency against a teacher are among the most serious and most detrimental to a teacher's career because teachers are viewed by a trusting society as the experts in their particular field or discipline. When the mission of public schools is to transmit knowledge and a teacher is shown to be incapable of fulfilling that mission, students and society suffer. Defining "competency" is difficult for administrators and school boards and so nearly impossible for the courts that they generally hesitate to interfere with the decisions of educators.

An incompetent teacher is unable to perform required contractual duties reasonably expected of the teacher by supervisors, parents, and students. A teacher's certificate and educational background create such a strong presumption of competency that the school board has a difficult burden when required to show in court why a teacher should be dismissed for incompetency. When a teacher has attained tenure, charges of incompetency become even more difficult to impose. Incompetency obviously includes lack of knowledge of subject matter and inability to transmit knowledge to students. Physical and mental disabilities have also resulted in teachers being ruled incompetent. The courts become involved when school boards attempt to dismiss teachers on grounds of incompetency and the teacher believes the charges are fallacious.

A continuing problem for most teachers since the beginning of public schools is the maintenance of classroom discipline so that students are able to learn. Although one or two days of unruly classroom behavior cannot be used to support charges of incompetency, the courts have been willing to uphold the dismissal of teachers who are incapable of creating and maintaining an orderly classroom. In 1909 an Indiana teacher admitted he was unable to discipline his classroom and once had had to threaten to call the police to regain control. The court upheld his dismissal for incompetence because the teacher was "wanting in practical efficiency and discipline" (*Biggs v. School City of Mt. Vernon,* 1909). Nearly 50 years later the Kentucky Supreme Court upheld a teacher's dismissal for incompetency and inefficiency because she was unable to maintain discipline:

> [The teacher], during much of her teaching career, was a poor disciplinarian. Not only was she unable to preserve proper order in the classrooms over which she presided, but she was deficient in controlling pupils placed under her care on the playground. Her pupils were unhappy and ill at ease, her classroom was full of tension and confusion, with the result that group work and individual incentive were lacking. She was transferred from school to school, five in all, in an effort to adjust her to a general atmosphere in which she could instruct effectively, but such transfers failed to bring about any beneficial results. Wherever she taught, demands by telephone and by letter were made by parents that she be transferred out of that school, or their children be moved to another teacher (*Guthrie v. Board of Education of Jefferson County,* 1957).

In 1978 a teacher was dismissed for insubordination, incompetency, and conduct unbecoming a teacher when he used excessive physical force in attempting to discipline students. The court ruled that his extreme overreaction to student misconduct made him incompetent as a teacher (*Kinsella v. Board of Education of Central School District No. 7 of Towns of Amherst and Tonawanda, Erie County,* 1978). All four supervisors in an Illinois school district recommended that a teacher be dismissed for failing to maintain classroom discipline even though she was tenured, had taught for 21 years, and was 66 years old. In court the witnesses consistently described a lack of discipline that led the court to uphold her dismissal:

> The observers also noted that students entered and left the room at will, did not work on home economics assignments, created disturbances such as fight-

> ing, and that [the teacher's] class was so unruly that the ensuing noise and disturbances interfered with other classes in nearby rooms (*Stamper v. Board of Education of Elementary School District No. 143,* 1986).

Generally, inability to control a classroom indicates other problems in a teacher's competence as an instructor of children. In many cases that have reached the courts, evidence of incompetency came from several sources. In 1944 a teacher was observed teaching errors in geography, using incorrect oral and written English, failing to correct students' use of improper English, neglecting to use maps in geography, and demonstrating little knowledge of technical teaching skills. In addition, only six or eight students seemed to know what was going on, the room was in constant confusion, and the students were allowed to cheat on tests. The court upheld her dismissal (*Appeal of Mulhollen,* 1944).

A Louisiana teacher challenged her dismissal for incompetency based on claims that she was lax, indifferent, and inefficient in performing duties, that she could not or would not maintain discipline, and that she lacked education in essentials of spelling, grammar, and punctuation. Her obesity meant she could not move around among students, resulting in widespread cheating on tests and inattentiveness among students. Several parents and students testified that she slept during class and used a record player to entertain the students during her naps. When her class was tested after she was dismissed, more than half of her students failed to attain scores that would allow promotion to the next grade. The court pointed out that a school board must take action when a teacher is incompetent:

> The parish school boards . . . are charged with the duty of exerting their best endeavors in promoting the cause of public education. . . . Certainly the cause of public education demands competent teachers. . . . Should the school board be aware of the incompetency of a teacher employed in its school system and fail to institute proper dismissal proceedings, it would then be derelict in its duty (*Singleton v. Iberville Parish School Board,* 1961).

All too often, teachers are allowed to continue teaching for several years before school administrators confront them for incompetent teaching. In 1975 a teacher who had taught for 25 years was dismissed for inadequate knowledge of subject matter, poor planning, improper use of grammar, inability to use audiovisual equipment, and failure to keep required records. When the United States Court of Appeals, Fifth Circuit, heard that she attempted to teach spelling before her students had mastered the alphabet, her dismissal was upheld (*Blunt v. Marion County School Board,* 1975). The incompetency of a science teacher led to his dismissal in 1980. He was unable to maintain discipline in class, used films every other day, did not meet district guidelines for science demonstrations and experiments, failed to cooperate with administrators who tried to help him, and tried to attribute his teaching difficulties to high blood pressure. The court stated that "a school district is not married to mediocrity but may dismiss personnel who are neither performing high quality work nor improving in performance" (*Board of Directors of Sioux City Community School District v. Mroz,* 1980).

Some claims of incompetency have not been supported by the courts. In 1959 a school board informed a teacher that her services had been unsatisfactory and incompetent over the past year. The court said "incompetency" was a relative term that could be employed to mean lack of legal qualifications or moral unfitness due to physical, intellectual, or moral fitness. Because "incompetency" did not adequately explain the charges against the teacher, the court overturned her dismissal (*County Board of Education of Clarke County v. Oliver,* 1959). To sustain a charge of incompetency, school boards must have documented evidence of a teacher's incapability to perform teaching tasks.

The issue of physical and mental competence of teachers has come before the courts, and the school board is usually faced with the task of showing that the teacher lacks the capacity to teach. In 1927 a teacher could not hear ordinary conversation and could not correct students' oral answers or hear the vile and obscene language being used regularly in the classroom. A California court upheld his dismissal (*Alexander v. Manton Joint Union School District in Tehama and Shasta Counties,* 1927). In New York, a psychiatrist testified in court that an industrial arts teacher was "unable to render consistent and effective service as a teacher," and the teacher's dismissal was upheld (*Coriou v. Nyquist,* 1969). A California teacher who was hospitalized twice in two years for schizophrenic-paranoia was ruled incompetent to continue as a teacher (*Alford v. Department of Education,* 1970). In 1986 a teacher who was claiming disability benefits appealed her dismissal, but the court ruled in favor of the school board, which said she lacked the physical ability to teach for a prolonged period of time (*State v. Lillard,* 1986).

Although claims of incompetency are difficult to support in court, school officials have an obligation to students and society to conduct regular, reasonable, fair evaluations of all teachers as required by law. Statutory requirements that a first-year teacher be given a written performance review became the issue in a North Dakota case in 1988. The teacher claimed that the report of the session where she and the principal met and discussed attainment of educational goals was not a performance review. The North Dakota Supreme Court ruled that the signed document and evidence presented by the principal that the goals were not met were sufficient to uphold her nonrenewal (*Retzlaff v. Grand Forks Public School District No. 1,* 1988).

Structured evaluation and documentation procedures should be in place for all teachers in all school districts. Even tenured teachers cannot use tenure as a shield if they cannot maintain classroom discipline, if they lack the basic knowledge of subject matter, and if they are physically or mentally unable to instruct. Teachers should realize that they must demonstrate updated knowledge of their field, conduct an orderly classroom where students are able to learn, and uphold the standards of their profession.

Principle VI

A public school teacher may be suspended or dismissed for insubordination, neglect of duty, or the willful refusal to obey reasonable orders from the employing school board or supervisor. A teacher is expected to follow all valid policies, regulations, and contract provisions applicable to the teacher's professional position.

Public school teachers are expected to cooperate with the school board, administrators, and other teachers in fulfilling the mission and goals of the school. Refusal to obey reasonable rules, regulations, and contract provisions may constitute insubordination, which is grounds for dismissal in most districts. Lack of cooperation, neglect of duty, or willful disregard for duty are also used in statutes and court cases to indicate that a teacher has refused to fulfill expectations of the school board or administrators. One act of defiance or occasional behavior contrary to the rules usually cannot lead to suspension or dismissal unless the solitary act was extensive enough to disrupt the school or irreparably harm the teacher-employer relationship. The courts become involved, often reluctantly, when teachers and school boards disagree on the severity of the sanction for the teacher's alleged insubordinate behavior or neglect of duty.

A teacher cannot be forced to obey an order or to follow a policy that is illegal or that violates the teacher's constitutional rights. Suspension or dismissal actions will be overturned by the courts when teachers are able to show that the dismissal resulted from their refusal to do something against the law or that infringed on their rights. Similarly, principals and superintendents may not take action against teachers who refuse to perform duties that violate board policy (*Hovland v. School District No. 52,* 1954). In 1957 a court ruled that a teacher could not be dismissed for insubordination because he refused to resign in person at a school board meeting. The court stated that the board had no legal power to force the teacher to submit his resignation at a board meeting (*Millar v. Joint School District No. 2, Village of Wild Rose,* 1957). Charges of insubordination will be upheld in court only when the teacher deliberately refuses to obey reasonable and lawful rules, policies, and orders from supervisors and the school board.

"Constant or continuing intentional refusal to obey a direct or implied order, reasonable in nature, and given by and with proper authority" constitutes a definition of insubordination often used by the courts (*Shockley v. Board of Education, Laurel Special School District,* 1959). In 1972 a high school teacher refused to cooperate with the preparations being made for a visit by an accreditation team, including completing forms for the self-study. He told the principal that when the team visited the school, they were not to come to his classroom or he would leave the room. After the visit, he would not complete evaluation forms and told the principal not to harass him again. The court upheld his dismissal for insubordination (*Ray v. Minneapolis Board of Education, Special School District No. 1,* 1972). A tenured teacher who met with an unauthorized assembly of students was dismissed for contradicting statements of the principal and superintendent and for encouraging the students not to return to class. The United States Court of Appeals, Sixth Circuit, ruled that his dismissal for insubordination did not violate the First Amendment (*Whitsel v. Southeast Local School District,* 1973).

In 1973 a teacher claimed that his heated argument with the local board of education meant that it could not be impartial when a hearing was held to consider his dismissal for insubordination. Although he claimed he was being dismissed because of his involvement with the teachers' organization, the evidence showed he was late to class, did not supervise his classes, failed to cooperate in the preparation for the high school evaluation, and had been found for unexplained and unauthorized reasons in the administrative offices and stockrooms of the high school. The court upheld his dismissal:

> A school system may justifiably demand more from its teachers than competent classroom instruction; a chronic refusal to comply with reasonable administrative obligations can surely have a disruptive effect on students, fellow teachers and administrators alike and consequently poses a distinct threat to an optimum learning environment (*Simard v. Board of Education of Town of Groton,* 1973).

A teacher who informed the superintendent by note that she was taking a one-week vacation trip was dismissed for insubordination because she left in spite of the superintendent denying her permission for the trip. The court upheld her dismissal because her "conduct has the marks of a persistent, sustained, and unreasonable course of defiance" (*Fernald v. City of Ellsworth Superintending School Committee,* 1975). Refusal to take his turn on hall duty led to the dismissal of a tenured teacher for insubordinate conduct (*Lockhart v. Board of Education of Arapahoe County School District No. 6,* 1986). A teacher's failure to heed warnings that he should cease residing with a 16-year-old male student, who had formerly been in his class, led to the teacher's dismissal. He had encouraged the youth to leave home over the mother's objections (*Weaver v. Board of Education of Pine Plains Central School District,* 1987). Fifty-three acts of misconduct, including insubordination, continuing neglect of duty, failure to prepare and grade final examinations, and manipulation of student test scores, led to a teacher's dismissal in 1987 (*Carlan v. Board of Education of Lawrence Union Free School District,* 1987). The courts upheld these dismissals based on charges of insubordination.

Neglect of duty, sometimes closely related to insubordination, has also led to cases where teachers have challenged their dismissals. In 1962 the principal asked the industrial arts teacher to have his class build the forms to be used in pouring a cement sidewalk at the school. The teacher refused, saying it was construction work. The court upheld the school board's decision to dismiss the teacher:

> It is not the function of a court to sit in judgment on the propriety of school curriculum, methods of teaching and demonstrations which school officials have determined necessary and proper (*State ex rel. Williams v. Avoyelles Parish School Board,* 1962).

A physical education teacher's request to miss two days of school to attend meetings unrelated to his teaching duties was denied. The meetings were of interest to him as vice-president of the teachers' associations, but the school district had already arranged to be represented at the meetings. When he attended the meetings anyway, he was dismissed for willful neglect of duty, and the court upheld his dismissal (*Yuen v. Board of Education of School District No. U-46,* 1966).

In 1979 the United States Supreme Court heard a case of a teacher claiming that her Fourteenth Amendment rights had been violated when she was dismissed for willful neglect of duty. A school district policy requiring teachers to earn five semester hours of college credit every three years to receive salary increases had been ignored by the teacher, who did not receive any salary increases for several years. The state board of education then mandated that the credits be earned, and the district had no choice but to dismiss the teacher when she continued to refuse to earn the credits. The Supreme Court ruled that she had not been denied either equal protection rights or due process of law (*Harrah Independent School District v. Martin*, 1979).

A teacher who failed to report to his assigned school on the first day of the academic year claimed that he had not been informed of the date school would start. The court upheld his dismissal, saying that the school was not responsible for getting him to the right school at the right time (*Franklin v. Alabama State Tenure Commission,* 1985). Distributing an original short story of questionable taste to her class led to a teacher's dismissal for neglecting professional duty, which the courts supported (*Harvey v. Jefferson County School District No. R-1,* 1985). The courts also upheld the termination of a tenured teacher for neglect of duty when she was reported to have been drinking beer with students in a motel room while serving as a cheerleader sponsor (*Blaine v. Moffat County School District RE. No. 1,* 1985). In 1986 an athletic director failed to follow published regulations on purchasing and to account for moneys received during games and fund-raising activities. In addition, he attempted to circumvent and undercut the authority of the superintendent and school board by taking his grievances to the mayor and board of aldermen and the citizens at large. The court upheld his dismissal for insubordination, neglect of duty, and incompetence:

> There is a further dimension to the insubordination point. [The athletic director] was not an ordinary school teacher. He was [the school district's] athletic director and high school football coach. Beyond his formal employment assignment, [he] was obviously a popular and influential person within the community, no doubt in part due to the competitive successes of the [high school] athletic teams. He possessed a capacity to undermine the authority of the Superintendent and the School Board far beyond that of almost all other district employees. For this reason the Superintendent and the School Board had broad discretionary authority to act decisively to assure the orderly operation of the District's educational programs (*Merchant v. Board of Trustees of Pearl Municipal Separate School District,* 1986).

However, some allegations of insubordination have been found too vague to support the dismissal of some teachers. In an Arizona case, the court implied that although a charge of insubordination without other facts satisfied the requirements for nonrenewal of a probationary teacher's contract, it would be insufficient to justify the dismissal of a tenured teacher (*School District No. 8, Pinal County v. Superior Court of Pinal County,* 1967). In another 1967 case, the teacher was told by school officials that he was guilty of insubordination because he refused to cooperate with the principal of his school. The court, supporting the teacher, said a mere complaint of noncooperation could be charged against anyone and was insufficient to prove insubordination (*Osborne v. Bullitt County Board of Education,* 1967).

Insubordination is a common reason for teacher dismissal. Teachers must recognize that as professional employees, they are obligated to follow the reasonable and lawful directives from the school board and supervisors as well as written policies, regulations, and contract provisions. Insubordination or neglect of duty may not be used as a guise to dismiss teachers; dismissal of tenured teachers requires documented evidence of continual refusal to obey rules, to follow procedures, or to perform required duties. School boards and administrators should recognize that insubordinate teachers can be dismissed or suspended but that all due process required by law and policy must be observed.

Principle VII

A public school teacher may be suspended or dismissed for immorality, immoral conduct, or moral turpitude, all of which encompass actions inconsistent with the standards of good conscience as applied to a professional teaching position.

A common reason for teacher suspension or dismissal is immorality. In the past, even rumors of immoral behavior that violated the social morés of the community could lead to a teacher's immediate dismissal if he or she did not agree to resign quietly and quickly. The definition of immorality has always varied from community to community and has changed over time. Today immoral conduct usually has to be shown to have adverse effects on the teacher's professional performance before a teacher may be dismissed for that reason. The courts have long struggled to derive a legal definition of "immorality." One definition often used in education cases came from a New Jersey court in 1951:

> "Immorality" is not necessarily confined to matters sexual in their nature. In a given context the word may be construed to encircle acts which are ... inconsistent with rectitude and the standards of conscience and good morals. Its synonyms are: corrupt, indecent, depraved, dissolute; and its antonyms are: decent, upright, good, right (*Appeal of Schneider,* 1951).

Teachers have always been expected to be role models for students, and their failure to meet community standards of behavior, even in their personal lives, has led to dismissal for immorality. When claims of teacher immorality have come before the courts, they have had to balance teacher rights to privacy against school board rights to employ exemplary teachers.

An often-quoted teacher discharge case heard in 1939 involved a teacher who was dismissed because she worked in her husband's restaurant as a waitress and bartender after school hours and during the summer. She also had been seen occasionally drinking beer in the restaurant, serving beer to customers, shaking dice with customers for drinks, playing the pinball machine, and showing customers how to play the machine. Her dismissal was upheld as the court emphasized the importance of a teacher setting an example for students:

> It has always been the recognized duty of the teacher to conduct himself in such way as to command the respect and good will of the community, though one result of the choice of a teacher's vocation may be to deprive him of the same freedom of action enjoyed by persons in other vocations. Educators have always regarded the example set by the teacher as of great importance, particularly in the education of the children in the lower grades such as those attending

the school in which this teacher had been employed (*Horosko v. Mount Pleasant Township School District,* 1939).

In a 1950 case, several teachers who cheated while taking state qualifying examinations for recertification were dismissed for immoral and unprofessional conduct (*Shirer v. Anderson,* 1950). A Florida teacher who falsely stated on his application for certification that he was a United States citizen was dismissed for immorality when his naturalization ceremony seven years later was publicized (*Negrich v. Dade County Board of Public Instruction,* 1962). When a teacher was convicted of swindling two fellow teachers out of several thousand dollars, the school district dismissed him for immoral conduct unbecoming a teacher (*Matter of Shelton,* 1987). The courts upheld all of these dismissals.

Teacher conduct with students has always been held to a high standard of morality. Referring to a student as a "slut" and implying that she was a prostitute led to the teacher's dismissal for immoral and cruel conduct (*Bovino v. Board of School Directors of Indiana Area School District,* 1977). In 1983 a wrestling coach had a freshman wrestler misrepresent his status and weigh in for an older wrestler so that the overweight older boy could participate in a tournament. The coach was dismissed for professional inefficiency, immorality, and willful and persistent violation of reasonable regulations (*Florian v. Highland Local School District Board of Education,* 1983). A Kentucky teacher was dismissed for immoral and unbecoming conduct for smoking marijuana off campus with 15-year-old female students (*Board of Education of Hopkins County v. Wood,* 1986). In 1987 a teacher was dismissed on grounds of immorality for directing one obscene remark at a student even though she had taught for several years with an unblemished record (*Fiscus v. Board of School Trustees of Central School District of Greene County,* 1987). The courts in all cases upheld the dismissals of the teachers.

Sexual relations with students almost always lead to suspension or dismissal because such conduct is "inherently harmful to the teacher-student relation, and thus to the school district" (*Denton v. South Kitsap School District No. 402,* 1973). A court ruled that fondling of students caused irreparable damage to the students and to the school and that the teacher's dismissal was justified (*Fadler v. Illinois State Board of Education,* 1987). A teacher who invited two students to a party where they drank beer and smoked marijuana was dismissed for improper conduct. After the party, the teacher had taken one of the girls home in his car, and the court ruled that that action alone was enough to sustain dismissal (*Barcheski v. Board of Education of Grand Rapids Public Schools,* 1987). Even if the stipulated cause for dismissal is not immorality, the courts will generally uphold the dismissals of teachers who have had any type of sexual relationship with students.

In the past, teachers were dismissed for private sexual conduct with consenting adults if such conduct did not fit the traditional proprieties of the community. Few teachers challenged the school board when they were dismissed on grounds of immorality for adultery, fornication, pregnancy outside of wedlock, and homosexual behavior. However, challenges of dismissals for this type of sexual conduct are now coming before the courts. In 1973 a teacher was dismissed for immorality because she and her husband participated in a "swingers club." The California Supreme Court upheld the dismissal, stating that "a teacher in the public school system is regarded by the public and pupils in the light of an exemplar, whose words and actions are likely to be followed by the children coming under her care and protection" and that the teacher's "illicit and indiscreet actions disclosed her unfitness to teach in public elementary schools" (*Pettit v. State Board of Education,* 1973).

However, not all teacher dismissals on the grounds of immoral conduct have been sustained by the courts. In 1973 the court ruled that a school board had been unreasonable in dismissing a teacher who had allowed friends of her son to stay in her one-bedroom apartment when they had been visiting. Although the school board had not accused the teacher of immoral conduct, it had said she was guilty of "social misbehavior that is not conducive to the maintenance of the integrity of the public school system." Noting the difference in age between the teacher and her son's friends, the openness of the teacher in introducing the men to school personnel, and the general knowledge throughout the town that the guests were college friends of the son, the court ordered her reinstated (*Fisher v. Snyder,* 1973). Another teacher was dismissed for immorality based on rumors she had a man living with her in the school-owned trailer, that she played cards, and that she did not go to church. The United States Court of Appeals, Tenth Circuit, overturned her dismissal (*Stoddard v. School District No. 1, Lincoln County, Wyoming,* 1979). A teacher who lived with a male friend for a month while her trailer was being repaired was dismissed for lacking good moral character. The court ordered her reinstated because neither her students nor her effectiveness as a teacher had been adversely affected by her conduct (*Sherburne v. School Board of Suwannee County,* 1984).

Pregnant, unmarried teachers may not be automatically dismissed for immorality. A New Mexico school board stated in court that it had dismissed a teacher because pregnancy of an unmarried teacher was evidence of her having engaged in premarital sexual intercourse, which was considered immoral in that community. However, the court ruled that the termination was arbitrary, unreasonable, and not supported by substantial evidence (*New Mexico State Board of Education v. Stoudt,* 1977; also *Avery v. Homewood City Board of Education,* 1982).

The case law involving homosexual teachers indicates that the courts have begun to look for a nexus between a teacher's private conduct and professional activities before dismissing the teacher. However, in 1977 a Washington teacher was dismissed for immorality because he was a known homosexual, having admitted it to a student. The court upheld his dismissal because the widespread knowledge about his homosexuality impaired his efficiency as a teacher:

> After [the teacher's] homosexual status became publicly known, it would and did impair his teaching efficiency. A teacher's efficiency is determined by his relationship with his students, their parents, the school administration and fellow teachers. If [the teacher] had not been discharged after he became known as a homosexual, the result would be fear, confusion, suspicion, parental concern and pressure on the administration by students, parents and other teachers (*Gaylord v. Tacoma School District No. 10,* 1977).

In other cases, teachers have shown that some "immorality" statutes are unconstitutionally vague or that their personal sexual preferences have no effect on their teaching. An Oregon teacher's dismissal because of her being a lesbian was overturned by the court, which ruled the immorality statute vague:

> This statute vests in the school board the power to dismiss teachers for immorality. However, the statute does not define immorality. Immorality means different things to different people, and its definition depends on the idiosyncracies of the individual school board members. It may be applied so broadly that every teacher in the state could be subject to discipline. The potential for arbitrary and discriminatory enforcement is inherent in such a statute. . . . A statute so broad makes those charged with its enforcement the arbiters of morality for the entire community. In doing so, it subjects the livelihood of every teacher in the state to the irrationality and irregularity of such judgments (*Burton v. Cascade School District Union High School No. 5,* 1973).

In 1977 a teacher who was arrested but never charged with homosexual solicitation in a public restroom was dismissed from his position even though students, other teachers, and the community were unaware of the arrest. The court overturned the teacher's dismissal because no connection could be shown between the alleged incident and his classroom performance:

> Although [the teacher] was charged with "immoral or unprofessional conduct" . . . we have previously held that the determinative test was fitness to teach; the terms "immoral" or "unprofessional conduct" are so broad and vague that, standing alone, they could be constitutionally infirm; hence the proper criteria is fitness to teach. . . . Proof that [the teacher's] act was unknown to his students, testimony that he would not repeat such conduct, the absence of evidence that he had by word or example influenced students to engage in improper activity all combine to indicate the insubstantiality of any risk that students would imitate his conduct (*Board of Education of Long Beach Unified School District of Los Angeles County v. Jack M.,* 1977).

Therefore, although charges of immorality may lead to justifiable teacher dismissals, school boards must be prepared to show that the allegedly immoral conduct will have a negative effect on the teacher's classroom performance if he or she is allowed to continue teaching. Sexual misconduct is becoming more difficult to use as a basis for dismissal because of society's changing definition of "immorality." Although dismissals based on teachers' sexual relationships with students will usually be supported in court, dismissals for other types of sexual conduct may not be upheld. However, many courts continue to favor the standard of the teacher as an exemplar, thus finding a nexus between most questionable conduct and school duties. The Massachusetts Supreme Court gave a perspective on this standard in 1983:

> We note that statutes from colonial days forward recognize the unique position of teachers as examples to our youth and charge them to "exert their best endeavors to impress on the minds of children and youth committed to their care and instruction" the values basic to our society . . . requiring school committees to have full and satisfactory evidence of [teachers'] moral character. This

special role of teachers on impressionable and not fully tutored minds distinguishes them from other public officials (*Dupree v. School Committee of Boston,* 1983).

Teachers must realize that their private conduct may not be protected if their classroom performance is adversely affected, either by the action itself or by resultant publicity. Automatic dismissal for immoral conduct is no longer possible, and dismissal for this reason requires due process.

Principle VIII

A public school teacher may be suspended or dismissed for good cause, which may include any possible wrong. Although "good cause" by itself is a vague term, it is often included in lists of statutory reasons for discharge to allow a school district some flexibility in resolving unforeseen problems that could lead to a teacher's valid suspension or dismissal.

Because of the impossibility of anticipating and including all reasons for teacher suspension or dismissal in a statute or policy, some kind of "other just cause" or "good cause" clause is usually included in spite of claims in court that such a reason is vague. School boards have to be allowed some legal discretion to dismiss teachers for unforeseen reasons:

> The teacher is intrusted [*sic*] with the custody of children and their high preparation for useful life. His habits, his speech, his good name, his cleanliness, the wisdom and propriety of his unofficial utterances, his associations, all are involved. . . . How can all of these things be provided for and offenses against them be particularly specified in a single statute? (*Goldsmith v. Board of Education of Sacramento City High School District,* 1924).

"Good cause" may not be used by a school board *carte blanche* to dismiss teachers. All substantive and procedural due process must be followed during dismissal proceedings. Tenure clauses, constitutional rights, and other limitations on teacher suspension and dismissal must be observed. The dismissal of a teacher for "good cause" may not be for an arbitrary or capricious reason, and the reason for dismissal must usually have a relationship to fitness for classroom performance. A Massachusetts court explained the concept of "good cause":

> Good cause includes any ground which is put forward by the [school board] in good faith and which is not arbitrary, irrational, unreasonable, or irrelevant to the [board's] task of building up and maintaining an efficient school system (*Rinaldo v. Dreyer,* 1936).

The courts become involved when school boards dismiss teachers for good cause and the teachers claim that the reason is vague or invalid. The cases generally arise when teachers fail to fulfill expectations of administrators and school boards but the teachers' infractions do not fit into any more specific category.

In 1936 a teacher-principal was dismissed for good and just cause when he refused to cooperate with the superintendent, school board, and state school officials in fulfilling necessary administrative duties, including allowing a new program to continue in his school. The court upheld his dismissal, stating that "ability and willingness to co-operate are . . . reasonably related to the fitness or capacity of a teacher" (*Stiver v. State ex rel. Kent,* 1936). A teacher who was arrested four times for public intoxication, spent one night in jail, and missed several days of school because of drunkenness was dismissed for cause, and the court upheld the school board action:

> It is the opinion of this court that a teacher is something of a leader to pupils of tender age, resulting in admiration and emulation, and that the Board might properly fear the effect of social conduct in public, not in keeping with the dignity and leadership they desired from teachers (*Scott v. Board of Education of Alton, Community Unit School District #11,* 1959).

An Arizona teacher's dismissal for good cause was upheld by the courts in 1966. After a confrontation in a bar, the teacher had been arrested and had pleaded guilty to disturbing the peace while under the influence of intoxicants, attempting to fight, and displaying a gun (*Williams v. School District No. 40 of Gila County,* 1966).

In 1974 a 54-year-old teacher who went through sex-reassignment surgery was dismissed for reasons of just cause because of alleged incapacity to teach children. Paul Monroe Grossman notified his superiors of his impending absence for surgery but did not inform them of its nature until he returned two months later as Paula Miriam Grossman. She was allowed to complete the academic year in male attire, and then she began living openly as a woman under her new name, at which time she was dismissed. The courts had a difficult time defining incapacity in this case, but the New Jersey Superior County finally ruled that although her dismissal from this particular school district was justified, it did not question her fitness to continue teaching elsewhere:

> We think it would be wrong to measure a teacher's fitness solely by his or her ability to perform the teaching function and to ignore the fact that the teacher's presence in the classroom might, nevertheless, pose a danger of harm to the students for a reason not related to academic proficiency. We are convinced that where, as has been found in this case, a teacher's presence in the classroom would create a potential for psychological harm to the students, the teacher is unable properly to fulfill his or her role and his or her incapacity has been established within the purview of the statute (*In re Grossman,* 1974).

A teacher who stole a check from a student's locker was dismissed for just cause even though she claimed her misdeed was an isolated reaction to grief and depression. The court ruled her action irremediable, especially because she pleaded guilty to theft in court (*McBroom v. Board of Education, District No. 205,* 1986). The Washington Supreme Court upheld the dismissal for sufficient cause of a teacher of mentally retarded children because his visual and hearing impairments endangered the safety of the children in his charge (*Clarke v. Shoreline School District No. 412, King County,* 1986). In 1987 a New York social studies teacher was accused of altering answers on his students' state regents examinations. Of 705 answers on 15 students' tests, 79 were altered by someone other than the student; a handwriting expert, after analyzing the tests, stated that the teacher had made the alterations. The court upheld the teacher's dismissal:

> [The teacher's] offense goes to the heart of one of the most integral aspects of the education process: integrity in conducting examinations. Altering the answers given on an examination, or even ignoring alterations obviously not made by the student, amounts to a serious breach of a teacher's obligations. The Commissioner was entitled to take serious action and dismissal is not so shocking in light of the offense as to warrant annulment (*Carangelo v. Ambach,* 1987).

Because "just cause" can never be defined exactly, many teachers who challenged their dismissals based on this reason have succeeded in court. A teacher who became the focus of a community squabble was dismissed for good cause when several incidents resulted in the board questioning her professional judgment. Children who went to the restroom during class lost their recess time; a child who complained of excessive bus speed was placed at the back of the bus; a child was taken from school to the home of another parent to solve a discipline problem. Yet, the community problem was not of her making, and the court ruled that she was to be reinstated with damages from the date of her dismissal to the date of reinstatement (*Kersey v. Maine Consolidated School District No. 10,* 1964).

In 1968 a teacher who knew his car had had a slight collision with the fender of an unoccupied parked car denied it to a witness and a police officer and left the scene of the accident. Even though there was no damage to either vehicle, he was arrested and charged under a city ordinance with having been involved in a traffic accident and failing to stop and furnish requested information. He pleaded no contest and paid a $20 fine. Later he was dismissed for inefficiency and other good and just cause. However, the court said his "crime" had to have been more serious than this one to constitute cause for termination (*Hale v. Board of Education, City of Lancaster,* 1968). In a Wyoming case, a teacher was dismissed for failure to establish rapport with the students. The court overturned his dismissal:

> "Good cause" cannot be just any reason that the Board deems sufficient for the discharge of the teacher. . . . We hold that a general charge of "inability to establish rapport with his students," unsupported by definition and specific facts going straight to the charge, is insufficient, standing alone, to constitute "other good or just cause" under the statute, or the good cause which is necessary to insulate the order of termination or dismissal against capriciousness and arbitrariness (*Powell v. Board of Trustees of Crook County School District No. 1,* 1976).

State statutes and teacher dismissal policies must include a general clause to which school boards can turn when teachers' inappropriate, but unique, actions make them unfit for classroom duties. No statute can be devised to anticipate every quirk of human behavior. When "good cause" can be applied to teacher behavior that adversely affects classroom performance, the courts will uphold a dismissal on that basis.

However, school boards and teachers need to realize that "good cause" cannot be used to dismiss teachers for exercising constitutional rights or for participating in other activities that may simply disagree with board members' preferences for teacher conduct. "Good cause" is not an excuse for ignoring a teacher's rights to due process.

Principle IX

A public school teacher may be discharged when a school district faces financial exigency, declining enrollments, or district reorganization and must reduce its teaching staff. When reduction in force is a temporary measure, the most senior tenured teachers generally must be furloughed last and called back to open positions first.

Although schools have never had as much money as many educators would desire to provide an optimum education for every child, financial exigency has been a major problem faced by a significant number of the nation's schools only twice: during the Great Depression of the 1930s and during the 1970s and 1980s. The affluent 1950s and 1960s saw great support for school programs from government and individuals as schools tried to keep up with the expanding needs of the baby boom generation's move through the education system. The rampant double-digit inflation of the 1970s, followed by recession and growing demands for government aid for other social needs, reduced the number of real and inflation-adjusted dollars available from government for education. The decrease in numbers of school-age children and the redistribution of school population from city to suburbs and from industrial states to the Sun Belt resulted in declining enrollments in many school districts, qualifying them for fewer state and federal funds. Buildings became dilapidated and facilities and equipment obsolete as needed repairs and updated technology were postponed indefinitely. Statutes mandating that school districts provide free and appropriate education for children formerly neglected—particularly the handicapped and impoverished—increased the per-pupil cost of education. Societal problems such as drug and alcohol abuse, one-parent families, teen mothers, and child abuse resulted in schools needing more counselors, psychologists, and social workers to deal with problems not directly related to the classroom but which impact education. And, to exacerbate an already dismal financial picture for education, taxpayers revolted, passing ceilings on property tax rates and decreasing the tax base for education.

In the 1980s, school budgets were slashed and the meager dollars redistributed within the bounds of school finance statutes. Sometimes in the middle of the year, anticipated shortfalls in state tax revenues meant immediate excision of programs and personnel. Education is a labor-intensive business with teacher salaries the largest single item in the budget, sometimes accounting for 80 percent of allocated funds. Although most school districts try to trim every other budget area first, teachers eventually have to be dismissed when financial crises occur. Some states have passed statutes outlining reduction in force (RIF) procedures, but, where no statutes exist, districts have had to determine which teachers to suspend, the order of layoff, ramifications for seniority and tenure, recall policies, and applicable due process. Teachers' associations have been active in protecting teacher rights in RIF situations, and collective bargaining contracts usually dictate procedures to be followed by districts.

The courts have heard many cases involving reduction in force issues. Nontenured and tenured teachers who are faced with losing their jobs often turn to the courts for relief. The courts in such circumstances have had to determine if a district was indeed facing financial exigency, if due process was followed, and if tenure laws or negotiated agreements were violated.

Although individual schools have faced financial problems throughout history, the school districts of the nation were first faced with having to terminate large numbers of teachers because of lack of money during the Depression. Few states had tenure laws at that time, and dismissal of teachers because of budgetary problems was sometimes arbitrary or a guise for eliminating particular teachers. In 1934 the economic situation in a New Jersey city was critical because of a bank failure and the city's inability to collect taxes. Because financing of schools was difficult and because the number of elementary students had decreased by 1,400 in four years, the district decided to close two schools. At a school board meeting, transfers of teachers for the next year were first confirmed; then school closures were announced. Of the 34 teachers affected by the school closures, 26 had just been transferred to those schools. The terminated teachers were primarily married women and women who lived outside the school district—groups that had been heavily criticized by the school board president. When the teachers took their case to court, their dismissals were upheld:

> In general the board had a right to dispense with the services of such number of teachers selected from the entire school district as it in good faith deemed necessary to effect the economy which its financial condition demanded, and whose services were no longer necessary because of the diminution of the number of pupils (*Downs v. Board of Education of Hoboken District,* 1934).

Even some tenured teachers were dismissed in the 1930s, and the courts upheld their dismissals. In another 1934 case, the board of education abolished a full-time physical education position and created a new position requiring credentials in both physical education and English. The current physical education teacher was not qualified in English and so was dismissed even though she had tenure. The court ruled the decision was based on public economy and supported the board's decision (*Wieder v. Board of Education of Borough of High Bridge,* 1934). The kindergarten program in a Pennsylvania school district was abolished for "instructional efficiency" and "as a matter of good school business administration" in 1939. The kindergarten teacher claimed she could not be dismissed because she had tenure, but the court said the tenure law did not prevent the school district from operating schools in an economic manner (*Ehret v. School District of Borough of Kulpmont,* 1939). In 1939 the number of students enrolled in one teacher's courses decreased after the initiation of a commercial course of study. The decline in enrollment in her program resulted in her dismissal, which the court upheld:

> It is the administrative function of the school directors and superintendents to meet changing educational conditions through the creation of new courses, reassignment of teachers, and rearrangement of curriculum.... [To deny the board this power] would transfer much of the discretion accorded to these

administrative boards to the teachers, that they might preserve their positions in perpetuity (*Jones v. Holes,* 1939).

However, in states that had tenure acts during the 1930s, tenured teachers generally could not be dismissed while nontenured teachers holding positions for which tenured teachers were qualified were retained. The Indiana Supreme Court expressed this view in 1939:

> The principal purpose of the [Tenure] Act was to secure permanency in the teaching force. If a justifiable decrease in the number of teaching positions should be held to give to the trustee the power to choose between tenure and nontenure teachers, both of whom are licensed to teach in the teaching position which remains, he is thereby given the power to nullify the Teachers' Tenure Act, and to discharge without cause a teacher who has, by reason of having served satisfactorily as a teacher during the specified period, secured a tenure status and an indefinite permanent contract. To countenance such an interpretation of the law would be to permit the trustee to do indirectly that which the law expressly forbids him to do directly (*Watson v. Burnett,* 1939).

In 1942 when an administrative position was not mandated by law but merely created by the school board, the court ruled that the board was allowed to abolish it when a decline in enrollment and financial deficits required some economic measures to be taken (*State ex rel. Frank v. Meigs County Board of Education,* 1942). However, the abolishment of a position could not be a subterfuge for terminating an administrator, especially when that person held tenure as a teacher. In 1949 the position of principal was abolished and a teacher-principal position created. The principal was terminated and a teacher named as teacher-principal with only the duties of principal. The court ruled that the position of principal was never really abolished, and the former principal was eligible for reinstatement (*Viemeister v. Board of Education of Borough of Prospect Park, Passaic County,* 1949).

In the 1970s the second rush of cases dealing with reduction in force issues reached the courts, many involving the same questions as had arisen 40 years earlier. For example, a New York appellate court ruled that the fractionalization of an administrative position did not violate the tenure law where the position of Director of Guidance was abolished and the administrative duties reassigned to the guidance counselors (*Beers v. Nyquist,* 1972). In 1974 the position of attendance teacher was abolished and the duties divided among the principals and assistant principals in the district. The court also upheld this dismissal:

> Faced with spiraling operating costs and ever increasing demands on their tax bases, school districts must have sufficient latitude within the law to manage their affairs efficiently and effectively. This implies, where appropriate, the power to consolidate and abolish positions for economic reasons (*Young v. Board of Education of Central School District No. 6, Town of Huntington,* 1974).

The termination of a combination English–social studies position was upheld by the Minnesota Supreme Court, which said that "the choice of which of the tenured teachers should be retained is an administrative decision for the . . . school board" (*Jordahl v. Independent School District No. 129,* 1974). A Kansas school district discontinued a special education cooperative program, and the court agreed that that was good cause for the dismissal of a tenured special education teacher (*Sells v. Unified School District No. 429, Doniphan County,* 1982). Another court ruled that a physical education teacher abandoned her right to tenure when she refused transfer to other positions and then was dismissed for financial exigency (*O'Toole v. Forestal,* 1986). In Pennsylvania an elementary school music teacher was suspended from his nonmandated position because of the district's severe economic difficulties. The court upheld his suspension:

> Where a school board eliminated a school program in accordance with a recommended curriculum change, the suspension of a teacher as a result thereof was "required by law". . . . The burden was upon the school board to establish that the suspension was motivated by a desire to provide a more efficient and effective school system and that "a department may not be abolished merely to circumvent the [tenure law] and to accomplish the dismissal of a teacher for political or arbitrary reasons by unlawful subterfuge" (*Glendale School District v. Feigh,* 1986).

The courts are often asked to evaluate documentation indicating that faculty cuts are necessary. In 1974, 43 probationary teachers who received notice of nonreemployment because of a decline in the average daily attendance in all schools in the district were able to show in court that the amount of decline meant that only 13 teachers needed to be released. The court ordered the school district to reconsider the criteria for nonrenewal of contracts (*Karbach v. Board of Education of Lawndale School District,* 1974). However, in 1977 a school board was able to show statistically that the student enrollment in the district was declining and would continue to do so in the future, necessitating the dismissal of four teachers. The teachers argued that high school enrollment was projected to increase slightly in some of the years, but the court upheld the school board. The court stated that the school board had the discretion to determine enrollment impact, and the courts would not intervene unless the school board acted arbitrarily (*Tressler v. Upper Dublin School District,* 1977). In Minnesota a school district placed 34 teachers on unrequested leave because of financial limitations. The court ruled that the district did not need to prove financial limitations specific to each position but could not arbitrarily pick which teachers to place on furlough (*Bye v. Special Intermediate School District No. 916,* 1986).

Many states now have specific provisions for handling reduction in force, and violation of those provisions nullifies the dismissal of teachers. In Pennsylvania all administrative positions in a district were eliminated, and those administrators, all of whom were also certificated as business education teachers, were assigned to teaching positions. This action resulted in one superfluous business education teacher. The teacher chosen for subsequent suspension had the lowest "quality rating" among all the business education teachers. However, the only reasons allowed for suspending teachers for financial reasons were specific:

1. substantial decrease in enrollment
2. curtailment of educational program on recommendation of superintendent, concurred in by the school board, and approved by the Department of Public Instruction
3. consolidation of schools
4. reorganization of school districts.

Because the teacher was suspended to reduce operating expenses, a reason not specified in the state statute, the court ordered his reinstatement (*Warwick Board of School Directors v. Theros,* 1981). Missouri provides another example of an explicit reduction in force statute: a school board is allowed to place temporary and tenured teachers on unrequested leave only for declining enrollment, district reorganization, or financial condition of the district (*Elrod v. Harrisonville Cass R-IX School District,* 1986).

The order in which teachers are suspended becomes a major issue in reduction in force cases. Generally, tenured teachers are entitled to positions until all nontenured teachers holding positions for which the tenured teacher is qualified have been released *(Coats v. Board of Education, Unified School District No. 353, Sumner County,* 1983; *Sto-Rox School District v. Horgan,* 1982). When all teachers are tenured, then seniority usually is a factor. For example, the courts upheld a decision to close a secondary school in West Virginia involving the dismissal of the secondary principal with the least seniority, not the principal of the school that was closed (*State ex rel. Board of Education of County of Kanawha v. Casey,* 1986). In 1987 the number of third grade positions in an Iowa school district was decreased because of budgetary problems, declining enrollment, and need for efficient utilization of staff. A third grade teacher was shifted to the sixth grade, which meant that a sixth grade teacher with less seniority was dismissed. The sixth grade teacher claimed she was wrongfully dismissed because five teachers with less seniority had not been included in the reduction in force plan. The court upheld her dismissal because each of the five teachers in question had special qualifications in areas of special education, art, learning disabilities, reading, and music, which the sixth grade teacher did not possess (*Pocahontas Community School District v. Levene,* 1987).

When positions are available again in a school district that has had a reduction in force, generally the most senior tenured teachers qualified for the open positions must be recalled first (*Walter v. Board of Education of Quincy School District No. 172,* 1982). New appointments cannot be made as long as suspended teachers are available who are properly certified to fill such vacancies (*Portage Area School District v. Portage Area Education Association,* 1977).

Another issue that arises in RIF cases concerns affirmative efforts by school districts to hire more minority teachers. When the collective bargaining contract, state law, or tradition calls for the last teacher hired to be the first laid off, minority teachers may always be the ones furloughed first, thereby defeating efforts to employ greater numbers of minority teachers. The United States Supreme Court in 1984 ruled in a case involving firefighters that bona fide seniority systems are valid as long as patterns of discrimination against individual minority workers cannot be shown:

> Mere membership in the disadvantaged class is insufficient to warrant a seniority award; each individual must prove that the discriminatory practice had an impact on him. . . . Even when an individual shows that the discriminatory practice has had an impact on him, he is not automatically entitled to have a nonminority employee laid off to make room for him (*Firefighters Local Union No. 1784 v. Stotts,* 1984).

Considering the many issues involved in discrimination cases, the courts are likely to look at the issues involving teachers and school districts on a case-by-case basis, reviewing past employment practices of the district, past and present master contracts, and teacher discharge patterns before ruling on a case alleging discriminatory RIF policies.

Reduction in force has resulted in many court cases because declining enrollments, budget deficits, and reorganization of staff have required the dismissal of teachers, both tenured and nontenured. So that due process is guaranteed all teachers, school districts should have reduction in force procedures in place before financial limitations necessitate the release of teachers. Such policies must adhere to state statutes for reduction in force, tenure, and dismissal of professional staff. Teachers often feel vulnerable when reduction in force procedures are implemented, but sometimes the termination of faculty is the only answer to serious financial problems. Administrators should notify all teachers who may be eligible for RIF far enough in advance of such a process that teachers have an opportunity to seek other employment. Teachers, administrators, and board members must abide by all mandated procedures to ensure that the rights of teachers who are being suspended from their positions are not violated.

Principle X

A public school teacher who is wrongfully discharged may seek reinstatement as well as recovery of damages, including lost salary, benefits, legal fees, and punitive damages.

When a person is wrongfully deprived of a property interest, the value of which can be determined, the person is generally eligible to recover that amount in damages. For a teacher who is wrongfully discharged, the most common remedies available are reinstatement and back pay, and the granting of one remedy does not preclude the other. State statutes govern the availability of damages and the procedures to be followed to recover them. Traditionally, reinstatement to the former teaching position with all previous rights and privileges was the most common remedy for teachers who were wrongfully dismissed. Back wages were also granted for the time during which the teacher was not working because of illegal discharge. With the value of fringe benefits constituting a substantial portion of a teacher's salary, recovery of damages now includes not only wages but also the value of such benefits as retirement payments and health and medical insurance premiums. Depending on state laws, interest is sometimes granted on the value of the lost salary, and teachers may be eligible for attorney fees. The courts have become involved in questions of damages when a teacher seeks reinstatement, damages, and attorney fees as a consequence of having shown that he or she was wrongfully discharged.

The most familiar type of remedy has always been reinstatement with back pay. The United States Court of Appeals, Eleventh Circuit, voiced this traditional view:

> Reinstatement is a basic element of the appropriate remedy in wrongful employee discharge cases and, except in extraordinary cases, is required (*Allen v. Autauga County Board of Education,* 1982).

However, to bring the wrongfully discharged teacher to the position in which he or she would have been had the wrongful action never occurred usually involves more than reinstatement and back pay. As early as 1919, a teacher who was wrongfully discharged was awarded the expenses he incurred while seeking another position (*Sams v. Board of Commissioners of Creek County,* 1919; also, *McBeth v. Board of Education of DeVall's Bluff School District No. 1, Arkansas,* 1969).

When a school district becomes liable for back pay for a teacher whose case has been pending in court for some time, the amount can be substantial. In 1979 the United States Court of Appeals, Tenth Circuit, ruled that a small school district in Wyoming had to pay a teacher who was dismissed without cause $33,000 in back salary (*Stoddard v. School District No. 1, Lincoln County, Wyoming,* 1979). The Eighth Circuit Court awarded a principal who was dismissed for exercising his First Amendment right of free speech $25,348 for lost wages. The trial court had awarded him an additional $5,000 for violation of his First Amendment rights, but the appellate court ruled that no evidence supported an award of constitutional damages (*Lewis v. Harrison School District No. 1,* 1986). Because the value of constitutional rights is indeterminate, "presumptive damages" could not be awarded under a United States Supreme Court ruling in *Memphis Community School District v. Stachura* (1986). An Arkansas school board attempted to claim that a nonprobationary teacher who was removed from her position without cause was only entitled to salary for her one-year contract. However, the court ruled for her reinstatement and her eligibility for back pay for the entire period she was unemployed (*Western Grove School District v. Strain,* 1986). In 1986 an Indiana teacher recovered $104,694.19 in back pay and wages, loss of retirement income, health and life insurance benefits, retirement severance pay, costs, and prejudgment interest on lost salary and wages. The court commented on the amount of the award:

> A judgment is not excessive unless the amount is so large it cannot be explained upon any reasonable hypothesis other than prejudice, passion, partiality, corruption, or some other improper element (*Greater Clark County School Corporation v. Myers,* 1986).

A teacher who is wrongfully discharged is obligated to seek another teaching position to mitigate the damages. However, a teacher does not have to accept just any employment to show a good faith effort to mitigate damages. The position should not be inferior to the one held before discharge. In 1963 a North Dakota teacher was dismissed for moving from the school district, thereby breaching the residency provision of his contract. In ruling in the teacher's favor, the court awarded him the wages he would have been paid under his contract from the date of discharge to the end of the contract term less the money he had earned parking cars, the only employment that had been available in the small town (*Miller v. South Bend Special School District No. 1, McHenry County,* 1963). The United States Court of Appeals, Fourth Circuit, ruled that a principal did not have to accept a job as a teacher because his acceptance of the teaching position might have implied that he was not qualified for another principalship (*Williams v. Albemarle City Board of Education,* 1974). In 1985 a teacher was ordered reinstated and awarded damages because she had been forced to take a job at a lower salary when she was wrongfully discharged. She received the wages she would have received for her teaching contract less the amount she had earned at her nonteaching job (*Board of Education of Taos Municipal Schools v. Singleton,* 1985).

The amount of damages awarded has become complex with the allowance for the value of lost fringe benefits as well as contract salary. A teacher who was suspended improperly was ruled eligible for past salary less the amount that would have been deducted for retirement contributions but plus the interest on each salary payment from the date of accrual to the date of court judgment (*Mass v. Board of Education of San Francisco Unified School District,* 1964). In 1966 a teacher who was wrongfully dismissed was ruled eligible for the value of her rent-free living quarters as well as her salary. However, she was not entitled to the expenses she incurred in moving to Montana from Colorado after her contract was breached by the school district. The court explained her award:

> The [teacher] should receive a sum which, when added to the benefits already received under the contract, will give her an economic status identical to that which she would have enjoyed had the contract been performed (*Wyatt v. School District No. 104, Fergus County,* 1966).

An orchestra teacher was reinstated with back pay after he was improperly dismissed. However, the court ruled he was not entitled to his extra duty salary (*Board of Education of Berwyn School District No. 100, Cook County v. Metskas,* 1982). A principal whose contract was not renewed won in court and was entitled to reinstatement and damages. Because he had taken a position in a town 50 miles away while the case was pending, he was granted lost wages, payment of life and health insurance premiums, housing and fringe benefits, retirement system payments, travel expenses to and from the job he held in the other town minus the value of carpooling arrangements, interest on the compensation he lost, and attorney fees (*Hyde v. Wellpinit School District No. 49,* 1982).

The issue of attorney fees has arisen only in the last few years, and they are usually awarded as expenses under state or federal statutes. In 1982 a teacher who incurred $6,000 in attorney fees to recover $4,000 in unpaid salary and benefits was awarded the attorney fees. She had been caught in a power struggle between the superintendent, who refused to sign her paychecks for four months because he wanted her assigned to a different school, and the school board, which had made her assignment (*Doyal v. School Board of Liberty County,* 1982).

The observance of mandated procedures in suits to recover damages is required of both parties. All due process must be afforded any teacher who is discharged; failure to follow due process will usually result in the court ordering the teacher reinstated, at least until due process requirements are met (*State ex rel. Charbonnet v. Jefferson Parish School Board,* 1966). However, teachers must adhere to procedure as well. In dismissing a case, the court stated that a tenured teacher had to exhaust all administrative remedies before turning to the courts to seek damages for improper termination (*Cahill v. Board of Education of City of Stamford,* 1985).

Today the issue of damages is coming before the courts more frequently than in the past because of laws that allow payment of attorney fees. Teachers who are able to show that they were wrongfully discharged are almost always eligible for reinstatement and back pay plus compensation for all reasonable fringe benefits. A lengthy court case can become expensive for school districts when teachers can be eligible for recovery of all damages. Teachers and school boards need to recognize that the costs of taking cases to court are increasing and work to follow all due process so that neither teachers nor school districts are forced to expend scarce resources unnecessarily.

Summary

To fulfill the mission of today's public schools, school boards must recruit, employ, and retain qualified, committed teachers. To accomplish this goal, school boards must also be able to discharge teachers who are not fit for classroom duties or when the services of teachers are no longer needed. Because of tenure or continuing contract laws in most states, the discharge of teachers can no longer be accomplished on pretext. All teachers are protected from arbitrary and capricious discharge or discharge based on the teachers' exercise of constitutional rights. In addition, tenured teachers have attained property and interest rights that the Fourteenth Amendment guarantees cannot be violated without due process of law. The extent of due process is determined by the type of discharge being effected, state laws, school board policies, and collective bargaining agreements. A school board must observe all due process when discharging a nontenured teacher under contract or a tenured teacher at any time.

The most common types of discharge are nonrenewal of contract, suspension, dismissal, and reduction in force. The nonrenewal of a nontenured teacher's contract usually requires no due process, although some states and districts provide for timely notice and a statement of reasons to be given the teacher. A tenured teacher may be suspended or dismissed only for statutory reasons, which often include incompetence, insubordination, immorality, and just cause. Reduction in force is allowed when a school district is facing financial exigency, declining enrollments, or staff reorganization, and tenure and seniority status usually determine the order for layoff and recall.

Statutory grounds for teacher suspension and dismissal have been general enough to adapt to changing definitions over time. Incompetence is often used to justify suspension or dismissal, but there must be clear evidence to overcome the presumption of competence attached to teachers' certification credentials. Insubordination or neglect of duty continue to be common bases for dismissal because teachers are expected to obey the reasonable rules and directives of school boards and supervisors. Where a teacher once could be ruled immoral for any action from drinking a beer off campus after school hours to having a baby out of wedlock, the courts have had difficulty applying consistent rules for moral behavior as social morés change. Almost all grounds for dismissal may be challenged for vagueness, and a connection between the teacher's questioned behavior and classroom performance must often be shown before dismissal will be allowed by the courts. A teacher who is wrongfully discharged is almost always reinstated and may be eligible for damages.

The courts will continue to be asked to balance the rights of teachers to employment against the rights of school boards as employers. Tenure protects teachers from unreasonable discharge, but teachers who violate the standards of the profession and state laws cannot legally hide behind tenure. School boards and administrators must implement fair, consistent, regular evaluation processes to document that teachers are fulfilling the mission of public schools. They must be willing to take action to discharge those teachers who are not qualified to teach, but they must also ensure that all elements of due process are observed.

Questions and Responses

1. What is tenure?

Because teachers historically had no protection from arbitrary and capricious employment decisions of school boards, the concept of tenure started to be applied to public schools after the American Association of University Professors developed it to protect professors in higher education. Tenure is a status conferred on a public school teacher who has satisfactorily completed a probationary period of employment. Most states normally require a teacher to work two to five years and to receive positive position evaluations that satisfy state or district criteria. Other requirements may also exist. Tenured teachers have property and liberty interests in their employment interests, which entitle them to protection under the Fourteenth Amendment. A teacher who is tenured may not be discharged without due process of law. Because tenure usually cannot be transferred to other states or even to other districts within the same state, districts often gain the benefit of having a cohort of experienced, qualified teachers because they are less likely to leave once they are tenured. Tenure ended the absolute power of school boards over teacher employment, but the difficulty of terminating tenured teachers has initiated much criticism of the practice. However, tenure does not guarantee a teacher his or her position regardless of actions the teacher may take that may indicate unfitness for teaching. Tenure just means that a teacher's job may not be terminated without application of due process.

2. What are the common types of teacher discharge?

"Discharge" can take several forms, including nonrenewal of contract, suspension, dismissal, termination of contract, furlough, and reduction in force. "Nonrenewal of contract" generally applies to a nontenured teacher who is not rehired at the end of a school year. "Suspension" is a temporary severance of the employment relationship between a teacher and a school district, which may be a disciplinary action in itself, may be a prelude to other disciplinary actions, or may be another term for "furlough" or "reduction in force." "Dismissal" is the permanent severance of the employment relationship between a teacher and a school district when the teacher has not initiated ending the relationship by resigning or the relationship has not ended by mutual agreement. "Reduction in force" and "furlough" are usually used when a school district must release teachers because of financial exigency, declining enrollments in the district or specific program areas, loss of revenue, or reorganization of the staff. "Termination of contract" is often used for any permanent end of the employment relationship. Many of these terms are used interchangeably in statutes and case law, and application of the terms depends on the state and school district.

3. On what grounds may a teacher lose his or her job?

In most states, a teacher may be suspended or dismissed only for statutory reasons. Some common grounds are incompetency, insubordination, immorality, neglect of duty, unprofessional conduct, moral turpitude, and just cause. The last term, "just cause," is included in most statutes to allow the school board some discretion to discharge a teacher for behavior that may not fit under other reasons and yet is so shocking to the conscience or so evident of the teacher's lack of professional fitness for the position that he or she should be removed form the classroom. Reduction in force statutes usually define the exact reasons for releasing teachers from duty because their services are no longer needed. Financial limitations, declining enrollments, changes in curriculum or reorganization of staff are some of the reasons for RIF actions.

The role of the building principal as the supervisor of teachers becomes key in the dismissal of a teacher. A school district should have sound evaluation and documentation practices in place so that every teacher, tenured or nontenured, knows the types of evaluation processes to be employed and the records to be kept of his or her performance throughout the year. Failure to have adequate documentation of a teacher's actions that are leading to a claim that he or she should be dismissed for statutory reasons may result in the district's inability to dismiss the teacher.

4. Why can a nontenured teacher be denied employment for the next year without due process?

A nontenured teacher signs a contract for a specific period of time, usually one academic year. At the end of the year, the terms of the contract have been met by both parties to the contract, and neither party is obligated to the other. A nontenured teacher has gained no constitutionally protected property or liberty interests in employment and is not protected under the due process clause of the Fourteenth Amendment. Because no teacher, tenured or nontenured, may be denied the right to exercise constitutional freedoms, nonrenewal of a nontenured teacher's contract must not be based on the exercise of such protected rights as free speech or association. In most districts, nontenured teachers must receive notice of nonrenewal early enough that they have an opportunity to seek other employment for the next year. Sometimes they may also request a statement of the reasons for nonrenewal, but they are seldom eligible for a hearing on the reasons.

5. What is the difference between suspension and dismissal?

Suspension is a temporary severance of the employment relationship; dismissal is permanent. Suspension can be imposed before a formal hearing is held when a teacher's continued presence in the school is inappropriate, a hazard to others, or not in the teacher's best welfare. Teachers may be suspended while other disciplinary actions, including civil or criminal court cases, are pending. Suspension may be a disciplinary action by itself or may be a prelude to dismissal or other disciplinary actions. Suspension is sometimes used in reduction in force cases when the RIF action is not viewed as permanent. As an intermediate step to other disciplinary actions, suspension must be based on the same grounds as dismissal, and all appropriate due process must be observed. Suspension is in effect until the problem leading to the suspension is resolved or other action is taken. Dismissal is the last and most serious disciplinary action a school district may take.

6. What is a RIF action?

"RIF" stands for "reduction in force," which is the action taken by a school district that must release teachers from their employment because of financial exigency, declining enrollments, loss of funds, or reorganization of curriculum or staff. Statutes and collective bargaining agreements usually stipulate the procedures to be used in reducing the number of teachers in a district. Generally, nontenured teachers must be released first and then tenured teachers in order of seniority. However, special qualifications and credentials must be considered. A tenured teacher who is not qualified to teach a certain subject may not be retained even if he or she has more seniority than the teachers qualified to teach that subject. If the district's financial situation changes and teachers are recalled, they must usually be recalled in reverse order of layoff: tenured teachers with the most seniority are called back first, and no new teachers may be hired until all teachers affected by the RIF action are offered the positions first.

7. When may a teacher be discharged for incompetency?

Incompetency is difficult for a school board to use as grounds for discharge because a teacher's certificate and educational background create a presumption of qualification. To discharge a teacher, administrators must have concrete evidence of a teacher's lack of knowledge of subject matter, use of erroneous information, inability to maintain classroom discipline, inability to correct students' errors, and similar documentation of incompetency. A few days of unruliness in a classroom would not constitute incompetency, but a history of chaos in a class that makes learning impossible for the majority of the students could be used as evidence in court to demonstrate incompetency as a teacher.

8. When may a teacher be discharged for insubordination?

A teacher is expected to abide by statutes, board policies, contract provisions, and reasonable directives from supervisors. Refusal to obey the district policies and procedures, failure to adhere to state laws, and disregard for orders from administrators constitute insubordination. A teacher may not be discharged for disobeying rules that are illegal or that contradict policies. When a teacher is caught between written policies or rules and oral directives, the teacher should abide by the written rules.

9. When may a teacher be discharged for immoral conduct?

Immoral conduct involves much more than sexual misconduct. Although almost any behavior that contradicts community values or standards was once considered "immoral," the courts will usually seek a connection between the teacher's actions and his or her classroom performance before ruling that a discharge may be effected for immoral conduct. Social morés are changing, and community values will be considered by the courts. The exercise of constitutional rights may not be the basis for discharge, and a person's private behavior is usually constitutionally protected if it has no adverse effect on job performance. However, any type of inappropriate behavior involving students is usually upheld as a valid reason for discharge of a teacher.

10. When may a teacher be discharged for "good cause"?
"Good cause" or "just cause" are often included in statutes to allow school boards some flexibility in employment decisions. No statute could ever include all possible reasons for discharging a teacher, and "good cause" clauses allow school boards to discharge a teacher whose behavior makes him or her unfit as a teacher but which does not fit exactly under one of the other grounds for discharge. By itself, such a clause is vague, and many cases have arisen because of its use as a basis for discharge. The courts will uphold a discharge for "good cause" when a teacher's actions shock the conscience or obviously show unfitness for classroom performance.

Case References

Adkins v. Children's Hospital of the District of Columbia, 261 U.S. 525 (1923).
Alexander v. Manton Joint Union School District in Tehama and Shasta Counties, 255 P. 516 (Cal. App. 1927).
Alford v. Department of Education, 91 Cal. Rptr. 843 (Cal. App. 1970).
Allen v. Autauga County Board of Education, 685 F.2d 1302 (11th Cir., 1982).
Andrews v. Union Parish School Board, 184 So. 574 (La.App. 1938).
Appeal of Mulhollen, 39 A.2d 283 (Pa. Super. 1944).
Appeal of Schneider, 79 A.2d 865 (N.J. Super, 1951).
Avery v. Homewood City Board of Education, 674 F.2d 337 (5th Cir., 1982).
Barcheski v. Board of Education of Grand Rapids Public Schools, 412 N.W.2d 296 (Mich. App. 1987).
Beers v. Nyquist, 338 N.Y.S.2d 745 (1972).
Bethel Park School District v. Krall, 445 A.2d 1377 (Pa. Cmwlth. 1982).
Biggs v. School City of Mt. Vernon, 90 N.E. 105 (Ind. App. 1909).
Blaine v. Moffat County School District RE. No. 1, 709 P.2d 96 (Colo. App. 1985).
Blunt v. Marion County School Board, 515 F.2d 951 (5th Cir., 1975).
Board of Directors of Sioux City Community School District v. Mroz, 295 N.W.2d 447 (Iowa 1980).
Board of Education of Argo-Summit School District No. 104, Cook County v. Hunt, 487 N.E.2d 24 (Ill. App. 1 Dist. 1985).
Board of Education of Berwyn School District No. 100, Cook County v. Metskas, 436 N.E.2d 587 (Ill. App. 1982).
Board of Education of Hopkins County v. Wood, 717 S.W.2d 837 (Ky. 1986).
Board of Education of Long Beach Unified School District of Los Angeles County v. Jack M., 566 P.2d 602 (Cal. 1977).
Board of Education of Taos Municipal Schools v. Singleton, 712 P.2d 1384 (N.M. App. 1985).
Board of Regents of State Colleges v. Roth, 408 U.S. 564 (1972).
Bovino v. Board of School Directors of Indiana Area School District, 377 A.2d 1284 (Pa. Cmwlth. 1977).

Brubaker v. Board of Education, School District 149, Cook County, Illinois, 502 F.2d 973 (7th Cir., 1974).
Burk v. Unified School District No. 329, Wabaunsee County, Kansas, 646 F.Supp. 1557 (D. Kan. 1986).
Burton v. Cascade School District Union High School No. 5, 353 F.Supp. 254 (D. Ore. 1973).
Bye v. Special Intermediate School District No. 916, 379 N.W.2d 653 (Minn. App. 1986).
Cahill v. Board of Education of City of Stamford, 502 A.2d 410 (Conn. 1985).
Carangelo v. Ambach, 515 N.Y.S.2d 665 (N.Y.A.D. 3 Dept. 1987).
Carlan v. Board of Education of Lawrence Union Free School District, 513 N.Y.S.2d 202 (N.Y.A.D. 2 Dept. 1987).
Casada v. Booneville School District No. 65, 686 F.Supp. 730 (W.D.Ark. 1988).
Chicago Board of Education v. Payne, 430 N.E.2d 310 (Ill. App. 1981).
Clarke v. Shoreline School District No. 412, King County, 720 P.2d 793 (Wash. 1986).
Coats v. Board of Education, Unified School District No. 353, Sumner County, 662 P.2d 1279 (Kan. 1983).
Conley v. Board of Education of City of New Britain, 123 A.2d 747 (Conn. 1956).
Cook v. Board of Education for County of Logan, 671 F.Supp. 1110 (S.D.W.Va. 1987).
Cooley v. Board of Education of Forrest City School District, 453 F.2d 282 (8th Cir., 1972).
Coriou v. Nyquist, 304 N.Y.S.2d 486 (N.Y. App. Div. 1969).
County Board of Education of Clarke County v. Oliver, 116 So.2d 566 (Ala. 1959).
Denton v. South Kitsap School District No. 402, 516 P.2d 1080 (Wash. App. 1973).
DeVito v. Board of Education, 317 S.E.2d 159 (W. Va. 1984).
Downs v. Board of Education of Hoboken District, 171 A. 528 (N.J. 1934).
Doyal v. School Board of Liberty County, 415 So.2d 791 (Fla. App. 1982).
Dupree v. School Committee of Boston, 446 N.E.2d 1099 (Mass. App. 1983).
Ehret v. School District of Borough of Kulpmont, 5 A.2d 188 (Pa. 1939).
Ellis v. Ambach, 508 N.Y.S.2d 624 (N.Y.A.D. 3 Dept. 1986).
Elrod v. Harrisonville Cass R-IX School District, 706 S.W.2d 465 (Mo. App. 1986).
Fadler v. Illinois State Board of Education, 506 N.E.2d 640 (Ill. App. 5 Dist. 1987).
Fernald v. City of Ellsworth Superintending School Committee, 342 A.2d 704 (Me. 1975).
Ferris v. Special School District No. 1, 367 F.Supp. 459 (D. Minn. 1973).
Firefighters Local Union No. 1784 v. Stotts, 467 U.S. 561 (1984).
Fiscus v. Board of School Trustees of Central School District of Greene County, 509 N.E.2d 1137 (Ind. App. 1 Dist. 1987).
Fisher v. Snyder, 476 F.2d 375 (8th Cir., 1973).
Florian v. Highland Local School District Board of Education, 493 N.E.2d 249 (Ohio App. 1983).
Foster v. Carson School District No. 301, Skamania County, 385 P.2d 367 (Wash. 1963).
Franklin v. Alabama State Tenure Commission, 482 So.2d 1214 (Ala. Civ. App. 1985).
Gaylord v. Tacoma School District No. 10, 559 P.2d 1340, (Wash. 1977), cert. denied, 434 U.S. 879 (1977).
Gilliland v. Board of Education of Pleasant View Consolidated School District No. 622 of Tazewell County, 365 N.E.2d 322 (Ill. 1977).
Glendale School District v. Feigh, 513 A.2d 1093 (Pa. Cmwlth. 1986).
Goldberg v. Kelly, 397 U.S. 254 (1970).
Goldsmith v. Board of Education of Sacramento City High School District, 225 P. 783 (Cal. App. 1924).
Greater Clark County School Corporation v. Myers, 493 N.E.2d 1267 (Ind. App. 4 Dist. 1986).
Greminger v. Seaborne, 584 F.2d 275 (8th Cir., 1978).
Grissom v. Board of Education of Buckley-Loda Community School District No. 8, 388 N.E.2d 398 (Ill. 1979).

Guthrie v. Board of Education of Jefferson County, 298 S.W.2d 691 (Ky.App. 1957).
Hale v. Board of Education, City of Lancaster, 234 N.E.2d 583 (Ohio 1968).
Hanlon v. Board of Education of Parkway School District, 695 S.W.2d 930 (Mo. App. 1985).
Harrah Independent School District v. Martin, 440 U.S. 194 (1979).
Harvey v. Jefferson County School District No. R-1, 710 P.2d 1103 (Colo. 1985).
Hawkins v. Linn County School District No. 14, 517 P.2d 330 (Or. App. 1973).
Horosko v. Mt. Pleasant Township School District, 6 A.2d 866 (Pa. 1939).
Hovland v. School District No. 52, 278 P.2d 211 (Mont. 1954).
Hyde v. Wellpinit School District No. 49, 648 P.2d 892 (Wash. App. 1982).
In re Grossman, 316 A.2d 39 (N.J. Super. 1974).
In re Swink, 200 A. 200 (Pa. Super. 1938).
Jones v. Holes, 6 A.2d 102 (Pa. 1939).
Jordahl v. Independent School District No. 129, 225 N.W.2d 224 (Minn. 1974).
Karbach v. Board of Education of Lawndale School District, 114 Cal. Rptr. 84 (Cal. App. 1974).
Keefe v. Geanakos, 418 F.2d 359 (1st Cir., 1969).
Kersey v. Maine Consolidated School District No. 10, 394 P.2d 201 (Ariz. 1964).
Kinsella v. Board of Education of Central School District No. 7 of Towns of Amherst and Tonawanda, Erie County, 407 N.Y.S.2d 78 (1978).
Lewis v. Harrison School District No. 1, 805 F.2d 310 (8th Cir., 1986).
Lockhart v. Board of Education of Arapahoe County School District No. 6, 735 P.2d 913 (Colo. App. 1986).
Lucia v. Duggan, 303 F.Supp. 112 (D. Mass. 1969).
Mailloux v. Kiley, 323 F.Supp. 1387 (D. Mass.); aff'd., 448 F.2d 1242 (1st Cir., 1971).
Mass v. Board of Education of San Francisco Unified School District, 394 P.2d 579 (Cal. 1964).
Matter of Shelton, 408 N.W.2d 594 (Minn. App. 1987).
McBeth v. Board of Education of DeVall's Bluff School District No. 1, Arkansas, 300 F.Supp. 1270 (E.D. Ark. 1969).
McBroom v. Board of Education, District No. 205, 494 N.E.2d 1191 (Ill. App. 2 Dist. 1986).
Memphis Community School District v. Stachura, 477 U.S. 299 (1986).
Merchant v. Board of Trustees of Pearl Municipal Separate School District, 492 So.2d 959 (Miss. 1986).
Meyer v. Nebraska, 262 U.S. 390 (1923).
Millar v. Joint School District No. 2, Village of Wild Rose, 86 N.W.2d 455 (Wis. 1957).
Miller v. Grand Haven Board of Education, 390 N.W.2d 255 (Mich. App. 1986).
Miller v. South Bend Special School District No. 1, McHenry County, 124 N.W.2d 475 (N.D. 1963).
Mott v. Endicott School District No. 308, 713 P.2d 98 (Wash. 1986).
Mt. Healthy City School District Board of Education v. Doyle, 429 U.S. 274 (1977).
Myers v. Greater Clark County School Corporation, 464 N.E.2d 1323 (Ind. App. 1984).
Negrich v. Dade County Board of Public Instruction, 143 So.2d 498 (Fla. App. 1962).
New Mexico State Board of Education v. Stoudt, 571 P.2d 1186 (N.M. 1977).
Northeast Community Education Association v. Northeast Community School District, 402 N.W.2d 765 (Iowa 1987).
Osborne v. Bullitt County Board of Education, 415 S.W.2d 607 (Ky. 1967).
O'Toole v. Forestal, 511 A.2d 1236 (N.J. Super. A.D. 1986).
Perry v. Sindermann, 408 U.S. 593 (1972).
Pettit v. State Board of Education, 513 P.2d 889 (Cal. 1973).
Pickering v. Board of Education, 391 U.S. 563 (1968).
Pocahontas Community School District v. Levene, 409 N.W.2d 698 (Iowa App. 1987).
Portage Area School District v. Portage Area Education Association, 368 A.2d 864 (Pa. Cmwlth. 1977).

Powell v. Board of Trustees of Crook County School District No. 1, 550 P.2d 1112 (Wyo. 1976).
Rankin v. Independent School District No. I-3, Noble County, Oklahoma, 876 F.2d 838 (10th Cir., 1989).
Ray v. Minneapolis Board of Education, Special School District No. 1, 202 N.W.2d 375 (Minn. 1972).
Retzlaff v. Grand Forks Public School District No. 1, 424 N.W.2d 637 (N.D. 1988).
Rinaldo v. Dreyer, 1 N.E.2d 37 (Mass. 1936).
Robinson v. Jefferson County Board of Education, 485 F.2d 1381 (5th Cir., 1973).
Ryan v. Aurora City Board of Education, 540 F.2d 222 (6th Cir., 1976).
Sams v. Board of Commissioners of Creek County, 178 P. 668 (Okl. 1919).
School District No. 8, Pinal County v. Superior Court of Pinal County, 433 P.2d 28 (Ariz. 1967).
Scott v. Board of Education of Alton, Community Unit School District #11, 156 N.E.2d 1 (Ill. App. 1959).
Sells v. Unified School District No. 429, Doniphan County, 644 P.2d 379 (Kan. 1982).
Sherburne v. School Board of Suwannee County, 455 So.2d 1057 (Fla. App. 1984).
Shirck v. Thomas, 486 F.2d 691 (7th Cir., 1973).
Shirer v. Anderson, 88 F.Supp. 858 (E.D.S.C. 1950).
Shockley v. Board of Education, Laurel Special School District, 149 A.2d 331 (Del. 1959).
Silver, Burdett and Company v. Indiana State Board of Education, 72 N.E. 829 (Ind. App. 1904).
Simard v. Board of Education of Town of Groton, 473 F.2d 988 (2d Cir., 1973).
Singleton v. Iberville Parish School Board, 136 So.2d 809 (La. App. 1961).
Smith v. Board of Education of Fort Madison Community School District, 293 N.W.2d 221 (Iowa 1980).
Sparks v. Board of Education of Ashland Independent School District, 549 S.W.2d 323 (Ky. App. 1977).
Stamper v. Board of Education of Elementary School District No. 143, 491 N.E.2d 36 (Ill. App. 1 Dist. 1986).
State v. Lillard, 521 A.2d 1110 (Del. Super. 1986).
State ex rel. Board of Education of County of Kanawha v. Casey, 349 S.E.2d 436 (W. Va. 1986).
State ex rel. Charbonnet v. Jefferson Parish School Board, 188 So.2d 143 (La. App. 1966).
State ex rel. Frank v. Meigs County Board of Education, 44 N.E.2d 455 (Ohio 1942).
State ex rel. Richardson v. Board of Regents of University of Nevada, 261 P.2d 515 (Nev. 1953).
State ex rel. Williams v. Avoyelles Parish School Board, 147 So.2d 729 (La. App. 1962).
Stiver v. State ex rel. Kent, 1 N.E.2d 1006 (Ind. 1936).
Sto-Rox School District v. Horgan, 449 A.2d 796 (Pa. Cmwlth. 1982).
Stoddard v. School District No. 1, Lincoln County, Wyoming, 590 F.2d 829 (10th Cir., 1979).
Swab v. Cedar Rapids Community School District, 494 F.2d 353 (8th Cir., 1974).
Swayne v. Board of Education of Rock Island School District No. 41, 494 N.E.2d 906 (Ill. App. 3 Dist. 1986).
Szabo v. Board of Education of Community Consolidated School District 54, 454 N.E.2d 39 (Ill. App. 1983).
Terry v. Houston County Board of Education, 342 S.E.2d 774 (Ga. App. 1986).
Thompkins v. Stuttgart School District No. 22, 858 F.2d 1317 (8th Cir., 1988).
Tichenor v. Orleans Parish School Board, 144 So.2d 603 (La. App. 1962).
Tressler v. Upper Dublin School District, 373 A.2d 755 (Pa. Cmwlth. 1977).
Vail v. Board of Education of Paris Union School District No. 95, 706 F.2d 1435 (7th Cir., 1983); aff'd., 466 U.S. 377 (1984).
Valley National Bank of Phoenix v. Glover, 159 P.2d 292 (Ariz. 1945).
Viemeister v. Board of Education of Borough of Prospect Park, Passaic County, 68 A.2d 768 (N.J. Super. 1949).

Walter v. Board of Education of Quincy School District No. 172, 442 N.E.2d 870 (Ill. 1982).
Warwick Board of School Directors v. Theros, 430 A.2d 268 (Pa. 1981).
Watson v. Burnett, 23 N.E.2d 420 (Ind. 1939).
Weaver v. Board of Education of Pine Plains Central School District, 514 N.Y.S.2d 473 (N.Y.A.D. 2 Dept. 1987).
Weissman v. Board of Education of Jefferson County School District No. R-1, 547 P.2d 1267 (Colo. 1976).
Wertz v. Southern Cloud Unified School District No. 334, 542 P.2d 339 (Kan. 1975).
Western Grove School District v. Strain, 707 S.W.2d 306 (Ark. 1986).
Whitsel v. Southeast Local School District, 484 F.2d 1222 (6th Cir., 1973).
Wieder v. Board of Education of Borough of High Bridge, 170 A.631 (N.J. 1934).
Williams v. Albemarle City Board of Education, 508 F.2d 1242 (4th Cir., 1974).
Williams v. School District No. 40 of Gila County, 417 P.2d 376 (Ariz. App. 1966).
Wyatt v. School District No. 104, Fergus County, 417 P.2d 221 (Mont. 1966).
Young v. Board of Education of Central School District No. 6, Town of Huntington, 315 N.E.2d 768 (N.Y. App. 1974).
Yuen v. Board of Education of School District No. U-46, 222 N.E.2d 570 (Ill. App. 1966).

6 Leaves of Absence

Leaves of absence for teachers were informally awarded in the early history of public schools. Schoolmasters themselves decided when school would and would not be held, usually trying to accommodate the needs and wishes of parents and the community. As schools were organized into districts and operated as businesses, teachers' leaves of absence became part of negotiations for compensation and contract specifications.

For teachers a leave of absence is time spent temporarily away from regular professional duties and responsibilities. The circumstances and type of absence determine whether a leave is approved, nonapproved, mandatory, discretionary, voluntary, involuntary, paid, or unpaid. Reasons for leave have expanded in recent years, but they generally can be classified as professional or personal. Professional leave may be granted for sabbaticals, conference attendance, professional development, or exchange teaching, while personal leave may be allowed for illness, disability, military service, religious observances, jury duty, childbirth, bereavement, or service in public office. School districts may at times place a teacher on a leave of absence for the welfare of the teacher or the school. Financial exigency has sometimes forced districts to place teachers on temporary leave.

Policies governing leaves of absence are generally established by local school boards as part of teacher employment guidelines. Local policies must adhere to state statutes and state board mandates as well as collective bargaining agreements because leaves of absence have become major negotiating items for teachers and school boards. Teachers are pressing for greater flexibility to develop leave policies in line with those of business and government, while school boards view leaves of absence in terms of financial expenditure and possible decrease in efficiency and quality of education. Generally, a teacher who takes a leave of absence after following all policies and procedures established by the board, the master contract, and the teacher's individual contract cannot lose tenure or seniority in the district.

Teachers' leaves of absence have become subjects for litigation when boards have violated statutes, collective bargaining clauses, their own policies, or individual teacher's rights and when teachers have abused leave of absence privileges. Although teachers view leaves of absence as important fringe benefits, school boards and parents are questioning the ability of substitute teachers to provide a continuing quality of education, and leaves of absence are increasingly becoming grounds for contract disputes. The courts likely will continue to be called upon to rule in cases involving temporary leave for teachers.

Legal Principles

Principle I *Board Regulation*

Although they must adhere to constitutional or statutory requirements, local boards of education retain responsibility for the establishment of policies granting and regulating leaves of absence for teachers. Local boards may create almost any type of reasonable leave and establish rules and procedures for its governance.

Principle II *No Gifts*

No public funds or property may be distributed in the form of a gift. Consequently, continued payment of salary, full or part, to a teacher during a period of temporary absence is unlawful unless such absence is designed to promote efficiency and competence from which the school district will benefit.

Principle III *Maternity Leave*

Maternity leave regulations may not needlessly, arbitrarily, or capriciously impinge upon a person's decision to bear or to beget a child. Policies governing leaves of absence may not discriminate against a pregnant teacher.

Principle IV *Nondiscriminatory Leave*

Leaves of absence must be administered on a nondiscriminatory basis.

Principle V *Public Service*

Where required by law, a leave of absence must be granted a teacher because of public service demands of the federal, state, and local governments. Continuation or reinstatement of salary and benefits will depend on the type of public service leave granted.

Principle VI *Involuntary Leave*

A local board may require a teacher to take a leave of absence when a defensible reason exists for a temporary severance of the teacher's connection with the school. Financial exigency may require putting a teacher on a leave of absence.

Discussion

Principle I

Although they must adhere to constitutional or statutory requirements, local boards of education retain responsibility for the establishment of policies granting and regulating leaves of absence for teachers. Local boards may create almost any type of reasonable leave and establish rules and procedures for its governance.

The courts have declared consistently that the authority of a school board to have charge of public schools and control the employment of teachers includes the power to decide within reasonable limits the rules governing temporary absences (*Malcolm v. City of Boston,* 1899; *Wood v. City of Haverhill,* 1899; *Averell v. City of Newburyport,* 1922; *School City of East Chicago v. Sigler,* 1941; *Giordano v. Ambach,* 1986). After World War II, teachers began working with school boards through contract negotiations to determine better leave of absence policies, bringing education employment practices more in line with those of business and government. Once boards of education recognized professional and personal leaves as attractive employment benefits for teachers, most boards established policies governing such leaves, removing much of the arbitrariness from the granting of leaves. Local policies and procedures must adhere to controlling statutes, state board of education policies, and collective bargaining agreements and must not infringe on the constitutional rights of teachers. When teachers challenge board leave policies or when boards overstep their authority in regulating leaves for teachers, the courts may become involved in settling the dispute.

Early court cases established that school board guidelines governing leaves of absence must be reasonable. For example, in 1950 a teacher applied for a one-semester sabbatical, which was refused because the teacher had hand delivered the application instead of sending it through registered mail as the guidelines stipulated. The teacher's right to a sabbatical was upheld (*State ex rel. Scoggins v. Vernon Parish School Board,* 1950).

Teachers also had to learn that reasonable procedures for requesting leave are to be strictly followed. In early 1967 a teacher asked for and was granted a leave of absence for the rest of the school year because of illness. Although she had had only one conversation with a school administrator after she took leave, she requested in August to be returned to her teaching position and filed suit when her request was refused. Because the school district policy gave no guarantee of reinstatement and because she had not followed the procedures for requesting reinstatement, the Arkansas Supreme Court ruled she had no right to her former position (*Special School District of Fort Smith v. Lynch,* 1967).

In the 1970s policies for leaves of absence became more defined by school districts and the courts. State appellate courts ruled that teacher leave time was a negotiable item (*Kenai Peninsula Borough School District v. Kenai Peninsula Education Association,* 1977), that school districts may not ignore their own policies regarding payment for approved leave (*Bettendorf Education Association v. Bettendorf Community School District,* 1978), and that voluntary extended maternity leave may not be counted toward active service in computing eligibility for sabbatical leaves (*Newell v. Orleans Parish School Board,* 1979). As paid personal leave became available to teachers, some abuses occurred, and teachers who violated district leave of absence policies did not prevail in court. The courts ruled that state statutes governing teacher leave did not allow a teacher to use paid personal leave to participate in an illegal teachers' strike (*Board of Education of Marshallton-McKean School District v. Sinclair,* 1977) nor another teacher to serve as a chaperon for her child's field trip to a hamburger establishment (*Green v. Fairfield City Board of Education,* 1978).

Many challenges to the authority of school boards to establish rules for leaves of absence arose in the 1980s. Two California cases involved defining the state statute governing differential compensation for sick leave. The teachers claimed that the statute meant that as soon as their sick leave was exhausted they were entitled to the difference between the cost of hiring a substitute and the teacher's normal salary. Their boards of education, however, interpreted the statute to mean that differential pay could be paid only for continuous illness or injury that extended beyond the time a teacher's sick leave was exhausted. In both cases, the California appellate courts ruled in favor of the teachers because the boards were extending application of the statute beyond its legal meaning (*Jefferson Classroom Teachers Association v. Jefferson Elementary School District,* 1982; *California Teachers' Association v. Parlier Unified School District,* 1984).

Differing interpretations of policies for sick and personal leave have resulted in other state court cases. An Oklahoma teacher was absent four days with administrative approval for personal business. She filed suit when two days' salary for a substitute teacher was deducted from her paycheck even though no substitute had been hired. The court affirmed that the deductions were in line with the negotiated agreement that allowed only two days of paid personal leave for teachers (*Earnest v. School Board of Independent District No. 16 of Stillwater, Oklahoma,* 1983). The Iowa Supreme Court ruled that a school district could deduct a full day's absence from a teacher's accrued sick leave even though the district was being reimbursed 60 percent from workmen's compensation for each day missed by the teacher. The teacher thought he should lose only 40 percent of a day for each day missed (*Drinnen v. Heartland Area Education Agency 11,* 1983).

On the other hand, disciplinary action against teachers who take leaves of absence that do not violate board policy will not be upheld. In 1982 a teacher was discharged because she had been absent 21 percent of the school days during the preceding four years. The court did not uphold her dismissal because all absences had been covered by sick leave, personal leave, or leave without pay (*San Dieguito Union High School District v. Commission on Professional Competence,* 1982). In another case, an Illinois physical education teacher, who was also the soccer coach at the local community college, was dismissed when the board was informed that the 12 personal or sick leave days he had taken over the past two years conformed to the schedule of soccer matches played away from the local campus. The court overturned the teacher's dismissal because his conduct was ruled remediable, he had never received formal notice of violation of policy, and the students, school, and faculty had not been harmed by his actions (*Szabo v. Board of Education of Community Consolidated School District 54,* 1983).

The courts not only have heard cases involving personal leaves of absence but also have ruled on questions of professional leave. The most common professional leave of absence is the sabbatical where teachers work a specified number of years and then may be eligible for a semester or a year of leave, usually for professional development and often at full or partial salary and continuation of benefits. Local boards of education generally establish guidelines for sabbatical and professional leaves, assess the eligibility of teachers who request such leave, and determine the policies for reassigning teachers returning from professional leave. Both teachers and boards have been accused of violating professional leave policies and have taken their cases to court. For example, in 1982 a Pennsylvania teacher applied for a sabbatical leave six and one-half years after his last yearlong sabbatical. His request was denied because the state statute said seven full years of service, not to include the year of sabbatical, had to be given after a sabbatical before a teacher could be eligible for another. His claim was not supported by the court (*Pennsbury School District v. Walker,* 1982).

Generally, a district must reassign a teacher to a comparable position when the teacher returns from a sabbatical leave. However, an administrative aide who took a yearlong sabbatical was reassigned to teach seventh grade geography when he returned. He filed suit, claiming entitlement to the position of administrative aide. His reassignment was upheld because the school code specifically stated that teachers, principals, and superintendents had to be returned to positions equivalent to former positions, but other administrative positions, such as the aide position, were not addressed (*Thrash v. Board of Education, School District No. 189,* 1982).

Several Pennsylvania cases have involved questions of sabbatical leave for teachers during times when districts were experiencing financial problems. In 1984 several teachers were granted sabbatical leaves for the following year but later were notified of their suspensions because of a drop in student enrollment. The court ruled the teachers were entitled to sabbatical leaves and could become eligible for suspension only after the year of leave:

> An inducement to enter and remain in the teaching field is the prospect of a sabbatical leave. [The teachers] have fulfilled their contractual and teaching obligations, and have met the statutory requirements for a sabbatical leave as well; therefore, they cannot be denied a benefit for which they have qualified (*Bristol Township School District v. Karafin,* 1984).

Citing *Bristol,* the same Pennsylvania court upheld a teacher's right to a sabbatical when she was furloughed for the year she was eligible for a leave of absence. She was then recalled to a half-time position. The court stated that she was to be granted a sabbatical for the following year at one-half salary for her full-time position, not the one-half of her half-time salary, which had been offered by the district (*Nelson v. Western Beaver County School District,* 1985). In 1986 three teachers in another district were eligible for sabbatical leaves the same year they were furloughed. The court ruled they were wrongfully denied their one-half salaries that were part of their leaves (*School District of City of Duquesne v. Duquesne Education Association PSEA/NEA,* 1986). The Pennsylvania appellate court ruled that a teacher's two years as a permanent substitute were allowed to be counted with her years as a regular teacher in determining her eligibility for sabbatical leave. The court observed that during those two years, the teacher had worked the full school year and had been paid in the same manner as regular teachers were paid (*Scranton School District v. Weiss,* 1988).

In summary, teacher abuse of personal and sick leave may encourage boards to decrease such privileges for teachers, while the arbitrary granting of personal and professional leave may force teachers to write leave policies into negotiated contracts to guarantee reasonable, equitable leave policies. Teachers, administrators, and school boards should know and observe their local policies governing personal and professional leaves of absence.

Principle II

No public funds or property may be distributed in the form of a gift. Consequently, continued payment of salary, full or part, to a teacher during a period of temporary absence is unlawful unless such absence is designed to promote efficiency and competence from which the school district will benefit.

Laws generally forbid public funds or property to be given in the form of gifts. Therefore, payment of salary is usually not allowed during a teacher's temporary leave of absence unless the school district can be shown to be a beneficiary of the leave. The question most often arises in connection with sick leaves and sabbatical leaves because such leaves of absence generally allow for full or partial salary and continuation of benefits during the leave. The courts have been asked to rule in cases where teachers claim the right to salary during leave and school boards either forbid payment or request return of salary at the conclusion of a leave.

One of the first cases to consider this issue was *Whittaker v. City of Salem* (1914). A school principal who worked unusually hard during the school year and who donated his vacation time to working for the district was given a contract for the following school year but was then allowed a leave of absence with pay because of his work the previous year. Although his health was impaired because of his work, the court ruled that leave with pay was a gift of public moneys beyond the power of a school board to grant.

The courts have consistently upheld paid sick leave for teachers because an obvious benefit accrues to the school from having healthy teachers in the classroom. Limited numbers of personal leave days—usually no more than one or two per year—are generally recognized as another valid benefit for both teachers and school districts. Paid sabbatical leaves for teachers who bring advanced education, professional development, increased experience and knowledge, or renewed vigor back to the schools are a worthwhile investment for school districts. However, teachers who fail to return to the district for a reasonable (and usually policy-mandated) length of time after a sabbatical leave may be found guilty of illegal receipt of public moneys and may be forced to return any compensation, salary and benefits, received during the leave.

Numerous cases have challenged the right of school boards to require a teacher to return to the district or to repay compensation received while on sabbatical leave. In 1982 an industrial arts teacher was granted a year's sabbatical but then resigned to take an administrative position in another school system before the next school year began. The court upheld the school district's action to recover the gross salary, retirement, social security, and health insurance paid the teacher while on leave (*Trumansburg Central School District v. Chalone,* 1982).

Rules governing sabbaticals are also subject to statute and collective bargaining agreements. In 1984 a school district sued a teacher for the return of her sabbatical salary and all benefits paid her when she refused a teaching position after her leave was over. The court ruled she was contractually required to return the salary, but because the collective bargaining agreement governing sabbaticals did not mention the return of fringe benefits, she could not be forced to return those indirect payments (*Bellevue School District No. 405 v. Bentley,* 1984).

This "beneficiary test" has been applied only to paid leaves of absence that could be interpreted as involving gifts of public moneys. The rules governing unpaid leaves are generally at the discretion of the school board within the bounds of state statutes and contracts. Long-term leave is occasionally granted for health-related disabilities, but generally the disabled teacher receives no salary during that time. Although some types of short-term personal leave are obviously beneficial to the schools, professional leave, which may be for a longer period of time and have a greater impact on the school operation, must demonstrate a benefit to the school before it is granted. Teachers and school boards must carefully consider what benefits a sabbatical leave will accrue to the district before requesting or granting such leaves. To avoid claims of unlawful distribution of public moneys as gifts, the rules for return of compensation and benefits to the district must be closely followed by those taking sabbatical or other professional development leaves of absence.

Principle III

Maternity leave regulations may not needlessly, arbitrarily, or capriciously impinge upon a person's decision to bear or to beget a child. Policies governing leaves of absence may not discriminate against a pregnant teacher.

No other leave of absence issue has involved more teachers and led to more litigation than has maternity leave. In early schools, female teachers were required to sign contracts to the effect that they would not become pregnant during a school year. Bearing a child usually meant the end of a teaching career for women, who were then expected to be full-time mothers. As social customs relaxed, women were allowed to continue to teach after becoming mothers, but they were expected to go on lengthy, unpaid leaves of absence as soon as pregnancy was confirmed and not to return to teaching for a year or more after childbirth. The health and welfare of both mother and child were supposedly safeguarded by mandatory unpaid maternity leaves, while students and the school were protected from the alleged embarrassment caused by the teacher's condition. Modern medical science and the acceptance of pregnancy and childbirth as natural phenomena that affect individual women differently gradually led to less stringent maternity leave policies. Yet, until the 1970s most school maternity policies mandated cutoff dates by which pregnant teachers were to begin maternity leave and allowed women to return to teaching only after a specified number of months following childbirth, regardless of an individual teacher's health and desire to resume teaching or her physician's advice. Maternity leave was unpaid, and accumulated sick leave and insurance benefits could not be applied to pregnancy or childbirth. When women began claiming violation of equal protection rights, court cases proliferated.

The United States Supreme Court has declared that the right to bear children is protected by the Constitution under due process, equal protection, and liberty rights of the Fourteenth Amendment (*Skinner v. Oklahoma ex rel. Williamson, Attorney General,* 1942; *Griswold v. Connecticut,* 1965). However, school boards and society in general did not recognize that inflexible maternity policies, including mandated cutoff and return dates as well as extended unpaid leaves of absence, greatly restricted a teacher's freedom to bear children. One of the first cases to challenge such a policy was *State ex rel. Sepulvado v. Rapides Parish School Board* (1959), in which the teacher said the maternity policy was arbitrary, unreasonable, and illegal. The board had established that no teacher could teach after the third month of pregnancy, nor could she return for 15 months after childbirth and then only at the beginning of a session after filing a certificate from a doctor stating that she was physically fit to return. The Louisiana Supreme Court upheld the policy:

> No one will quarrel with the fact that a maternity leave is mandatory on the school board, but although the law was intended to benefit expectant mothers in the teaching profession, the needs of the school system cannot be overlooked. The schools have the duty of securing enough teachers for each term and must arrange the teachers' maternity leaves in such a way as not to disrupt the operation of the schools. . . . In adopting the resolutions involved here we think the school board properly considered the welfare not only of the teacher but of the school children and the school system, and we see nothing unreasonable or arbitrary in the time fixed for such leaves of absence both before and after childbirth *(State ex rel. Sepulvado v. Rapides Parish School Board,* 1959).

In 1964 the Civil Rights Act was passed, and shortly thereafter teachers began using Title VII of that act and the equal protection clause of the Fourteenth Amendment to challenge maternity policies that allegedly were discriminatory against women. The courts began supporting these claims in the early 1970s, although they ruled that Title VII cannot be applied retroactively (*Schwabenbauer v. Board of Education of City School District of City of Olean,* 1985). In 1971 a probationary teacher, who was terminated when she informed the superintendent she was pregnant, sued the school district. The board claimed that if nontenured teachers were allowed maternity leave, they could gain tenure without sufficient evaluation. A Georgia federal court pointed out that the board could extend the probationary period if so desired and that other types of leave presented the same problems for evaluation. The maternity policy was ruled in violation of the equal protection clause (*Jinks v. Mays,* 1971).

In 1972 the United States Court of Appeals, Sixth Circuit, ruled that a pregnant teacher could take legal action when she was forced to take a full year's leave of absence even though her baby was born just nine days after the start of school (*Garner v. Stephens,* 1972). In *Green v. Waterford Board of Education* (1973), the Second Circuit Court handed down a ruling that would be quoted by the United States Supreme Court the next year. Instead of going on mandatory maternity leave after five months of pregnancy, the teacher in *Green* asked to remain on the job as long as her doctor deemed the health of her unborn child and her own health were not being endangered. The school board claimed the leave policy was to protect the health of the teacher and her child, but the court stated that the policy was discriminatory:

> The heart of [the teacher's] case is that disqualifying a physically capable woman from working because of a condition related solely to her sex is unconstitutionally discriminatory. [The teacher] admits the obvious, that men do not become pregnant, but points out that men, being human, are also subject to crises of the body, some of which, like childbirth, give ample warning. A cataract operation or a prostatectomy, for example, may be planned months ahead.

> Because male teachers are not forced by [the board] to take premature leave because of a known forthcoming medical problem, female teachers should not be treated differently. Thus stated, the argument is persuasive, even compelling. One realizes with a shock what so many women now proclaim: Old accepted rules and customs often discriminate against women in ways that have long been taken for granted or have gone unnoticed.
>
> Why the Board should choose, by means of an inflexible rule, to manifest particular concern with the health of a pregnant woman, but not, for example, with the health of a teacher (male or female) recuperating from a heart attack is nowhere explained (*Green v. Waterford Board of Education,* 1973).

The school board also advanced the argument that the teacher and the school system should be protected from giggling children making remarks about the teacher's pregnant condition. The court discounted this argument:

> We regard any such interest as almost too trivial to mention; it seems particularly ludicrous where, as here, [the teacher] taught only high school students. Whatever may have been the reaction in Queen Victoria's time, pregnancy is no longer a dirty word (*Green v. Waterford Board of Education,* 1973).

The court declared that the only substantial justification for mandatory maternity leave policies was for continuity of classroom education and administrative efficiency and convenience. However, where, as in this case, the teacher provided the board with a definite date for commencement of leave, those problems no longer existed. Thus, the court concluded the maternity leave policy was discriminatory and furthered no legitimate state interests. The teacher was awarded damages (*Green v. Waterford Board of Education,* 1973).

Also in 1973 an untenured teacher claimed violation of her civil rights and the Fourteenth Amendment because of a district policy mandating termination of a teacher's employment at the end of six months of pregnancy. The United States Court of Appeals, Tenth Circuit, relying on the opinions of the Sixth and Fourth Circuits, said that the state must demonstrate a compelling state interest to justify its maternity leave policy because the teacher's interest was a fundamental one: (1) it concerned the acknowledged right of the teacher to bear children and (2) it demanded that a schoolteacher select either employment or pregnancy. The court overturned the board policy because "the regulation penalizes the feminine school teacher for being a woman and, therefore, it must be condemned on that ground" (*Buckley v. Coyle Public School System,* 1973).

The United States Supreme Court ended much of the controversy surrounding mandatory maternity leave when it ruled in *Cleveland Board of Education v. LaFleur* and *Cohen v. Chesterfield County School Board* in 1974. The teachers in these cases desired to teach beyond their school board policy cutoff dates of the fourth and the fifth months of pregnancy, respectively, and also desired to return to teaching after childbirth sooner than board policy allowed. The Supreme Court first stated that marriage and family life are protected liberties under the Fourteenth Amendment:

> By acting to penalize the pregnant teacher for deciding to bear a child, overly restrictive maternity leave regulations can constitute a heavy burden on the exercise of these protected freedoms (*Cleveland Board of Education v. LaFleur* and *Cohen v. Chesterfield County School Board,* 1974).

The school boards contended that firm cutoff dates were necessary to maintain continuity of classroom instruction and that some teachers became physically incapable of performing teaching duties in the latter part of their pregnancies. The Supreme Court disagreed with these "irrebuttable presumptions":

> The arbitrary cutoff dates embodied in the mandatory leave rules before us have no rational relationship to the valid state interest of preserving continuity of instruction. As long as the teachers are required to give substantial advance notice of their condition, the choice of firm dates later in pregnancy would serve the boards' objectives just as well, while imposing a far lesser burden on the women's exercise of constitutionally protected freedom.
>
> The provisions amount to a conclusive presumption that every pregnant teacher who reaches the fifth or sixth month of pregnancy is physically incapable of continuing. There is no individualized determination by the teacher's doctor—or the school board's—as to any particular teacher's ability to continue at her job. The rules contain an irrebuttable presumption of physical incompetency, and that presumption applies even when the medical evidence as to an individual woman's physical status might be wholly to the contrary (*Cleveland Board of Education v. LaFleur* and *Cohen v. Chesterfield County School Board,* 1974).

The Cleveland policy governing the return of teachers after maternity leave was also struck down because it suffered from the same constitutional deficiencies. The policy required a mother to wait until her child reached the age of three months before she was eligible to return to work. However, the Chesterfield County requirements that a teacher submit a medical certificate from her physician and that return to work be guaranteed no later than the beginning of the next school year were ruled valid protections of the board's interests in teacher fitness and continuity of education.

A flurry of court activity resulted from this decision as lower courts awaiting the United States Supreme Court rulings overturned mandatory maternity leave and return policies and school districts rushed to rewrite policies to be in line with *Cleveland* and *Cohen* (*Kornblum v. Newark Unified School District,* 1974; *Bradley v. Cothern,* 1974; *Paxman v. Wilkerson,* 1975; *Richards v. Omaha Public Schools,* 1975; *Freeport Area School District v. Commonwealth, Human Relations Commission,* 1975; *Black v. School Committee of Malden,* 1976; *Fabian v. Independent School District No. 89 of Oklahoma County, Oklahoma,* 1976). The Iowa Supreme Court in 1975 emphasized that gender discrimination was inherent in one maternity leave policy:

> Every human, regardless of sex, is subject to crises or physiological disabilities of the body. Here the regulation isolates pregnancy from all other disabilities or physical conditions and makes it subject to the restrictive provisions therein

> provided. Noticeably, in the case of other illnesses or debilitating conditions an individual is not required to cease employment at a fixed time and return to work following recovery at a set date regardless of the employee's wishes or medical advice. Any person affected by a disability, other than pregnancy, ceases employment and thereafter returns to work when he or she alone deems it proper to do so. But this is not the case where the individual becomes pregnant. Unquestionably, such discriminate treatment is linked to sex alone (*Cedar Rapids Community School District v. Parr,* 1975).

Similarly, a federal district court in Massachusetts overturned a collective bargaining agreement clause that violated the Fourteenth Amendment rights of pregnant teachers:

> While it might be unusual, a teacher might physically require no more than several weeks to bear a child and recuperate, a time span no longer than a winter or spring vacation in many school systems. To carry this idea to the extreme, can it be irrebuttably presumed that a teacher would not be able to bear a child and recuperate in a matter of days, thereby missing very few teaching days, or none if the child was born on a weekend? Although the natural reaction of many might be to strongly disapprove of a mother who returned to work so quickly after bearing a child, that is something which a court can not take into account. . . . In reality, such an occurrence is most unlikely and is only raised here to clarify the Court's position that mandatory cutoff dates, however brief they make a mandatory maternity leave, create irrebuttable presumptions as to the physical competency of a teacher experiencing pregnancy and the recuperation after childbirth (*Rodgers v. Berger,* 1977).

Most unconstitutional maternity leave policies had been eliminated or rewritten by 1980 to conform with United States Supreme Court decisions, but women teachers in Michigan brought individual and class action suits against seven school districts in 1981. All district policies that included the following stipulations were ruled in violation of Title VII of the Civil Rights Act of 1964:

1. Disparate treatment of individuals with pregnancy-related disabilities in the availability of sick leave, employer-paid fringe benefits, and seniority, tenure, retirement and salary increment credit for time on leave as compared to individuals on non-pregnancy disability leave;
2. Required notice of pregnancy within a certain number of months, often as a prerequisite to receiving pregnancy leave;
3. Required medical verification of a pregnant teacher's ability to perform her duties;
4. Mandatory leave commencement dates at a specified month of pregnancy unrelated to individual ability to work;
5. Length of service requirements for eligibility for pregnancy leaves; and
6. Disparate treatment of women returning from pregnancy leave as compared to those returning from non-pregnancy disability leave in such matters as

> placement and date of reinstatement (*Thompson v. Board of Education of Romeo Community Schools,* 1981).

The question of marital status of pregnant teachers did not arise in early cases. However, in 1986 an unmarried teacher, who was forced to take a leave of absence while she was pregnant, filed suit under a constitutional right of privacy and Title VII. The court ruled that the school board's interest of protecting schoolchildren from exposure to an unmarried, pregnant teacher did not outweigh the teacher's interest in exercising her constitutional right to bear a child out of wedlock and that she had been discriminated against in violation of Title VII (*Ponton v. Newport News School Board,* 1986).

Related to mandatory maternity leave policies is the issue of paid sick leave and continuation of benefits during maternity leave. Historically, women were not allowed to use accumulated sick leave for maternity and at times lost their rights to seniority and tenure when on maternity leave. Several court rulings in cases not directly related to education impacted school district policies on the payment of benefits to teachers on maternity leave. Until 1978 the lower courts, following the lead of the United States Supreme Court, ruled that exclusion of pregnancy and maternity conditions from sick leave and disability insurance coverage did not violate the Constitution nor Title VII. Because pregnant women did not constitute a protected class, discrimination could not be shown (*Geduldig v. Aiello,* 1974; *General Electric Company v. Gilbert,* 1976; *Narragansett Electric Company v. Rhode Island Commission for Human Rights,* 1977; *Nashville Gas Company v. Satty,* 1977). The cases involving teachers' maternity leave cited these court decisions, and teachers continued to be denied benefits during maternity leave (*Richards v. Omaha Public Schools,* 1975; *Tawney v. Board of Education of County of Boone,* 1977; *Lewis v. Los Angeles City Unified School District,* 1977).

In 1978 Congress passed the Pregnancy Discrimination Act, which stated that pregnancy-related illness and disability could be treated no differently from other disabilities under employee benefit plans. In a California case pending at the time this bill passed, the United States Court of Appeals, Ninth Circuit, ruled that discrimination did exist when teachers were not allowed to use sick leave for maternity (*deLaurier v. San Diego Unified School District,* 1978).

The issue of maternity benefits is still not settled in many states. A 1982 case involved a New Jersey statute that stated sick leave could not be used for child-rearing purposes by a nondisabled teacher. A school board policy implemented the state law by allowing accumulated disability leave benefits to be used by pregnant teachers 30 days before and 30 days after the birth of a child but then requiring a physician's certificate before a teacher could qualify for additional paid sick leave. The court upheld this policy (*Matters of Hackensack Board of Education,* 1982). On the other hand, a Pennsylvania teacher wanted to use her 30 days of accumulated sick leave during her pregnancy and then go on unpaid maternity leave. The board granted her unpaid maternity leave beginning on the date she desired to begin leave but refused to grant her sick leave. The court ruled that this action constituted unlawful gender discrimination:

> The refusal to allow the use of accumulated sick leave in conjunction with maternity leave fails to recognize the disability caused by pregnancy, and the

> District's policy treats disability from pregnancy differently than other disabilities. . . . Under District policy, certification of disability from any cause other than pregnancy results in compensation; certification of disability from pregnancy results in the denial of compensation (*Dallastown Area School District v. Commonwealth, Pennsylvania Human Relations Commission,* 1983).

In 1986 a New York appellate court ruled that requiring a pregnant teacher to choose between taking unpaid maternity leave for an extended period of time or taking paid sick leave for perhaps a shorter period of time was not inherently discriminatory (*West Hempstead Union Free School District v. State Division of Human Rights,* 1986). The Pennsylvania appellate court ruled that a school district's leave policy was reasonable when a teacher was not allowed to accrue sick leave during the 10 months she voluntarily chose not to work after her baby was born and her paid maternity leave had ended (*Grim v. West Chester Area School District,* 1987).

Tenure and seniority rights of teachers on maternity leave have also been issues for many school districts. In a Massachusetts school district, maternity leave was considered a break in service and terminated all prior service credit for purpose of tenure. A federal court ruled that this policy violated the Fourteenth Amendment:

> The damage that results from the . . . [teacher's] ineligibility to attain tenure status is a most severe penalty. . . . To rule that the differentiation established by [the board] is valid places [the teacher] in an extremely unreasonable position: She must decide whether to sacrifice any service she has accumulated toward receiving tenure by taking maternity leave or to forego childbirth until she has attained that status. To be forced to make such a choice places a heavy burden on a teacher's personal choice in matters of family life (*Rodgers v. Berger,* 1977).

However, in other cases teachers' claims regarding maternity leave have been ruled invalid. A New York teacher was told when she was hired that she had to have a master's degree or complete 30 hours of graduate study over the next five years. The next year she was granted a five-year maternity leave. At the end of the five years, her license to teach was terminated for failure to comply with the education requirement. Her claim that she should have been allowed an extension of time equal to the length of her maternity leave was not upheld by the court (*New York City Board of Education v. New York State Human Rights Appeal Board,* 1976). In 1982 a teacher's contract was not renewed after her maternity leave because of decreasing enrollments in the district. She filed suit that she was entitled to seniority credit for her maternity leave and that her dismissal was discriminatory. However, the collective bargaining agreement said sick and maternity leave could not be used in calculating seniority, and the court upheld the negotiated clause (*Burton v. School Committee of Quaboag Regional School District,* 1982).

Almost all maternity leave cases have been litigated under Title VII of the Civil Rights Act of 1964. However, in 1982 the United States Supreme Court ruled in a maternity leave case filed under Title IX of the Education Amendments of 1972. The tenured teacher in the case was not rehired after her one-year maternity leave, and the school board said the Department of Health, Education, and Welfare and Title IX had no jurisdiction in the case. The Supreme Court opened the door to new grounds for maternity leave suits by ruling that the case could be tried under Title IX (*North Haven Board of Education v. Bell,* 1982).

Claims for maternity or child-rearing benefits by men have generally not been successful in education cases. In 1974 a teacher claimed he was a victim of discrimination when he was refused child care leave when his wife had a baby. He took leave without permission from the end of September through the rest of the school year and then sued for back pay. The court refused to consider his claim (*Ackerman v. Board of Education of City of New York,* 1974). Because some cases are succeeding in lower courts, male teachers may be able to claim entitlement to leave for child care purposes in the future.

In summary, teachers' leaves of absence for maternity have been the center of controversy for several years. Except for some questions regarding payment of benefits and child care leave for men, most maternity leave issues have been settled and conclude that teachers who become pregnant may not be subjected to discrimination. Mandatory cutoff and return dates are unconstitutional, and teachers may usually use accumulated sick leave and other benefits during maternity. Notice of commencement of maternity leave and reasonable rules that allow for the return of the teacher at a convenient time during the school year have been upheld on the basis of ensuring continuity of education. School officials must be certain that district maternity leave policies are in line with court decisions and not in violation of teachers' constitutional and civil rights. Teachers, too, must know what district maternity leave policies are so as not to violate policies that protect both the teachers' and the district's interests.

Principle IV

> Leaves of absence must be administered on a nondiscriminatory basis.

Once United States Supreme Court decisions and acts of Congress banned discrimination caused by mandatory maternity leave policies and denial of benefits for maternity leave, other challenges to policies governing teachers' leaves of absence were made. The courts have been called upon to make decisions when claims of discriminatory administration of leaves of absence have involved gender, religion, and race.

Gender discrimination was claimed by a tenured teacher, who was placed on an unrequested partial leave of absence for budgetary reasons, when he was not offered a position when it became available. The suit arose when the school board did not view him as qualified to teach girls' physical education and to coach girls' sports, even though he was so certified and had formerly taught and coached girls' sports. The court ordered him reinstated with damages (*Walter v. Independent School District No. 457, Trimont,* 1982).

Several cases in which teachers claimed religious discrimination in leave policies have been heard. A teacher who was a member of the Worldwide Church of God needed to miss eight days of school each year to observe holy days. Understanding that his salary would be cut for the days not covered by personal leave, he chose to take unpaid leave. Despite having been assured his job was not in jeopardy if he took leave without pay for religious reasons, he was terminated. He challenged his dismissal on grounds of violation of his free exercise of religion and due process rights. Stating that accommodating a teacher's religion by allowing five to ten days' absence per year was not an undue hardship on the school system, the court ordered him reinstated with back pay and damages (*Niederhuber v. Camden County Vocational and Technical School District Board of Education,* 1980).

The courts ruled that loss of pay was not a valid basis for a claim of religious discrimination in two cases involving Jewish teachers. Both teachers believed that having to use personal leave days and then unpaid leave to observe the two days of worship required for both Yom Kippur and Rosh Hashanah was discriminatory. However, the courts ruled they had not been prevented from observing their religious holidays, and loss of pay was not an abuse of religious freedom (*Pinsker v. Joint District No. 28J of Adams and Arapahoe Counties,* 1983; *King v. Iowa Civil Rights Commission,* 1983). In 1985 a Catholic teacher brought action under the free exercise clause of the First Amendment when the school district refused to grant him paid leave to observe two holy days in addition to the three days allowed for religious observances. Although the Catholic church did not require their faithful members to refrain from working on those days and the parish provided masses outside of working hours, the teacher said his personal beliefs prevented him from working. The district allowed him to use paid personal leave days to practice his religious beliefs; therefore, the court ruled that his rights under the First Amendment had not been violated (*DiPasquale v. Board of Education, Williamsville Central School District,* 1985).

Charges of racial discrimination in administering leave of absence policies often involve involuntary leaves, or layoffs, of teachers when school districts are under court-ordered desegregation regulations. Although some teachers attempt to challenge their layoffs, the courts almost always uphold board actions taken to bring the racial composition of faculties into compliance with judicial orders. Layoff plans usually include provisions for order of recall, which also must be nondiscriminatory.

The ruling case on involuntary leave of absence policies involving race issues is *Wygant v. Jackson Board of Education* (1986). The Michigan school district, adhering to the collective bargaining agreement with the teachers' association, laid off teachers according to seniority. However, the negotiated contract also contained an exception to the seniority rule: at no time was a greater percentage of minority personnel to be laid off than the percentage of minority personnel employed at the time of layoff. Nonminority teachers brought suit against the school district when they were laid off and minority teachers with less seniority were retained. The school district claimed that role models for minority schoolchildren were needed and that societal discrimination would be remedied by their layoff policy. However, the United States Supreme Court ruled against the district's policy. Because the district was not under court orders to remediate past discrimination, the court said that other, less intrusive means of accomplishing their purposes existed, such as adopting stronger nondiscriminatory hiring practices.

In summary, leaves of absence may not be administered on any discriminatory basis. The courts continue to take a close look when discrimination based on such characteristics as gender, race, and religion is alleged against a school district's leave of absence policy. School boards should ensure that district leave policies do not discriminate or violate the rights of any individual or class of teachers. At the same time, teachers should not take advantage of leave of absence policies nor claim discrimination unless evidence exists to support such a claim.

Principle V

Where required by law, a leave of absence must be granted a teacher because of public service demands of the federal, state, and local governments. Continuation or reinstatement of salary and benefits will depend on the type of public service leave granted.

Few court cases have arisen concerning leaves of absence for teachers who are required or who desire to meet public service demands. School districts usually are allowed to establish reasonable requirements for notice prior to a teacher taking such leave, for suspension or payment of salary, for continuation or suspension of fringe benefits, and for notice of intent to return. Yet, the teacher who is meeting the demands of the federal, state, or local government may not be subjected to discrimination or recrimination. These policies and protections are accorded to teachers in public service that offers statutory employment protection and may differ from those available to teachers holding temporary or paid public offices.

Public service leaves of absence may be granted for relatively long-term service in the military or Peace Corps or for short-term service such as jury duty, court appearances, and congressional hearings. State and local policies may determine how salary and fringe benefits are handled during such a leave of absence, but when requirements are met by the teacher who takes leave, all benefits and privileges of a former position must usually be reinstated upon the person's return to a teaching position.

Eligibility for credit for military service has been disputed since the Vietnam conflict. In New Jersey the courts upheld the state board's policy that allowed veterans who held only emergency teaching certificates at the time they went into the service to be eligible for military service credit when they obtained standard teaching certificates. One court also ruled that five months of military service entitled the teacher to one full year of employment credit (*Camden County Vocational Technical Association v. Board of Education of Camden County Vocational Technical Schools, Camden County,* 1986). In 1987 a Kentucky teacher who was not given credit for his two years in the military filed suit against the school district. The district claimed he had been employed by a different school district at the time he went into the army and so his benefits could not be restored. The court upheld the teacher's claims, citing state statutes granting experience credit for time in the military (*Watkins v. Oldham,* 1987). Three teachers in a Montana school district resigned in 1970 to join the armed forces and were later rehired when they left the military. Although their time in the service counted for seniority, they did not get credit on the salary schedule. The United States Court of Appeals, Ninth Circuit, ruled that under the Vietnam Era Veterans' Readjustment Assistance Act of 1982, the teachers were to receive credit on the salary schedule for their military service (*Lang v. Great Falls School District No. 1 and A,* 1988).

Because federal and state statutes often govern public service leaves, teachers and school boards must be familiar with these regulations. A teacher may not be kept from meeting public service obligations but must, at the same time, observe the rules established by the district to provide for continuity and quality of education.

A local board may require a teacher to take a leave of absence when a defensible reason exists for a temporary severance of the teacher's connection with the school. Financial exigency may require putting a teacher on a leave of absence.

Principle VI

Leaves of absence are usually considered a privilege and benefit for those teachers who qualify to be absent temporarily from their positions. However, circumstances do arise when school officials require a teacher to take a leave of absence when the teacher would not ordinarily choose to do so. The school board may place a teacher on an involuntary leave of absence when the welfare of the teacher, students, or school must be considered before the desire of a teacher to remain in a position. All statutes and board policies must be strictly followed to avoid infringing upon a teacher's right of employment. The courts have become involved when teachers have claimed involuntary leaves of absence were violations of due process, equal protection, property rights, or liberty interests.

Many reasons may cause a school board to require a teacher to take a leave of absence. Among the most common are a teacher's illness or disability, involvement in criminal court proceedings, and candidacy for public office. A district's financial problems that force a temporary reduction in the teaching staff may also result in involuntary leaves of absence for teachers. Involuntary leaves of absence are also known as suspensions (particularly when a school district disciplinary action or a court case is pending) and furloughs (often used in temporary reduction in force situations). Court cases have addressed all of these reasons for required leaves of absence.

A school district's action of placing a teacher on a medical leave of absence has been challenged in court when the teacher has not recognized that a mental or physical disability was endangering his or her own welfare and also the welfare of students and fellow employees. However, districts must establish and follow policies that safeguard the teacher's constitutional rights when taking such action.

For example, in 1978 a tenured teacher was placed on an involuntary health leave after several psychiatric examinations ordered by the board all reported him to have residual paranoid schizophrenic tendencies that would make him incapable of managing a classroom. The court, however, found that the district had violated the teacher's due process rights by placing him on involuntary leave without a hearing. Although he was not automatically reinstated, he was entitled to a hearing where he could confront the doctors and challenge their reports with his own evidence (*Doe v. Anker,* 1978). In a similar case where a tenured teacher was placed on involuntary medical leave without pay when an administration-ordered medical examination found her unfit to teach, the court remanded the case with instructions that she was eligible for back pay as well as reinstatement. Her due process rights had been denied, and she had had no opportunity to dispute the evidence or to see her medical records (*Newman v. Board of Education of City School District of New York,* 1979).

On the other hand, a teacher filed suit in a 1982 case for deprivation of property rights in employment when he was placed on an extended medical leave of absence. Adhering to all due process requirements, the principal had ordered him to submit to two examinations; the examinations had verified that the teacher was not psychologically stable enough to continue teaching. The court ruled that the board's action was reasonable (*Dusanek v. Hannon,* 1982). An Iowa guidance counselor went on immediate sick leave with the understanding that he could return for a 30-day probationary period if he furnished a certificate from a psychiatrist that stated he was fully capable of returning to his duties as a counselor. When he failed to furnish the certificate, he was terminated. The state supreme court ruled that the board could terminate him, although the teacher was not barred from seeking reinstatement (*Smith v. Fort Madison Community School District,* 1983).

Many court challenges to involuntary leaves of absence have involved teachers who were candidates for public office and those who were elected to office. Because teaching is considered a public office, any teacher running for a political office was once viewed as having a conflict of interest. Therefore, a teacher could be required to take a leave of absence without pay while campaigning for any public office and could be required to resign if elected. The courts formerly upheld this view, often citing *School City of East Chicago v. Sigler* (1941) as the authority on this issue:

> It will be conceded that [the teacher] has the same privilege as any other citizen to become a candidate for public office. Such candidacy should not be and is not ground for cancellation of his contract as a permanent teacher. But anyone who has been a candidate recognizes that political activity is apt to interfere with one's usual avocation and this fact, independent of any possible involvement of the school system in political controversies, affords a sound reason for a temporary severance of the candidate's connection with the schools. This rule, general in terms and applying to all teachers, does not to us seem such an unreasonable exercise of the board's powers as to warrant judicial interference. The board, not the courts, is charged with the duty of managing the school system and so long as it acts with fairness its decisions on matters within its discretion are not subject to judicial review (*School City of East Chicago v. Sigler,* 1941).

However, teachers began to press for their rights as public citizens to be involved in the electoral process, and the courts supported them. In 1978 a school administrator announced his candidacy for the state house of representatives. Shortly afterward, the school board passed a rule that required employees to take unpaid leaves of absence while campaigning for elective political office. The administrator took leave on three occasions and lost over $11,000 in salary. The United States Supreme Court upheld the lower court ruling that the regulation imposed substantial economic disincentives for employees seeking public office and thus had the effect of discrimination (*Dougherty County, Georgia, Board of Education v. White,* 1978). Following this Supreme Court ruling, the Kentucky Court of Appeals ruled that a board policy requiring leaves of absence for teachers who were political candidates violated teachers' rights of free speech and association and added that there was no showing that seeking political office was an activity which would hinder teachers in the performance of their duties (*Allen v. Board of Education of Jefferson County,* 1979).

State statutes differ on when teachers must take unpaid leaves of absence to hold political office. When dual allegiance questions arise, the courts have split on whether or not teachers, who work in the executive branch of government, may concurrently act as legislators in the legislative branch (*Monaghan v. School District No. 1, Clackamas County,* 1957; *Begich v. Jefferson,* 1968). Whether or not teachers may be members of state boards of education also depends on which state is involved (*Amador v. New Mexico State Board of Education,* 1969; *Hoskins v. Walker,* 1974).

In most states, membership of a teacher on the local school board is a conflict of interest, but states are not clear on whether a teacher must take a leave of absence or resign before holding a position on the school board. This issue arose when a teacher was elected to a Florida school board. The next year Florida passed a law stating that a state employee could not hold office as a member of the governing board that was the person's employer. When the teacher's term on the board expired, she took leave without pay from teaching and was reelected. The state commission on ethics found her in violation of the law, noting that because she had tenure, she was still an employee of the board. The court disagreed with this interpretation of the statute:

> It is undisputed that [the teacher] performs no teaching services for, nor does she receive any compensation from, the School Board. While she is on leave, the School Board does not and cannot exercise any control over her. Therefore, we conclude that [the teacher], by taking a leave of absence without pay, is no longer an "employee" of the School Board. In a very real sense, she has surrendered her employee status. The mere fact of her continuing contract creates only an expectancy of future employment. . . . The fact that she may or may not return to the classroom is a prospective event which neither the Commission nor this Court need be concerned with at this time (*Wright v. State Commission on Ethics,* 1980).

Both tenured and nontenured teachers have been placed on temporary furlough or involuntary leave of absence when their school districts have faced financial crises because of unexpected revenue losses, reductions in student enrollment, legislative action, consolidation of school districts, and other economic problems. The 1980s saw many cases come before the courts when teachers challenged school boards' rights to abolish positions and place teachers on unpaid leaves of absence. However, when due process is observed, the courts uphold school district actions that result from financial exigency (*Elrod v. Harrisonville Cass R-IX School District,* 1986).

Minnesota has been the locus for several court cases involving reduction in force issues. In 1982 an art teacher whose position was discontinued found that his leave of absence was legal because the courts were bound by state statute:

> The school board may place on unrequested leave of absence, without pay or fringe benefits, as many teachers as may be necessary because of discontinuance of position, lack of pupils, financial limitations, or merger of classes caused by consolidation of districts. The unrequested leave shall be effective at the close

of the school year (as quoted in *Herfindahl v. Independent School District No. 126, Clara City,* 1982).

In another Minnesota case, the district collective bargaining agreement was found binding when it provided that teachers be placed on unrequested leaves of absence in inverse order of seniority in reduction in force cases. The teacher in the case was admittedly hardworking, capable, and popular but also least senior. Because the entire district, but especially the social studies department, had suffered a large reduction in enrollment, decreasing the number of teachers was justified. The court ruled that the board had not acted arbitrarily when it placed the teacher on an unrequested leave of absence for financial limitations, lack of pupils, and discontinuance of position (*Laird v. Independent School District No. 317, Deer River, Minnesota,* 1984). Sixteen teachers in another Minnesota district were placed on unrequested leave because of financial limitations and declining enrollment. The court upheld all of the leaves except one where accreditation of the program would be in jeopardy if the teacher-pupil ratio were increased (*Bye v. Special Intermediate School District No. 916,* 1986). However, in another case the Minnesota Court of Appeals ruled that a district that placed teachers on leave when they failed to request a hearing and rescinded leave for those who did request hearings had acted arbitrarily and capriciously even though the board claimed the leaves were necessary for financial reasons (*Roseville Education Association v. Independent School District No. 623,* 1986).

Probationary teachers are in a vulnerable position when budget problems force districts to reduce the teaching staff. The St. Louis Teachers Union claimed that nontenured teachers were entitled to be placed on leaves of absences rather than being terminated when they were not rehired because of insufficient funds. The court disagreed, stating that under that type of leave of absence plan a probationary teacher who taught just one day before being placed on leave of absence could gain tenure with no assessment nor experience (*St. Louis Teachers Union Local 420 v. St. Louis Board of Education,* 1984).

In all cases where teachers are placed on unrequested leave, due process must be observed. In 1984 a special education director, who was also certified and experienced as a math teacher, was placed on unrequested leave. At the same meeting where the board conducted a hearing and eliminated the special education position, a new math teacher and part-time special education consultant were hired. The court ruled that serious procedural due process violations had occurred, infringing on the teacher's constitutional and seniority rights. He was entitled to reinstatement and back pay for the entire period he was on an involuntary leave of absence (*Pearson v. School Board of Independent School District No. 381,* 1984).

Therefore, a school board has the right to place a teacher on an unrequested leave of absence, and that right is usually supported by statute or board policy. However, due process guidelines should be included in such a policy and then be strictly observed as ethical as well as legal implications arise from depriving a person of a teaching position. The welfare of students and the school must be considered, but the teacher's constitutional rights may not be violated. All policies allowing teachers to be placed on involuntary leaves of absence for whatever reason should be carefully written to protect the rights of both the district and the teacher.

Summary

Leaves of absence have become an important employment issue for teachers, and a major bargaining item during collective negotiations in many districts. The policies governing teacher leaves of absence have become more clearly defined as negotiated contracts and court decisions have so demanded. Arbitrary granting of personal and professional leave has been largely replaced by guidelines that ensure equitable, nondiscriminatory leave policies.

Discrimination that once pervaded many district leave policies has been ruled unconstitutional by the United States Supreme Court, particularly in the case of maternity leave. Following the lead of landmark Supreme Court decisions and realizing the protection afforded by the Civil Rights Act of 1964 as well as the Fourteenth Amendment, many teachers have challenged discriminatory leave policies and forced districts to rewrite their guidelines. Litigation over leaves of absence continues when gender, religion, and race discrimination, violation of equal protection and due process, and denial of property and liberty interests are claimed. To avoid violating teacher rights, districts must follow due process in administering leaves of absence.

In the future, more cases may arise when female teachers claim a right to more flexibility in maternity leave and benefits policies and when male teachers claim a right to child care leave. School districts desiring to put teachers on temporary leave when they are allegedly unfit to continue in the classroom will be challenged unless boards establish and then follow strict procedures that guarantee district and teacher rights. As school districts face budget crises and attempt to reduce the teaching staff by furloughing teachers, court cases involving seniority and tenure will be brought by the teachers who are victims of financial exigency.

Personal and professional leaves of absence are benefits that attract many professional persons to teaching careers. Tenure and seniority generally must remain intact when a teacher takes a leave of absence. When school districts have reasonable and equitable leave policies and when teachers observe the requirements of their leave policies, both will benefit.

Questions and Responses

1. Who establishes the regulations and policies governing teachers' leaves of absence?

Local school boards generally have the authority and obligation to establish reasonable policies for teacher leaves of absence in their district. However, local guidelines must observe all state statutes, state board of education mandates, collective bargaining agreements, and court decisions related to that district. Leaves of absence have become a major negotiating item in many districts.

2. On what grounds may a teacher claim discrimination in leave of absence issues?

Teachers often use Title VII of the Civil Rights Act of 1964 and the Fourteenth Amendment to the Constitution to show that their equal protection, due process, civil rights, and property interests in employment have been violated by discriminatory leave policies. The United States Supreme Court has also ruled that Title IX of the Education Amendments of 1972 may be used to support claims of discriminatory leave of absence policies based on gender.

3. When may a teacher be required to go on unrequested leave of absence?

A school board may determine that the welfare of the teacher, students, or the school may benefit from a teacher taking a leave of absence even when the teacher does not desire such a leave. Mental or physical disability unrecognized by the teacher may require a temporary leave of absence until the teacher is able to return to the classroom, usually as determined by a physician's certification. Disciplinary action against a teacher by the district may include suspension, and a teacher may be put on a leave of absence when involved in criminal or civil court proceedings. Teachers who are elected or appointed to some public offices may be required to take a leave from regular teaching duties. Districts facing budget problems may reduce the teaching staff temporarily by furloughing teachers. Discontinuance of position, decrease in student enrollment, and consolidation of districts may result in teachers being placed on unrequested leaves of absence.

4. When may a school board overrule a teacher's jury duty, military service, or Peace Corps service?

In most states, laws require that a leave of absence be granted a teacher who desires or who is obligated to perform certain types of public service. Jury duty, congressional hearings, and court appearances are usually mandatory, and a teacher must be given the short-term leave of absence necessary to fulfill the obligation. Service in the military or the Peace Corps often requires a long-term leave of absence, and districts are usually bound to grant leaves of absence for such service. However, to provide for continuity of education and to safeguard the welfare of students and the school, federal, state, and local guidelines for public service leaves of absence usually call for notice of departure date, anticipated length of leave, and intent to return. Pay and fringe benefits may normally be suspended for public service leave, especially for long-term commitments, but all benefits must usually be reinstated upon the return of the teacher.

5. Why may a teacher be forced to repay the salary and benefits received during a sabbatical leave?

Most states have laws that forbid the distribution of public funds in the form of a gift. Because a sabbatical leave usually grants a teacher a leave of absence with full or partial pay and continuation of full or partial benefits, such payment would be considered an illegal gift of public moneys if the teacher did not return to the district. A teacher is granted a sabbatical leave in anticipation of a return with increased knowledge, experience, education, or vigor from which the district will benefit. Compensation for sabbatical leave is justified by this "beneficiary test," but when the teacher does not return to the district, the teacher may be required to pay back the salary and benefits received because the individual, not the district, will be the beneficiary of the leave.

6. When may teachers claim violation of religious freedom caused by leave of absence policies?

Many school districts provide one or two personal leave days per year for a teacher to use as desired, including to observe holy days or to participate in religious activities. When additional days of leave are desired in order to practice religion, the teacher must usually take leave without pay. The courts have ruled that the granting of leave without pay for purposes of religious observances and activities is permissible so long as no undue hardship is placed upon the school district by excessive absences. However, when teachers claim violation of religious freedom because they are forced to take leaves without pay for worship purposes, they are often overruled by the courts. The denial of pay generally does not infringe on free exercise of religion.

7. What have the courts ruled about mandatory maternity leave policies?

In the landmark cases of *Cleveland Board of Education v. LaFleur* and *Cohen v. Chesterfield County Board of Education* (1974), the United States Supreme Court struck down mandatory maternity leave policies. District policies may not establish cutoff dates prior to childbirth when pregnant teachers must begin maternity leave. Also, districts may not establish return policies that dictate specific dates after childbirth before which a teacher may not return to teaching. Such policies rely on "irrebuttable presumptions" that all pregnant teachers are disabled and unable to carry on teaching responsibilities after and before board-established dates related to childbirth. No flexibility for individual teacher health or physician advice is allowed by these policies. The Supreme Court ruled that teachers' rights under the Fourteenth Amendment were thus being violated. Within the guidelines handed down by the Supreme Court, lower courts have ruled on other maternity leave policies, including benefits.

8. How can a school district ensure continuity of education is maintained when mandatory maternity leave has been ruled unconstitutional?

A teacher may be required to give prior notice of the date she plans to begin her maternity leave. She may also be required to give notice of her intent to return to teaching and an anticipated date of return. These dates of leave and return are thus established by the teacher, not by the district. Substitute teachers and teaching assignments may then be arranged so that the teacher's rights are guaranteed while continuity of education is safeguarded. Continuity of education may not be used as justification for violating a teacher's rights. However, a district may establish a policy whereby a teacher may not be guaranteed return to a position until the beginning of a semester or term after maternity leave; continuity in the classroom is thus provided if such a policy also adheres to state rules and court decisions binding on the district. The unpredictability of pregnancy is no greater than for other illnesses and injuries that may befall any teacher. Therefore, the inability of school districts to predict maternity leave requirements is no greater than their inability to predict teacher absences for other reasons.

9. What have the courts determined about benefits for maternity leave? Depending on applicable state statutes, collective bargaining agreements, and court decisions, teachers who go on maternity leave must receive the same benefits and must observe the same guidelines as any teacher who goes on any type of sick or disability leave. The sick leave policy for a district must usually be enforced for maternity leave as well as for other illnesses, and a teacher may use accumulated sick leave during maternity leave. A teacher may not lose seniority credit or tenure by taking maternity leave.

10. What have the courts stated about child care leave for male teachers? Few significant cases have come before the courts where male teachers have claimed the right to child-rearing or child care leave. However, the issue is becoming more recognized in business and government as well as in education, and more cases will probably arise that may eventually establish some guidelines for leaves of absence for purposes of child care by male teachers.

Case References

Ackerman v. Board of Education of City of New York, 387 F.Supp. 76 (S.D.N.Y. 1974).
Allen v. Board of Education of Jefferson County, 584 S.W.2d 408 (Ky. App. 1979).
Amador v. New Mexico State Board of Education, 455 P.2d 840 (N.M. 1969).
Averell v. City of Newburyport, 135 N.E. 463 (Mass. 1922).
Begich v. Jefferson, 441 P.2d 27 (Alaska 1968).
Bellevue School District No. 405 v. Bentley, 684 P.2d 793 (Wash. App. 1984).
Bettendorf Education Association v. Bettendorf Community School District, 262 N.W.2d 550 (Iowa 1978).
Black v. School Committee of Malden, 341 N.E.2d 896 (Mass. 1976).
Board of Education of Marshallton-McKean School District v. Sinclair, 373 A.2d. 572 (Del. 1977).
Bradley v. Cothern, 384 F.Supp. 1216 (E.D. Tex. 1974).
Bristol Township School District v. Karafin, 478 A.2d 539 (Pa. Cmwlth. 1984).
Buckley v. Coyle Public School System, 476 F.2d 92 (10th Cir., 1973).
Burton v. School Committee of Quaboag Regional School District, 432 N.E.2d 725 (Mass. App. 1982).
Bye v. Special Intermediate School District No. 916, 379 N.W.2d 653 (Minn. App. 1986).
California Teachers' Association v. Parlier Unified School District, 204 Cal.Rptr. 20 (Cal. App. 5 Dist. 1984).
Camden County Vocational Technical Association v. Board of Education of Camden County Vocational Technical Schools, Camden County, 503 A.2d 890 (N.J. Super. A.D. 1986).
Cedar Rapids Community School District v. Parr, 227 N.W.2d 486 (Iowa 1975).
Cleveland Board of Education v. LaFleur, 414 U.S. 632 (1974).
Cohen v. Chesterfield County School Board, 414 U.S. 632 (1974).
deLaurier v. San Diego Unified School District, 588 F.2d 674 (9th Cir. 1978).
Dallastown Area School District v. Commonwealth, Pennsylvania Human Relations Commission, 460 A.2d 878 (Pa. Cmwlth. 1983).
DiPasquale v. Board of Education, Williamsville Central School District, 626 F.Supp. 457 (W.D.N.Y. 1985).
Doe v. Anker, 451 F.Supp. 241 (S.D.N.Y. 1978).
Dougherty County, Georgia, Board of Education v. White, 439 U.S. 32 (1978).

Drinnin v. Heartland Area Education Agency 11, 332 N.W.2d 328 (Iowa 1983).
Dusanek v. Hannon, 677 F.2d 538 (7th Cir., 1982), cert. denied, 459 U.S. 1017 (1982).
Earnest v. School Board of Independent District No. 16 of Stillwater, Oklahoma, 666 P.2d 1287 (Okl. 1983).
Elrod v. Harrisonville Cass R-IX School District, 706 S.W.2d 465 (Mo. App. 1986).
Fabian v. Independent School District No. 89 of Oklahoma County, Oklahoma, 409 F.Supp. 94 (W.D. Okl. 1976).
Freeport Area School District v. Commonwealth, Human Relations Commission, 335 A.2d 873 (Pa. Cmwlth. 1975).
Garner v. Stephens, 460 F.2d 1144 (6th Cir., 1972).
Geduldig v. Aiello, 417 U.S. 484 (1974).
General Electric Company v. Gilbert, 429 U.S. 125 (1976).
Giordano v. Ambach, 509 N.Y.S.2d 203 (N.Y.A.D. 3 Dept. 1986).
Green v. Fairfield City Board of Education, 365 So.2d 1217 (Ala. Civ. App. 1978).
Green v. Waterford Board of Education, 473 F.2d 629 (2d Cir., 1973).
Grim v. West Chester Area School District, 529 A.2d 71 (Pa. Cmwlth. 1987).
Griswold v. Connecticut, 381 U.S. 479 (1965).
Herfindahl v. Independent School District No. 126, Clara City, 325 N.W.2d 36 (Minn. 1982).
Hoskins v. Walker, 315 N.E.2d 25 (Ill. 1974).
Jefferson Classroom Teachers Association v. Jefferson Elementary School District, 187 Cal.Rptr. 542 (Cal. App. 1982).
Jinks v. Mays, 332 F.Supp. 254 (N.D. Ga. 1971).
Kenai Peninsula Borough School District v. Kenai Peninsula Education Association, 572 P.2d 416 (Alaska 1977).
King v. Iowa Civil Rights Commission, 334 N.W.2d 598 (Iowa 1983).
Kornblum v. Newark Unified School District, 112 Cal.Rptr. 457 (Cal. App. 1974).
Laird v. Independent School District No. 317, Deer River, Minnesota, 346 N.W.2d 153 (Minn. 1984).
Lang v. Great Falls School District No. 1 and A, 842 F.2d 1046 (9th Cir., 1988).
Lewis v. Los Angeles City Unified School District, 429 F.Supp. 935 (C.D. Cal. 1977).
Malcolm v. City of Boston, 53 N.E. 812 (Mass. 1899).
Matters of Hackensack Board of Education, 446 A.2d 170 (N.J. Super. A.D. 1982).
Monaghan v. School District No. 1, Clackamas County, 315 P.2d 797 (Or. 1957).
Narragansett Electric Company v. Rhode Island Commission for Human Rights, 374 A.2d 1022 (R.I. 1977).
Nashville Gas Company v. Satty, 434 U.S. 136 (1977).
Nelson v. Western Beaver County School District, 491 A.2d 964 (Pa. Cmwlth. 1985).
New York City Board of Education v. New York State Human Rights Appeal Board, 387 N.Y.S.2d 873 (App. Div. 1976).
Newell v. Orleans Parish School Board, 370 So.2d 655 (La. App. 1979).
Newman v. Board of Education of City School District of New York, 594 F.2d 299 (2d Cir., 1979).
Niederhuber v. Camden County Vocational and Technical School District Board of Education, 495 F.Supp. 273 (D.N.J. 1980).
North Haven Board of Education v. Bell, 456 U.S. 512 (1982).
Paxman v. Wilkerson, 390 F.Supp. 442 (E.D.Va. 1975).
Pearson v. School Board of Independent School District No. 381, 356 N.W.2d 438 (Minn. App. 1984).
Pennsbury School District v. Walker, 447 A.2d 1089 (Pa. Cmwlth. 1982).
Pinsker v. Joint District No. 28J of Adams and Arapahoe Counties, 554 F.Supp. 1049 (D. Colo. 1983).

Ponton v. Newport News School Board, 632 F.Supp. 1056 (E.D. Va. 1986).
Richards v. Omaha Public Schools, 232 N.W.2d 29 (Neb. 1975).
Rodgers v. Berger, 438 F.Supp. 713 (D. Mass. 1977).
Roseville Education Association v. Independent School District No. 623, 380 N.W.2d 512 (Minn. App. 1986).
St. Louis Teachers Union Local 420 v. St. Louis Board of Education, 666 S.W.2d 25 (Mo. App. 1984).
San Dieguito Union High School District v. Commission on Professional Competence, 185 Cal.Rptr. 203 (Cal. App. 1982).
School City of East Chicago v. Sigler, 36 N.E.2d 760 (Ind. 1941).
School District of City of Duquesne v. Duquesne Education Association PSEA/NEA, 512 A.2d 103 (Pa. Cmwlth. 1986).
Schwabenbauer v. Board of Education of City School District of City of Olean, 777 F.2d 837 (2d Cir., 1985).
Scranton School District v. Weiss, 537 A.2d 910 (Pa.Cmwlth. 1988).
Skinner v. Oklahoma ex rel. Williamson, Attorney General, 316 U.S. 535 (1942).
Smith v. Fort Madison Community School District, 334 N.W.2d 701 (Iowa 1983).
Special School District of Fort Smith v. Lynch, 413 S.W.2d 880 (Ark. 1967).
State ex rel. Scoggins v. Vernon Parish School Board, 44 So.2d 385 (La. App. 1950).
State ex rel. Sepulvado v. Rapides Parish School Board, 108 So.2d 96 (La. 1959).
Szabo v. Board of Education of Community Consolidated School District 54, 454 N.E.2d 39 (Ill. App. 1 Dist. 1983).
Tawney v. Board of Education of County of Boone, 426 F.Supp. 528 (S.D. W.Va. 1977).
Thompson v. Board of Education of Romeo Community Schools, 526 F.Supp. 1035 (W.D. Mich. 1981).
Thrash v. Board of Education, School District No. 189, 435 N.E.2d 866 (Ill. App. 1982).
Trumansburg Central School District v. Chalone, 449 N.Y.S.2d 92 (N.Y.A.D. 1982).
Walter v. Independent School District No. 457, Trimont, 323 N.W.2d 37 (Minn. 1982).
Watkins v. Oldham, 731 S.W.2d 829 (Ky. App. 1987).
West Hempstead Union Free School District v. State Division of Human Rights, 497 N.Y.S.2d 721 (N.Y.A.D. 2 Dept. 1986).
Whittaker v. City of Salem, 104 N.E. 359 (Mass. 1914).
Wood v. City of Haverhill, 55 N.E. 381 (Mass. 1899).
Wright v. State Commission on Ethics, 389 So.2d 662 (Fla. App. 1980).
Wygant v. Jackson Board of Education, 476 U.S. 267 (1986).

7 Academic Freedom

The concept of academic freedom dates back at least as far as the time of Plato, who claimed the right to follow an argument wherever it may lead. Throughout history, other educational philosophers have discussed, supported, and died for the freedom to think, to learn, and to teach. Scholars have argued that the right to investigate, to question, to evaluate, and to criticize existing values, theories, and practices is fundamental to political, social, economic, and scientific progress. Thomas Jefferson was among the first to advocate intellectual freedom in the United States when he explained that his University of Virginia would be based on the "illimitable freedom of the human mind."

Academic freedom as espoused and practiced by institutions of higher education has a different connotation when applied to public schools. The mission of higher education differs from that of public schools, and the role of academic freedom differs accordingly. The scholars of universities and colleges are charged with discovering truth; the teachers of public schools are charged with transmitting knowledge to the nation's children. University students are legal adults responsible for distilling the information they glean from their education into their own definition of truth. They are voluntarily attending classes, choosing courses of study, conducting research, analyzing ideas, and applying concepts to their lives. The students of public schools are minors, and teachers are responsible for instructing them in the theoretical and practical knowledge they will need to become productive citizens in a democratic society. Under compulsory education laws, public school children become a captive audience with few choices in courses or teachers. Still in their formative, impressionable years, they cannot be expected to discern truth from opinion or fact from prejudice. Therefore, public school educators establish curricula to ensure that accepted theories and concepts are being taught in the nation's schools and children are not being proselyted or indoctrinated with ideas antithetical to the interests of society.

However, public school teachers have a claim to academic freedom, which has been defined as a constitutional right under the First Amendment. Academic freedom gives teachers the right to speak freely in their classrooms about their subjects. The courts become involved when the rights of teachers and the broad interests of the state must be protected against narrow local or individual interests that would curtail a teacher's academic freedom. When teachers insist that anything they say, any book or materials they use, and any teaching method they employ must be protected by the shield of academic freedom, the courts are again called upon to confirm that the ideals of academic freedom are applied differently in public schools than in colleges and universities. Academic freedom is critical to education at all levels in a democratic society. The nation's courts, including the United States Supreme Court, become involved when that freedom is threatened or is used as a guise for unprofessional conduct, illegal actions, or the right to violate the protected rights of others.

Legal Principles

Principle I *No Interference*

A teacher in a public school has the right to teach the subject matter to which he or she is assigned without undue interference from school officials or parents and to create an atmosphere in which knowledge may be freely transmitted.

Principle II *Controversial Ideas*

A teacher has the right to discuss controversial topics, ideas, and philosophies in a classroom as long as the topic is related to the subject matter that the teacher has been assigned to teach.

Principle III *In-Class Speech*

A teacher's in-class speech may be restricted when continued utterances will be disruptive to the educational process of the school.

Principle IV *Textbooks*

Within limits imposed by state statutes and board of education policies, a teacher generally has the right to use any textbooks, materials, and teaching methods that relate to the subject matter that the teacher has been assigned to teach. No pornographic, obscene, or other illegal material may be used in a classroom.

Discussion

Principle I

A teacher in a public school has the right to teach the subject matter to which he or she is assigned without undue interference from school officials or parents and to create an atmosphere in which knowledge may be freely transmitted.

An important purpose of academic freedom is to allow teachers to create and to protect an atmosphere in which knowledge may be transmitted from teacher to student. Academic freedom is protected under the First Amendment, and teachers are entitled to all First Amendment freedoms. According to the United States Supreme

Court, "it can hardly be argued that either students or teachers shed their constitutional rights to freedom of speech or expression at the schoolhouse gate" (*Tinker v. Des Moines Independent Community School District,* 1969). However, like all constitutional rights, the right to academic freedom is not absolute. The courts become involved when the academic freedom of teachers must be balanced against the competing rights of society, including school administrators, boards of education, and parents, all of whom may desire to curtail a teacher's rights.

Most battles for academic freedom have been fought by institutions of higher education; however, public schools have benefited from court decisions upholding the same basic ideals. Many cases where academic freedom was defined were heard in the 1950s and 1960s and involved challenges to loyalty oaths required of university professors and public school teachers. In ruling against the New York loyalty oath in 1967, the United States Supreme Court handed down a decision that would be quoted in later academic freedom cases:

> Our Nation is deeply committed to safeguarding academic freedom, which is of transcendent value to all of us and not merely to the teachers concerned. That freedom is therefore a special concern of the First Amendment, which does not tolerate laws that cast a pall of orthodoxy over the classroom. . . . The classroom is peculiarly the "marketplace of ideas." The Nation's future depends upon leaders trained through wide exposure to that robust exchange of ideas which discovers truth "out of a multitude of tongues, [rather] than through any kind of authoritative selection" (*Keyishian v. Board of Regents of the University of the State of New York,* 1967).

No classroom, whether in a university or a public school, should suffer from a "pall of orthodoxy." Threats to teachers' rights to instruct in their subjects in the manner they believe most appropriate have come from many sources. State legislatures that pass laws mandating restrictive curricula (*Meyer v. State of Nebraska,* 1923; *Epperson v. Arkansas,* 1968; *Edwards v. Aguillard,* 1987), schools boards that desire to winnow textbooks because they allegedly contain material or sentiments that conflict with board members' values (*Cary v. Board of Education of Adams-Arapahoe School District 28-J,* 1979; *Board of Education, Island Trees Union Free School District No. 26 v. Pico,* 1982), and parents who insist that classroom teachings adhere to their narrow beliefs (*Stachura v. Memphis Community School District,* 1985; *Mozert v. Hawkins County Board of Education,* 1987; *Smith v. Board of School Commissioners of Mobile County,* 1987) have all been challenged before the courts for attempting to limit academic freedom. The courts, in consistently upholding the rights of teachers, have "[applied] the First Amendment's mandate in our educational system where essential to safeguard the fundamental values of freedom of speech and of inquiry and of belief" (*Epperson v. Arkansas,* 1968).

Ideally, all teachers are capable of determining the best methods, materials, and textbooks to use in transmitting their assigned subject matter to students. However, claiming that teachers may teach anything in public school classrooms, completely free from restraint, is a convolution of the concept of academic freedom. The state, exercising its police powers, has a compelling interest in the welfare of its children and so may regulate to some degree teacher conduct and curriculum content in the classroom. School boards, as the governing bodies for schools, retain the right to establish some regulations to which teachers must adhere. Parents have a fundamental right to guide and direct the education of their children and so may, to a limited extent, impact instruction in schools. Therefore, a teacher may not overstep the reasonable limits of academic freedom as applicable to public schools, limits that have been upheld when challenged in court.

Academic freedom protects teachers from the arbitrary notions of school boards and the community about the content that should be taught in public school classrooms as well as the methods and materials to be used in instruction. Teachers are generally recognized as professionals who have the expertise to transmit knowledge to their students. The protection of academic freedom guarantees their being allowed to practice their profession without undue external interference. However, teachers must realize that academic freedom has some bounds when applied to public schools. Although limited in their control over teacher activities, legislatures, boards of education, parents, and the community have a valid interest in the education of young, impressionable students, and the academic freedom of teachers will be weighed against the competing rights of these others when challenges to teacher materials and methods arise.

Principle II

A teacher has the right to discuss controversial topics, ideas, and philosophies in a classroom as long as the topic is related to the subject matter that the teacher has been assigned to teach.

Teachers in public schools are generally assigned to teach subjects in which they have expertise as evidenced by state certification, college degrees, and experience. Under contract to teach specific curricula, teachers must usually abide by state curriculum guides, state and local textbook committee adoption lists, and district subject matter policies. A public school teacher generally may not deviate from assigned subject matter to delve into unrelated topics because the mission of the school is to transmit knowledge; each teacher contributes to that mission by instructing in his or her assigned area. These expectations may not be used to set unreasonable limits on class discussion of a course subject; students must be able to explore questions and controversies with their teachers in school. However, court cases are brought when teachers discuss controversial topics unrelated to the subject matter they are to be teaching.

Restrictions on discussion of controversial ideas may not limit a teacher's freedom to instruct about new theories or information even if the new body of knowledge conflicts with established beliefs of the community. One of the first important cases in America's quest for academic freedom involved a biology teacher in Tennessee who insisted on teaching the controversial theories of Charles Darwin. William Jennings Bryan and Clarence Darrow argued John Scopes's fate in the "monkey trial," and, in spite of Darrow's "inherit the wind" speech pleading for academic freedom in America's classrooms, Scopes's dismissal was upheld (*Scopes v. State,* 1927).

Although evolution continues to be a debated subject, one of the last antievolution statutes was overturned by the United States Supreme Court in 1968. An Arkansas biology teacher challenged the state statute forbidding the teaching of evolution and mandating the dismissal of teachers who violated the law. The Supreme Court ruled that a state may not prohibit the teaching of a particular segment from a body of knowledge:

> The State's undoubted right to prescribe the curriculum for its public schools does not carry with it the right to prohibit, on pain of criminal penalty, the teaching of a scientific theory or doctrine where that prohibition is based upon reasons that violate the First Amendment (*Epperson v. Arkansas,* 1968).

In 1987 the evolution issue again came before the United States Supreme Court but with a different focus. Louisiana's "balanced treatment" statute required teachers to give instruction in the theory of creation science, as taught in Genesis, whenever the theory of evolution was taught. The Supreme Court ruled the statute unconstitutional because it violated the establishment clause of the First Amendment by promoting a particular type of religion (*Edwards v. Aguillard,* 1987).

Biology is not the only course where controversial topics are part of the generally accepted curriculum. History, government, economics, and civics are among the subjects almost impossible to teach without discussion of events and ideas that give rise to conflicting points of view. In 1974 a Texas civics teacher was accused of introducing controversial topics in his class, including a statement that he was not opposed to interracial marriage. The school board accepted the teacher's argument that avoiding controversy in a senior political science course was impossible, but he was later dismissed. In overturning his termination, the federal district court issued two caveats regarding academic freedom:

1. The freedom of speech of a teacher and a citizen of the United States must not be so lightly regarded that he stands in jeopardy of dismissal for raising controversial issues in an eager but disciplined classroom.
2. However, it must also be that teacher's duty to be exceptionally fair and objective in presenting his personally held opinions, to actively and persuasively present different views, in addition to open discussion. It is the duty of the teacher to be cognizant of and sensitive to the feelings of his students, their parents, and their community (*Sterzing v. Ft. Bend Independent School District,* 1972).

The relationship of the controversial topic to the assigned subject matter is important to the courts in determining if a teacher's rights have been violated. A speech teacher in Milwaukee was dismissed for immoral behavior in 1961 after discussing explicit sexual topics in his class. The Wisconsin Supreme Court upheld the dismissal (*Wasilewski v. Board of School Directors of the City of Milwaukee,* 1961). An Ohio teacher who was in a car accident on the way to school spent time in her Spanish class making derogatory comments about police. Her written reprimand was upheld in court (*Petrie v. Forest Hills School District Board of Education,* 1982). A Montana teacher was dismissed after he made comments in his junior high class that his girlfriend had to move out of his house because people did not like their living arrangements. He also had introduced the subject of abortion, which was not part of his science curriculum, by asking how many of the boys would want their girlfriends to get abortions if they became pregnant, and he had brought an aborted human fetus to class in a plastic bag. The state supreme court upheld his dismissal when the teacher admitted that his teaching performance had been adversely affected by his actions (*Yanzick v. School District No. 23, Lake County, Montana,* 1982).

The courts recognize that the educational process is often facilitated by open discussion of new and sometimes controversial ideas and philosophies. A federal court in Florida explained the role of teachers in guiding such a discussion:

> This Court realizes that from time to time it may be necessary for a school teacher to delve into thought provoking discussions with students that may well concern areas of interest other than English, Biology, American History, or the like. Even then a teacher, above all, has a serious responsibility in that the teacher is guiding a student in the development of his mind and may well leave an immeasurable impact on that student's mind (*Moore v. School Board of Gulf County, Florida,* 1973).

Therefore, teachers should realize that while they are generally free to discuss controversial topics related to their subject matter, they should present more than one side of the issue. Academic freedom allows teachers to explore with students the body of knowledge generally accepted within a course of study, but teachers who overstep reasonable limits set by the state, local board, or professional standards will not prevail in court.

Principle III

A teacher's in-class speech may be restricted when continued utterances will be disruptive to the educational process of the school.

When teachers express themselves in their classrooms, they must be certain the speech does not interfere with the normal operation of the school. In-class speech, verbal or symbolic, unrelated to the course topic and disruptive to the educational atmosphere of the school will not be protected in court by claims of academic freedom. The 1970s saw many cases come to court where teachers claimed that the First Amendment applied to speech within their classrooms. Most of these cases cited *Tinker v. Des Moines Independent Community School District* (1969), in which teachers' constitutional rights to free expression were recognized. The standard generally used by the courts was that of "material and substantial disruption" as established in *Tinker.*

Among the first cases to go before the courts was one brought by a civilian instructor of English at an air force base in Texas. Deriding the United States military role in Vietnam, the teacher said that those who burned themselves to death in protest of the war were the true heroes. When he was dismissed, he claimed that his academic freedom had been infringed and that he had been subjected to anti-Semitism. However, the United States Court of Appeals, District of Columbia, upheld his dismissal (*Goldwasser v. Brown,* 1969).

Using the classroom as a forum to criticize school administrators and policies is often ruled to be disruptive. An English teacher in Illinois spent most of two class periods discussing the school administration's dismissal of the swim coach because he had grown a beard. She stated that the swim team could boycott future meets to show their displeasure. This probationary teacher's dismissal was based on several grounds and was upheld in court (*Robbins v. Board of Education of Argo Community High School District 217,* 1970). In 1972 an economics teacher, who became angry over the way a substitute teacher had handled her class, used the incident as an opportunity to instruct her students in political unrest. She continued to encourage her students to ignore school disciplinary rules even after she was warned several times to return to teaching the subject of economics. The United States Court of Appeals, Eighth Circuit, upheld her dismissal (*Ahern v. Board of Education of School District of Grand Island,* 1972). In a similar case involving a Florida biology teacher who criticized school administrators after they asked him to end his discussions of personal experiences with prostitutes, homosexuals, and masturbation, the court expressed its view of a teacher's right to free speech:

> [The teacher] has the right to criticize his employers and the school administration but is limited in the exercise of that right to the extent that its exercise may not invade the classroom occupied by fifteen year olds and must be balanced against the need for meaningful school administration. . . . It would appear to this Court that criticisms of a school board, Superintendent and school administration in the classroom could well lead students to hold these officials as well as some of their teachers in various degrees of contempt. This is certainly no assistance to the educational processes (*Moore v. School Board of Gulf County, Florida,* 1973).

Teachers who use academic freedom to protect their espousal of personal political or religious views in their classrooms will probably not be supported by the courts. In 1974 a mathematics teacher discussed with his class the presence of army recruiters in the school. He suggested that the students throw apples (which had been distributed by a student organization that morning to promote an unrelated school program) at the recruiters and "get them in a crowd and push them and kick them, make them feel like they [aren't] wanted." He also suggested that the 4,000 students could get the ROTC off their campus if they tried. The United States Court of Appeals, Eighth Circuit, upheld the teacher's dismissal:

> The District Court found that the [teacher's] statements, both in class and in the hallway, interfered with the educational process. The statements were completely irrelevant to [the teacher's] duties of teaching mathematics and diverted the time and attention of both students and teacher from the prescribed curriculum. They embodied, as well, an attempt to defeat a school policy by improper means. But, beyond matters of school policy and curriculum, it was found that [the teacher's] statements were "infused with the spirit of violent action" to the degree that the school authorities found a situation of potential disruption (*Birdwell v. Hazelwood School District,* 1974).

An art teacher in New York was dismissed for using class time to proselyte students to join a religious organization. She urged students to recruit other students, offered transportation to meetings, encouraged Bible reading in class, and preached her religion under the guise of counseling. Her dismissal was upheld in court (*LaRocca v. Board of Education of Rye City School District,* 1978). In 1988 a Pennsylvania science teacher was warned that he must cease from promoting his personal religious views in class. He did not deny the allegations against him and stated that "he was a Christian and that part of his mission was in a sense evangelistic." After several additional incidents, including one where the teacher required a student to pray with him in the hallway as a condition of reentering the classroom, the teacher was dismissed. The court upheld the board's action (*Rhodes v. Laurel Highlands School District,* 1988).

Derogatory epithets uttered by teachers in class will not be supported in court. In 1983 a Nebraska teacher was dismissed for calling black students "dumb niggers" in a racially mixed class. The state high court upheld the midyear dismissal on grounds of immorality:

> Few would argue that calling young black students in a racially mixed classroom "dumb niggers" is not indecent and shameless conduct showing moral indifference to the opinions of respectable members of the community, and as such offends the moral sense of the community, or that such behavior does not directly affect the teacher's fitness to teach. . . . The question . . . is whether it is immoral for a teacher to teach white students that it is all right to engage in conduct which is humiliating, painful, and harmful to individuals, which subjects a class of people to public disdain and ridicule, and which is in violation of rules and regulations adopted by the Board for the purpose of putting an end to racial discrimination. Of necessity, such action must be considered immoral, just as if [the teacher] had instructed the students how to cheat on an examination (*Clarke v. Board of Education of School District of Omaha,* 1983).

Obscene speech will not be upheld in court, as shown by a 1987 case. Although an elementary school teacher in Indiana had an unblemished record for 12 years, her contract was terminated when she directed a common obscene expression at a child who had admittedly been a discipline problem in her class. The court agreed that her action was immoral (*Fiscus v. Board of School Trustees of Central School District of Greene County,* 1987).

Controversial symbolic speech has been upheld by the courts when the teacher's expression has not disrupted the school. Two such cases were heard in the United States Court of Appeals, Second Circuit, which relied on the reasoning of *Tinker* in supporting teachers who had been dismissed. One teacher wore a black armband to school to protest the Vietnam War. He did not discuss the armband in class and no disruption occurred, but the administrators feared that "the armband would tend to be disruptive" (*James v. Board of Education of Central District No. 1,* 1972). Another teacher refused to salute the flag or to recite the Pledge of Allegiance but stood quietly at attention with her arms at her sides when these activities transpired (*Russo v. Central School District No. 1,* 1972).

Therefore, the courts will defend a teacher's exercise of the constitutional right of free speech in classrooms as long as that speech does not materially disrupt the school environment. A Texas federal court expressed the view of most courts:

> The State, through the local school board, has a vital, if not compelling, interest in the welfare of the students. If a classroom speech has a disruptive effect on the students or interferes with discipline in the schools, then the school administration or the board may seek to control a teacher's academic freedom (*Dean v. Timpson Independent School District,* 1979).

Teachers must understand that not everything they say in class will be protected by a claim of academic freedom. Utterances that are unrelated to the subject they are assigned to teach, that are disruptive to the school, that indoctrinate or proselyte students, or that are obscene may result in disciplinary actions that will be upheld in court. At the same time, school boards must recognize that teachers' First Amendment rights of free speech do extend into the classroom.

Principle IV

Within limits imposed by state statutes and board of education policies, a teacher generally has the right to use any textbooks, materials, and teaching methods that relate to the subject matter that the teacher has been assigned to teach. No pornographic, obscene, or other illegal material may be used in a classroom.

The textbooks and materials used by teachers are an integral part of their academic freedom in public schools. Yet, in most states, textbook selection is not the exclusive prerogative of teachers. In some states, the legislature, board of education, or department of education establishes guidelines for textbook selection and compiles lists of approved texts from which local boards or teachers may make their selection. In other states, local school boards establish textbook adoption committees comprised of administrators, teachers, and parents. In few districts are teachers allowed to select any textbook they desire. Supplementary books and materials are generally less controlled but sometimes also face rigorous procedures to gain approval from appropriate committees. Teaching methods are usually less subject to prior scrutiny, but new, experimental, or nontraditional approaches may be questioned by parents and school boards. The courts hesitate to become involved in matters of professional expertise because they prefer that educators make such decisions. Yet, cases have come before the courts when teachers' claims of freedom to use certain books or methods have conflicted with parents' and board members' rights to ensure that children are receiving an appropriate education.

Since the 1960s, constant challenges to teachers' choices of books, materials, and methods have been brought before the courts. One of the first textbook selection cases was heard in 1966 by the United States Court of Appeals, Fourth Circuit, which affirmed the dismissal of a psychology teacher whose offense was assigning *Brave New World* by Aldous Huxley to his classes as a supplementary reading (*Parker v. Board of Education of Prince George's County, Maryland,* 1966). A series of lower court cases beginning in 1969 established legal standards for teachers' academic freedom in the use of materials and methods in the classroom.

In the first case, the teacher assigned an article from *Atlantic Monthly* to his senior English class. The next evening he was called before the school board and asked to defend his use of the article, which contained a vulgar word (one used to mean "an incestuous son"). He was suspended when he refused to agree not to use the article again. The United States Court of Appeals, First Circuit, did not find the word obscene in the context of the article and so supported the teacher:

> The question in this case is whether a teacher may, for demonstrated educational purposes, quote a "dirty" word currently used in order to give special offense, or whether the shock is too great for high school seniors to stand. If the answer were that the students must be protected from such exposure, we would fear for their future. We do not question the good faith of the [board] in believing that some parents have been offended. With the greatest of respect to such parents, their sensibilities are not the full measure of what is proper education (*Keefe v. Geanakos,* 1969).

The next year a case was heard involving an Alabama English teacher who was dismissed for assigning a short story, "Welcome to the Monkey House" by Kurt Vonnegut, Jr., to her junior classes as an outside reading. The next morning the teacher was called into the principal's office where the principal and the assistant superintendent described the story as "literary garbage" that condoned "the killing off of elderly people and free sex." The federal court discussed the academic freedom of the teacher when it ordered her reinstated and the record of her dismissal expunged:

> Although academic freedom is not one of the enumerated rights of the First Amendment, the Supreme Court has on numerous occasions emphasized that the right to teach, to inquire, to evaluate and to study is fundamental to a democratic society.... Since the [board has] failed to show either that the assignment was inappropriate reading for high school juniors, or that it created a significant disruption to the educational processes of this school, this Court concludes that [the teacher's] dismissal constituted an unwarranted invasion of her First Amendment right to academic freedom (*Parducci v. Rutland,* 1970).

The third case that is referenced in many later academic freedom cases was heard in 1971 and affirmed by the United States Court of Appeals, First Circuit. Relating to teaching methods rather than textbooks, this case involved a teacher who wrote a vulgar word on the board in the context of a discussion on taboo words. (The word means "sexual intercourse.") The next day he was suspended for seven days with pay and later was dismissed for conduct unbecoming a teacher. Although the court admitted that such a teaching method might not be appropriate, his dismissal was overturned because he had used the method in good faith and had never been warned not to use it (*Mailloux v. Kiley,* 1971).

The same taboo word was the issue in a Louisiana case of a fifth grade teacher. Concerned over the increasing use of vulgar language by his students, he required two girls to write the word 1,000 times. When dismissed for incompetence, the teacher claimed his academic freedom should protect his choice of disciplinary sanctions, but the court said the First Amendment did not entitle a teacher to require young students to use vulgar words when no educational purpose was served (*Celestine v. Lafayette Parish School Board,* 1973).

The courts have ruled in favor of other teachers and their materials and methods, often citing *Keefe, Parducci,* and *Mailloux.* In 1976 an English teacher, who returned *Catcher in the Rye* by J. D. Salinger to the curriculum over the protests of parents and the instructions of the school board, was dismissed for insubordination. The courts, however, in ruling in her favor, stated it would not support censorship (*Harris v. Mechanicsville Central School District,* 1976). A tenured psychology teacher in Texas was dismissed for using a survey from *Psychology Today* as a supplement to her teaching of sex roles. She had previously been warned by the superintendent and principal about bringing questionable materials into her class. However, the court ordered her reinstated with back pay because she had not violated any policy:

> A teacher has a constitutional right protected by the First Amendment to engage in a teaching method of his or her own choosing, even though the subject matter may be controversial or sensitive (*Dean v. Timpson Independent School District,* 1979).

Another teacher in Texas was dismissed for using a nontraditional simulation exercise to teach post–Civil War history. Because the simulation evoked strong feelings among students on racial issues, she was told not to discuss blacks in American history or anything else controversial. The United States Court of Appeals, Fifth Circuit, overruled her dismissal (*Kingsville Independent School District v. Cooper,* 1980). A Tennessee case arose in 1978 when parents protested the materials used in teaching a life science class even though the textbook had been approved by the school board and the films had been used for several years. The teacher had consulted with and obtained approval for his teaching methods, including the unit on human reproduction, from the principal. In spite of having taken all these precautionary steps, the teacher was dismissed and claims that he was a "sex maniac" were widely publicized. Eventually, the courts found all charges to be false, that he had been suspended without a fair hearing, and that his reputation had suffered from the stigma that accompanied the dismissal. He was awarded $321,000 in damages, although the United States Surpreme Court decreased the amount of damages, ruling that individuals cannot be compensated for the abstract value of their constitutional rights (*Stachura v. Memphis Community School District,* 1985, and *Memphis Community School District v. Stachura,* 1986).

Other methods and materials have not been protected by the First Amendment, even though teachers attempted to claim their academic freedom had been violated when their cases came before the courts. Three junior high teachers in Illinois were dismissed for distributing movie brochures about the 1969 Woodstock rock music festival. The court upheld their dismissals because the brochures contained vulgar pictures and words and promoted positive views of drug use that contradicted state law (*Brubaker v. Board of Education, School District 149, Cook County, Illinois,* 1974). Three nontenured teachers in Wyoming were not rehired because of their use of such unorthodox methods as playing loud rock music and discussing only current events in their classes. The court stated that they did not "have an unlimited liberty as to structure and content of the courses" (*Adams v. Campbell County School District, Campbell County, Wyoming,* 1975). All English teachers in a Colorado district filed suit against the school board when it banned 10 books of 1,285 on a reading list for language arts classes. Although the court said that teachers "cannot be made to simply read from a script prepared or approved by the board," the procedures used by the board had been in line with the collective bargaining agreement and so the board action was upheld (*Cary v. Board of Education of Adams-Arapahoe School District 28-J,* 1979). The Washington Supreme Court ruled that history teachers could be required to teach in a conventional manner when not enough students requested their team-teaching technique to make offering more than one section feasible (*Millikan v. Board of Directors of Everett School District No. 2,* 1980). An Alaska social studies teacher's dismissal for violating the district's book approval policy was upheld. He had used a controversial book as a supplement to a unit on homosexuals even though he had been warned that the policy would be enforced (*Fisher v. Fairbanks North Star Borough School District,* 1985).

Pornographic or obscene materials are not protected under the First Amendment, and teachers who introduce such materials into their classrooms risk serious sanctions. In 1982 a high school photography teacher was dismissed for knowingly showing to his classes pornographic movies which he had filmed. The New York appellate court upheld his dismissal (*Shurgin v. Ambach,* 1982). Another teacher handed out "Fritz the Cat" cartoons to her eighth grade class, not knowing they contained objectionable materials. Upholding the teacher's nine-month suspension without pay, the West Virginia Supreme Court did overturn her dismissal for willful neglect of duty (*DeVito v. Board of Education,* 1984). A language arts teacher, who distributed one of her original short stories that contained objectionable language to her classes, claimed her dismissal violated her academic freedom. However, the court affirmed her dismissal because she was also guilty of neglecting other professional duties (*Harvey v. Jefferson County School District No. R-1,* 1985).

Some teachers have risked their professional careers by showing R-rated videos in their classes. In 1986 a teacher who had taught for 25 years rented a video to show to his fourth and fifth grade classes but admitted in court that he did not know what the *R* meant, as he had not been to a movie for several years. His dismissal for willful neglect of duty was overturned in spite of his having been present and figuring grades while the movie was being shown, apparently oblivious to the profanity in the movie (*Terry v. Houston County Board of Education,* 1986). A Kentucky teacher, who showed an R-rated movie on the last day of class without knowing anything about the movie or previewing it, was dismissed in 1987. She left the room during the movie after asking a student who had seen it to edit the unsuitable parts, which he did by holding up a file folder to cover the 25-inch screen. When confronted by the principal, the teacher claimed the movie had an educational purpose of portraying alienation between people and the repressiveness of the educational system. Her dismissal was upheld, and the United States Supreme Court refused to hear the case (*Fowler v. Board of Education of Lincoln County, Kentucky,* 1987). A nontenured teacher in Illinois was dismissed after showing an R-rated film to her high school English class. The federal district court upheld her dismissal in spite of her claim of violation of First Amendment rights (*Krizek v. Board of Education of Cicero-Stickney Township High School District No. 201, Cook County, Illinois,* 1989).

Cases involving the use of the Bible and other religious materials in public schools have been brought before the courts, beginning with *School District of Abington Township, Pennsylvania v. Schempp* (1963). In this case, the United States Supreme Court ruled that beginning the school day with readings from the Bible violated the establishment clause of the First Amendment, although the court did not state that study of the Bible was always unconstitutional:

> One's education is not complete without a study of comparative religion or the history of religion and its relationship to the advancement of civilization. It certainly may be said that the Bible is worthy of study for its literary and historic qualities. Nothing we have said here indicates that such study of the Bible or of religion, when presented objectively as part of a secular program of education, may not be effected consistently with the First Amendment (*School District of Abington Township, Pennsylvania v. Schempp,* 1963).

In 1983, a federal district court in Virginia overturned a Bible study class but further defined when study of the Bible is appropriate:

> The Supreme Court has recognized the importance of the Bible independent of its religious significance and the influence that this book has had on Western civilization cannot be gainsaid . . . [I]t becomes obvious that a basic background in the Bible is essential to fully appreciate and understand both Western culture and current events (*Crockett v. Sorenson,* 1983).

However, the courts have not upheld teachers' use of the Bible in school as a religious book. The Pennsylvania appellate court upheld the dismissal of an elementary school teacher who had conducted religious activities in his class, including daily reciting of the Lord's Prayer and reading of a Bible story (*Fink v. Board of Education of Warren County School District,* 1982). Teachers, students, and parents in Michigan brought suit against a school superintendent who had directed that religious activities in classrooms be stopped. The federal district court ruled in favor of the superintendent because praying, reading from the Bible, and telling stories with a biblical basis violated the establishment clause (*Breen v. Runkel,* 1985).

When teachers recognize the limits of their choice in textbooks, materials, and methods—limits imposed by statute and policy but often also suggested by professional ethics and common sense—the courts will uphold their First Amendment rights. A balance exists between a teacher's exercise of academic freedom and the rights of others interested in the welfare of children:

> A teacher's methods are not without limits. Teachers occupy a unique position of trust in our society, and they must handle such trust and the instruction of young people with great care. On the other hand, a teacher must not be manacled with rigid regulations, which preclude full adaptation of the course to the time in which we live (*Sterzing v. Ft. Bend Independent School District,* 1972).

Teachers must recognize that their freedom to select textbooks, materials, and methods is sometimes limited because of their importance to the teaching of assigned subjects. Where laws and policies allow, teachers should participate on textbook selection committees and work to ensure that new methods and materials are fully approved before use. School boards should recognize the rights and interests of teachers, as educational experts, in selecting books and materials. Open communication between teachers and parents about the educational value of books and methods will decrease misunderstanding and the likelihood of court challenges brought by parents.

Summary

Academic freedom is a precious right for American educators, a right that must be protected but not abused. For public school teachers, academic freedom does not imply total freedom to pursue truth because teachers of the nation's children hold a different charge than do university professors. To exercise their right to safeguard an educational environment where students may freely inquire and learn and teachers may freely transmit knowledge and teach is a definition of academic freedom for public school teachers.

As society becomes more diverse and the knowledge base expands, more challenges to academic freedom may be anticipated. Old ideas, books, and methods may no longer be applicable, and teachers will be the pioneers for new philosophies and materials. Teachers must be willing to introduce new concepts that are part of the body of knowledge encompassed by the subject they are assigned to teach. Sometimes they may be called upon to defend that subject matter against the parochial prejudice of the local community. School boards and parents have recognized interests in the education of children, but they may not mandate that facts or theories accepted by the greater society be neglected in favor of narrow beliefs.

At the same time, teachers may not ignore laws and policies that regulate the curriculum and how it is handled in the schools. Professional judgment indicates appropriate textbooks and teaching methods to most teachers. Those who desire to overstep professional limits may wrongfully claim protection under academic freedom, and the courts will likely not support such claims.

From the case law defining academic freedom, criteria may be derived for determining when teaching methods and materials are appropriate for public school instruction:

1. Disruption of the class or the normal educational atmosphere of the school must be avoided.
2. Efforts to indoctrinate, proselytize, or propagandize are inappropriate in public schools.
3. The assignment, method, or materials must have educational value.
4. The material or method must be relevant to the curriculum and valid educational objectives of the course.

5. The material or method must be suitable to the age and maturity of the students.
6. Obscene or pornographic materials must never be used in any class.
7. State and local boards of education in most states have the authority to regulate the curriculum in the public schools under their jurisdiction and to reject textbooks, materials, and methods that do not achieve educational purposes. Teachers are obligated to adhere to such statutes and policies provided they do not infringe on individual constitutional rights.

Free speech and academic freedom should be cherished rights to teachers, who have not always enjoyed them. The courts will uphold teachers' rights as long as the teachers themselves exercise these rights in a professional manner, keeping the welfare of the students and the school foremost in their minds.

Questions and Responses

1. What is academic freedom?
Academic freedom has long been an ideal for scholars as they seek the truth, wherever it may be found. However, for public school teachers, academic freedom may be defined as the right to transmit knowledge about assigned subject matter to students in an atmosphere conducive to learning and teaching. Academic freedom has been recognized as a protected right under the free speech clause of the First Amendment.

2. When may a teacher discuss controversial topics in class?
A teacher may discuss controversial topics, ideas, or philosophies in class as long as they pertain to the subject matter the teacher has been assigned to teach. Students should be encouraged to explore new ideas through discussion with teachers and peers in a disciplined classroom. Teachers have an obligation to guide the education of impressionable students in an open, objective manner. Discussing many sides of a controversial topic and avoiding personal opinions will benefit students' educational experiences.

3. When may a teacher's in-class speech be restricted?
A teacher's in-class speech should relate to the subject matter he or she has been assigned to teach. Obscene speech as well as utterances that lead to disruption of the educational process may be restricted. A teacher may not use the students in a classroom as a captive audience for purposes of indoctrinating, preaching, proselyting, or propagandizing.

4. When may a teacher use a classroom as a forum for expressing personal religious views?
Proselyting or mandating religious beliefs or observances is inappropriate behavior on the part of public school teachers. Any speech that may be interpreted as promoting or deriding religion should be avoided. However, the role of religion in the context of such subjects as history, sociology, art, music, or literature may be discussed.

5. When may teachers criticize school administrators or policies in class?
Open criticism of school administrators and policies in class is inappropriate. Inciting students to break school rules, condoning damage to school property, or making derisive comments about the school, other teachers, the school board, or the administration has the potential of disrupting the educational process and could lead to charges of insubordination or improper conduct being levied against the teacher.

6. Why must a teacher follow guidelines from the state regarding textbook selection?
State legislatures and boards of education have a legal responsibility to oversee the education of the children of the state. Therefore, statutes and policies governing textbook selection must be followed by teachers. Rules on textbook selection vary from state to state, and teachers must follow the rules of their particular state.

7. When may a teacher exercise a right to controversial symbolic expression in class?
Symbolic expression is protected under the free speech clause of the First Amendment. As long as the symbolic speech, which may be exercised in such ways as through dress or actions, is not disruptive, a teacher may exercise that right.

8. What are the laws or rules governing pornographic or obscene materials in classrooms?
Pornography and obscenity are not protected by the First Amendment. Therefore, material that may be determined by community standards or professional ethics to be pornographic or obscene should never be used in classrooms. Textbooks or supplementary readings that contain vulgar words should have a valid educational purpose before being used.

9. When may R-rated movies or videos be shown in schools?
Good judgment would normally preclude a teacher from showing an R-rated movie to schoolchildren. The motion picture industry's rating system suggests that persons under the age of 17 not view these films because of the amount of vulgarity, profanity, nudity, or violence. Movies shown in schools should have some identifiable educational purpose. Even movies shown solely for entertainment in a school should adhere to reasonable standards of decency appropriate for the age of the students involved.

10. What criteria should teachers use in selecting textbooks, materials, and methods for use in their classrooms?
Teachers who use the following criteria when selecting books, materials, and teaching methods will ensure that they are not overstepping the limits on academic freedom in public schools:

a. Disruption of the class or the normal educational atmosphere of the school must be avoided.
b. Efforts to indoctrinate, proselytize, or propagandize are inappropriate in public schools.
c. The assignment, method, or materials must have educational value.

d. The material or method must be relevant to the curriculum and valid educational objectives of the course.
e. The material or method must be suitable to the age and maturity of the students.
f. Obscene or pornographic materials must never be used in any class.
g. State and local boards of education in most states have the authority to regulate the curriculum in the public schools under their jurisdiction and to reject textbooks, materials, and methods that do not achieve educational purposes. Teachers are obligated to adhere to such statutes and policies provided they do not infringe on individual constitutional rights.

Case References

Adams v. Campbell County School District, Campbell County, Wyoming, 511 F.2d 1242 (10th Cir., 1975).
Ahern v. Board of Education of School District of Grand Island, 456 F.2d 399 (8th Cir., 1972).
Birdwell v. Hazelwood School District, 491 F.2d 490 (8th Cir., 1974).
Board of Education, Island Trees Union Free School District No. 26 v. Pico, 457 U.S. 853 (1982).
Breen v. Runkel, 614 F.Supp. 355 (W.D.Mich. 1985).
Brubaker v. Board of Education, School District 149, Cook County, Illinois, 502 F.2d 973 (7th Cir., 1974).
Cary v. Board of Education of Adams-Arapahoe School District 28-J, 598 F.2d 535 (10th Cir., 1979).
Celestine v. Lafayette Parish School Board, 284 So.2d 650 (La. App. 1973).
Clarke v. Board of Education of School District of Omaha, 338 N.W.2d 272 (Neb. 1983).
Crockett v. Sorenson, 568 F.Supp. 1422 (W.D. Va. 1983).
Dean v. Timpson Independent School District, 486 F.Supp. 302 (E.D. Tex. 1979).
DeVito v. Board of Education, 317 S.E.2d 159 (W.Va. 1984).
Edwards v. Aguillard, 482 U.S. 578 (1987).
Epperson v. Arkansas, 393 U.S. 97 (1968).
Fink v. Board of Education of Warren County School District, 442 A.2d 837 (Pa.Cmwlth, 1982).
Fiscus v. Board of School Trustees of Central School District of Greene County, 509 N.E.2d 1137 (Ind. App. 1 Dist. 1987).
Fisher v. Fairbanks North Star Borough School District, 704 P.2d 213 (Alaska 1985).
Fowler v. Board of Education of Lincoln County, Kentucky, 819 F.2d 657 (6th Cir., 1987), cert. denied, 484 U.S. 986 (1987).
Goldwasser v. Brown, 417 F.2d 1169 (D.C. Cir., 1969), cert denied, 397 U.S. 992 (1970).
Harris v. Mechanicville Central School District, 382 N.Y.S.2d 251 (1976).
Harvey v. Jefferson County School District No. R-1, 710 P.2d 1103 (Colo. 1985).
James v. Board of Education of Central District No. 1, 461 F.2d 566 (2d Cir., 1972).
Keefe v. Geanakos, 418 F.2d 359 (1st Cir., 1969).
Keyishian v. Board of Regents of the University of the State of New York, 385 U.S. 589 (1967).
Kingsville Independent School District v. Cooper, 611 F.2d 1109 (5th Cir., 1980).
Krizek v. Board of Education of Cicero-Stickney Township High School District No. 201, Cook County, Illinois, 713 F.Supp. 1131 (N.D.Ill. 1989).
LaRocca v. Board of Education of Rye City School District, 406 N.Y.S.2d 348 (App. Div. 1978).
Mailloux v. Kiley, 323 F.Supp. 1387 (D. Mass), aff'd. 448 F.2d 1242 (1st Cir., 1971).
Memphis Community School District v. Stachura, 477 U.S. 299 (1986).
Meyer v. State of Nebraska, 262 U.S. 390 (1923).
Millikan v. Board of Directors of Everett School District No. 2, 611 P.2d 414 (Wash. 1980).

Moore v. School Board of Gulf County, Florida, 364 F.Supp. 355 (N.D. Fla. 1973).
Mozert v. Hawkins County Board of Education, 827 F.2d 1058 (6th Cir., 1987).
Parducci v. Rutland, 316 F.Supp. 352 (M.D. Ala. 1970).
Parker v. Board of Education of Prince George's County, Maryland, 237 F.Supp. 222 (D. Md.), aff'd. 348 F.2d 464 (4th Cir., 1965).
Petrie v. Forest Hills School District Board of Education, 449 N.E.2d 786 (Ohio App. 1982).
Rhodes v. Laurel Highlands School District, 544 A.2d 562 (Pa.Cmwlth. 1988).
Robbins v. Board of Education of Argo Community High School District 217, 313 F.Supp. 642 (N.D. Ill. 1970).
Russo v. Central School District No. 1, 469 F.2d 623 (2d Cir., 1972).
School District of Abington Township, Pennsylvania v. Schempp, 374 U.S. 203 (1963).
Scopes v. State, 289 S.W. 363 (Tenn. 1927).
Shurgin v. Ambach, 436 N.E.2d 1324 (N.Y. App. 1982).
Smith v. Board of School Commissioners of Mobile County, 827 F.2d 684 (11th Cir., 1987).
Stachura v. Memphis Community School District, 763 F.2d 211 (6th Cir., 1985).
Sterzing v. Ft. Bend Independent School District, 376 F.Supp. 657 (S.D. Tex. 1972).
Terry v. Houston County Board of Education, 342 S.E.2d 774 (Ga. App. 1986).
Tinker v. Des Moines Independent Community School District, 393 U.S. 503 (1969).
Wasilewski v. Board of School Directors of the City of Milwaukee, 111 N.W.2d 198 (Wis. 1961).
Yanzick v. School District No. 23, Lake County, Montana, 641 P.2d 431 (Mont. 1982).

Personal Freedoms 8

Historically, teachers have been allowed few of the personal freedoms available to other citizens. Until the post–World War II era, any person who signed a contract to teach in America's public schools simultaneously signed away the right to exercise many individual constitutional freedoms. Since colonial days, teachers have been reprimanded, suspended, dismissed, fined, and jailed for real and imagined violations of public standards. In 1925 John Scopes was in trouble for going dancing on weekends long before he was fired for teaching Darwinism. Among the most frequently cited reasons for teacher dismissal in the 1930s were insubordination, marriage, childbirth, neglect of duty, immorality, rumors of immorality, general unpopularity, unprofessional conduct, and political activity.

By the 1950s, dismissal of teachers based on their private conduct had decreased, primarily because many states began to enact tenure laws. Taking their cue from professors in higher education, public school teachers began to realize that they should not have to choose between employment and exercise of their basic rights. They sought the passage of tenure laws to protect them from dismissal for reasons that violated constitutional freedoms. The 1970s saw a shift in societal views which resulted in several landmark court decisions supporting teachers who were challenging unreasonable dismissal actions.

However, some teachers continue to have problems freely exercising their personal rights. The teacher whose personal conduct conflicts with community expectations of teacher behavior, the teacher who speaks out in contradiction of the popular viewpoint, or the teacher whose social, religious, or political opinions appear unorthodox to the majority may have to struggle to exercise freedoms taken for granted by other citizens. Some school boards and administrators continue to subtly encourage teachers to leave by giving them poor evaluations, transferring them to undesirable schools, assigning them to unpopular classes, or scheduling them to unpleasant extra duties. "Immorality" and "unprofessional conduct"—among other common statutory grounds for teacher dismissal—continue to be used when the propriety of teachers' actions outside of teaching duties is questioned.

Where once they had no advocate, many teachers now turn to the courts when their personal freedoms are threatened. Every state has statutes governing teacher conduct, legislating their personal freedoms, and defining grounds for dismissal. Therefore, most personal freedom cases are heard in state courts, although cases involving constitutional rights may be heard in federal courts. Because so few cases dealing with individual freedoms of teachers have reached the United States Supreme Court, rulings from state and federal courts do not always give clear guidance to teachers or school boards concerned about the exercise of personal freedoms by teachers.

Legal Principles

Principle I *Free Speech*

A public school teacher's speech outside of school on issues of public importance may not be the basis for dismissal or other disciplinary sanction unless the teacher knowingly or recklessly makes false statements or statements that harm the public interest. A teacher who engages in obscene, slanderous, or other speech not protected by the First Amendment may be subject to disciplinary action.

Principle II *Grievances*

A public school teacher's complaints about internal working conditions, policies, or procedures of the school or district may not be protected as an exercise of free speech if a substantial public interest is not involved or if the educational process is disrupted.

Principle III *Politics*

A teacher's political philosophy, affiliation, or speech may not be the basis for dismissal or other disciplinary action. A teacher's political activities may be restricted only if the activities are criminal, disrupt the educational process, or interfere with the teacher's effectiveness in the classroom.

Principle IV *Dress and Grooming*

A teacher's appearance or dress usually may not be restricted unless it disrupts the educational process or interferes with the teacher's effectiveness in the classroom.

Principle V *Private Conduct*

Generally, the personal or social philosophies, creeds, or affiliations of a teacher may not be restricted. The private conduct of a teacher is of no concern to the employing school district unless the conduct interferes with the educational process or the teacher's effectiveness in the classroom.

Principle VI *Criminal Activities*

Dishonest conduct or conviction of a crime or a civil wrongdoing can generally be shown to interfere with a teacher's effectiveness in the classroom, thereby establishing grounds for teacher suspension or dismissal.

Principle VII *Contagious Diseases*

Affliction with a contagious disease may not provide the basis for discrimination against a teacher who is otherwise qualified to continue in his or her teaching position.

Discussion

Principle I

A public school teacher's speech outside of school on issues of public importance may not be the basis for dismissal or other disciplinary sanction unless the teacher knowingly or recklessly makes false statements or statements that harm the public interest. A teacher who engages in obscene, slanderous, or other speech not protected by the First Amendment may be subject to disciplinary action.

Freedom of speech was one of the first unique rights Americans gained after the Revolutionary War, second only to religion as an enumerated guaranteed right. Yet, expression by teachers outside the classroom has traditionally been curtailed because anything they said was assumed to reflect upon the school and influence the attitudes of students. The out-of-class speech most suspect has always been that which is critical of school administration, policies, and procedures. Until the 1960s, a teacher who spoke against the school board or administration was likely to be dismissed for insubordination and disruption of the school process.

In 1964 the United States Supreme Court reviewed a libel case that was later used to support teachers' rights to free speech. In *New York Times Company v. Sullivan* (1964), the court ruled that a public official could recover damages for libel only if the person making the statement showed "actual malice," that is, "with knowledge of its falsity or with reckless disregard of whether it was false or not."

In 1968 this definition was used by the United States Supreme Court in the controlling decision on the rights of teachers to speak freely outside the classroom. An Illinois teacher wrote a letter to the editor denouncing the school administration's use of tax moneys. The school board, after a full hearing, said the letter was "detrimental to the best interests of the schools" and dismissed him. The Supreme Court, in overturning the dismissal, balanced the teacher's rights as a citizen to speak upon matters of public concern with the school's interest in promoting the efficiency of the educational process:

> Free and open debate is vital to informed decision-making by the electorate. Teachers are, as a class, the members of a community most likely to have informed and definite opinions as to how funds allotted to the operation of the schools should be spent. Accordingly, it is essential that they be able to speak out freely on such questions without fear of retaliatory dismissal (*Pickering v. Board of Education of Township High School District 205,* 1968).

The controversial letter, greeted with apathy by everyone except the school board, included several false statements. However, relying on *Times,* the court said that "absent proof of false statements knowingly or recklessly made by him, a teacher's exercise of his right to speak on issues of public importance may not furnish the basis for his dismissal" (*Pickering v. Board of Education of Township High School District 205,* 1968).

Tenure laws generally protect the tenured teacher from dismissal for exercising the right of free speech outside the classroom unless disruption of the school operation occurs. However, probationary teachers or teachers in states and districts with no tenure policy remained vulnerable until the United States Supreme Court ruled that a nontenured teacher cannot be deprived of constitutional rights. Teachers who are not protected by tenure statutes may not be dismissed for exercising their right to free speech unless a public interest is harmed:

> Even though a person has no "right" to a valuable governmental benefit and even though the government may deny him the benefit for any number of reasons, there are some reasons upon which the government may not rely. It may not deny a benefit to a person on a basis that infringes his constitutionally protected interests—especially, his interest in freedom of speech (*Perry v. Sindermann,* 1972).

In the 1970s, the courts often cited *Pickering* and *Perry* in voiding teacher punishments for exercising out-of-class speech rights when such speech had not disrupted the operation of the school system, harmed a public interest, nor interfered with the normal superior-subordinate relationship (*Gieringer v. Center School District No. 58,* 1973; *Adcock v. Board of Education of San Diego Unified School District,* 1973; *Lusk v. Estes,* 1973; *Zoll v. Eastern Allamakee Community School District,* 1978). However, the courts ruled against other dismissed teachers because their actions had disrupted the schools (*Jones v. Battles,* 1970; *Gilbertson v. McAlister,* 1975; *Gray v. Union County Intermediate Education District,* 1975; *Swilley v. Alexander,* 1978).

When teachers began claiming that the exercise of free speech protected them from disciplinary sanction regardless of other conduct in which they had engaged, no matter how unprofessional the conduct, the courts again became involved in defining teachers' rights. The United States Supreme Court's ruling in *Mt. Healthy City School District Board of Education v. Doyle* (1977) solved a problem posed by the *Pickering* decision, which had implied that a school board could not dismiss an employee who had engaged in First Amendment activity even if the board had legitimate reasons that had nothing to do with the protected rights. The *Mt. Healthy* ruling established a standard that first required the teacher to show that his or her speech was protected under the First Amendment. Once the teacher showed that the speech was protected, the burden of proof shifted to the school board to show that the teacher would have been fired regardless of the protected speech. Under this "if but for" standard (if but for the exercise of a protected right, the teacher would have been dismissed), teachers were no longer able to claim absolute protection under the free speech clause.

Teachers' freedom of expression was extended to private communication in 1979. In 1971 a teacher was dismissed for complaining to her principal about the racial segregation policies of the school. The United States Court of Appeals, Fifth Circuit, upheld the dismissal on the grounds that the complaint was private communication not protected under the First Amendment. The United States Supreme Court ruled that private communication is protected and remanded the case for consideration of issues outside the First Amendment. In 1982 the Fifth Circuit Court finally resolved the ten-year-old case by stating the teacher was to be rehired with back pay (*Givhan v. Western Line Consolidated School District,* 1979; on remand, *Ayers v. Western Line Consolidated School District,* 1982).

In the 1980s, free speech claims continued to come before the courts. In a case heard by the United States Court of Appeals, Sixth Circuit, a teacher was dismissed for telling the black principal and assistant principal that she "hated all black folks." Her dismissal was upheld because most of the children in the school were black (*Anderson v. Evans,* 1981). In 1982 the Fifth Circuit Court ruled that threatening to kill the school athletic director did not qualify as protected speech and that the teacher's dismissal was not a violation of the First Amendment (*White v. South Park Independent School District,* 1982). Similarly, a teacher's dismissal for challenging the superintendent to a fistfight and behaving in an "insolent, abusive, loud and out of control" manner was upheld (*Kurlander v. School Committee of Williamstown,* 1983). In New Jersey a school board recognized the right of teachers to speak at public meetings of the board but dismissed a teacher for his sarcastic, disruptive, and belligerent manner. The state superior court upheld the dismissal:

> A board may expect a member of its professional staff to maintain a deportment appropriate to a public meeting of a local government entity. . . . We are satisfied that even if this constituted the sole reason for the local board's decision not to renew [the teacher's] contract, it does not rise to the stature of a violation of First Amendment privileges (*Dore v. Board of Education of Township of Bedminster, Somerset County,* 1982).

A Nebraska school counselor claimed his dismissal was for filing a grievance against district insurance policies. The evidence showed, however, that he had neglected his position by not registering seniors for classes needed for graduation and not notifying parents that their children were not going to graduate. The court ruled his dismissal was unrelated to First Amendment rights (*Bickford v. Board of Education of School District No. 82 of Hall County,* 1983). A junior high principal was dismissed after being warned that he was ineffective as an administrator, difficult to work with, disloyal to the schools, unresponsive and condescending to parents, and intrusive in making unwelcomed and unscheduled visits to parents of black children. However, he claimed his dismissal was impermissible because of its being based on his public refusal to support a bond issue, his complaint to the board about maintenance problems, and his contact with the local news media about enrollment inaccuracies. The United States Court of Appeals, Fifth Circuit, ruled that the dismissal was not in retaliation for his exercise of constitutional rights (*Yielding v. Crockett Independent School District,* 1983).

When teachers are able to show that they were disciplined solely for exercising their right to free speech, the courts will rule in their favor. In 1983 an assistant coach publicly criticized the head football coach for using excessive corporal punishment. Press coverage of his words resulted in community uproar, and the assistant coach was transferred to a less desirable school. The United States Court of Appeals, Eighth Circuit, ruled that his speech was protected because of public interest in the welfare of children (*Bowman v. Pulaski County Special School District,* 1983). A high school principal who spoke in a special board meeting against the transfer of his wife from her position as an English teacher at the high school to the junior high was notified a month later that his contract would not be renewed. The jury concluded that his speech was the major factor in his termination and ruled that he was eligible for reinstatement and back pay (*Lewis v. Harrison School District No. 1,* 1986).

In the *Lewis* decision, the United States Court of Appeals, Eighth Circuit, defined a three-step process, adapted from the *Mt. Healthy* decision, for determining whether or not the dismissal of a teacher is in violation of the First Amendment free speech clause:

1. The court must determine whether the speech is protected under the Constitution.
2. The employee must show that the speech was a substantial or motivating factor in the adverse employment decision.
3. The employer must show that the employment action would have been taken even in the absence of the protected speech (*Lewis v. Harrison School District No. 1,* 1986).

Citing this standard, the courts have ruled in support of some teachers' free speech claims. A group of Arkansas teachers wrote a letter to the state department of education with specific complaints about the failure of the district special education administrator to implement P.L. 94-142 to benefit special education students. Of those who signed the letter, the principal and one teacher were forced to resign, and three other teachers did not have their contracts renewed. The court found the teachers were exercising their First Amendment rights as citizens in regard to matters of public concern—the quality of education in the community and observance of federal policy. Their request for damages from the board was upheld (*Southside Public Schools v. Hill,* 1987). A Chicago librarian was transferred to another school and denied a promotion because of her remarks in a feature news story about the quality of education in the Chicago school system. The federal district court ruled that her comments were of vital public concern and so constitutionally protected. She was awarded damages of $15,000 from the school board and $15,000 from the superintendent in his official capacity to compensate her for emotional distress, humiliation, and injury to her reputation (*Thompson v. Board of Education of the City of Chicago,* 1989).

Teachers have occasionally claimed that their free expression rights were violated when they have been dismissed for speech not protected under the First Amendment. In 1984 a teacher who made harassing phone calls to the principal was dismissed for unbecoming behavior after he was convicted of disorderly behavior. The court upheld the dismissal (*Matter of Tanelli,* 1984). Another teacher was arrested for making obscene phone calls and was terminated when his voice was identified as the one making the calls. However, the jury in the criminal trial acquitted him because evidence was presented to show that the phone company equipment could have malfunctioned in tracing the calls (*Williams v. Southfield School, Inc.,* 1986). Although few cases have arisen, teachers cannot expect greater protection for their speech than that due other citizens. Speech that does not merit constitutional protection if spoken or written by an ordinary citizen will not be protected when the speaker is a teacher.

In summary, the courts have ruled that teachers do not give up their constitutional rights to free speech outside the classroom just because they are teachers. As long as a teacher does not knowingly or recklessly make false statements, disrupt the educational process, or harm a public interest, teachers may speak on any matter of public importance, including school policies that impact the public. Yet, a teacher's constitutionally protected speech cannot be an absolute shield against possible disciplinary action. If a teacher would have been subject to disciplinary action had he or she not exercised the right to free speech, disciplinary sanctions may still apply. Obscene, slanderous, or libelous speech is never protected. Teachers, realizing that they are free to exercise their First Amendment rights to speech and expression, may speak as informed citizens on issues of public importance. School boards and administrators should recognize and safeguard the free speech rights of teachers.

Principle II

A public school teacher's complaints about internal working conditions, policies, or procedures of the school or district may not be protected as an exercise of free speech if a substantial public interest is not involved or if the educational process is disrupted.

A teacher's free speech rights outside the classroom on topics of public interest have been supported by the courts since the 1970s. Even when public concern focused on educational issues and teachers spoke or wrote for or against a board or administrative stance or policy, the courts supported, even encouraged, teachers to exercise their rights to speak as informed citizens. As long as the teacher's expression did not disrupt education or relationships with superiors or colleagues, did not harm the public interest, and was not slanderous, libelous, or obscene, a teacher could speak about internal policies and procedures of the school or district. When some teachers began taking matters regarding the operation of the schools to the public, whether or not the concerns were of public interest, the courts became involved in yet another speech issue.

In 1983 the United States Supreme Court ruled that public employee speech concerning matters of only personal interest was not protected under the First Amendment because no public interest was involved. Although *Connick v. Myers* (1983) did not involve school personnel, the Supreme Court cited *Pickering* when considering whether or not the discharge of an assistant district attorney was in violation of the First Amendment. According to the record, the employee had created a "mini-insurrection" in the department because she was to be transferred. The court concluded that the woman's questionnaire about the district attorney office's employment policies was not a matter of public concern:

> When employee expression cannot be fairly considered as relating to any matter of political, social, or other concern to the community, government officials should enjoy wide latitude in managing their offices, without intrusive oversight by the judiciary in the name of the First Amendment. . . . We hold only that when a public employee speaks not as a citizen upon matters of public concern, but instead as an employee upon matters only of personal interest, absent the most unusual circumstances, a federal court is not the appropriate forum in which to review the wisdom of a personnel decision taken by a public agency allegedly in reaction to the employee's behavior.

> To presume that all matters which transpire within a government office are of public concern would mean that virtually every remark—and certainly every criticism directed at a public official—would plant the seed of a constitutional case. While as a matter of good judgment, public officials should be receptive to constructive criticism offered by their employees, the First Amendment does not require a public office to be run as a roundtable for employee complaints over internal office affairs (*Connick v. Myers,* 1983).

In light of the *Connick* decision, complaints by teachers over the internal policies and procedures of a school or district may not give rise to a First Amendment question. In a case before the United States Court of Appeals, Eleventh Circuit, a social studies teacher complained about the school's collegiate registration process and about teacher assignments, particularly the filling of vacancies in social studies with physical education teachers and coaches. The next year he was assigned to ninth and tenth grade history courses instead of the junior and senior level courses he had traditionally taught. He sued, claiming the course assignments were in retaliation against his exercise of free speech. Citing *Connick,* the court said his speech was not on matters of public concern but only a series of grievances over internal school policies, and his suit was dismissed (*Ferrara v. Mills,* 1986).

In 1988 the United States Court of Appeals, Seventh Circuit, ruled on two cases of alleged violations of free speech rights. In the first case, a probationary industrial arts teacher was asked to resign as the junior varsity basketball coach and was later informed that his teaching contract had been canceled. He claimed that his nonrenewal was in retaliation for remarks made to the local newspaper when he was interviewed about the coaching position. The court ruled that the article had quoted "a self-serving statement on a matter of private concern" and upheld his discharge (*Vukadinovich v. Bartels,* 1988), In the other case, the transfer of an Illinois teacher was ruled not to have been motivated by his sarcastic memoranda directed to school officials; the subject matter of the notes was not of public concern (*Hesse v. Board of Education of Township High School District No. 211, Cook County, Illinois,* 1988).

Free speech claims became complex in the 1980s. For example, in 1985 a teacher-coach was allegedly given negative evaluations, denied a day of personal leave, removed as assistant baseball coach, and transferred to an elementary school position because he spoke directly to the school board about his concerns instead of following school district policy of taking complaints to the superintendent first. His concerns involved his classroom assignments, his evaluations, the district grievance procedures, inequitable mileage allowances, and inadequate liability insurance for coaches. The United States Court of Appeals, Seventh Circuit, determined that some of the teacher's complaints involved public concerns and some, notably classroom assignments and evaluations, did not. The policy requiring all complaints to be channeled through the superintendent was ruled to be an improper restriction on speech. The court's decision required the teacher's record to be expunged, the teacher to be reinstated to his former teaching and coaching positions, and compensatory damages to be paid him. However, the appellate court remanded the damage award to the district court because it found $514,333 excessive, advising an amount between $200,000 and $400,000 (*Knapp v. Whitaker,* 1985).

In 1989, the United States Court of Appeals, Fourth Circuit, ruled that a teacher's letter to the editor in the school newspaper addressed a matter of public concern because it was in reply to allegations of sexual discrimination in the physical education department. The case was remanded for purpose of determining if the letter entitled the teacher to First Amendment protection from a negative evaluation and resulting loss of his increment pay raise (*Seemuller v. Fairfax County School Board,* 1989).

Therefore, before a teacher's speech will be protected by the First Amendment, it must be more than a complaint or grievance about the operation of the school or district on matters of interest only to the teacher. A substantial public interest must be involved. Teachers must realize that the courts have established a stricter standard under *Connick* than was available under *Pickering* and take private concerns through proper administrative channels, not to the public, for resolution. However, matters that are of public interest may be properly brought to the attention of the people by teachers, and school boards and administrators should realize that the use of a public forum for such concerns is a proper exercise of free speech rights by teachers.

Principle III

A teacher's political philosophy, affiliation, or speech may not be the basis for dismissal or other disciplinary action. A teacher's political activities may be restricted only if the activities are criminal, disrupt the educational process, or interfere with the teacher's effectiveness in the classroom.

The political activities of teachers have often been embroiled in legal conflict. The First Amendment gives the right to assemble peaceably, which has been extended to include the right to associate with groups of one's choice. Political activities are thus protected by the Constitution, as demonstrated when the Sedition Act of 1778 was declared unconstitutional because it conferred a penalty upon those who criticized the government and public officials. Traditionally, public employees, including schoolteachers, have been curbed from participation in partisan political activity. This philosophy was espoused by Justice Oliver Wendell Holmes who, as a member of the Massachusetts Supreme Court, upheld the dismissal of a city policeman who had solicited support for a political candidate: "The petitioner may have a constitutional right to talk politics, but he has no constitutional right to be a policeman" (*McAuliffe v. Mayor of City of New Bedford,* 1892). Bans on partisan political speeches and activities within the classroom have been upheld in court (*Goldsmith v. Board of Education of Sacramento City High School District,* 1924), but statutes forbidding teachers from exercising their political rights as citizens outside of school are being successfully challenged by teachers who represent a cross-section of American political ideology.

The legal history of the political activity issue would be shorter and simpler had the precedent of the earliest cases been followed. In 1884 the political activity of a superintendent of schools in Virginia resulted in his dismissal. However, the Supreme Court of Appeals of Virginia struck down the statute that prohibited teacher participation in politics (*Louthan v. Commonwealth,* 1884).

Throughout the twentieth century, the United States has faced threats to its national security. Fears that the country could be infiltrated by those with ideas inimical to democratic ideals and that the government could be overthrown by subversives have led to attempts to restrict political rights. School children have seemed particularly vulnerable to being influenced by anti-American propaganda from their teachers. Therefore, many teachers, as well as other public officials, have been forced to sign elaborate loyalty oaths and to declare their membership in or association with all organizations; refusal to cooperate has been termed evidence of guilt, and nonsigners have risked losing their jobs.

During the 1940s and 1950s, cold war fears of socialism and communism resulted in government-sanctioned actions to identify teachers, professors, labor leaders, military personnel, and movie producers whose political views might be "un-American." In 1952, the United States Supreme Court upheld a New York statute that precluded members of organizations advocating the overthrow of the government by force from holding positions in public schools. The teacher claimed that the law was an abridgment of his right to free speech and assembly, but the Supreme Court disagreed:

> It is clear that [persons employed in the public schools of the State] have the right under our law to assemble, speak, think and believe as they will. . . . It is equally clear that they have no right to work for the State in the school system on their own terms. . . . They may work for the school system upon the reasonable terms laid down by the proper authorities. . . . If they do not choose to work on such terms, they are at liberty to retain their beliefs and associations and go elsewhere. Has the State then deprived them of any right to free speech or assembly? We think not (*Adler v. Board of Education of City of New York,* 1952).

This ruling influenced teacher associations, loyalty oaths, and political activities for the next 15 years, although other cases were successfully argued in favor of teachers and their free speech and association rights (*Wieman v. Updegraff,* 1952; *Sweezy v. New Hampshire,* 1957; *Shelton v. Tucker,* 1960; *Cramp v. Board of Public Instruction of Orange County,* 1961; *Baggett v. Bullitt,* 1964; *Elfbrandt v. Russell,* 1966). By 1967 most loyalty oaths had been overturned, and the United States Supreme Court was ready to reject the *Adler* rationale. Three teachers filed suit after being dismissed for refusing to sign certificates avowing they had never been members of the Communist party. Influenced by Justice William O. Douglas's dissent in *Adler,* the Supreme Court struck down the New York statute. *Keyishian v. Board of Regents of the University of the State of New York* (1967) became the authoritative voice in rejecting guilt by association for teachers, as it distinguished mere membership in a controversial organization from participation in unlawful activities.

Loyalty oaths *per se* are not unconstitutional and can be prerequisite to employment, as illustrated by the Presidential Oath of Office and rulings from the United States Supreme Court (*American Communications Association v. Douds,* 1950). Pledges to bear allegiance to the government and sustain the constitutions of federal and state governments have been upheld (*Knight v. Board of Regents of University of State of New York,* 1967; *Hosack v. Smiley,* 1967; *Ohlson v. Phillips,* 1969; *Schmid v. Lovette,* 1984). The courts have struck down negative oaths or those that prohibit certain actions and imply the recision of constitutional rights. In *Connell v. Higginbotham* (1971), the United States Supreme Court upheld the first clause in the Florida oath:

"I do hereby solemnly swear or affirm that I will support the Constitution of the United States and of the State of Florida." The following clause was declared unconstitutional: ". . . and that I do not believe in the overthrow of the Government of the United States or of the State of Florida by force or violence." However, the United States Supreme Court reaffirmed the right of a state to require a loyalty oath when it upheld the following oath in 1972:

> I do solemnly swear (or affirm) that I will uphold and defend the Constitution of the United States of America and the Constitution of the Commonwealth of Massachusetts and that I will oppose the overthrow of the government of the United States of America or of this Commonwealth by force, violence or by any illegal or unconstitutional method (*Cole v. Richardson,* 1972).

The rulings in many of these cases affirm that mere membership in organizations may not result in disciplinary action although participation in illegal activities conducted by an organization would not be protected. In the *Keyishian* decision, the United States Supreme Court clearly differentiated between belief and action:

> Under our traditions beliefs are personal and not a matter of mere association, and . . . men in adhering to a political party or other organization . . . do not subscribe unqualifiedly to all of its platforms or asserted principles.
>
> A law which applies to membership without the "specific intent" to further the illegal aims of the organization infringes unnecessarily on protected freedoms. It rests on the doctrine of "guilt by association" which has no place here (*Keyishian v. Board of Regents of the University of the State of New York,* 1967, quoting *Schneiderman v. United States,* 1943, and *Elfbrandt v. Russell,* 1966).

Many cases that have arisen over First Amendment rights of association have involved political activity within school districts rather than over state or national issues. Because of teachers' inherent interests in school issues, the courts have generally upheld teachers' rights to be involved in school district politics and have ruled against attempts to foreclose those rights. Retaliatory action against teachers who support candidates for the school board has not been upheld in most cases (*Guerra v. Roma Independent School District,* 1977; *Miller v. Board of Education of the County of Lincoln,* 1978; *Childers v. Independent School District No. 1 of Bryan County, State of Oklahoma,* 1982).

In 1985 the United States Court of Appeals, Eleventh Circuit, ruled that a teacher, who claimed his dismissal violated his constitutional rights, was entitled to a hearing in court whether or not he had pursued administrative relief. The teacher alleged that his political activity in running for superintendent and advocating a change in the method of selecting school board members had led to his dismissal (*Holley v. Seminole County School District,* 1985). In 1986 a guidance counselor who was not reemployed after 11 years in the district claimed the dismissal was in retaliation for his support of a recall petition against three board members and his opposition to the election of the superintendent. Although the district alleged they needed only one guidance counselor and he was the less senior, the court called the action a "sham" and required the teacher to be reinstated with back pay (*Claiborne County Board of Education v. Martin,* 1986).

Teachers who have become involved in teacher organizations have occasionally had their First Amendment rights violated when association views and activities conflicted with those of the board or administration. The California Supreme Court ruled that the teachers' union could circulate petitions protesting cutbacks in educational funds and calling for a restructure of the tax formula (*Los Angeles Teachers Union, Local 1021, American Federation of Teachers v. Los Angeles City Board of Education,* 1969). Distribution of letters protesting a proposed teacher competency testing program had to be allowed by the school board in an Alabama case (*Hall v. Board of School Commissioners of Mobile County, Alabama,* 1982). In 1986 a teacher was discharged for insubordination after she became active in the teachers' association and criticized the school administration. The United States Court of Appeals, Eighth Circuit, overturned her dismissal (*Cox v. Dardanelle Public School District,* 1986).

The right of teachers to organize was challenged in a 1981 Illinois case when the teachers formed an affiliate of the National Education Association (NEA). The superintendent took the organization of the teachers as a personal attack, even though he also belonged to the NEA. The association was denied permission to meet in the school, and members were prohibited from talking about association business on school premises during school hours and from using the faculty mailboxes for communication. The faculty senate was abolished, and some teachers were deprived of summer program employment. New "supervisor" positions were created, but no association member was named to one of the new positions. The courts ruled the administration guilty of violating First Amendment rights of association and free speech (*Lake Park Education Association v. Board of Education of Lake Park High School District No. 108, DuPage County, Illinois,* 1981).

Therefore, protected political freedoms involve all levels of politics from national and state partisan politics to teacher organizations and local political issues. School boards must be just as careful to protect political rights on the local level as on the state or national level. Teachers must avoid influencing students with political propaganda, but they may freely participate in the political process as citizens outside of school. School boards should ensure that improperly worded loyalty oaths and rules about disclosure of association ties have been rescinded in accordance with court rulings and recognize the rights of teachers to associate with controversial groups. In the emotional mood of a McCarthy era, a Vietnam War, or the organization of a local teachers' union, school boards must evaluate objectively the regulations affecting the political activities of teachers and preserve their constitutional rights.

Principle IV

A teacher's appearance or dress usually may not be restricted unless it disrupts the educational process or interferes with the teacher's effectiveness in the classroom.

Because dress and grooming standards for teachers were not an important issue in public schools before the 1960s, court challenges to such standards are not prevalent. However, a few cases arose at the same time student dress codes were being tested in courts. Two types of cases have been brought before the courts: those involving contemporary dress and grooming fads and those involving religious clothing. Only a few cases concerning teachers' rights to determine their own grooming and appearance standards have been heard in appellate courts, and the United States Supreme Court has refused to hear dress code cases for students or teachers.

Many of these cases involve the right of male teachers to wear beards, mustaches, sideburns, and hair longer than the styles preferred by most men at the time. One of the first cases involved a California teacher who wore a beard in violation of the principal's personal administrative policy and so was assigned to home teaching. The court, relying on liberty claims under the Fourteenth Amendment and symbolic expression rights under the First Amendment, ordered the teacher reinstated, saying, "The wearing of a beard is a form of expression of an individual's personality" (*Finot v. Pasadena City Board of Education,* 1967). A Massachusetts teacher was suspended for insubordination and failure to set a proper example when he grew a beard in violation of an unwritten policy. The court did not rule on the teacher's right to wear a beard but said his right could not be taken away without due process (*Lucia v. Duggan,* 1969).

A person who wears a beard or hairstyle that reflects ethnic, racial, or religious values or beliefs may be entitled to more protection than a person whose choice of grooming is simply personal preference. In 1969 the only black teacher in a Florida high school was dismissed when he refused to shave off his beard. In court the board was unable to show that the teacher's goatee had caused disruption of the educational process. The teacher was to be reinstated because his Fourteenth Amendment liberty rights and First Amendment freedom of expression rights had been denied:

> The wearing of a beard by a teacher has been held to be a constitutionally protected liberty under the due process clause of the fourteenth amendment to the Constitution of the United States . . . and the wearer of the goatee here involved deserves no less protection; furthermore where, as here, it is worn as an "appropriate expression of his heritage, culture and racial pride as a black man" its wearer also enjoys the protection of first amendment rights (*Braxton v. Board of Public Instruction of Duval County, Florida,* 1969).

Following these cases, the courts usually decided in favor of teachers on the basis of liberty, expression, due process, and equal protection rights. After 1972, though, the courts started ruling more frequently in favor of school boards, showing reluctance to interfere with the educational responsibilities of local boards. The constitutional rights of teachers were recognized but deemed "frivolous" compared with school boards' interests in maintaining local control of educational decisions (*Morrison v. Hamilton County Board of Education,* 1973; *Miller v. School District No. 167, Cook County, Illinois,* 1974). For example, in a 1982 Louisiana case, a dress code prohibiting the wearing of beards was extended to all school employees. The United States Court of Appeals, Fifth Circuit, acknowledged a constitutional liberty interest in choosing one's hairstyle but ruled that grooming may be regulated if policies are reasonable:

> Here, the school board has made a quite rational determination to limit its employees' choice of hairstyle, and we therefore will not intervene. In the high school environment, a hairstyle regulation is a reasonable means of furthering

> the school board's undeniable interest in teaching hygiene, instilling discipline, asserting authority, and compelling uniformity (*Domico v. Rapides Parish School Board,* 1982).

As dress styles became casual in the 1960s, teachers claimed the right to wear clothes of their personal choice, a right that was sometimes challenged by administrators and school boards asserting that teachers should be role models of decorum for students. In 1969 a Louisiana teacher refused to wear a tie, as required by school board policy. The court refused to substitute its judgment for that of the board because the purpose of the rule—to enhance the professional image of teachers—was not unreasonable (*Blanchet v. Vermilion Parish School Board,* 1969). A high school teacher who wore miniskirts was not rehired, and the court refused to extend constitutional protection to clothing preferences (*Tardif v. Quinn,* 1976). A Connecticut teacher argued that his refusal to wear a coat and tie was protected as a form of symbolic expression under the First Amendment. However, the United States Court of Appeals, Second Circuit, said that such an argument would "trivialize the Constitution" (*East Hartford Education Association v. Board of Education of the Town of East Hartford,* 1977).

With the conservative shift in clothing and hairstyles in the 1970s, the controversy over dress and grooming standards quieted. The issue is not settled, however, and school boards that believe dress codes are necessary should review them for fairness and their rational relationship to the school's educational goals. Personal preference should not be a part of grooming and appearance standards set by school boards or administrators. At the same time, teachers should realize that extreme styles that cause a commotion in school will probably not be protected by any alleged constitutional right.

Clothing and hairstyles worn to adhere to religious mandates or to symbolize religious beliefs introduce different issues from those that arise when teachers choose styles at odds with traditional dress and grooming standards. The right to free exercise of religious beliefs is generally claimed by teachers who wear distinctive religious clothing to public schools.

The first cases addressing this issue involved Roman Catholic nuns and priests who taught in public schools. In districts with no policy to the contrary, the courts have ruled that clergymen and nuns, like all teachers, may dress as they please (*Hysong v. School District of Gallitzin Borough,* 1894; *Gerhardt v. Heid,* 1936; *State ex rel. Johnson v. Boyd,* 1940; *New Haven v. Torrington,* 1945; *Rawlings v. Butler,* 1956; *Moore v. Board of Education,* 1965). However, school policies that forbid the wearing of religious clothing have been upheld (*O'Connor v. Hendrick,* 1906; *Commonwealth v. Herr,* 1910; *Zellers v. Huff,* 1951).

Since the 1960s, the cases concerning religious dress have involved members of Far Eastern, Muslim, Sikh, and Hare Krishna sects, whose traditional garb may cause comment and questions about religious beliefs that skirt the separation of church and state issue. In 1986 the Oregon Supreme Court heard a case brought by a teacher whose certificate was revoked for violating Oregon's statute forbidding the wearing of religious dress while teaching. The teacher had become a Sikh, married, changed her name from Janet Cooper to Karta Kaur Khalsa, and donned the white clothes and white turban required by her new religion. The court upheld the revocation of her certificate on the grounds that the teacher's religious dress would be an "inescapable visual reminder" of the teacher's religious commitment and violate the children's free exercise of religion:

> [The law's] concern is that the teacher's appearance in religious garb may leave a conscious or unconscious impression among young people and their parents that the school endorses the particular religious commitment of the person whom it has assigned the public role of teacher. This is what makes the otherwise privileged display of a teacher's religious commitment by her dress incompatible with the atmosphere of religious neutrality that [the law] aims to preserve (*Cooper v. Eugene School District No. 4J,* 1986).

No court has ruled the wearing of small decorative or symbolic caps, badges, or jewelry impermissible. A small Christian cross, a Star of David, a Muslim fez, a Mennonite cap, or a Jewish *yarmulke* would probably cause no disruption of the school and so violate no religious right. Teachers who insist on wearing "exotic" religious garb, as the court described the teacher's dress in *Cooper,* may be asked to dress more traditionally.

Therefore, teachers generally have the right to dress for school in the clothing and grooming style most comfortable for them as long as no disruption of the school occurs and the teacher's classroom performance is not hampered. However, reasonable school board regulations will generally be upheld because the courts have ruled dress and grooming issues too trivial for court review. Teachers who belong to religious sects with strict dress requirements may have to determine whether or not their religious clothing will detract from the educational process, but school boards may not make regulations against religious clothes or any other style of dress or hairstyle simply because of personal preference.

Principle V

Generally, the personal or social philosophies, creeds, or affiliations of a teacher may not be restricted. The private conduct of a teacher is of no concern to the employing school district unless the conduct interferes with the educational process or the teacher's effectiveness in the classroom.

Even though the Constitution does not specifically mention a right of privacy, the United States Supreme Court has noted that privacy is a fundamental right and that "the First Amendment has a penumbra where privacy is protected from governmental intrusion" (*Griswold v. Connecticut,* 1965). Teachers whose lives have long been an open, public record may now claim a legal right to privacy. Although most teachers may no longer feel as though they live in a fishbowl, the number of court cases contesting dismissal for personal misconduct bears out the contention that teachers often enjoy less freedom in their private lives than do other citizens.

Personal and social beliefs, affiliations, and conduct should seldom have negative consequences for teachers, but sometimes those who desire to exercise their constitutional rights have to turn to the courts to ensure that community expectations for teacher conduct do not infringe upon teacher rights. The courts often insist that a nexus, or connection, must exist between the teacher's personal misconduct and the effectiveness of his or her classroom performance before the conduct may lead to disciplinary sanctions.

Teachers once were primarily young, unmarried women who expected to lose their teaching jobs as soon as they married. The rules governing out-of-school conduct of teachers were so strict that dating and courting were nearly impossible without the entire community taking the role of chaperon. A breach of village standards of morality usually left the schoolteacher with neither a job nor a husband. "Immorality" and "rumors of immorality" have long been labels for sexual misconduct even though definitions have changed over time. In the 1880s mere suspicion of immoral behavior was reason to dismiss a teacher (*Tingey v. Vaughn,* 1885). Now, however, teachers often question dismissals based on charges of immorality because shifting attitudes and values of society have blurred the definition of "immorality."

Traditionally, a couple living together without marriage were committing fornication, which was illegal as well as immoral and never condoned by society, much less by a school board. However, court standards have changed because of or in spite of community standards. Card playing, obesity, not going to church, and rumors of cohabitation were reasons for a Wyoming school board to dismiss a teacher for immorality in 1979. However, the United States Court of Appeals, Tenth Circuit, ordered her reinstated and awarded her $33,000 in back pay (*Stoddard v. School District No. 1, Lincoln County, Wyoming,* 1979).

Another teacher, dismissed for living with her boyfriend, claimed the Missouri immorality statute was too vague. The court, ruling the law constitutional but finding no relationship between the teacher's behavior and her job performance, ordered her reinstated (*Thompson v. Southwest School District,* 1980). In 1984 a Florida court overturned a school board's decision to deny a contract to a teacher who had lived with a male friend while her trailer was being repaired:

> We are led to conclude . . . that private, off-campus conduct ostensibly involving a consensual sexual relationship between a teacher and an adult of the opposite sex cannot, in and of itself, provide "good cause" for a school board's rejection of a teacher nominated for employment by the superintendent unless it is shown that such conduct adversely affects the ability to teach.
>
> The Board's action . . . strongly suggests that in . . . denying [the teacher] a continuing contract . . . the Board was concerned more with what it considered to be an affront to its members' own personal moral standards, than with [the teacher's] possible adverse effects on the students (*Sherburne v. School Board of Suwannee County,* 1984).

Pregnancy out of wedlock was once considered proof of illicit behavior, and pregnant single teachers were automatically dismissed and shunned by a condemning society. Most cases now indicate that unless an unwed pregnant teacher's conduct negatively affects her classroom performance, she probably cannot be dismissed. In 1982 the United States Court of Appeals, Fifth Circuit, stated that "the school board offered no support for the assertion that unwed parenthood is *per se* proof of immorality and that a parent of an illegitimate child is an unfit role model" (*Avery v. Homewood City Board of Education,* 1982).

In 1986 an unmarried teacher who became pregnant had her pay cut, was removed as adviser to the student council and cheerleader squad, was not allowed to organize fund-raisers or field trips, and was not allowed to attend graduation exercises. When she decided to raise her child as a single mother, she was discharged. In ruling for the teacher, the trial court awarded her $2,000,000 in compensatory damages, which the appellate court dropped to $750,000. Punitive damages of $10,000 to $500,000 per person were levied against individual board members (*Eckmann v. Board of Education of Hawthorn School District No. 17,* 1986).

Although sexual relationships between teachers and other adults of the opposite sex may no longer provide grounds for a teacher's automatic dismissal, sexual misconduct involving teachers with students is almost always regarded in a much stricter light. Almost all cases of sexual misconduct of teachers with students, including a teacher's allowing sexual harassment of one student by other class members and a teacher's dating a student with parental approval, have been resolved against the teacher (*Potter v. Kalama Public School District No. 402,* 1982; *Clark v. Ann Arbor School District,* 1983; *Shipley v. Salem School District 24J, Marion County,* 1983; *Welch v. Board of Education of Chandler Unified School District No. 80 of Maricopa County,* 1983; *Katz v. Ambach,* 1984; *Lewis v. East Feliciana Parish School Board,* 1984; *Libe v. Board of Education of Twin Cedars Community School District,* 1984; *Lile v. Hancock Place School District,* 1985; *Board of Education of Santa Fe Public Schools v. Sullivan,* 1987).

Homosexual behavior between consensual adults has not traditionally been accepted as an appropriate lifestyle for teachers in most communities. Until homosexuals began claiming their constitutional rights on many fronts, homosexual teachers stayed "in the closet," knowing they would be dismissed if their beliefs or actions were known. Legal trends in cases involving homosexual teachers show the courts moving with societal trends in granting more constitutional rights to homosexuals. Before "immorality" or "moral turpitude" may be charged against a homosexual teacher and lead to dismissal, the school district must show that the teacher's classroom effectiveness has been impaired because general knowledge about his or her lifestyle has disrupted the school. The case that solidified the concept of "nexus" in cases concerning teachers' personal conduct was *Morrison v. State Board of Education* (1969), in which a teacher was reinstated because one past isolated incident of homosexual behavior was said by the court to have no connection to his current job performance.

In Oregon a lesbian teacher was reinstated when the court agreed that the immorality statute on which she was dismissed was unconstitutionally vague (*Burton v. Cascade School District Union High School No. 5,* 1973). This case has been cited in other attempts to claim some statutory grounds for teacher dismissal unconstitutional for reason of vagueness, but few have prevailed with this argument.

Another case came to trial in 1974 involving a teacher who was transferred to a nonteaching position and eventually denied a new contract because of his being homosexual; he took his case to the news media, appearing on CBS's "60 Minutes." Even though the court denied the teacher his position on other grounds, the case set precedent for homosexual teacher cases:

> The time has come today for private, consenting adult homosexuality to enter the sphere of constitutionally protectable interests. Intolerance of the uncon-

> ventional halts the growth of liberty (*Acanfora v. Board of Education of Montgomery County,* 1973).

In 1977 a teacher, who was arrested but never charged with public lewd conduct after allegedly soliciting a police officer, was discharged after he told his principal about the incident. The court found no reason to believe him unfit to teach and ordered him reinstated with back pay (*Board of Education of Long Beach Unified School District of Los Angeles County v. Jack M.,* 1977). However, in another 1977 case, a teacher was dismissed for immoral conduct after telling a student he had been a homosexual for 20 years. During the trial for reinstatement, the court held that the teacher's conduct was immoral because the teacher obviously thought so himself or he would not have kept his homosexuality secret for 20 years. According to this court, a known homosexual's fitness to teach was impaired to the point to justify his discharge (*Gaylord v. Tacoma School District No. 10,* 1977).

In 1984 the United States Court of Appeals, Tenth Circuit, heard the National Gay Task Force's challenge to Oklahoma's state statute that provided for the dismissal or suspension of teachers who engaged in public homosexual activity. The court ruled as follows on each section of the law:

1. There was no constitutional problem with teachers being refused employment, dismissed, or suspended for homosexual activity.
2. The definition of public homosexual activity was not unconstitutionally vague.
3. Classification based on choice of sexual partners was not suspect and so was not subject to strict scrutiny by the courts.
4. The portion of the statute that allowed punishment of teachers for advocacy of public or private homosexual activity was unconstitutionally overbroad (*National Gay Task Force v. Board of Education of City of Oklahoma City,* 1984).

Therefore, current cases indicate that homosexual teachers are generally not guaranteed reinstatement if dismissed on grounds of immorality because of their sexual conduct. However, a connection between teacher conduct and adverse job performance must usually be made before dismissal will be upheld by the courts.

The issue of who sets standards for teacher morality arose when a teacher was dismissed for immorality in the form of engaging in homosexual actions in an arcade booth that had public access in an adult bookstore. The Supreme Court of Oregon remanded the case to the Fair Dismissal Appeals Board, stating that the Board was not to determine whether the teacher's conduct was "immoral" by reference to vague "community moral standards" but was to exercise its own judgment:

> Difficult issues arise if the law is viewed as incorporating moral standards of private individuals or social groups external to the agency to which the legislature has delegated the duty to interpret and apply the statutory standard. Among these issues are whether "immorality" refers to what people profess or what they do, and what part of the public is entitled to set standards of morality

> for the population as a whole. There are issues whether "immorality" refers to conduct that those admitted to the standard-setting "public" consider immoral for themselves, or more particularly for their children, or for school teachers (*Ross v. Springfield School District No. 19,* 1986).

However, community standards generally still determine court attitudes and subsequent rulings, resulting in different court rulings in similar cases in different jurisdictions. In many areas of the country, teachers are still viewed as role models, and violation of their exemplar responsibility is enough to establish nexus between a teacher's personal conduct and job performance. On the issue of teachers' rights of personal conduct, no clear guidelines emerge because no major case has reached the United States Supreme Court. As society becomes more liberal, the courts seem to be moving toward enforcing fewer restraints on teacher behavior. With the exception of misconduct with students, immoral conduct must usually be shown to have an adverse effect on job performance before most courts today will uphold a teacher's discharge:

> The private conduct of a man, who is also a teacher, is a proper concern to those who employ him only to the extent it mars him as a teacher, who is also a man. Where his professional achievement is unaffected, where the school community is placed in no jeopardy, his private acts are his own business and may not be the basis of discipline (*Jarvella v. Willoughby-Eastlake City School District Board of Education,* 1967).

The issue of teacher privacy will continue to come before the courts as traditional values, attitudes, and morés are questioned. That teachers have rights as private citizens is well established in theory; however, when individual conduct and community values clash, teachers' rights may often still be abridged for the sake of larger state interests. Administrators and school board members should be aware of state statutes and pertinent court decisions when attempting to establish restraints on the private lives of teachers.

Principle VI

Dishonest conduct or conviction of a crime or a civil wrongdoing can generally be shown to interfere with a teacher's effectiveness in the classroom, thereby establishing grounds for teacher suspension or dismissal.

Society has long held that teachers should be proper role models for children and set the example by perfect decorum both in and out of the classroom. Therefore, teachers have been dismissed for "immorality" or "conduct unbecoming a teacher" when they have broken laws or trampled on the oblique morés of the community. Traditionally, courts accepted the premise that any conduct that breached the law was grounds for a teacher's dismissal. However, teachers are beginning to challenge the idea that their actions off campus, even if in violation of the law, have a relationship to their effectiveness in the classroom.

A community's sensitivity about appropriate teacher behavior was easily offended prior to the 1960s. In 1939 a teacher who worked during holidays in her husband's restaurant as a bartender was dismissed for incompetency and immorality because she was seen playing pinball and shaking dice for drinks. Her dismissal was upheld (*Horosko v. Mt. Pleasant Township School District,* 1939).

At one time a teacher's drinking of an alcoholic beverage would have been sufficient to justify dismissal. Now, alcohol abuse, often as evidenced by "driving while intoxicated" charges, may or may not result in dismissal of a teacher (*Lindgren v. Board of Trustees, High School District No. 1,* 1976; *Turk v. Franklin Special School District,* 1982). However, the dismissal of a teacher for using alcohol on school premises during the school day was upheld by the North Carolina Supreme Court:

> We do not hesitate to conclude that these men and women are intended by parents, citizenry, and lawmakers alike to serve as good examples for their young charges. Their character and conduct may be expected to be above those of the average individual not working in so sensitive a relationship as that of teacher to pupil. It is not inappropriate or unreasonable to hold our teachers to a higher standard of personal conduct, given the youthful ideals they are supposed to foster and elevate (*Faulkner v. New Bern-Craven County Board of Education,* 1984).

When teachers and students are together in settings where alcohol is available, the courts generally take a firm stance on the role of teachers. The dismissal of a teacher for allowing students to get drunk in his home, even though the students had provided the alcohol, was upheld (*Coupeville School District No. 204 v. Vivian,* 1984). Another teacher was dismissed for drinking beer with students in a motel while on a trip to an athletic contest. That dismissal was also upheld (*Blaine v. Moffat County School District RE. No. 1,* 1985).

With the growing use of illegal drugs in society, the number of drug-related cases of teacher misconduct has increased. A major issue in drug cases is the example the teacher sets for students. Because drug use, possession, or advocacy is not listed as a specific ground for teacher dismissal in many states, automatic dismissal is usually not possible; dismissal charges must be brought on grounds of "immoral conduct," "unfitness to teach," or "just cause."

A teacher was dismissed for immoral conduct after she testified in court on behalf of a friend that she thought marijuana was not harmful and that she had used it daily for 15 years with nothing but beneficial effects. The court upheld the board's claim that her nationally publicized advocacy of an illegal drug would encourage students to follow her example (*Governing Board of Nicasio School District of Marin County v. Brennan,* 1971). Resultant publicity also determined the different outcomes of two similar California cases. In one case, the teacher's arrest in Hawaii for possession of marijuana was reported in the city newspaper, and the court upheld his dismissal (*Jefferson Union High School District v. Jones,* 1972). Because no one knew of the second teacher's conviction for possession of marijuana, the revocation of his certificate was overturned (*Comings v. State Board of Education,* 1972).

Whether or not teachers can be effective in their classrooms after breaking drug laws has not been settled. In 1975 the cultivation of one marijuana plant was not judged to be moral turpitude, even though the teacher was convicted of a felony (*Board of Trustees of Santa Maria Joint Union High School District v. Judge,* 1975). In 1977 a teacher's arrest for delivery of 114 pounds of marijuana did not imply the teacher was unfit to teach (*Fischler v. Achew,* 1977). But in 1981, the growing of 52 marijuana plants was judged a sign of moral turpitude, and the teacher's dismissal was upheld (*Adams v. State Professional Practices Council,* 1981). Two arrests for possession of marijuana and cocaine were sufficient to demand the dismissal of a Chicago teacher in 1981. The court referred to the adverse effect the teacher's conduct would have on his classroom performance:

> We are aware of the special position occupied by a teacher in our society. As a consequence of that elevated stature, a teacher's actions are subject to much greater scrutiny than that given to the activities of the average person. We do not doubt that knowledge of a teacher's involvement in illegalities such as possession of marijuana would have a major deleterious effect upon the school system and would greatly impede that individual's ability to adequately fulfill his role as perceived by the Board (*Chicago Board of Education v. Payne,* 1981).

In 1982 a New York school board issued a reprimand to a teacher who had pleaded guilty in court to four counts of possession of a controlled substance. He contended the penalty was too severe and appealed to the state commissioner of education, who ordered him dismissed. The court agreed with the harsher sanction:

> We have no hesitation in stating that the penalty of reprimand for these offenses does not shock us as unduly severe. On the contrary, it is so lenient, and the panel's reasons for imposing it so insubstantial, as to be arbitrary and capricious and an abuse of discretion (*Riforgiato v. Board of Education of City of Buffalo,* 1982).

In 1983 a junior high teacher was indicted for possession with intent to distribute cocaine and was subsequently suspended from teaching pending the outcome of the criminal proceedings. He said his indictment arose from "off duty" conduct unrelated to his teaching responsibilities. The lower court granted him back pay, but the appellate court reversed the decision:

> There are . . . circumstances where the crime charged, no matter where or when performed, is so inimical to the duties inherent in the employment that an indictment for that crime is for misconduct in office. . . . Teachers . . . are in a position of special public trust. As role models for our children they have an "extensive and peculiar opportunity to impress [their] attitude and views" upon their pupils. . . . More particularly, they also have special obligations to their pupils as to drugs (*Dupree v. School Committee of Boston,* 1983).

However, local concern about drug use sometimes does result in infringement of teachers' personal rights. An elementary school teacher was arrested for possession of illegal alcohol and marijuana after a police search of the nightclub he and his brother operated. The brother acknowledged ownership of the illegal substances and testified that the teacher had had no knowledge of their presence on the premises. The State Professional Practices Council found no probable cause for disciplinary action, but the school board dismissed him. The court overturned the board action:

> We must reject this argument, otherwise whenever a teacher is accused of a crime and is subsequently exonerated with no evidence being presented to tie the teacher to the crime, the school board could, nevertheless, dismiss the teacher because the attendant publicity has impaired the teacher's effectiveness (*Baker v. School Board of Marion County,* 1984).

In 1986 a teacher was dismissed for the alleged manufacture, cultivation, and possession of marijuana plants, which constituted immorality and misconduct in office. The police had taken pictures of marijuana plants in the teacher's garden, but when they had returned with a search warrant, no marijuana plants were found. The court ordered the teacher reinstated with back pay because he was able to show he did not have exclusive control over access to the garden (*Forehand v. School Board of Washington County,* 1986).

Some school boards are finding dismissals of teachers for drug-related conduct difficult to enforce because of interpretation of laws and court procedures. A Maryland teacher pleaded guilty to charges of possession of marijuana and drug paraphernalia when she was arrested in connection with a police search of an apartment where she sometimes lived with her boyfriend. However, Maryland law stipulated that upon successful completion of probation, first-time offenders in certain drug-related cases could have their arrest and conviction expunged. Her dismissal was overturned because her probationary period had still been in effect at the time of the board's action (*Tate v. Board of Education of Kent County,* 1985).

A permanent substitute teacher, who was arrested and charged with a misdemeanor count of marijuana possession after the police searched his house, was suspended without pay. When the criminal charges were dismissed because of a defect in the search warrant, he filed for reinstatement. The school board held a hearing and dismissed him because the charges had been dropped on a technicality. They believed he had a reputation as a drug user, making him unable to function as a role model or example of morality. The court ordered him reinstated because the notoriety had resulted from the board's role in prolonging action on the case (*Rogliano v. Fayette County Board of Education,* 1986).

A tenured elementary school principal, arrested and charged with possession of marijuana with intent to distribute, was dismissed on grounds of dishonesty and willful neglect. He argued that his removal hearing should not have been held before the criminal charges were resolved, but the court ruled that an administrative removal hearing and a criminal trial were entirely separate and independent proceedings:

> By his actions [the principal] demonstrated that he lacked an uncompromising adherence to the highest principles and ideals . . . . Furthermore, as a school principal [he] had a duty to the public to cultivate respect for authority among the younsters [*sic*] under his supervision, surely being guilty of acts constituting a felony exhibits a "willful neglect" of that duty. Finally, public policy and

> common sense dictate that a School Board have [*sic*] the power to remove a teacher found guilty of acts constituting a serious felony, especially one involving a serious social problem such as drug abuse . . . . Involvement with illegal drugs is a plague that most often pursues our youth, even on school grounds. The school board would be remiss in its duties if it did not properly dismiss [the principal] for his involvement with illegal drugs (*Summers v. Vermilion Parish School Board,* 1986).

Therefore, when the use or possession of drugs tends to destroy or diminish a teacher's capacity to teach, a school board is justified in dismissing the teacher. However, a nexus between the behavior and the teacher's lessened capacity to teach must usually be established and all constitutional rights of the teacher must be observed. A school board would be wise to note that the dismissal of teachers involved with drugs cannot be automatic but must depend on the facts of the individual situation.

In other cases where teachers break the law, much variation in court rulings also exists. Shoplifting cases have been decided both in favor of and against teachers (*Lesley v. Oxford Area School District,* 1980; *Gillett v. Unified School District No. 276, Jewell County,* 1980; *Golden v. Board of Education of County of Harrison,* 1981). A teacher could not be dismissed for immorality in Ohio merely because he was convicted of hit-and-run driving (*Hale v. Board of Education, City of Lancaster,* 1968). A school board in 1977 charged a teacher with immorality based on his conviction of felonious restraint, aggravated assault, theft, and violation of the Uniform Firearms Act. The teacher argued that his effectiveness as a teacher was not impaired, but the court rejected his plea (*Skripchuk v. Austin,* 1977). In 1986 a teacher pleaded guilty to criminal negligent homicide in the traffic fatality of a teenager on a bicycle and was sentenced to one year in the county jail. The state commissioner of education imposed a two-year suspension without pay for conduct unbecoming a teacher and neglect of duty, and the teacher appealed. The court upheld the suspension:

> [The teacher's] conviction established that he had grossly deviated from the standard of care a responsible citizen owes to other users of the public highways. It was hardly irrational for the Commissioner to infer that this well-publicized dereliction by a teacher would adversely impact on his ability to "function as an example for students," . . . particularly youths just converging on the significant adolescent milestone of learning to drive (*Ellis v. Ambach,* 1986).

Lying and stealing have been ruled immoral and sufficient reasons for dismissal of teachers in several cases (*Bethel Park School District v. Krall,* 1982; *Balog v. McKeesport Area School District,* 1984; *Kenai Peninsula Borough Board of Education v. Brown,* 1984; *Kimble v. Worth County R-III Board of Education,* 1984; *In re Dowden,* 1984). Welfare fraud (*Perryman v. School Committee of Boston,* 1983) and filing false income tax returns (*Logan v. Warren County Board of Education,* 1982; *United States v. Tolla,* 1986) have also led to teacher dismissals that have been upheld in court.

Misuse of position and dishonesty on the job have also led to disciplinary actions against teachers, even when they have claimed that their conduct had no connection to their classroom performance. A Mississippi athletic director was dismissed for insubordination, violation of purchasing policies, unauthorized sale of shirts, jackets, and pop, and failure to account to the student activity fund for moneys received. His dismissal was upheld (*Merchant v. Board of Trustees of the Pearl Municipal Separate School District,* 1986). Stating "the school teacher has traditionally been regarded as a moral example for the students," the court upheld the dismissal of a teacher who was supposed to be teaching homebound students but called in sick and drove a coal truck to the next state (*Board of Education of Laurel County v. McCollum,* 1986). A driver's education teacher's contract was not renewed because the teacher took the driver's education car on a two-day trip without authorization, asked two students to lie for him, and reported he had taught driving on days when he had not taught (*Noel v. Andrus,* 1987). A Minnesota teacher who swindled two fellow teachers out of the funds they had invested in their corporation was dismissed for immoral conduct and conduct unbecoming a teacher. The court upheld his dismissal:

> While [the teacher] may be genuinely sorry for, and may be unlikely to repeat, his conduct, the record does support the school board's conclusion that [the teacher's] continued presence in this small school district will result in faculty disorder and an unsatisfactory learning environment (*Matter of Shelton,* 1987).

Therefore, teachers who break the law or engage in conduct that violates reasonable standards of ethical behavior may expect to be subject to disciplinary action. Society continues to hold teachers to standards of conduct that can be used by students as examples of good citizenship. The Oregon Supreme Court stated this philosophy in 1963:

> A teacher in a public school is the key factor in teaching by precept and example the subjects of honesty, morality, courtesy, obedience to law, and other lessons of a steadying influence which tend to promote and develop an upright and desirable citizenry (*Bay v. State Board of Education,* 1963).

Teachers should respect and obey the law and adhere to professional standards of conduct. Criminal activities or civil wrongdoing may result in school boards determining that a teacher's effectiveness in the classroom has been impaired. School boards, however, must be certain that all due process is observed when dismissing a teacher for violation of the law.

Principle VII

Affliction with a contagious disease may not provide the basis for discrimination against a teacher who is otherwise qualified to continue in his or her teaching position.

With the advances in medical science, many diseases that once led to deadly epidemics have been eradicated, illnesses that once led to premature death are curable, and sicknesses that once incapacitated the victims are controlled. These rapid changes in medicine have forced changes in attitudes toward teachers who contract diseases. Teachers were formerly forced to end their careers when such noncontagious diseases as cancer, polio, or epilepsy struck because the prognosis for recovery was negligible. The fear of the spread of smallpox, scarlet fever, or whooping cough meant that teachers who contracted these contagious diseases were sometimes quarantined and then often lost their jobs because of the lack of adequate medical leave policies. Because the life expectancy of the victims of many diseases was once short and because afflicted teachers in the past could easily infect children, the issue of teachers continuing in their positions while having contagious but controlled diseases has only recently been raised. The courts have become involved when teachers have claimed a right to continued employment and school boards have attempted to remove them from contact with children.

The first case in recent years to gain national attention concerning a teacher with a contagious disease was heard in 1987. A Florida teacher, who had taught for nearly 14 years, was dismissed after suffering a third relapse of tuberculosis within two years. Filing suit in federal court, she claimed protection as a handicapped person under Section 504 of the Rehabilitation Act of 1973. The United States Supreme Court ruled in the teacher's favor, stating that her hospitalization for tuberculosis established a "record of impairment," which classified her as a handicapped individual. Although "one or more of her major life activities [were] substantially limited by her impairment," one definition of "handicap" under Section 504, the school board could not discriminate against her as long as she was "otherwise qualified" to teach:

> Allowing discriminations based on the contagious effects of a physical impairment would be inconsistent with the basic purpose of Section 504, which is to ensure that handicapped individuals are not denied jobs or other benefits because of the prejudiced attitudes or the ignorance of others. By amending the definition of "handicapped individual" to include not only those who are actually physically impaired, but also those who are regarded as impaired and who, as a result, are substantially limited in a major life activity, Congress acknowledged that society's accumulated myths and fears about disability and disease are as handicapping as are the physical limitations that flow from actual impairment. Few aspects of a handicap give rise to the same level of public fear and misapprehension as contagiousness. Even those who suffer or have recovered from such noninfectious diseases as epilepsy or cancer have faced discrimination based on the irrational fear that they might be contagious. The Act is carefully structured to replace such reflexive reactions to actual or perceived handicaps with actions based on reasoned and medically sound judgments: the definition of "handicapped individual" is broad, but only those individuals who are both handicapped *and* otherwise qualified are eligible for relief (*School Board of Nassau County, Florida v. Arline,* 1987).

In this case, the Supreme Court relied on the American Medical Association's (AMA) list of factors to be considered about the risk to others of having a teacher with a contagious disease in a school:

1. the nature of the risk (how the disease is transmitted)
2. the duration of the risk (how long is the carrier infectious)
3. the severity of the risk (what is the potential harm to third parties)

4. the probabilities the disease will be transmitted and will cause varying degrees of harm (Brief for American Medical Association as *Amicus Curiae* 19).

One year later, a second case arose, this one involving a California teacher with acquired immune deficiency syndrome (AIDS). Subsequent to his being diagnosed as having AIDS, the teacher was transferred from his classroom of hearing-impaired students to an administrative position in the district. Citing the *Arline* case, the United States Court of Appeals, Ninth Circuit, ruled that the teacher was a handicapped person as defined by Section 504. The most current medical information about AIDS at that time was used to show that the teacher was not a risk to students under the AMA standards stated in *Arline.* The court granted a preliminary injunction reinstating the teacher to his classroom, noting the importance of time in the decision:

> Here, [the teacher] is not claiming future monetary injury; his injury is emotional and psychological—and immediate. Such an injury cannot be adequately compensated for by a monetary award after trial. . . . Studies and statistics of etiology and terminus of AIDS show that although the time during which such a person may be quick and productive varies, the virus is fatal in all recorded cases. Presently [this teacher] is fully qualified and able to return to work; but his ability to do so will surely be affected in time. A delay, even if only a few months, pending trial represents precious, productive time irretrievably lost to him (*Chalk v. United States District Court Central District of California,* 1988).

Even though the United States Supreme Court in the *Arline* case specifically stated in a footnote that its decision would not necessarily apply to AIDS victims, the decision by the Ninth Circuit Court established that courts will, indeed, use the *Arline* decision, current medical data, and the AMA standards when a teacher's rights to employment are threatened by a contagious disease. As new medical information becomes available, the courts will be faced with the difficult task of making decisions based on new knowledge as well as case precedent. School boards should realize, however, that teachers with contagious diseases in remission or that pose negligible risk of transmittal to students may qualify for protection under Section 504 of the Rehabilitation Act of 1973.

Summary

Teachers currently enjoy greater personal freedoms than they have ever had in the past. The 1960s and 1970s were years of great social change in America, and those changes influenced education. The freedoms young teachers take for granted today go back to landmark court decisions granting constitutional rights to teachers. Because the legal issues of personal freedoms for teachers are relatively recent developments, no clear guidelines exist in many instances. Where the United States Supreme Court has ruled, such as in free speech and association cases, the trial courts have direction and decisions are consistent. Otherwise, as in cases involving drug use or homosexual activity, no unanimity in current court decisions exists. As the courts uphold drug testing of persons in certain occupations, cases will surely arise when teachers suspected of illicit drug use are asked or required to submit to drug tests. The issue of the rights of teachers with contagious or infectious diseases is so new that court decisions are limited and rely heavily on medical data, which may change as research advances.

Should a teacher claim infringement of personal freedoms, school officials must realize that the burden of proof will fall on them to show that a need to limit a teacher's constitutional rights existed. If no disruption of the educational process occurred or could have reasonably been expected, the courts will generally support teachers' rights. The courts are ordering the reinstatement of many teachers dismissed for exercising their constitutional rights, and local school districts can be held liable for back pay and damage awards. However, teachers should not let the exercise of their rights detract from the educational process.

Questions and Responses

1. When will a teacher be successful in challenging a dismissal from a teaching position on the grounds that the dismissal was based on a statute that is unconstitutionally vague?

If vagueness of the statute is the only claim the teacher is making in the court, the dismissal will probably be upheld because the courts are reluctant to declare laws unconstitutional. However, if a statute or policy can be shown to be so vague that a person of ordinary intelligence cannot tell when a violation has occurred, it will be struck down as infringing on constitutional rights.

2. When will a teacher automatically be dismissed for using illegal drugs?

Most states rely on "immoral conduct," "conduct unbecoming a teacher," or "other just cause" clauses to dismiss a teacher for possession, use, distribution, or advocacy of illegal drugs. Sometimes, if a teacher's conviction on possession charges is viewed as a little-known, isolated incident, the teacher will not be dismissed. On the other hand, if the teacher's conduct has gained publicity or if an adverse relationship between the drug issue and the teacher's classroom performance can be shown, the dismissal will probably be upheld. In states where a conservative community attitude toward drugs exists, a teacher would have a difficult time challenging a drug-related conviction on the grounds that it is unrelated to the teacher's job performance. Automatic dismissal of a teacher is seldom possible; all due process must be observed when a teacher is dismissed, regardless of the reason.

3. When can a school board enforce a dress and grooming code for teachers?

In the 1960s and 1970s when student dress codes were being challenged in the courts, a few cases involving teacher dress codes were also heard. Because the cases were tried only in lower courts in several states under differing circumstances, no consistent trend concerning the validity of dress and grooming codes can be seen. However, the latest cases that reached the appellate courts were decided against the teachers, either because the courts ruled that such claims were frivolous or because the courts determined that such issues were the prerogative of the board. Generally, reasonable dress and grooming codes will be upheld by the courts as not in violation of teachers' rights.

4. Under which amendments of the Constitution are cases involving the personal freedoms of teachers usually filed?

Most cases where teachers challenge disciplinary sanctions based on accusations of misconduct in their personal lives are filed under First and Fourteenth Amendment clauses. Violations of the First Amendment rights of free speech and privacy are most often claimed when a teacher's personal conduct outside the classroom is questioned. The due process and equal protection clauses of the Fourteenth Amendment are also usually cited. A teacher who is dismissed may claim loss of a property right or a liberty interest without observance of applicable procedural due process or may claim that the disciplinary sanction was discriminatory.

5. When may a teacher be dismissed for speech outside of the classroom?

The United States Supreme Court has ruled that a teacher may speak as a citizen on any issue in which the public has an interest. This speech may be oral, written, or symbolic but must not disrupt the educational process. A teacher may not engage in obscene, slanderous, libelous, or other speech that is not protected under the First Amendment. Even if the speech concerns school issues, a teacher may freely speak for or against the issue as long as it is a matter of public concern and the teacher does not knowingly or recklessly make false statements.

6. When may a teacher's complaints about school policies or procedures result in disciplinary action against the teacher?

Whenever a school issue is a private concern involving only internal working conditions, a teacher may not take the issue to the public forum. Grievances about personnel, policies, or procedures should be handled through proper internal channels unless a public interest is involved. The United States Supreme Court has ruled that teachers who use a public forum to voice complaints that are only personal matters may be subject to disciplinary actions because their speech is not protected by the First Amendment.

7. When may a teacher be dismissed for belonging to an unpopular political party?

The First Amendment right of free assembly gives teachers the right to belong to any organization—social, religious, or political—or to associate with any group without fear of retaliation. The freedom to believe is absolute, and no one may restrain membership in an organization because of the popular or unpopular views held by the group. However, a teacher's participation in a group's illegal activities would not be protected.

8. When may a school board restrict the wearing of religious clothing by a teacher?

Small caps, badges, or jewelry that symbolize religious beliefs or affiliations have never been successfully challenged in court because they generally cause no disruption of the educational process nor infringe on First Amendment religious clauses.

However, religious garb or clothing has sometimes been ruled disruptive as well as a violation of the establishment clause.

9. When may a teacher's private lifestyle result in disciplinary sanctions?

A teacher's personal conduct is of no concern to the employing school board unless it has a disruptive influence on the educational process or adversely affects the teacher's performance in the classroom. Sexual preferences and private activities that once automatically led to a teacher's dismissal are usually disregarded by the courts unless the educational environment is affected. Notoriety about the teacher's personal activity is often used by school boards and courts as one indicator that the conduct has negatively affected classroom performance.

10. When may a school board dismiss a teacher who has been convicted of a crime?

Most criminal or civil wrongdoings can be shown to have a negative effect on the teacher's classroom performance and can lead to the teacher's dismissal. Society continues to hold teachers to a higher standard of conduct because they are considered examples for students to emulate. Teachers with criminal records are generally not considered appropriate role models of good citizenship for students. However, court procedures that overturn convictions on technical, procedural errors sometimes result in school boards being faced with a dilemma about the status of a teacher. Administrative hearings can usually be held that are separate from courtroom proceedings in order for boards to take action to dismiss a teacher in spite of court rulings. School boards must be careful to protect a teacher's due process rights and to ensure that teachers who are wrongfully accused of illegal actions are not punished.

Case References

Acanfora v. Board of Education of Montgomery County, 359 F.Supp. 843 (D.Md. 1973), aff'd. on other grounds, 491 F.2d 498 (4th Cir., 1974), cert. denied, 419 U.S. 836 (1974).

Adams v. State Professional Practices Council, 406 So.2d 1170 (Fla. App. 1981).

Adcock v. Board of Education of San Diego Unified School District, 513 P.2d 900 (Cal. 1973).

Adler v. Board of Education of City of New York, 342 U.S. 485 (1952).

American Communications Association v. Douds, 339 U.S. 382 (1950).

Anderson v. Evans, 660 F.2d 153 (6th Cir., 1981).

Avery v. Homewood City Board of Education, 674 F.2d 337 (5th Cir., 1982).

Baggett v. Bullitt, 377 U.S. 360 (1964).

Baker v. School Board of Marion County, 450 So.2d 1194 (Fla. App. 5 Dist. 1984).

Balog v. McKeesport Area School District, 484 A.2d 198 (Pa. Cmwlth. 1984).

Bay v. State Board of Education, 378 P.2d 558 (Or. 1963).

Bethel Park School District v. Krall, 445 A.2d 1377 (Pa. Cmwlth. 1982).

Bickford v. Board of Education of School District No. 82 of Hall County, 336 N.W.2d 73 (Neb. 1983).

Blaine v. Moffat County School District RE. No. 1, 709 P.2d 96 (Colo. App. 1985).

Blanchet v. Vermilion Parish School Board, 220 So.2d 534 (La. App. 1969).

Board of Education of Laurel County v. McCollum, 721 S.W.2d 703 (Ky. 1986).

Board of Education of Long Beach Unified School District of Los Angeles County v. Jack M., 566 P.2d 602 (Cal. 1977).

Board of Education of Santa Fe Public Schools v. Sullivan, 740 P.2d 119 (N.M. 1987).

Board of Trustees of Santa Maria Joint Union High School District v. Judge, 123 Cal.Rptr. 830 (Cal. App. 1975).

Bowman v. Pulaski County Special School District, 723 F.2d 640 (8th Cir., 1983).

Braxton v. Board of Public Instruction of Duval County, Florida, 303 F.Supp. 958 (M.D. Fla. 1969).

Burton v. Cascade School District Union High School No. 5, 353 F.Supp. 254 (D. Or. 1973).

Chalk v. United States District Court Central District of California, 840 F.2d 701 (9th Cir., 1988).

Chicago Board of Education v. Payne, 430 N.E.2d 310 (Ill. App. 1981).

Childers v. Independent School District No. 1 of Bryan County, State of Oklahoma, 676 F.2d 1338 (10th Cir., 1982).

Claiborne County Board of Education v. Martin, 500 So.2d 981 (Miss. 1986).

Clark v. Ann Arbor School District, 344 N.W.2d 48 (Mich. App. 1983).

Cole v. Richardson, 405 U.S. 676 (1972).

Comings v. State Board of Education, 100 Cal.Rptr. 73 (Cal. App. 1972).

Commonwealth v. Herr, 78 A. 68 (Pa. 1910).

Connell v. Higginbotham, 403 U.S. 207 (1971).

Connick v. Myers, 461 U.S. 138 (1983).

Cooper v. Eugene School District No. 4J, 723 P.2d 298 (Or. 1986).

Coupeville School District No. 204 v. Vivian, 677 P.2d 192 (Wash. App. 1984).

Cox v. Dardanelle Public School District, 790 F.2d 668 (8th Cir., 1986).

Cramp v. Board of Public Instruction of Orange County, 368 U.S. 278 (1961).

Domico v. Rapides Parish School Board, 675 F.2d 100 (5th Cir., 1982).

Dore v. Board of Education of Township of Bedminster, Somerset County, 449 A.2d 547 (N.J. Super. A.D. 1982).

Dupree v. School Committee of Boston, 446 N.E.2d 1099 (Mass. App. 1983).

East Hartford Education Association v. Board of Education of the Town of East Hartford, 562 F.2d 838 (2d Cir., 1977).

Eckmann v. Board of Education of Hawthorn School District No. 17, 636 F.Supp. 1214 (N.D. Ill. 1986).

Elfbrandt v. Russell, 384 U.S. 11 (1966).

Ellis v. Ambach, 508 N.Y.S.2d 624 (A.D. 3 Dept. 1986).

Faulkner v. New Bern-Craven County Board of Education, 316 S.E.2d 281 (N.C. 1984).

Ferrara v. Mills, 781 F.2d 1508 (11th Cir., 1986).

Finot v. Pasadena City Board of Education, 58 Cal.Rptr. 520 (Cal. App. 1967).

Fischler v. Askew, 349 So.2d 227 (Fla. App. 1977).

Forehand v. School Board of Washington County, 481 So.2d 953 (Fla. App. 1 Dist. 1986).

Gaylord v. Tacoma School District No. 10, 559 P.2d 1340 (Wash. 1977), cert. denied, 434 U.S. 879 (1977).

Gerhardt v. Heid, 267 N.W. 127 (N.D. 1936).

Gieringer v. Center School District No. 58, 477 F.2d 1164 (8th Cir., 1973), cert. denied, 414 U.S. 832 (1973).

Gilbertson v. McAlister, 403 F.Supp. 1 (D. Conn. 1975).

Gillett v. Unified School District No. 276, Jewell County, 605 P.2d 105 (Kan. 1980).

Givhan v. Western Line Consolidated School District, 439 U.S. 410 (1979); on remand, *Ayers v. Western Line Consolidated School District,* 691 F.2d 766 (5th Cir., 1982).

Golden v. Board of Education of County of Harrison, 285 S.E.2d 665 (W.Va. 1981).

Goldsmith v. Board of Education of Sacramento City High School District, 225 P. 783 (Cal. App. 1924).

Governing Board of Nicasio School District of Marin County v. Brennan, 95 Cal.Rptr. 712 (Cal. App. 1971).

Gray v. Union County Intermediate Education District, 520 F.2d 803 (9th Cir., 1975).
Griswold v. Connecticut, 381 U.S. 479 (1965).
Guerra v. Roma Independent School District, 444 F.Supp. 812 (S.D. Tex. 1977).
Hale v. Board of Education, City of Lancaster, 234 N.E.2d 583 (Ohio 1968).
Hall v. Board of School Commissioners of Mobile County, Alabama, 681 F.2d 965 (5th Cir., 1982).
Hesse v. Board of Education of Township High School District No. 211, Cook County, Illinois, 848 F.2d 748 (7th Cir., 1988).
Holley v. Seminole County School District, 755 F.2d 1492 (11th Cir., 1985).
Horosko v. Mount Pleasant Township School District, 6 A.2d 866 (Pa. 1939).
Hosack v. Smiley, 276 F.Supp. 876 (D. Colo. 1967), aff'd. 390 U.S. 744 (1968).
Hysong v. School District of Gallitzin Borough, 30 A. 482 (Pa. 1894).
In re Dowden, 446 So.2d 853 (La. App. 2 Cir. 1984).
Jarvella v. Willoughby-Eastlake City School District Board of Education, 233 N.E.2d 143 (Ohio 1967).
Jefferson Union High School District v. Jones, 100 Cal.Rptr. 73 (Cal. App. 1972).
Jones v. Battles, 315 F.Supp. 601 (D. Conn. 1970).
Katz v. Ambach, 472 N.Y.S.2d 492 (N.Y.A.D. 3 Dept. 1984).
Kenai Peninsula Borough Board of Education v. Brown, 691 P.2d 1034 (Alaska 1984).
Keyishian v. Board of Regents of the University of the State of New York, 385 U.S. 589 (1967).
Kimble v. Worth County R-III Board of Education, 669 S.W.2d 949 (Mo. App. 1984).
Knapp v. Whitaker, 757 F.2d 827 (7th Cir., 1985).
Knight v. Board of Regents of University of State of New York, 269 F.Supp. 339 (S.D.N.Y. 1967), aff'd, 390 U.S. 36 (1968).
Kurlander v. School Committee of Williamstown, 451 N.E.2d 138 (Mass. App. 1983).
Lake Park Education Association v. Board of Education of Lake Park High School District No. 108, DuPage County, Illinois, 526 F.Supp. 710 (N.D. Ill. 1981).
Lesley v. Oxford Area School District, 420 A.2d 764 (Pa. Cmwlth. 1980).
Lewis v. East Feliciana Parish School Board, 452 So.2d 1275 (La. App. 1 Cir. 1984).
Lewis v. Harrison School District No. 1, 805 F.2d 310 (8th Cir., 1986).
Libe v. Board of Education of Twin Cedars Community School District, 350 N.W.2d 748 (Iowa App. 1984).
Lile v. Hancock Place School District, 701 S.W.2d 500 (Mo. App. 1985).
Lindgren v. Board of Trustees, High School District No. 1, 558 P.2d 468 (Mont. 1976).
Logan v. Warren County Board of Education, 549 F.Supp. 145 (S.D. Ga. 1982).
Los Angeles Teachers Union, Local 1021, American Federation of Teachers v. Los Angeles City Board of Education, 455 P.2d 827 (Cal. 1969).
Louthan v. Commonwealth, 79 Va. 196 (1884).
Lucia v. Duggan, 303 F.Supp. 112 (D. Mass. 1969).
Lusk v. Estes, 361 F.Supp. 653 (N.D. Texas 1973).
Matter of Shelton, 408 N.W.2d 594 (Minn. App. 1987).
Matter of Tanelli, 477 A.2d 394 (N.J. Super. A.D. 1984).
McAuliffe v. Mayor of City of New Bedford, 29 N.E. 517 (Mass. 1892).
Merchant v. Board of Trustees of the Pearl Municipal Separate School District, 492 So.2d 959 (Miss. 1986).
Miller v. Board of Education of the County of Lincoln, 450 F.Supp. 106 (S.D. W.Va. 1978).
Miller v. School District No. 167, Cook County, Illinois, 495 F.2d 658 (7th Cir., 1974).
Moore v. Board of Education, 212 N.E.2d 833 (Ohio 1965).
Morrison v. Hamilton County Board of Education, 494 S.W.2d 770 (Tenn. 1973).
Morrison v. State Board of Education, 82 Cal.Rptr. 175 (1969).
Mt. Healthy City School District Board of Education v. Doyle, 429 U.S. 274 (1977).

National Gay Task Force v. Board of Education of City of Oklahoma City, 729 F.2d 1270 (10th Cir., 1984).
New Haven v. Torrington, 43 A.2d 455 (Conn. 1945).
New York Times Company v. Sullivan, 376 U.S. 254 (1964).
Noel v. Andrus, 810 F.2d 1388 (5th Cir., 1987).
O'Connor v. Hendrick, 77 N.E. 612 (N.Y. 1906).
Ohlson v. Phillips, 304 F.Supp. 1152 (D. Colo. 1969), aff'd. 397 U.S. 317 (1970).
Perry v. Sindermann, 408 U.S. 593 (1972).
Perryman v. School Committee of Boston, 458 N.E.2d 748 (Mass. App. 1983).
Pickering v. Board of Education of Township High School District 205, 391 U.S. 563 (1968).
Potter v. Kalama Public School District No. 402, 644 P.2d 1229 (Wash. App. 1982).
Rawlings v. Butler, 290 S.W.2d 801 (Ky. 1956).
Riforgiato v. Board of Education of City of Buffalo, 448 N.Y.S.2d 74 (N.Y.A.D. 1982).
Rogliano v. Fayette County Board of Education, 347 S.E.2d 220 (W.Va. 1986).
Ross v. Springfield School District No. 19, 716 P.2d 724 (Or. 1986).
Schmid v. Lovette, 201 Cal.Rptr. 424 (Cal. App. 1 Dist. 1984).
Schneiderman v. United States, 320 U.S. 118 (1943).
School Board of Nassau County, Florida v. Arline, 480 U.S. 273 (1987).
Seemuller v. Fairfax County School Board, 878 F.2d 1578 (4th Cir. 1989).
Shelton v. Tucker, 364 U.S. 479 (1960).
Sherburne v. School Board of Suwannee County, 455 So.2d 1057 (Fla. App. 1 Dist. 1984).
Shipley v. Salem School District 24J, Marion County, 669 P.2d 1172 (Or. App. 1983).
Skripchuk v. Austin, 379 A.2d 1142 (Del. Super 1977).
Southside Public Schools v. Hill, 827 F.2d 270 (8th Cir., 1987).
State ex rel. Johnson v. Boyd, 28 N.E.2d 256 (Ind. 1940).
Stoddard v. School District No. 1, Lincoln County, Wyoming, 590 F.2d 829 (10th Cir., 1979).
Summers v. Vermilion Parish School Board, 493 So.2d 1258 (La. App. 3 Cir., 1986).
Sweezy v. New Hampshire, 354 U.S. 234 (1957).
Swilley v. Alexander, 448 F.Supp. 702 (S.D. Ala. 1978).
Tardif v. Quinn, 545 F.2d 761 (1st Cir., 1976).
Tate v. Board of Education of Kent County, 485 A.2d 688 (Md. App. 1985).
Thompson v. Board of Education of the City of Chicago, 711 F.Supp. 394 (N.D.Ill. 1989).
Thompson v. Southwest School District, 483 F.Supp. 1170 (W.D. Mo. 1980).
Tingey v. Vaughn, 17 Ill. App. 347 (1885).
Turk v. Franklin Special School District, 640 S.W.2d 218 (Tenn. 1982).
United States v. Tolla, 781 F.2d 29 (2d Cir., 1986).
Vukadinovich v. Bartels, 853 F.2d 1387 (7th Cir., 1988).
Welch v. Board of Education of Chandler Unified School District No. 80 of Maricopa County, 667 P.2d 746 (Ariz. App. 1983).
White v. South Park Independent School District, 693 F.2d 1163 (5th Cir., 1982).
Wieman v. Updegraff, 344 U.S. 183 (1952).
Williams v. Southfield School, Inc., 494 So.2d 1339 (La. App. 2 Cir. 1986).
Yielding v. Crockett Independent School District, 707 F.2d 196 (5th Cir., 1983).
Zellers v. Huff, 236 P.2d 949 (N.M. 1951).
Zoll v. Eastern Allamakee Community School District, 588 F.2d 246 (8th Cir., 1978).

9 Labor Relations

Collective negotiations, the bargaining by representatives of the teachers and the school board of the terms to be included in a master teaching contract, has become a common practice in the nation's schools since the 1960s. Before that time, school boards held almost unilateral power to make the decisions affecting the operation of the schools. Although contract negotiations in the private sector date back to the unionization efforts in industry during the early 1900s, bargaining in the public sector, especially in school districts, has been much slower to develop. Because employment in the public sector has generally been considered a privilege with attendant benefits and job security, interest in and support for unionism among public employees did not develop to any great extent until the 1950s. Prior to the 1950s, teachers were members of national and state professional educational organizations, whose goals centered on furtherance of scholarly research into the academic disciplines, or of local teachers' associations, whose primary purpose was to provide social activities for the teachers.

By the late 1950s, however, changes in society and the teaching profession awakened new interest in the potential political clout of teachers' associations. As tenure laws were passed and courts recognized teachers' constitutional rights, the ranks of teachers' organizations swelled. Teachers began realizing that their collective strength in defending their rights and demanding a voice in the decision-making process was much greater than that of the individual teacher. Local teachers' organizations became affiliated with state and national associations. Over three-fourths of all teachers now belong to nationally recognized organizations involved in the labor relations between teachers and their employing school boards.

Early federal legislation (such as the National Labor Relations Act of 1935, the Taft-Hartley Act of 1947, and the Landrum-Griffin Act of 1959) governing labor relations in the private sector specifically excluded the public sector, which slowed the organization of public employees. By the early 1960s, however, government employees were clamoring for the right to organize and then for those organizations to be recognized as bargaining units. In January 1962, President John F. Kennedy issued Executive Order 10988, which gave federal government employees the right to form, join, and assist any employee organization freely and without fear of penalty or reprisal. The order also provided that a government agency had to recognize an employee organization as the exclusive representative of the employees in a unit. Dissatisfaction with this original order led to the issuance of Executive Order 11491 by President Richard M. Nixon in October 1969. This order included provisions for implementing collective bargaining practices, including the right to negotiate, in the public sector.

In 1959 Wisconsin became the first state to enact legislation allowing collective bargaining in the public sector. Approximately 30 states have passed some type of legislation authorizing collective bargaining for public employees, including teachers. In states where no statutory authorization for collective negotiations between teachers and school boards exists, court rulings and voluntary bargaining arrangements have sometimes allowed collective bargaining to occur.

Although differences between private and public sector employment have decreased as the same economic and technological challenges face both sectors, practical and philosophical differences still exist that influence the statutes, policies, and procedures governing employee-employer negotiations. School systems rely on state tax revenues and subsequent legislative appropriations for their operating funds, not on profits from the marketplace. Therefore, negotiations for teachers' salaries and benefits are bound by budget deadlines, tax collections, and the legislative process. State legislatures are the ultimate decision makers regarding educational policies and practices in each state, and laws may be enacted that drastically change contractual provisions, necessitating adjustments by both teachers and boards. Teachers also enjoy employment benefits protected by statute, including salary schedules, retirement systems, leaves of absence, and tenure. These employment protections cause many who do not enjoy such protections to question the need for collective negotiations for teachers. The rising militancy of teachers demanding additional constitutional rights and a voice in decisions affecting the schools has raised alarm in some who wonder why teachers, as public servants, should have more power in the decision-making process. When negotiations between teachers and school boards fail, many people believe that schoolchildren become the victims. Therefore, even in the states that allow collective bargaining by teachers and school boards, statutes either expressly forbid teachers the right to strike or allow strikes only after extensive statutory proceedings are exhausted. Seldom do such restrictions apply in the private sector.

Labor laws and court decisions vary greatly from state to state, making collective negotiations a difficult legal topic to generalize. Statutes and case law governing labor relations in education change rapidly as teachers' associations battle for greater voice in the decisions affecting them and school boards struggle to retain control of the decision-making process. Although labor relations is a relatively new topic in school law, it is one of the most dynamic as the outcome of the negotiating process defines the legal relationship between teachers and school boards in most of the nation's school districts today.

Legal Principles

Principle I *Right to Organize*

Teachers have the right to organize collectively, to form professional associations, and to join such organizations without interference from administrators or school boards.

(continued on next page)

Legal Principles (continued)

Principle II *State Statutes*

Where state statutes exist, collective negotiations between school boards and teachers are governed by those statutes. Collective bargaining statutes vary widely from state to state.

Principle III *Discretionary Authority to Bargain*

In the absence of a state statute, school boards ordinarily have the discretionary authority to bargain collectively with teachers. However, absent statutory authorization, a board need not recognize nor bargain with the teachers' association.

Principle IV *School Board Rights*

School boards cannot bargain away their statutory authority or rights. Generally, school boards have exclusive rights to make educational policy decisions.

Principle V *Scope of Negotiations*

The scope of collective negotiations is generally determined by state statute or by written agreements and case law where no state statute exists.

Principle VI *No Right to Strike*

Teachers, as public employees, have no inherent right to strike without statutory authorization. Neither may they impose other sanctions against a school board.

Discussion

Principle I

Teachers have the right to organize collectively, to form professional associations, and to join such organizations without interference from administrators or school boards.

The struggle by teachers to gain the right to organize into professional organizations vested with the authority to represent teachers collectively dates back to the 1930s. However, the struggle was generally unsuccessful for two decades because of the assumption, supported by the courts, that school boards had absolute authority over employment of teachers. Scholarly associations were viewed as proper outlets for the academic and intellectual interests of teachers. Local educational organizations, whose membership usually included all teachers, present or retired, as well as administrators, were seen as social clubs to promote school loyalty, out-of-school activities, and recognition of birthdays, holidays, and retirements. Efforts by national, state, or local associations to become involved in decisions considered the exclusive prerogative of school boards were squelched as threatening, inappropriate, and illegal.

Membership in associations with political agendas was kept small by actions of school boards to punish teachers who joined or to refuse to employ teachers suspected of membership.

The courts consistently ruled to support the authority of school boards in employment issues, following the teacher-as-a-public-servant concept extrapolated from Justice Oliver Wendell Holmes's statement that "the petitioner may have a constitutional right to talk politics, but he has no constitutional right to be a policeman" (*McAuliffe v. Mayor of City of New Bedford,* 1892).

Decision making in the public sector was seen as a sovereign prerogative of those elected by the citizens, and that power could not be shared. The Chicago Board of Education enacted a policy that no person would be employed as a teacher until first stating in writing that he or she was not and would not become a member of a teachers' organization. The Illinois Supreme Court upheld the policy, stating that no teacher has a right to demand employment:

> It is no infringement upon the constitutional rights of any one for the board to decline to employ him as a teacher in the schools, and it is immaterial whether the reason for the refusal to employ him is because the applicant is married or unmarried, is of fair complexion or dark, is or is not a member of a trades union, or whether no reason is given for such refusal (*People ex rel. Fursman v. City of Chicago,* 1917).

Before being employed in Seattle in the 1930s, teachers were to sign a declaration to the following effect:

> I hereby declare that I am not a member of the American Federation of Teachers, or any local thereof, and will not become a member during the term of this contract.

The American Federation of Teachers (AFT) brought court action to keep the school board from enforcing the resolution, but the Washington Supreme Court upheld the board's power to make employment decisions:

> The right of freedom of contract as it exists in this case to refuse for any reason or no reason at all to engage the professional services of any person is in no sense a denial of the constitutional right of that person to follow his chosen profession (*Seattle High School Chapter No. 200 of the AFT v. Sharples,* 1930).

During the 1940s and 1950s, interpretations by the United States Supreme Court of the right of assembly as guaranteed by the First Amendment brought a new perspective to the conflict between the school board's right to contract and the teacher's individual constitutional rights. In a series of decisions striking down loyalty oath requirements for employment, the high court supported the right of teachers to join associations. This right of association soon came to mean the right to belong to teachers' organizations, as well as political, religious, or fraternal organizations, without fear of sanction from disapproving boards of education.

In 1951 the case that first defined the rights of teachers to organize collectively was heard by an appellate court in Connecticut. *Norwalk Teachers' Association v. Board of Education of City of Norwalk* (1951) resolved many of the disputed issues regarding membership in and organization of teachers' associations. The Norwalk Teachers' Association (NTA), a voluntary association of 298 of Norwalk's 300 teachers, began negotiating with the school board over salaries in 1946 and served as the bargaining agent for teachers through 1951. However much uncertainty existed about application of state statutes, the rights and duties of both parties to the negotiations, and the scope of the negotiated contract. The union and the board decided to go to court to get some ruling on the legitimacy of their collective bargaining practices. The court ruled that teachers have the right to organize:

> Union organization in industry is now the rule rather than the exception. In the absence of prohibitory statute or regulation, no good reason appears why public employees should not organize as a labor union. . . . There is no objection to the organization of the [teachers] as a labor union, but if its organization is for the purpose of "demanding" recognition and collective bargaining the demands must be kept within legal bounds. . . . It means nothing more than that the [teachers] may organize and bargain collectively for the pay and working conditions which it may be in the power of the board of education to grant (*Norwalk Teachers' Association v. Board of Education of City of Norwalk,* 1951).

As membership in teachers' organizations increased rapidly, many state courts faced cases alleging discriminatory practices against member teachers, particularly those actively involved in organizing teachers. The Montana Supreme Court's statement supporting teachers' rights is representative of these decisions:

> It is sufficient to say that the School Trustees have no authority or power to discriminate between the teachers employed by it . . . because of their membership or lack of membership in a labor union (*Benson v. School District No. 1 of Silver Bow County,* 1959).

In 1968 a group of Illinois teachers brought their case against the superintendent and school board to federal court, claiming violation of First Amendment rights. Because their affiliation with the AFT had led to their not being rehired, they filed a claim under Section 1983 of the Civil Rights Act of 1871. The United States Court of Appeals, Seventh Circuit, emphatically declared that teachers' constitutional right of association extends to their membership in unions:

> It is settled that teachers have the right of free association, and unjustified interference with teachers' associational freedoms violates the Due Process Clause of the Fourteenth Amendment. . . . Public employment may not be subjected to unreasonable conditions, and the assertion of First Amendment rights by teachers will usually not warrant their dismissal. . . . Unless there is some illegal intent, an individual's right to form and join a union is protected by the First Amendment (*McLaughlin v. Tilendis,* 1968).

The United States Court of Appeals, Eighth Circuit, agreed that public employees may file suit for damages and injunctive relief under Section 1983 if they are forbidden from joining unions:

> The First Amendment protects the right of one citizen to associate with other citizens for any lawful purpose free from government interference. The guarantee of the "right of assembly" protects more than "the right to attend a meeting; it includes the right to express one's attitudes or philosophies by membership in a group or by affiliation with it or by other lawful means" (*American Federation of State, County, and Municipal Employees, AFL-CIO v. Woodward,* 1969).

Although the right of teachers to join national, state, and local teachers' organizations is now widely recognized as a freedom protected by the First Amendment, the courts still become involved when conflicts between an association and a school board lead to sanctions against the association or its individual members. In 1988 the Georgia Association of Educators brought action against a school district under Section 1983 when the board terminated an automatic payroll dues deduction service that had been in effect for 20 years. The superintendent had become hostile toward the local teachers' organization because it was affiliated with the NEA [National Education Association] and admitted nonprofessional school personnel to associate membership. After a bus mechanic, a member of the local association, brought a grievance to the board, the superintendent sent a memo to board members:

> If we go beyond the law and permit anyone to address the Board, we can be assured that the GCAE-NEA union will be here every month with some disgruntled employee. . . . I respectfully remind the Board that the NEA has twenty-five years of collective bargaining experience, has trained its employees thoroughly in techniques of divisiveness and militant action, is totally committed to the unionization of teachers, and is a formidable opponent. (*Georgia Association of Educators v. Gwinnett County School District,* 1988).

The board voted to terminate the payroll dues deduction service under the guise that the administrative cost of providing the service was an unauthorized expenditure of public funds. After the vote, the superintendent wrote to the association that "the school board and administration have tossed, instead of marshmallows, a few hardballs back to GCAE." Board members later admitted that the reason for their action was that association leaders had spoken to the board on behalf of its members and that the superintendent wanted to destroy the association. As a result of the termination of the dues deduction service, the local association lost 430 members and approximately $81,000 in dues revenues. The United States Court of Appeals, Eleventh Circuit, overturned a summary judgment in favor of the board and remanded the case for trial:

> The First Amendment protects the right of public employees to associate, speak and petition freely, as well as the right of associations to engage in advocacy on behalf of their members. The Government may not retaliate against individ-

> uals or associations for their exercise of First Amendment rights (*Georgia Association of Educators v. Gwinnett County School District,* 1988).

In 1989 a Connecticut teacher was transferred from one position to a less desirable position because he had sought help from the local association to pursue a grievance. The federal district court denied a motion for a summary judgment in favor of the Director of Pupil Personnel Services and the Superintendent of Schools because the transfer violated the teacher's First Amendment rights:

> The first amendment does not require the government to recognize or bargain with an association of employees, but it does protect the right of an individual "to associate with others, and to petition his government for redress of grievances. . . ." Thus, the state may not abridge the right of public employees to associate in a labor union and to seek redress of grievances through collective action, . . . nor may it retaliate against an employee for doing so. . . . Access to procedures for the redress of grievances is essential to a meaningful first amendment right to petition the government. . . . Where those procedures result from collective bargaining, the right to freedom of association is implicated as well (*Stellmaker v. DePetrillo,* 1989).

Therefore, teachers have the right to organize for their collective good or to join associations whose goals are to further the interests of teachers through collective bargaining. Those rights are guaranteed by the right of association protected by the First Amendment, and school boards and administrators may not interfere with either the organization or the individual teacher's right to affiliate with that organization.

Principle II

Where state statutes exist, collective negotiations between school boards and teachers are governed by those statutes. Collective bargaining statutes vary widely from state to state.

Because of the constitutional right of free assembly, teachers are able to join professional associations. However, the right of teachers' associations to negotiate collectively with school boards is not addressed by federal law. Even if their primary purpose is to protect and advance the rights of teachers through collective bargaining with school boards, teachers' associations are bound by statutes in states where the legislature has enacted laws governing labor relations in the public sector. Each state is free to establish laws that impact the bargaining process between teachers and school boards, including the method of selecting and certifying the bargaining unit. Over 30 states have enacted such legislation, some states expressly mandating teacher-board negotiations, some allowing such negotiations, and some expressly prohibiting recognition of collective agreements between teachers and boards.

Although no federal statute governing negotiations between teachers and school boards exists, many state statutes are closely patterned after the National Labor Relations Act and similar clauses in private industry contracts with labor unions. Examples of collective bargaining statutes that have been the focal point of judicial decisions demonstrate the variation in policies from state to state:

> Alaska (1977): Each city, borough, and regional school board shall negotiate with its certificated employees in good faith on matters pertaining to their employment and the fulfillment of their professional duties.
>
> Connecticut (1972): The town or regional board of education and the organization designated or elected as the exclusive representative for the appropriate unit, through designated officials or their representatives, shall have the duty to negotiate with respect to salaries and other conditions of employment about which either party wishes to negotiate, and such duty shall include the obligation of such board of education to meet at reasonable times . . . and confer in good faith with respect to salaries and other conditions of employment, or the negotiation of an agreement.
>
> Indiana (1984): The citizens of Indiana have a fundamental interest in the development of harmonious and cooperative relationships between school corporations and their certificated employees; recognition by school employers of the right of school employees to organize, and acceptance of the principle and procedure of collective bargaining between school employers and school employee organizations, can alleviate various forms of strife and unrest.
>
> Wisconsin (1984): "Collective bargaining" means the performance of the mutual obligation of a municipal employer, through its officers and agents, and the representatives of its employes, to meet and confer at reasonable times, in good faith, with respect to wages, hours and conditions of employment with the intention of reaching an agreement, or to resolve questions arising under such an agreement. The duty to bargain, however, does not compel either party to agree to a proposal or require the making of a concession. Collective bargaining includes the reduction of any agreement reached to a written and signed document. The employer shall not be required to bargain on subjects reserved to management and direction of the governmental unit except insofar as the manner of exercise of such functions affects the wages, hours and conditions of employment of the employes. In creating this subchapter the legislature recognizes that the public employer must exercise its powers and responsibilities to act for the government and good order of the municipality, its commercial benefit and the health, safety and welfare of the public to assure orderly operations and functions within its jurisdiction, subject to those rights secured to public employes (*sic*) by the constitutions of this state and of the United States.

The courts have become involved in interpreting state statutes when teachers' associations and school boards have disagreed on the application of the law. State court rulings also indicate the diversity in statutory enactments and interpretation of labor law relative to teachers and school board negotiations. Unless the legislation is discriminatory or its application has been arbitrary, the courts are reluctant to interfere with the legislative process. For example, in 1966 the Minnesota Public Employees Labor Relations Act excluded teachers, and the Federation of Teachers filed a discrimination suit. The conflict between the American Federation of Teachers and the National Education Association had brought to light the fact that exclusion from the act left teachers without statutory means for selecting an exclusive bargaining agent. The suit sought a judicial remedy, but the court upheld the statute:

> It is well recognized that the legislature may classify professions, occupations, and businesses according to natural and reasonable lines of distinction, and if such legislation affects alike all persons of the same class, it is not an invalid classification. . . . The legislature has historically treated teachers as a distinct classification, and this unique historical recognition is sufficient to classify the teachers for the purpose of this legislation. . . . We are committed to the principle that unless the law is unconstitutional beyond a reasonable doubt, it must be sustained (*Minneapolis Federation of Teachers Local 59, AFL-CIO v. Obermeyer,* 1966).

In 1969 a federal district court in North Carolina upheld a state law that voided contracts between government units and labor unions, stating, "There is nothing in the United States Constitution which entitles one to have a contract with another who does not want it" (*Atkins v. City of Charlotte,* 1969). The court explained that the decision to allow contracts between employees and employers in the public sector was a state decision having nothing to do with the federal Constitution. Five years later, this decision was quoted in another North Carolina case where the teachers' association claimed that the statute had a detrimental effect on membership in labor organizations because contracts were not recognized. The court said that the First Amendment right of association does not require governmental units to negotiate and enter into contracts with them (*Winston-Salem/Forsyth County Unit of the North Carolina Association of Educators v. Phillips,* 1974).

In the 1980s few states were added to the list of those with statutes addressing teacher-employer negotiations. However, many courts were asked to reaffirm state statutes when handing down rulings, as in 1987 when an Illinois appellate court said, "It is well settled in Illinois that school boards have the authority to enter into valid and binding collective bargaining agreements with public employee unions" (*Proviso Council of West Suburban Teachers Union, Local 571 v. Board of Education, Proviso Township High Schools, District 109, Cook County,* 1987).

State statutes allowing collective negotiations between teachers' associations and school boards vary from comprehensive laws defining the compulsory process specifically to general provisions granting minimal permission to public employees to bargain collectively. School boards and teachers' associations are bound by statutes wherever legislation exists, and when new laws are passed or former laws amended, collective bargaining processes must be updated accordingly.

Principle III

In the absence of a state statute, school boards ordinarily have the discretionary authority to bargain collectively with teachers. However, absent statutory authorization, a board need not recognize nor bargain with the teachers' association.

Although the majority of states have collective bargaining statutes governing negotiations between teachers' associations and school boards, other states have never enacted such legislation. Without statutory authorization, a school board legally does not need to recognize a teachers' association, although teachers cannot be forbidden from or punished for joining or forming a union. A school board cannot be forced to bargain with a teachers' association, and this refusal does not violate any federal law. A teacher has an individual right to join an organization, but an organization has no right to negotiate contracts.

However, when no state statute exists, individual school boards generally have the discretion to negotiate with a teachers' association. In some states, this discretionary authority has been articulated by attorney general opinions or by court rulings.

In the 1951 *Norwalk* ruling, the Connecticut appellate court observed that the state had no statute forbidding negotiations between teachers' organizations and school boards. Yet, as was true in many school districts across the nation, contracts were being negotiated by representatives of teachers and school boards. The court ruled that the contract between the Norwalk Teachers' Association and the Board of Education was valid:

> If [the school board] chooses to negotiate with the [teachers' association] with regard to the employment, salaries, grievance procedure and working conditions of its members, there is no statute, public or private, which forbids such negotiations. It is a matter of common knowledge that this is the method pursued in most school systems large enough to support a teachers' association in some form. It would seem to make no difference theoretically whether the negotiations are with a committee of the whole association or with individuals or small related groups, so long as any agreement made with the committee is confined to members of the association (*Norwalk Teachers' Association v. Board of Education of City of Norwalk,* 1951).

One school district where negotiations had been conducted between the teachers' union and the school board for several years before being challenged on the grounds that no legislative authority existed was Chicago. In 1966 a taxpayer claimed that the Chicago Teachers Union (CTU), with a membership of 12,000, had unlawfully disrupted the operation of the school system by striking and that the bargained contract between the school board and the CTU was illegal because it was not authorized by the school code or any other state statute. The Illinois Supreme Court upheld the negotiated agreement and the right of the board to make the agreement:

> We conclude that the Board of Education of the City of Chicago does not require legislative authority to enter into a collective bargaining agreement with a sole collective bargaining agency selected by its teachers, and we hold that such an agreement is not against public policy (*Chicago Division of the Illinois Education Association v. Board of Education of City of Chicago,* 1966).

Not all states that lack collective bargaining statutes allow districts to negotiate contracts with teachers' associations. Some courts strictly interpret their state laws when the issue of bargaining by teachers arises. In Virginia, a district school board had entered into several collective bargaining agreements with teachers' unions, and in 1977 the state sought to have the agreements declared void. The state supreme court relied on a series of past decisions to show that the legislature had never intended for the local boards to have the power to bargain with teachers collectively:

> The powers vested in local boards to enter into contracts and to hire employees and fix the terms and conditions of their employment are of ancient origin, conferred at a time when the concept of collective bargaining in the public sector had not emerged as a debatable issue. . . . Recent Virginia history of public employee collective bargaining is persuasive, if not conclusive, that the General Assembly, the source of legislative intent, has never conferred upon local boards, by implication or otherwise, the power to bargain collectively and that express statutory authority, so far withheld, is necessary to confer the power (*Commonwealth v. County Board of Arlington County,* 1977).

In Kentucky in 1980 a public agency could elect to negotiate with a representative of its employees but had no duty to do so. Also, the public agency could not be involved in designating an exclusive bargaining representative. The Fayette County Board of Education, after taking a poll that indicated the majority of teachers wanted collective bargaining and wanted the Fayette County Education Association (FCEA) to represent them, negotiated a contract with the FCEA. After the bargaining process was completed, the Professional Educators of Fayette County and the Independent Educators Association of Fayette County wanted to be involved in the ratification of the contract. The court ruled the agreement void because the board had no power to enter into an agreement recognizing one organization as the bargaining agent for all employees (*Fayette County Education Association v. Hardy,* 1980).

Although in many states without collective bargaining laws applicable to teachers, school boards have the discretionary authority to negotiate with teachers' associations, they must be cognizant of case law. Teachers' associations have no authority to force a school board to bargain with them if there is no statutory authorization for collective bargaining. Most states passed their collective bargaining statutes affecting teacher-employer relations in the 1960s and 1970s, and those states without statutes are not as likely to enact laws as they once may have been, even though teachers' associations are actively lobbying in some of those states.

School boards cannot bargain away their statutory authority or rights. Generally, school boards have exclusive rights to make educational policy decisions. **Principle IV**

The public ownership of schools was used as the argument against the initiation of collective bargaining between teachers and the public's representative—the school board—for many years and still influences the policies and practices of the negotiation process. Different from industry where management has full powers to bargain with employees, the public school board is accountable to the citizenry and, therefore, cannot bargain away its delegated authority or statutory rights. The New Jersey Supreme Court explained the differences between managerial power in the private sector and the power of the public school board:

> A private employer may bargain away as much or as little of its managerial control as it likes. . . . However, the very foundation of representative democracy would be endangered if decisions on significant matters of governmental policy were left to the process of collective negotiation, where citizen participation is precluded. This Court would be most reluctant to sanction collective agreement on matters which are essentially managerial in nature, because the true managers are the people. Our democratic system demands that governmental bodies retain their accountability to the citizenry (*Ridgefield Park Education Association v. Ridgefield Park Board of Education,* 1978)

In 1987 the Maryland Supreme Court emphasized that "local boards are state agencies, and, as such, are responsible to other appropriate state officials and to the public at large." Local boards must respond to the needs of the community, a requirement not made of private employers. Therefore, teachers are "but one of many groups in the community attempting to shape educational policy by exerting influence on local boards" (*Montgomery County Education Association, Inc. v. Board of Education of Montgomery County,* 1987).

The Oklahoma Supreme Court defined further differences between the freedom to contract in the private sector and the public schools:

> Public school matters differ from private matters where freedom to contract is virtually unlimited as public school matters are frequently subject to restrictive policies which reflect governmental interests and public concern. . . . Boards of education are merely representatives of the public interest and the public interest must, certainly at times, bind these representatives and limit or restrict their power to, in turn, bind the public which they represent. . . . It has been judicially observed that the public policy limitation on public sector collective bargaining statutes is necessary in order that the collective actions of public employees do not distort the normal political process for controlling public policy (*Mindemann v. Independent School District No. 6 of Caddo County,* 1989).

Therefore, the law is generally settled that school boards have certain statutory rights that cannot be bargained away or otherwise given to any other party. This concept was first explained by the *Norwalk* court in 1951 when it said, "To negotiate a contract which involves the surrender of the board's legal discretion, is contrary to law or is otherwise ultra vires" (*Norwalk Teachers' Association v. Board of Education of City of Norwalk,* 1951).

The courts become involved when the school board claims an item is an educational policy decision and, therefore, nonnegotiable, while the teachers' association claims the item is negotiable. Interpreting state statutes to determine where the exclusive managerial prerogative of the board lies has become the subject of much litigation. A case heard by the Alaska Supreme Court in 1977 illustrates the conflicting points of view between school boards and teachers' associations:

> The school boards contend that the submission of educational policies to a good faith collective bargaining requirement would remove the final decisions

> on such matters from the boards. . . . Delegation of part of the decision-making power on educational policy to labor unions is unconstitutional, they urge, because the union is a private organization, unaccountable to the public. The union can use the power for its own ends, and is under no duty to foster educational policies which are in the general public interest.
>
> The unions argue that such delegation is perfectly proper, and that there is no delegation of decision-making power inherent in a labor negotiations requirement. They further argue that they represent professional employees, and that their participation in good faith collective bargaining labor negotiations is an attempt by the legislature to provide professional advice to school boards on the management of the schools (*Kenai Peninsula Borough School District v. Kenai Peninsula Education Association,* 1977).

Although the court admitted that some doubt exists about what is bargainable in education, it ruled that control of educational policy cannot be shifted from school board to teachers' union. However, the court noted that the statute implicitly intended that the school boards meet and confer with the unions. Then teachers could give the boards the benefit of their expertise as policies are established.

The hiring and assignment of teachers are almost always nondelegable school board responsibilities. Yet, teachers' associations in many states have attempted to bring the procedures involved in employment decisions to the bargaining table. Bound by state statutes, the courts have settled these disputes by ruling on the exclusive managerial nature of the items. In 1976 a New Jersey board's appointment of an acting vice-principal allegedly violated a clause in the negotiated agreement that stated that vice-principals had to have tenure in the school district. The New Jersey Superior Court ruled that the agreement by the school board to confine itself to hiring only those applicants within the system was beyond the scope of bargaining because it involved a major educational policy. The violation of managerial prerogative was unenforceable (*Board of Education of Township of North Bergen v. North Bergen Federation of Teachers,* 1976). The New Jersey courts ruled in 1978 that the selection of the school in which a teacher works or the grade and subjects that he or she teaches was a managerial duty designed to promote the goal of providing students with a thorough and efficient education. Therefore, teacher assignment was not a mandatory subject of collective negotiations (*Ridgefield Park Education Association v. Ridgefield Park Board of Education,* 1978).

When the Boston school district needed to decrease the number of teachers because of dropping enrollments in the city's schools, the teachers' association claimed tenured teachers could not be laid off. However, the Massachusetts Supreme Court ruled that the board had the right to determine the size of the teaching staff annually as an area of exclusive managerial prerogative:

> It is by now well established in this State that public policy may limit the ability of a public employer to bind itself in a collective bargaining agreement. . . . This gloss on public sector collective bargaining statutes is deemed necessary in order that the collective actions of public employees do not distort the normal political process for controlling public policy. . . . In the context of public education, this court has held that specific appointment determinations, and de-

cisions to abolish positions are within the exclusive managerial prerogative of a school committee, and thus beyond the scope of collective bargaining (*Boston Teachers Union, Local 66 v. School Committee of Boston,* 1982).

The right to transfer teachers or to reduce the number of teachers is also a nondelegable right of local school boards in Illinois. In 1987 an appellate court ruled that evaluation of teacher qualifications in order to transfer, dismiss, or retain teachers required "the educational expertise of the school board" and could not be delegated (*Proviso Council of West Suburban Teachers Union, Local 571 v. Board of Education, Proviso Township High Schools, District 109, Cook County,* 1987). Similarly, the decision of a Michigan school board to terminate operation of a district special education center and transfer the students to an adjacent regional center was ruled an educational policy decision within the board's managerial discretion. The teachers' union had filed a complaint, claiming the district had refused to bargain over a decision to subcontract bargaining unit work. The Michigan Supreme Court upheld the board's action:

> It is within the scope of a local school board's management prerogative to determine its role in the delivery of educational services.... Faced with a projected budget deficit, the local board was forced to weigh the interests of employees protected by statute against the needs of children in perhaps the most vulnerable group of the student population.... A local school board must be able to exercise its management power in order to prudently discharge its fiscal responsibilities while also safeguarding the best interests of the students educated in the district (*Bay City Education Association v. Bay City Public Schools,* 1988).

An allegation by a teachers' association that a board decision should have been negotiated is often accompanied by the claim that the conflict should have been submitted to arbitration, especially in states with binding arbitration laws. In many states, submitting an issue to arbitration indicates the board's willingness to delegate its authority to a third party, and, because this action is unlawful, arbitration cannot be used as a means for settling disputes over managerial decisions. The courts have been asked to rule when a teachers' association has insisted that a decision be submitted to arbitration and the board has claimed the decision is theirs to make. In striking down the state binding arbitration clause, the Virginia Supreme Court explained how a binding arbitration statute can result in the delegation of board power:

> There can be no doubt that a delegation of power is involved in the binding arbitration provision. Indeed, the very section of the [statute] which provides that an arbitration panel shall have authority to make a final and binding decision also states that the local school board "hereby delegates such authority to the Panel" (*School Board of the City of Richmond v. Parham,* 1978).

A New York teacher who demanded a right to arbitration when he was denied the varsity football coaching position was told by the court that assessing qualifications of teachers for coaching positions was a nondelegable responsibility of the board

(*Riverhead Central School District v. Riverhead Central Faculty Association,* 1988). In 1989 a probationary teacher whose contract was not renewed and a tenured teacher who was not reappointed to his extra duty coaching position had the support of their association in demanding the issues be submitted to arbitration. The courts, however, interpreted Oklahoma's statute to limit the school board's ability to delegate decisions to binding arbitration:

> The Board could not lawfully limit its statutory authority to nonrenew a probationary teacher through a collective bargaining agreement notwithstanding its voluntary agreement to the contrary.
>
> [The statute] explicitly confers upon school boards the function of fixing teacher duties. We hence find a school board has the plenary power to discontinue the extra-duty assignments of a tenured teacher. Such power is essentially managerial in nature and not bargainable. The substantive decision to assign or not assign teachers' duties is basically a policy determination. To find otherwise would *significantly* interfere with the board's inherent managerial responsibility for the local educational policies and duty to maintain adequate standards for the benefit of the pupils and the school district.
>
> We conclude it was beyond the power of the Board to bind itself to arbitration through collective bargaining which would have the effect of superseding its nondelegable and exclusive authority to fix teachers' duties, in the absence of any legislation to the contrary (*Mindemann v. Independent School District No. 6 of Caddo County,* 1989).

In some states, courts have ruled that an arbitrator may have a limited role in making recommendations to the school board. In an Alaska case in 1985, the state supreme court ruled that the question of the reinstatement of a nontenured teacher could be submitted to arbitration because the arbitrator might recommend that the board exercise its discretion to reinstate the teacher. However, "the legislative edict is clear that [the] school district cannot negotiate away its authority to decide tenure, nonretention, reinstatement or other matters concerning educational policy or management prerogative" (*Jones v. Wrangell School District,* 1985).

School boards at times claim statutory authority to make decisions when they actually do not have that authority or have misinterpreted a statute or a contractual provision. In Washington, two part-time teachers were not appointed to full-time positions when there were openings for which they were qualified. The teachers filed grievances, claiming a right to be transferred to the full-time positions. The board claimed the teacher transfer policy meant that part-time teachers could be transferred only to equivalent part-time positions, not to full-time positions. After the arbitrator agreed with the teachers, the board went to court to claim the arbitrator had no jurisdiction over the dispute because the board had merely exercised its discretion in the employment of teachers. The state supreme court upheld the position of the teachers (*Lake Washington School District No. 414 v. Lake Washington Education Association/Washington Education Association,* 1987).

Because of the public's interest in the schools, school boards may not delegate to teachers' associations any of the rights given to them by the state. To do so would involve giving more decision-making power to teachers than the law allows. Matters of educational policy are generally the exclusive prerogative of the school boards, which should always exercise that authority in the best interest of the students and the schools. Teachers' associations sometimes attempt to negotiate agreements that grant to the association decision-making rights that belong to the board. When negotiating a contract or interpreting the terms of the contract, both school board and teachers' association should recognize that some areas of educational policy are exclusively the domain of the board, acting as a representative of the public interest.

Principle V

The scope of collective negotiations is generally determined by state statute or by written agreements and case law where no state statute exists.

From the earliest attempts by teachers' associations to negotiate contracts with school boards, the question of what subjects are negotiable has been asked. As school boards have worked to retain control over subjects they consider their exclusive managerial prerogative, teachers' associations have worked to bring more subjects to the bargaining table. Generally, the school has statutory authority to make educational policy, and subjects to be negotiated include wages, hours, and conditions of employment, as patterned after language in industry contracts with labor unions. However, the lines between managerial prerogative and conditions of employment are not as narrowly drawn in education as they are in industry, and the courts become involved when school boards and teachers' organizations cannot agree on the scope of negotiations.

Many states have enacted statutes to define the scope of teacher-employer negotiations, but not all issues can be anticipated or addressed by laws. The specificity of state statutes varies widely. Although many statutes merely state that wages, hours, and conditions of employment are subject to negotiation, others provide more definite guidelines. For example, in 1972 Oregon law restricted negotiable items to "salaries and related economic policies affecting professional services." Washington's statute, however, included a long list of negotiable items, including curriculum, textbook selection, in-service training, student teaching, personnel, hiring, salaries, and noninstructional duties. (Laws are cited in *West Hartford Education Association v. DeCourcy,* 1972.) California law in 1983 provided even more direction for collective bargaining:

> The scope of representation shall be limited to matters relating to wages, hours of employment, and other terms and conditions of employment. "Terms and conditions of employment" mean health and welfare benefits . . . leave, transfer and reassignment policies, safety conditions of employment, class size, procedures to be used for the evaluation of employees, organizational security . . . procedures for processing grievances . . . and the layoff of probationary certificated school district employees. . . . In addition, the exclusive representative of certificated personnel has the right to consult on the definition of educational objectives, the determination of the content of courses and curriculum, and the selection of textbooks to the extent such matters are within the discretion of the public school employer under the law. All matters not specifically enumerated are reserved to the public school employer and may not be a subject of

> meeting and negotiating, provided that nothing herein may be construed to limit the right of the public school employer to consult with any employees or employee organization on any matter outside the scope of representation (as cited in *San Mateo City School District v. Public Employment Relations Board,* 1983).

Statutes dealing with the scope of collective negotiations in the public sector, especially education, are changing continually. Before case law can be referenced, the state law at the time of the case must be studied. In general, the scope of collective negotiations between teachers' associations and school boards is broadening as teachers' associations influence legislation and written agreements that make more subjects negotiable.

Early cases often dealt with the issue of whether or not one specific item was negotiable. As lists of negotiable and nonnegotiable items grew, sometimes a third category evolved. Some subjects were not the board's exclusive prerogative, but neither were they mandated by statute to be negotiated. Thus, the board and teachers' association could agree to negotiate some items, a category sometimes called "permissive." Not all states were willing to recognize this third category, however. In 1978 a New Jersey teachers' association tried to use past court decisions to show that three categories of items existed in that state, including a permissive category, but the state supreme court disagreed. The court said that state law clearly indicated two categories: mandatorily negotiable terms and conditions of employment and nonnegotiable matters of governmental policy. Transfer of teachers fell into the latter category (*Ridgefield Park Education Association v. Ridgefield Park Board of Education,* 1978). A Maryland teachers' association attempted to use the same argument in 1987 when it wanted the school calendar and reclassification of positions to be negotiated after the board had unilaterally made decisions regarding these subjects. The association claimed that under Maryland law there were three categories of subjects: "mandatory" subjects of collective bargaining, which a local board must agree to negotiate; "permissive" subjects, which a local board may but need not agree to negotiate; and "illegal" subjects, which a local board may never agree to negotiate. In reviewing the issue, the Maryland Supreme Court agreed that some state courts use three categories because their statutes create or have been interpreted to create a "permissive" category. Other courts, including Maryland, recognize only a dichotomy between negotiable and nonnegotiable subjects, with no intermediate category. However, this court stated the dilemma so often facing school boards, teachers' associations, and the courts in trying to determine where the line between negotiable and nonnegotiable items lies:

> [Maryland law] suggests a dichotomy between "matters that relate to salaries, wages, hours, and other working conditions," which are negotiable, and matters of educational policy, which are not. As many courts have observed, however, no clear line distinguishes matters of educational policy from matters subject to collective bargaining. . . . For example, matters that fall directly under [the statute] such as salary levels and hours of work also implicate educational policy considerations: higher salaries for some teachers may be necessary to attract or retain qualified personnel, and longer hours may enhance educational

> achievement. . . . In fact, virtually every managerial decision in some way relates to "salaries, wages, hours, and other working conditions," and is therefore arguably negotiable. At the same time, virtually every such decision also involves educational policy considerations and is therefore arguably nonnegotiable (*Montgomery County Education Association, Inc. v. Board of Education of Montgomery County,* 1987).

In simplest terms, educational policy is generally not subject to collective negotiations, but wages, hours, and working conditions are negotiable. The New Jersey Supreme Court stated this differentiation in 1973:

> Major educational policies which indirectly affect the working conditions of the teachers remain exclusively with the Board and are not negotiable, whereas items which are not predominantly educational policies and directly affect the financial and personal welfare of the teachers do not remain exclusively with the Board and are negotiable (*Board of Education of City of Englewood v. Englewood Teachers Association,* 1973).

As more and more issues have become topics for litigation, some courts have developed various standards by which to decide whether or not a topic is negotiable. In 1974 the Nevada Supreme Court stated that "the government employer [is] required to negotiate if a particular item is found to *significantly* relate to wages, hours, and working conditions even though that item is also related to management prerogative" (*Clark County School District v. Local Government Employee Management Relations Board,* 1974). In 1984 the Wisconsin Supreme Court, quoting earlier Wisconsin cases, announced a "primarily related" standard by which to weigh the interests of the competing parties:

> In recognizing the interests of the employees and the interests of the municipal employer as manager and political entity, the statute necessarily presents certain tensions and difficulties in its application. Such tensions arise principally when a proposal touches simultaneously upon wages, hours, and conditions of employment and upon managerial decision making or public policy. To resolve these conflict situations, this court has interpreted [the statute] as setting forth a "primarily related" standard. . . . The standard requires [the court] . . . to determine whether the proposals are "primarily related" to "wages, hours and conditions of employment," to "educational policy and school management and operation," to "management and direction of the school system" or to "formulation or management of public policy" (*West Bend Education Association v. Wisconsin Employment Relations Commission,* 1984).

The Illinois Supreme Court has also used state statutes to establish a standard for defining the parameters of negotiable and nonnegotiable items. In Illinois, the subject must have a "direct" effect on wages, hours, and terms and conditions of employment before it is negotiable. The applicable Illinois statute implies this "direct" standard:

> Employers shall not be required to bargain over matters of inherent managerial policy, which shall include such areas of discretion or policy as the functions of the employer, standards of services, its overall budget, the organizational structure and selection of new employees and direction of employees. Employers, however, shall be required to bargain collectively with regard to policy matters directly affecting wages, hours and terms and conditions of employment as well as the impact thereon upon request by employee representatives (as cited in *Decatur Board of Education, District No. 61 v. Illinois Educational Labor Relations Board,* 1989).

The courts continue to struggle in ruling on the negotiability of items. Because state statutes, court decisions, and negotiated agreements vary so much, some items are negotiable in some states and not negotiable in others. The school calendar, for example, has been a disputed topic in many states. In 1967 the Wisconsin Supreme Court ruled the school calendar was a "condition of employment," subject to bargaining (*Joint School District No. 8, City of Madison v. Wisconsin Employment Relations Board,* 1967). Later that court ruled that the school board was required to meet and confer about the calendar but could not be required to concede to association demands (*City of Beloit v. Wisconsin Employment Relations Commission,* 1976). The Nevada Supreme Court in 1974 ruled the school calendar negotiable because it affected the teachers' working conditions and hours (*Clark County School District v. Local Government Employee Management Relations Board,* 1974). However, Connecticut, Alaska, Indiana, Oregon, and Maryland have all stated that the school calendar was not negotiable. (See *West Hartford Education Association v. DeCourcy,* 1972; *Kenai Peninsula Borough School District v. Kenai Peninsula Education Association,* 1977; *Eastbrook Community Schools Corporation v. Indiana Education Employment Relations Board,* 1983; *East County Bargaining Council v. Centennial School District No. 28JT,* 1984; *Montgomery County Education Association, Inc. v. Board of Education of Montgomery County,* 1987.) The Indiana appellate court's rationale was similar to that of other state courts when denying the negotiability of the school calendar:

> Although the school calendar necessarily affects the days and hours during which teachers work, we conclude . . . that the calendar's effect on students and other public interests outweigh the private interest of the teachers. The protection of the students' interests being the predominant goal, we must conclude that the school calendar is a matter of educational policy (*Eastbrook Community Schools Corporation v. Indiana Education Employment Relations Board,* 1983).

Class size is yet another item that has resulted in much court action. As of 1989, Alaska, Florida, Kansas, Maine, Nebraska, New York, Oregon, South Dakota, and Wisconsin courts had found class size to be a nonmandatory bargaining subject, and Connecticut, Massachusetts, Nevada, and Illinois courts had stated that class size was a mandatory topic for collective bargaining. The argument in favor of class size being a negotiable item was stated by an Illinois appellate court:

> Classroom size is a mandatory issue for bargaining in Illinois. . . . Class size is an element which obviously affects financial planning. The bargaining requirement may well create administrative problems, such as the need for additional teachers, or even additional buildings. The substantial fiscal problems faced by school boards must be a factor when determining whether class size should be subject to bargaining. At the same time, a teacher's work hours are definitely affected by class size. Classroom discipline requirements are subject to change based on the size of the class. It would appear that the amount of pressure on a teacher increases in proportion to the increase in class size (*Decatur Board of Education, District No. 61 v. Illinois Educational Labor Relations Board,* 1989).

Courts in many states have been asked to rule on the negotiability of other items. The Connecticut Supreme Court ruled in 1972 that the length of the school day, extracurricular activity assignments, and binding arbitration of grievances were nonnegotiable (*West Hartford Education Association v. DeCourcy,* 1972). A year later the South Dakota Supreme Court declared that elementary parent-teacher conferences, teachers' aides, elementary planning periods, the expansion of audiovisual facilities, teachers' budget allowances, expansion of the guidance and counseling program, and mandatory retirement of administrators were not "other conditions of employment" and so were not open to negotiation (*Aberdeen Education Association v. Aberdeen Board of Education, Aberdeen Independent School District,* 1974). In Nevada the state supreme court determined that professional improvement, student discipline, teacher evaluation, differentiated staffing, teacher load, and instructional supplies were all negotiable because they affected either the teachers' working conditions or hours (*Clark County School District v. Local Government Employee Management Relations Board,* 1974). In 1976 the Wisconsin Supreme Court ruled that teacher evaluations, access to and scope of teacher's files, "just cause" as a standard for disciplinary action against teachers, teacher layoffs, discipline of students who present a physical threat to teacher safety, teacher in-service training, and summer school were negotiable, but bargaining over the elementary reading program and assistance to teachers having difficulties was nonmandatory (*City of Beloit v. Wisconsin Employment Relations Commission,* 1976). In Alaska the court denied that elementary planning time, relief from nonprofessional chores, paraprofessional tutors, teacher specialists, teachers' aides, pupil-teacher ratio, a teacher ombudsman, teacher evaluation of administrators, selection of instructional materials, the use of secondary department heads, secondary teacher preparation and planning time, and teacher representation on school board advisory committees were negotiable (*Kenai Peninsula Borough School District v. Kenai Peninsula Education Association,* 1977). Indiana appellate courts have consistently ruled that school boards do not have to bargain with teachers about making up days on which they did not work because of emergency closings of schools (*Eastbrook Community Schools Corporation v. Indiana Education Employment Relations Board,* 1983; *Union County School Corporation Board of School Trustees v. Indiana Education Employment Relations Board,* 1984; *Halley v. Board of School Trustees of Blackford County School Corporation,* 1988). Teacher vacations and definition of the work year for salary purposes were ruled to be subject to mandatory collective bargaining in Oregon in 1984 (*East County Bargaining Council v. Cen-*

tennial School District No. 28JT, 1984). In 1988 teachers claimed that a North Dakota school district could not change the number of class periods in a standard day without negotiating. The court ruled that the district could change from a five-period to a six-period day, which did not change the number of hours in the standard day, without bargaining with the association (*Mandan Education Association v. Mandan Public School District No. 1,* 1988). New York teachers claimed that the decision about applying for state funds under an "Excellence in Teaching Apportionment Program" should be a mandatory subject of bargaining. The court disagreed (*City School District of City of Elmira v. New York State Public Employment Relations Board,* 1988). The District of Columbia appellate court ruled that the beginning date of the school year and Good Friday's status as a holiday were not mandatory subjects for negotiation (*Public Employee Relations Board v. Washington Teachers' Union Local 6, AFT,* 1989).

Regardless of the desire of teachers' associations and school boards to negotiate some items, they may not violate state statutes. Negotiated agreements that are beyond the scope of the law will be declared void when challenged in court. In 1909, for example, New Jersey enacted a tenure statute to "prevent school boards from abusing their superior bargaining power over teachers in contract negotiations." In 1982 the state supreme court upheld special education teachers who challenged a negotiated agreement that made them ineligible for tenure. The court ruled that the agreement violated the tenure law:

> It is now well settled that public employees and employers may not agree to contractual terms that contravene a specific term or condition of employment set by a statute. . . . We have specifically stated that the tenure provisions of [New Jersey law] constitute a mandatory contractual term that may not be waived or bargained away. . . . Whether certain teachers are entitled to tenure never depends on the contractual agreement between the teachers and the board of education. Tenure is a "statutory right imposed upon a teacher's contractual employment."
>
> As a practical matter, the protection of tenure would be greatly reduced if it were subject to contract principles. If tenure were subject to contract, it would be available to teachers only if school boards agreed to grant it to them. But the Legislature has explicitly mandated that teachers be granted tenure under certain conditions as a means to improve public education. Neither school boards nor teachers are free to disobey that mandate. Tenure is not dependent on agreement between the parties. Teachers are entitled to tenure because the Legislature has granted them that right (*Spiewak v. Board of Education of Rutherford,* 1982).

In 1989 New York teachers who had greater seniority as health teachers were ruled eligible to retain their positions over teachers who had taught health a shorter time but whose seniority was greater because of teaching time in other areas. The court ruled that the collective bargaining agreement that required teaching time in other areas to be applied to seniority status in new teaching positions violated an imperative provision in New York's education law (*Szumigala v. Hicksville Union Free School District Board of Education,* 1989).

In another New York case, the State Commissioner of Education had issued a regulation that preempted any school district obligation to negotiate a ban against smoking on school district buses. When the Public Education Relations Board ordered a school district to rescind its order banning smoking on buses because the order had not been negotiated, the court upheld the district (*Rush-Henrietta Central School District v. Newman,* 1989).

The scope of collective negotiations in the nation's school districts is constantly changing with new state laws, new negotiated agreements, and new court rulings. When either the school board or the teachers' association is dissatisfied with the current provisions of a negotiated agreement, it can take the counsel of the Washington Supreme Court: "If the [party] is dissatisfied with the current provisions, it may return to the bargaining table and seek to modify or eliminate them in future collective bargaining agreements" (*Lake Washington School District No. 414 v. Lake Washington Education Association/Washington Education Association,* 1987). As long as negotiations do not violate the law, teachers' associations and school boards can determine the items to be brought to the bargaining table.

Principle VI

Teachers, as public employees, have no inherent right to strike without statutory authorization. Neither may they impose other sanctions against a school board.

A major reason for reluctance to allow collective bargaining in the public sector was the fear it would lead to strikes by public employees. In the private sector, the right to strike is commonly viewed as an effective tool to be wielded by the union against management as long as national laws are observed. However, the traditional belief is that public employees serve the public welfare and have no right to threaten or interfere with the safety and welfare of the public by disruptive organized activities. President Calvin Coolidge said, "There is no right to strike against public safety by anybody anywhere at any time." President Franklin D. Roosevelt wrote, "A strike of public employees manifests nothing less than an intent on their part to prevent or obstruct the operations of Government until their demands are satisfied. Such action, looking toward the paralysis of Government by those who have sworn to support it, is unthinkable and intolerable." (Quotations cited in *Norwalk Teachers' Association v. Board of Education of City of Norwalk,* 1951.)

In states where collective bargaining is permitted or mandated by statute, the legislature usually does not allow and often expressly forbids strikes. In the few states where teacher strikes are permitted, many qualifications must be met and statutory procedures exhausted before a strike is legal.

The courts become involved when school boards seek injunctions to end a teachers' strike or to stall a threatened strike. Contempt of court charges have been brought against teachers and their organization if a strike continues in spite of an injunction or restraining order. Teachers' associations bring suit against school boards when they believe they have received unreasonable disciplinary sanctions for participating in or organizing a teachers' strike. The weight of judicial decisions is still against strikes and other types of interference by teachers' associations with the operation of the schools.

In the *Norwalk* case, the Connecticut court answered the question of whether or not strikes were an allowable aspect of collective bargaining:

> Under our system, the government is established by and run for all of the people, not for the benefit of any person or group. The profit motive, inherent in the principle of free enterprise, is absent. It should be the aim of every employee of the government to do his or her part to make it function as efficiently and economically as possible. The drastic remedy of the organized strike to enforce the demands of unions of government employees is in direct contravention of this principle (*Norwalk Teachers' Association v. Board of Education of City of Norwalk,* 1951).

In the 1960s, many teachers' associations in various states attempted to use strikes to influence school board decisions. Almost all strike efforts failed when the cases reached the courts. In a New Jersey district, 400 teachers did not report to work and set up picket lines when the school board did not meet their demands. At the urging of the national union representative, the strike continued for two days after the district obtained a restraining order. The court fined the union, the local president, and the national representative $1,000 each for contempt of court and fined other strike leaders $500 each. Strike leaders were also sentenced to jail terms of several months. The court stated that strikes thwart public purpose:

> When government undertakes itself to meet a need, it necessarily decides the public interest requires the service, and its employees cannot reverse or frustrate that decision by a concerted refusal to meet that need (*In re Block,* 1967).

With the increase of teacher strikes in many states, legislatures began passing laws explicitly prohibiting strikes in the public sector. In 1967, New York enacted the Taylor Act, which was to be challenged in several cases:

> No public employee or employee organization shall engage in a strike, and no employee organization shall cause, instigate, encourage, or condone a strike.

Almost immediately, the New York City School District's teachers' association challenged the Taylor Act by calling a strike. The association, its local president, and the national union president were found guilty of contempt of court for failing to obey a court order enjoining them from striking. The union claimed that its members were not on strike but had resigned. The court, however, pointed out that none of the 40,000 teachers' resignations had been transmitted to the school board. After fining the union $150,000 and the national president $250 and sentencing him to 15 days in jail, the court denounced strikes by teachers:

> From time immemorial, it has been a fundamental principle that a government employee may not strike. In this sensitive area, neither labor—the public employee—nor management—the governmental agency—in their mutual interdependence can afford the indulgence of arbitrary self-interest at the expense of the public.

> The defendant Union, powerful though it may be, is nevertheless insufficiently powerful to disdain, with impunity, the law and the Court. Our existence as a free people is dependent on a healthy respect for law and order. For ours is a society open and ordered, animate and free, and it can continue so only so long as we maintain our liberties *under law.* Ironic indeed is the fact that this basic lesson in elementary civics must be taught anew to, of all pupils, the very persons to whom we daily entrust our tender offspring for training and development as the leaders of tomorrow. . . . Law means nothing unless it means the same law for all. This strike by a powerful union against the public was a rebellion against the government; if permitted to succeed it would eventually destroy government with resultant anarchy and chaos (*Board of Education of City of New York v. Shanker,* 1967).

New York teachers again challenged the constitutionality of the Taylor Act in 1970 on the grounds it infringed on free association, free speech, and equal protection. The court, refusing to enjoin the board of education from making payroll deductions against teachers who had engaged in an illegal strike, ruled that the state could ban strikes by public employees (*Zeluck v. Board of Education of City School District of City of New Rochelle,* 1970).

A 1968 case began when a New Jersey school board refused to renew the contracts of two nontenured teachers. The teachers' association imposed sanctions against the district and announced through the local press that any teacher accepting employment in that district would be violating the professional code of ethics. Claiming that they were not striking but merely resigning as of a future date, 36 teachers walked off their jobs. The court refused to make a distinction, stating that work stoppages and blacklists in the public sector were illegal under New Jersey criminal code as obstruction of government (*Board of Education, Borough of Union Beach v. New Jersey Education Association,* 1968).

Indiana teachers were found in contempt of court when they ignored a restraining order and continued their strike. The state supreme court stated that "government employees may not engage in a strike for any purpose" (*Anderson Federation of Teachers, Local 519 v. School City of Anderson,* 1969).

A due process issue arose in Michigan when teachers did not report for work at the beginning of the school year because a prolonged labor dispute had resulted in no negotiated contract. In December the teachers again failed to report to work, and the school board adopted a resolution requiring teachers either to report for work or to submit letters of resignation. One teacher resigned, 38 reported for work, and the other 184 were terminated. The state supreme court ruled that tenured teachers who strike in violation of the public employee law could be disciplined without a prior hearing:

> When public employees strike, the public employer must, like a private employer, be able to hire substitute employees so that the public business is not interrupted. In order to hire competent replacements, it may be necessary for the public employer to offer permanent employment and thus displace strikers. Where essential services have been suspended, the hiring of replacements often

> cannot await time consuming adjudicatory processes (*Rockwell v. Board of Education of the School District of Crestwood,* 1975).

In 1976 the United States Supreme Court heard a Wisconsin case after members of the teachers' union went on strike when no agreement on a master contract was reached. Two days later, the superintendent sent a letter to all teachers, inviting them to return to work; a few did return. Three days later he sent another letter, asking the 86 teachers still on strike to return to work, but none did. Each striking teacher then received a notice about a disciplinary hearing and a warning that teachers' strikes were illegal in the state. After the hearing, the board voted to terminate the teachers. The board once again invited all teachers to reapply for their teaching positions. One did so, and replacements were hired to fill the other positions. The teachers filed suit, alleging their Fourteenth Amendment due process rights had been violated by inadequate notice and a hearing before the school board, which they believed was not an impartial tribunal. The Supreme Court ruled that "the Board's prior role as negotiator does not disqualify it to decide that the public interest in maintaining uninterrupted classroom work required that teachers striking in violation of state law be discharged" (*Hortonville Joint School District No. 1 v. Hortonville Education Association,* 1976). The high court further ruled that the teachers had no property right in the expectation that their jobs would remain open to them after they had left them to go on an illegal strike.

State courts continue to rule teachers' strikes illegal. The Alaska Supreme Court noted in 1982 that in the absence of express statutory permission, no state that had considered the question of strikes by public employees had found them to be legal, including Maryland, West Virginia, Connecticut, Illinois, Indiana, Kentucky, Minnesota, New Jersey, North Dakota, Ohio, Oklahoma, Rhode Island, Tennessee, and Washington. Alaska teachers had gone on strike to argue that they had no way of enforcing their views because state law did not allow teachers to strike or to submit their disputes to binding arbitration. Nonteaching employees had the right to strike in a school district, but teachers did not. However, the court upheld the state statutes:

> No court has held that the common law permits public employees to legally strike in the absence of explicit statutory consent. Our reasons for following the majority rule are not founded on the traditional fear of strikes as illegal conspiracies, . . . but rather on a recognition of the special role that teachers fill in society and our acknowledgment of the functional limitations of this court when attempting to make social policy decisions. Resolution of this controversy involves a delicate balancing of the citizens' need for a timely school year and of the teachers' need for an effective tool to influence their working conditions. . . . While a teachers' strike would not directly affect the public's safety as would a police officers' strike, nonetheless teachers can be considered indispensable to the daily functioning of society during the scheduled academic year (*Anchorage Education Association v. Anchorage School District,* 1982).

A Pennsylvania teachers' association claimed that a teachers' strike should not invoke the provisions of the state law prohibiting strikes that "create a clear and present danger or threat to the health, safety or welfare of the public." The court, however, stated that loss of state subsidies creates a clear and present danger to the public (*Jersey Shore Education Association v. Jersey Shore Area School District,* 1986). In 1987 a New Jersey teachers' association reasoned that a teachers' strike does not create a substantial and imminent threat to the public. The court remained unmoved; teachers' strikes are illegal in New Jersey (*Passaic Township Board of Education v. Passaic Township Education Association,* 1987). Citing earlier rulings, the Pennsylvania Commonwealth Court ruled in 1988 that loss of state subsidies (even if offset by decreases in operating expenses) plus the negative impact of a strike on students meant that striking teachers were creating a clear and present danger:

> The trial court determined that high school seniors were receiving instruction by supervisory employees but that it was deficient in quality; that high school seniors would be disadvantaged in applying to programs of higher education; that they would graduate too late to be admitted to summer school; that grades K–11 were receiving no instruction; that students in grades K–11 were subjected to the possibility of repeating a grade or receiving inadequate instruction in preparation for the next higher grade; that special education students would be adversely affected and that they were particularly vulnerable to interruption in their learning processes; that school lunch benefits would be lost to needy students; and that families with two working parents or one-parent families would be economically disadvantaged by the need to engage babysitters (*Armstrong Education Association v. Armstrong School District,* 1988).

The courts have ruled that many types of concerted actions against school districts can be classified as strikes because of interference with the operation of the schools. A work stoppage in an effort to reinstate provisions of an expired contract was ruled a strike in Michigan (*Warren Education Association v. Adams,* 1975). Refusal to perform assigned extracurricular duties was ruled to constitute a strike in New Jersey (*Board of Education of City of Asbury Park v. Asbury Park Education Association,* 1976). In 1984 teachers in Massachusetts engaged in a "work-to-rule" action when no agreement between the school board and the teachers' association was reached at the beginning of the school year. One teacher sent parents a letter stating that she would not work on school-related activities after 3:15 p.m., that she would cease sending home weekly evaluations, that she would cease publication of a monthly newsletter to parents, and that she would be available to meet with parents only during her planning period. Another teacher posted a similar letter on the bulletin board at school. The association published a letter in the local newspaper defining what "working-to-rule" meant:

> It means that the traditional work of the teacher, that is, correcting papers, planning lessons, conferring with parents, recording grades, etc. will be done during the confines of the school day.

The state supreme court agreed with a hearing officer and the Labor Relations Commission that teachers had a right to quit activities that were not required by their most recently expired contract (such as the newsletter and weekly evaluation reports of students) because those services were not traditional activities engaged in by all teachers. However, a concerted refusal by the teachers to perform tasks that were traditionally performed after school hours by teachers as a group constituted a strike justifying disciplinary measures (*Lenox Education Association v. Labor Relations Commission,* 1984).

Therefore, strikes by teachers are uniformly held to be illegal by the courts except in states with statutes that expressly allow strikes by public employees, including teachers. Even in those states, the procedures that must be exhausted and qualifications that must be met result in few legal teachers' strikes. Work stoppages and slowdowns, blacklisting, refusal to perform duties, and other types of concerted activities by teachers with the goal of interfering with the operation of the school are also generally ruled illegal by the courts.

Summary

Collective negotiations in the public sector, although lacking the sometimes violent history of the private sector, has had its own history of conflict and misunderstanding. Yet, the inherent differences between the private and public sector have resulted in laws and court decisions that recognize those differences. Looking to the private sector for examples, policies, or procedures does not generally assist labor relations in the public sector, as stated by the Pennsylvania Supreme Court:

> The distinction between the public and private sector cannot be minimized. Employers in the private sector are motivated by the profit to be returned from the enterprise whereas public employers are custodians of public funds and mandated to perform governmental functions as economically and effectively as possible. The employer in the private sector is constrained only by investors who are most concerned with the return for their investment whereas the public employer must adhere to the statutory enactments which control the operation of the enterprise. . . . The experiences gained in the private employment sector will not necessarily provide an infallible basis for a monolithic model for public employment (*Pennsylvania Labor Relations Board v. State College Area School District,* 1975).

General recognition of a teacher's right to join a professional association whose goal is to negotiate contracts or at least to influence the decisions of the school board did not come until the courts ruled that that right was protected by the First Amendment. Although the right to organize or to join a professional association does not imply a right for that organization to bargain with the school board, no sanctions can be levied against any teacher who chooses to become a member of any national, state, or local labor organization.

With the advent of collective bargaining between representatives of a recognized teachers' union and the school board, decision-making power has, in most districts, become more evenly distributed between the two parties. School boards maintain their managerial prerogative to make educational policy, a right that cannot be delegated or bargained away; yet, teachers have the right to negotiate decisions over their salaries and working conditions.

The majority of states have statutes governing collective bargaining in the public sector, and teachers' associations and school boards are bound by those laws. Failure to abide by state law can result in sanctions against the party in violation. Unless negotiations are expressly forbidden by state statute, a school board usually has the discretionary authority to choose to bargain with teachers in states where no collective bargaining statute exists.

The scope of collective negotiations is often determined by state statute, but varying interpretations of statutes have led to many disputes. Educational policy and teachers' working conditions cannot always be distinctly separated, and both parties often approach the bargaining table intent on expanding the scope of their own interests. Salaries and fringe benefits are clearly negotiable items in most districts, but such subjects as classroom size and the school calendar contain elements of educational policy as well as working conditions.

The courts have often been asked to rule in labor disputes between teachers' associations and school districts. By interpreting state statutes and master contracts, the courts have influenced the collective bargaining process in public schools. Teachers' associations and school boards have at times both asked for court injunctions to stop unfair labor practices by the other party. Because teachers' strikes are illegal in almost every state, the courts generally rule in support of school districts when teachers' associations have allowed or encouraged walkouts, slowdowns, work stoppages, mass resignations, blacklisting, working-to-rule, or other forms of organized activity that interrupt the operation of the school.

Labor relations in the public sector cannot be exactly equated to those conducted in the private sector. Although the controlling laws in most states are fairly well established, collective bargaining laws, policies, and procedures vary drastically from state to state, and movements to enact national labor laws for the public sector have not been successful. The courts undoubtedly will continue to be active in the area of collective negotiations in education.

Questions and Responses

1. What is collective bargaining in the public sector?

Collective bargaining is the process of negotiating a labor contract by representatives of labor (the employees) and management (the employer). Usually when employees and employers bargain collectively, the employees have organized into an association that has been formally recognized by the individual employees and by the employer to represent the interests of the whole employee group. The terms of the final contract must be mutually agreeable to the rank and file of the employees and to the employer. In the public sector, collective bargaining is undertaken by representatives of the public employees' organization and the public employer.

2. How does collective bargaining differ between the public and private sectors?

In the private sector, labor and management are the only two parties whose interests are at stake during negotiations. The terms of the contract have little or no impact on any other person or group. The primary interests of both groups are economic;

labor wants employees to benefit financially from the work they do, and management wants to ensure a profit for the company and its stockholders. If negotiations fail, each party generally has the power to bring serious sanctions against the other party, including strikes by employees and lockouts by employers. Labor relations in the private sector are governed by national labor laws, and labor unions and management must abide by the laws that control their negotiating procedures. Ideally, both parties will be the beneficiaries of the negotiated contract.

In the public sector, employees and employers are ultimately responsible for fulfilling some type of government service for the benefit of society. Denial or interruption of that service harms a third party—the public—that is in need of that service. Economic interests of both parties are secondary to the health, safety, and welfare of the public, whose tax dollars provide the funds for operation of the service as well as for salaries for the employees. If negotiations fail, the ultimate victim of any sanction by one party against the other is the public. Because of public outcry against strikes by public servants and the inability of employers to shut down a government agency or move its operation to another location, sanctions are limited in the public sector. Although national laws have little application to collective bargaining in the public sector, almost every state has statutes that define the allowable processes and scope of negotiations in the public sector in that state. Ideally, the public employee and employer will benefit from the terms of the negotiated contract, but both parties must guarantee that the public will be the continuous beneficiary of the government service provided by the agency involved in negotiations.

3. Are teachers allowed to organize or join teachers' associations?

The First Amendment to the United States Constitution guarantees the right of assembly, which has been interpreted to include the right of association. For many years, teachers, as public servants, were not allowed to organize or to join any type of labor union because of the suspicion that such organizations were subversive. However, the courts have recognized that as citizens of the United States, teachers do have constitutional rights that cannot be denied by their employing school boards. The right of association has been extended to include professional teachers' associations at the national, state, and local levels, including those whose goal is to negotiate collective agreements with school boards.

4. When may teachers' associations and school boards bargain collectively?

Most states have enacted legislation that allows collective bargaining in the public sector, including between teachers and school boards. However, teachers' associations have no inherent right to bargain with school boards, and a few states expressly forbid collective bargaining in school districts. In some states, as teachers' associations gained strength, they have influenced the passage of legislation that mandates collective negotiations. In the absence of legislation, school districts usually have the discretionary authority to bargain with representatives of the teachers' association.

5. What types of items can be brought to the bargaining table?

In school district negotiations, all subjects that concern the operation of the school generally fall into one of the following categories: (a) educational policy or (b) salary and working conditions. Most states have statutes that define the scope of collective bargaining in the public sector as limited to those items related to salary, wages, and working conditions. However, many more items are being considered as proper topics for collective bargaining as the demarcation between educational policy and working conditions becomes less definite. For example, assignment of extra duties, layoff policies, leave of absence policies, health and welfare benefits, and grievance procedures are among items often negotiated.

6. What is the managerial prerogative of the school board?
The school board has been delegated its powers and authority by the legislature of the state. Therefore, those powers cannot be delegated or bargained away. Generally, the power to determine educational policy for the district is the prerogative of the school board and, therefore, cannot be subject to negotiation. The school board has been charged with the responsibility of making the educational policy decisions for the welfare of the schools in the district, and those management rights are nonnegotiable.

7. Why are teachers generally not allowed to go on strike?
Teachers are public servants and are constrained by statutes that limit the sanctions that can be imposed by public employees against the government. The victims of teachers' strikes are not the school board members, who are acting in their capacity as elected or appointed officials representing the public; it is the public, and particularly students, who suffer when teachers strike. Therefore, public sentiment has almost always been against teachers striking or otherwise interfering with the operation of the schools. To enforce this view, most states have statutes expressly forbidding teachers from striking. Even in those states that allow teachers' strikes, many procedures have to be exhausted and qualifications met before teachers can legally walk off the job.

8. What happens when teachers and school boards cannot agree on the terms of a contract?
State statutes often describe the procedures that must be followed when negotiations fail to produce a contract between the teachers' association and the school board. These procedures vary widely from state to state and must be followed by both parties. Mediation, fact finding, arbitration, and binding arbitration are processes allowed in some states and mandated in others when an agreement cannot be reached. In only a few states may teachers go on strike and only after all other stages in the process have been exhausted. Usually, teachers continue working under the terms of the expired contract until the impasse is resolved and a new contract is ratified.

9. What types of sanctions may be brought against teachers and teachers' associations that interfere with the operation of schools by some illegal action?
School districts often go to court to get a restraining order or injunction ordering teachers back to work or to cease the interrupting activity. Failure to abide by the court order often leads to contempt of court rulings, which usually result in fines against the association, leaders, and participants. The courts have upheld disciplinary actions, including termination, against teachers who persist in engaging in illegal activities. State statutes must be obeyed by individual teachers and their associations.

10. What types of sanctions may be brought against a school district that breaches state law or the terms of a negotiated agreement?

School boards are also bound by state law. When the board is in breach of the negotiated contract, teachers' associations often go to court to obtain injunctions or writs of mandamus to force the board to perform its duties as dictated by the agreement. Teachers' associations often raise the public's awareness of violations of the contract through press releases, which may influence the election of board members. Teachers must also go through all processes mandated by state law when filing a grievance against the board, rather than engaging in illegal strikes or other destructive types of action.

Case References

Aberdeen Education Association v. Aberdeen Board of Education, Aberdeen Independent School District, 215 N.W.2d 837 (S.D. 1974).

American Federation of State, County, and Municipal Employees, AFL-CIO v. Woodward, 406 F.2d 137 (8th Cir. 1969).

Anchorage Education Association v. Anchorage School District, 648 P.2d 993 (Alaska, 1982).

Anderson Federation of Teachers, Local 519 v. School City of Anderson, 251 N.E.2d 15 (Ind. 1969); cert. denied, 399 U.S. 928 (1970).

Armstrong Education Association v. Armstrong School District, 542 A.2d 1047 (Pa. Cmwlth., 1988).

Atkins v. City of Charlotte, 296 F.Supp. 1068 (W.D. N.C. 1969).

Bay City Education Association v. Bay City Public Schools, 422 N.W.2d 504 (Mich. 1988).

Benson v. School District No. 1 of Silver Bow County, 344 P.2d 117 (Mont. 1959).

Board of Education, Borough of Union Beach v. New Jersey Education Association, 247 A.2d 867 (N.J., 1968).

Board of Education of City of Asbury Park v. Asbury Park Education Association, 368 A.2d 396 (N.J. Super. 1976).

Board of Education of City of New York v. Shanker, 283 N.Y.S.2d 548 (N.Y., 1967).

Board of Education of City of Englewood v. Englewood Teachers Association, 311 A.2d 729 (N.J. 1973).

Board of Education of Township of North Bergen v. North Bergen Federation of Teachers, 357 A.2d 302 (N.J. Super. A.D. 1976).

Boston Teachers Union, Local 66 v. School Committee of Boston, 434 N.E.2d 1258 (Mass. 1982).

Chicago Division of the Illinois Education Association v. Board of Education of City of Chicago, 222 N.E.2d 243 (Ill. App. 1966).

City of Beloit v. Wisconsin Employment Relations Commission, 242 N.W.2d 231 (Wis. 1976).

City School District of City of Elmira v. New York State Public Employment Relations Board, 536 N.Y.S.2d 214 (N.Y.A.D. 3 Dept. 1988).

Clark County School District v. Local Government Employee Management Relations Board, 530 P.2d 114 (Nev. 1974).

Commonwealth v. County Board of Arlington County, 232 S.E.2d 30 (Va. 1977).

Decatur Board of Education, District No. 61 v. Illinois Educational Labor Relations Board, 536 N.E.2d 743 (Ill.App. 4 Dist. 1989).

East County Bargaining Council v. Centennial School District No. 28JT, 685 P.2d 452 (Or. App. 1984).

Eastbrook Community Schools Corporation v. Indiana Education Employment Relations Board, 446 N.E.2d 1007 (Ind. App. 1983).

Fayette County Education Association v. Hardy, 626 S.W.2d 217 (Ky. App. 1980).

Georgia Association of Educators v. Gwinnett County School District, 856 F.2d 142 (11th Cir., 1988).

Halley v. Board of School Trustees of Blackford County School Corporation, 531 N.E.2d 1182 (Ind.App. 4 Dist. 1988).

Hortonville Joint School District No. 1 v. Hortonville Education Association, 426 U.S. 482 (1976).

In re Block, 236 A.2d 589 (N.J. 1967).

Jersey Shore Education Association v. Jersey Shore Area School District, 512 A.2d 805 (Pa.Cmwlth. 1986).

Joint School District No. 8, City of Madison v. Wisconsin Employment Relations Board, 155 N.W.2d 78 (Wis. 1967).

Jones v. Wrangell School District, 696 P.2d 677 (Alaska 1985).

Kenai Peninsula Borough School District v. Kenai Peninsula Education Association, 572 P.2d 416 (Alaska, 1977).

Lake Washington School District No. 414 v. Lake Washington Education Association/Washington Education Association, 745 P.2d 504 (Wash. 1987).

Lenox Education Association v. Labor Relations Commission, 471 N.E.2d 81 (Mass. 1984).

Mandan Education Association v. Mandan Public School District No. 1, 425 N.W.2d 917 (N.D. 1988).

McAuliffe v. Mayor of City of New Bedford, 29 N.E. 517 (Mass. 1892).

McLaughlin v. Tilendis, 398 F.2d 287 (7th Cir., 1968).

Mindemann v. Independent School District No. 6 of Caddo County, 771 P.2d 996 (Okl. 1989).

Minneapolis Federation of Teachers Local 59, AFL-CIO v. Obermeyer, 147 N.W.2d 358 (Minn. 1966).

Montgomery County Education Association, Inc. v. Board of Education of Montgomery County, 534 A.2d 980 (Md. 1987).

Norwalk Teachers' Association v. Board of Education of City of Norwalk, 83 A.2d 482 (Supreme Court of Errors of Conn., 1951).

Passaic Township Board of Education v. Passaic Township Education Association, 536 A.2d 1276 (N.J. Super. A.D. 1987).

Pennsylvania Labor Relations Board v. State College Area School District, 337 A.2d 262 (Pa. 1975).

People ex rel. Fursman v. City of Chicago, 116 N.E. 158 (Ill. 1917).

Proviso Council of West Suburban Teachers Union, Local 571 v. Board of Education, Proviso Township High Schools, District 109, Cook County, 513 N.E.2d 996 (Ill.App. 1 Dist. 1987).

Public Employee Relations Board v. Washington Teachers' Union Local 6, AFT, 556 A.2d 206 (D.C.App. 1989).

Ridgefield Park Education Association v. Ridgefield Park Board of Education, 393 A.2d 278 (N.J. 1978).

Riverhead Central School District v. Riverhead Central Faculty Association, 528 N.Y.S.2d 611 (N.Y.A.D. 2 Dept. 1988).

Rockwell v. Board of Education of the School District of Crestwood, 227 N.W.2d 736 (Mich. 1975).

Rush-Henrietta Central School District v. Newman, 542 N.Y.S.2d 440 (N.Y.A.D. 4 Dept. 1989).

San Mateo City School District v. Public Employment Relations Board, 663 P.2d 523 (Cal. 1983).

School Board of the City of Richmond v. Parham, 243 S.E.2d 468 (Va. 1978).

Seattle High School Chapter No. 200 of the AFT v. Sharples, 293 P. 994 (Wash. 1930).

Spiewak v. Board of Education of Rutherford, 447 A.2d 140 (N.J. 1982).

Stellmaker v. DePetrillo, 710 F.Supp. 891 (D.Conn. 1989).

Szumigala v. Hicksville Union Free School District Board of Education, 539 N.Y.S.2d 83 (N.Y.A.D. 2 Dept. 1989).

Union County School Corporation Board of School Trustees v. Indiana Education Employment Relations Board, 471 N.E.2d 1191 (Ind.App. 4 Dist. 1984).
Warren Education Association v. Adams, 226 N.W.2d 536 (Mich.App. 1975).
West Bend Education Association v. Wisconsin Employment Relations Commission, 357 N.W.2d 534 (Wis. 1984).
West Hartford Education Association v. DeCourcy, 295 A.2d 526 (Conn. 1972).
Winston-Salem/Forsyth County Unit of the North Carolina Association of Educators v. Phillips, 381 F.Supp. 644 (M.D.N.C. 1974).
Zeluck v. Board of Education of City School District of City of New Rochelle, 307 N.Y.S.2d 329 (N.Y., 1970).

10 Tort Liability

The old English common law of torts evolved as a result of the written law providing no remedy for the victim of an injurious intentional or negligent action by another person. As the common law expanded to take care of tortious actions, a person who caused injury to another person through violation of some legal duty was held liable to the injured party. Although a tort could also be a crime, the punishment of a tortfeasor under civil law was assessment of damages to compensate the victim for the injury rather than fines or jail terms for the wrongdoer. When the common law was transferred to the United States, these elements and procedures of tort law were eventually written down and formalized. Even though other areas of law have contributed to the increase in school-related litigation, torts continue to be the single greatest source for school law cases. The time and money involved when teachers, administrators, and school boards are named in lawsuits for alleged torts, the rising costs of liability insurance, and the negative publicity that often accompanies suits mandate that educators become aware of their rights and responsibilities under tort law.

Civil courts become involved in tort cases whenever one person alleges that another person has intentionally or negligently caused an injury and the injured party seeks damages. When the second party disputes the claim, the courts have to determine whether or not a tort has occurred and, if so, what damages should be levied. Almost all tort actions arise under state law; few cases are heard in the federal courts because federal rules of law are seldom involved. However, with the interpretation of Section 1983 of the Civil Rights Act of 1871 as a federal tort law under which victims of unconstitutional infringement of their civil rights are eligible for damages, some cases are being heard in the federal court system.

Three types of common law tort actions have been identified: intentional, strict liability, and unintentional. The perpetrator of an intentional tort meant to do injury or proceeded to act with disregard for whether or not an injury would occur. Strict liability involves behavior that automatically results in liability if an injury occurs. An unintentional tort is committed when a person is negligent and should have anticipated that an injury would occur and taken appropriate action to preclude it. Almost all tort cases involving teachers stem from claims of negligence.

A school district has inherent host powers, which obligate the school district and its agents to protect the safety and welfare of students, employees, and visitors. Negligence in carrying out the duty of care implied in a school's host powers may subject a school to tort action. The criteria that determine whether or not an unintentional tort has occurred have been refined over time and adapted by the courts to apply to situations today. To sustain a claim of negligence in court, the injured party must show that the claim meets all prerequisite standards:

1. A legal duty of care was owed to the injured party.
2. That duty of care was breached by the perpetrator.
3. The negligent act was the proximate cause of the injury.
4. Real harm or an actual injury was suffered by the party bringing suit.

If a claim of tort fails any one of these elements of proof, the suit will be dismissed. A person held to be negligent had to have done something that a reasonable and prudent person in the same situation would not have done, or failed to have done something that a reasonable and prudent person would have done. The "reasonable and prudent person" standard varies from community to community and must be adapted to the situation. In school settings, a teacher is usually held to the standard of a reasonable and prudent teacher, which is higher than that required of laypersons.

Because the remedy in tort is payment of damages, the courts have identified several types of damage awards. Actual or real damages compensate the injured party for the documented cost of the injury. Compensatory damages attempt to bring the injured party to the position in which he or she would have been had the tort not occurred. Punitive damages are levied to punish the tortfeasor, and nominal damages are awarded when damages are required by law but the court determines that the injured party is eligible for only a minimal amount.

School districts have historically been free from liability and the payment of damages because of the doctrine of governmental immunity. However, this doctrine has been at least partially abrogated by legislative or court action in most jurisdictions. Where such is the case, state law normally permits or requires the purchase of liability insurance to cover damages that may be charged against the school district or its employees acting in their official capacities. Teachers and other professional employees are generally provided insurance protection as a part of their fringe benefit packages or through their membership in a union or professional association. In some instances, teachers are provided indemnification by the state.

In this litigious age, educators are involved more and more frequently in expensive lawsuits. Familiarity with, not fear of, tort law may ease the anxieties of educators when they are accused of tortious actions that may lead to the courtroom.

Legal Principles

Principle I *In Loco Parentis*

Because a public school teacher assumes an *in loco parentis* relationship to the students in his or her charge, the teacher has a legal responsibility to provide for the students' health, safety, and welfare. Failure to fulfill this duty may lead to the teacher being charged with a tort.

(continued on next page)

Legal Principles (continued)

Principle II *Intentional Torts*

Intentional torts are actions undertaken by a tortfeasor with full knowledge and intent to harm another person. Many intentional torts may involve criminal as well as civil elements.

Principle III *Strict Liability*

Strict liability involves intentional behavior for which the tortfeasor is automatically liable if any damage or injury results.

Principle IV *Negligence*

An unintentional tort is a negligent action that a reasonable and prudent person would not have done, or the failure to do something that a reasonable and prudent person would have done in a similar situation. The negligent action becomes the proximate cause of an injury to a person to whom a duty of care is owed by the tortfeasor.

Principle V *Foreseeability*

A public school teacher may be charged with negligence if he or she does not anticipate and take action to prevent an event that could reasonably have been foreseen as a potential threat to the safety or welfare of students.

Principle VI *Assigned Duties*

A public school teacher may be charged with negligence if he or she fails to fulfill assigned duties and that failure leads to the injury of a student.

Principle VII *Contributory Negligence*

Actions by the injured student may result in his or her being charged in a tort action with contributory negligence, which may decrease the teacher's liability. However, students are not expected to have the same degree of foresight, caution, or judgment as a teacher.

Principle VIII *Assumption of Risk*

A student assumes some risk when he or she knowingly participates in activities known to involve some inherent hazard. A teacher is responsible for instructing students about risks and in correct procedures to reduce the chance of injury, for ensuring that equipment and facilities are safe, and for maintaining a safe instructional environment.

Principle IX *Federal Torts*

Teachers and other school officials may be held personally liable under the federal tort law if they knew or reasonably should have known that they were violating a student's constitutional or civil rights.

Discussion

Principle I

Because a public school teacher assumes an *in loco parentis* relationship to the students in his or her charge, the teacher has a legal responsibility to provide for the students' health, safety, and welfare. Failure to fulfill this duty may lead to the teacher being charged with a tort.

The common law concept of *in loco parentis* means, literally, "in place of the parent." It has governed the relationship between teachers and students since early days in England when young men were turned over to tutors who were expected to treat their charges as the boys' parents would. Although American public schools scarcely incorporate all aspects of the tutor-student relationship, the tradition of *in loco parentis* has dominated the legal aspects of the teacher-student relationship. Teachers are expected to treat students as parents would by providing for the students' health, safety, and welfare, furthering their best educational interests, and even disciplining them for their own good:

> [A teacher's] relationship to the pupils under his care and custody differs from that generally existing between a public employee and a member of the general public. In a limited sense the teacher stands in the parent's place in his relationship to a pupil . . . and has such a portion of the powers of the parent over the pupil as is necessary to carry out his employment (*Eastman v. Williams,* 1965).

The family image of public schools has been used by the courts to uphold a teacher's right to discipline unruly children and a student's duty to obey:

> In the school, as in the family, there exists on the part of the pupils the obligation of obedience to lawful commands, subordination, civil deportment, respect for the right of other pupils, and fidelity to duty. Those obligations are inherent in any proper school system, and constitute, so to speak, the common law of the school (*State ex rel. Burpee v. Burton,* 1878).

However, the *in loco parentis* concept has also been used to impress upon teachers that their roles are as parents, not as authoritarian disciplinarians or uncompromising taskmasters. When teachers have been found guilty of breaching that parental role, they have been held liable for resulting damages:

> At least in a limited sense the relation of a teacher to a pupil is that of one in loco parentis. We are not here concerned with the law applicable to the punishment of a pupil by a teacher; but rather with the law applicable to the duties of a teacher in the care and custody of a pupil. In the faithful discharge of such duties the teacher is bound to use reasonable care, tested in the light of the existing relationship. If, through negligence, the teacher is guilty of a breach of such duty and in consequence thereof a pupil suffers injury, liability results (*Gaincott v. Davis,* 1937).

With recent changes in laws governing child abuse and tort liability and with society's gradual recognition that not all parent-child relationships benefit the child, the *in loco parentis* tradition may be weakening as society redefines both parent-child and teacher-pupil relationships. Yet, in 1983 a football coach's relationship to his players was defined as *in loco parentis* when the coach was charged with causing injury to one of his players. The boy was injured during a game, and the complaint alleged that he should not have been allowed to play in the game because he had not attended the requisite number of practice sessions. The Illinois appellate court dismissed the complaint on grounds of statutory immunity because of *in loco parentis*:

> [The statute] conferred immunity on teachers and school districts from negligence in the supervision of activities connected with school programs. The court reasoned that the statute conferred the status in loco parentis on teachers for supervision of activities connected with school programs. Therefore, teachers standing *in loco parentis* should not be subjected to greater liability than parents. Since parents are not liable to their children for negligence, teachers are also not liable for negligence when they are acting *in loco parentis* (*Kain v. Rockridge Community Unit School District No. 300,* 1983).

The extent of teacher liability under *in loco parentis* continues to be the subject of court cases. In 1989 another Illinois appellate court noted that the state supreme court had interpreted state law as conferring upon educators the status of *in loco parentis* in disciplinary and nondisciplinary matters. Therefore, the court ruled that teachers could be subjected to the same, but not greater, liability as parents (*Templar v. Decatur Public School District,* 1989).

Because *in loco parentis* has helped define the teacher-student relationship since the beginning of schooling in America, it will likely continue to influence the courts in their decisions about possible breaches of that relationship. Regardless of laws and court decisions, the ideal relationship between teachers and students should be one where teachers are concerned for and protective of the welfare of their students. Anything less could lead to charges that a teacher is negligent in fulfilling his or her duties.

Principle II

Intentional torts are actions undertaken by a tortfeasor with full knowledge and intent to harm another person. Many intentional torts may involve criminal as well as civil elements.

Because most teachers would never be guilty of intentionally or maliciously causing injury to students, few teachers have been charged with intentional torts. Assault, battery, slander, libel, false imprisonment, and trespass are common examples of intentional tort, but few court cases involving educators have been predicated on these types of actions.

However, the history of corporal punishment in America's schools introduces the issue of teachers being charged with the intentional torts of assault and battery. Parents have traditionally had the right to discipline their children as they saw fit, and, under the *in loco parentis* concept, that privilege was transferred to the schools, giving teachers the right to discipline children when they deemed such punishment appropriate. Physical, or corporal, punishment has been one type of disciplinary measure used by parents and, hence, by teachers. When parents have disagreed with teachers on the necessity and appropriateness of corporal punishment, some charges of intentional tort have been levied against teachers.

Even in the middle 1800s, some teachers were accused of using excessive corporal punishment on students. In 1853 the Indiana Supreme Court said that a teacher could be guilty of assault and battery if chastisement were administered in anger or insolence (*Cooper v. McJunkin,* 1853). That court also said that a teacher was not justified in beating a student so severely as to wear out two whips, in striking two blows to the student's head with fists, and in kicking the student in the face because he misspelled a word and refused to try again (*Gardner v. State,* 1853). Another teacher beat a student with a small rawhide whip the day after the boy had called him "old Jack Seaver" while the boy was driving his father's cow past the teacher's house. Although the court admitted that a teacher "may not safely be trusted with all a parent's authority, for he does not act from the instinct of parental affection," it upheld the teacher's actions (*Lander v. Seaver,* 1859). The Alabama Supreme Court stated that corporal punishment may at times overstep the bounds of *in loco parentis:*

> When, in the judgment of reasonable men, the punishment inflicted is immoderate or excessive, and a jury would be authorized, from the facts of the case, to infer that it was induced by legal malice, or wickedness of motive, the limit of lawful authority may be adjudged to be passed. In determining this question, the nature of the instrument of correction used may have a strong bearing on the inquiry as to motive or intention (*Boyd v. State,* 1890).

Since World War II, corporal punishment by teachers and other school officials has come under increasing criticism as a disciplinary measure in schools. Yet, when a claim of intentional tort is alleged in corporal punishment cases, the courts have to determine such issues as the motive of the individual using corporal punishment, the extent of injury to the student, and whether or not the force used was excessive. In 1944 a Connecticut court ruled that a 190-pound principal used excessive force when he sat on the abdomen of a disobedient 10-year-old child (*Calway v. Williamson,* 1944). The standards used by many courts in ruling in corporal punishment cases were stated by the Alabama Supreme Court in 1954:

> To be guilty of an assault and battery, the teacher must not only inflict on the child immoderate chastisement, but he must do so with legal malice or wicked motives or he must inflict some permanent injury (*Suits v. Glover,* 1954).

In 1967 a physical education teacher was charged with assault when a student's arm was broken as the teacher attempted to remove the student from the basketball court. The teacher claimed that the student had threatened to strike him and the boy's arm was broken when the teacher tried to restrain him. On the other hand, the student claimed that after the teacher had menaced, chased, seized, lifted, and shaken him against the bleachers, the teacher had suddenly let him fall to the floor, fracturing his arm. The court found that the teacher, who weighed 230 pounds, could scarcely have been seriously threatened by the 101-pound boy and upheld the charges against him (*Frank v. Orleans Parish School Board,* 1967).

An Oregon teacher was similarly charged with assault and battery for allegedly shoving a pupil into a glass window, severely injuring the boy's arm. The teacher contended that he had been merely attempting to remove the student from the classroom because of his disruptive actions and that the injury had resulted from the boy's struggling. The court ruled for the teacher but gave a warning about the use of corporal punishment:

> But a teacher's right to use physical punishment is a limited one. His immunity from liability in damages requires that the evidence show that the punishment administered was reasonable, and such a showing requires consideration of the nature of the punishment itself, the nature of the pupil's misconduct which gave rise to the punishment, the age and physical condition of the pupil, and the teacher's motive in inflicting the punishment (*Simms v. School District No. 1, Multnomah County,* 1973).

In 1977 the United States Supreme Court became involved in the controversy over corporal punishment in public schools. *Ingraham v. Wright* (1977) was not premised on claims of intentional tort but on claims that corporal punishment violated the Eighth Amendment because it constituted a "cruel and unusual punishment." The high court ruled that corporal punishment of students did not violate the Eighth Amendment, which had been written to protect the rights of criminals, and that remedies available to students under civil tort law and criminal law were not available to prisoners:

> The openness of the public school and its supervision by the community afford significant safeguards against the kinds of abuses from which the Eighth Amendment protects the prisoner. In virtually every community where corporal punishment is permitted in the schools, these safeguards are reinforced by the legal constraints of the common law. Public school teachers and administrators are privileged at common law to inflict only such corporal punishment as is reasonably necessary for the proper education and discipline of the child; any punishment going beyond the privilege may result in both civil and criminal liability (*Ingraham v. Wright,* 1977).

The debate about the use of corporal punishment in the schools has led to many court cases where teachers have been charged with violating corporal punishment policies, using corporal punishment in states and districts that have banned its use, using excessive force, or causing serious or permanent injury to students. In some of these cases, damages have been levied against teachers found guilty of committing intentional torts; other cases have been brought under criminal law or other state statutes. More cases are being brought by students and parents who believe that corporal punishment is a form of child abuse. Controversy about the effectiveness of physical punishment, publicity about child abuse, and awareness of damage awards have also contributed to the number of cases.

In 1982 an assistant superintendent grabbed a student who had shouted a derisive name at him, took the student to a nearby classroom, and gave him a "substantial shaking." The student was never absent from school because of injuries; he went to a doctor three weeks later only because he needed a physical examination prior to track season. When the student brought criminal charges, the trial court found the administrator guilty of assault and sentenced him to 45 days in prison and fined him $1,000. However, the Ohio appellate court overturned the ruling (*State of Ohio v. Hoover,* 1982). A Georgia father brought action under state law against a principal who administered corporal punishment to his son. The boy had been sent to the principal's office because of his having disrupted the class by drawing explicit pictures of sexual intercourse and circulating them throughout the room. Given a choice between suspension and paddling, the boy had chosen paddling and was swatted four times with a wooden paddle by the principal with the assistant principal present. Afterwards, the boy returned to the classroom without exhibiting any pain, having any problem sitting down, or voicing any complaint about pain. In court, however, his parents swore he had received severe bruises to his buttocks and one thigh and that the principal had violated Georgia's corporal punishment law by administering excessive and unduly severe punishment. The court upheld the principal (*Maddox v. Boutwell,* 1985).

As long as corporal punishment is used in the schools as an approved form of discipline and those administering the punishment establish and then follow reasonable guidelines, teachers and administrators will not be found guilty of assault and battery. However, teachers who physically punish students in an unreasonable manner could be held liable for damages under intentional tort or penalized under criminal law. Teachers must follow all procedures for administering corporal punishment, including having a witness present and having someone else administer the punishment if the teacher is so angry that too much force may be exerted. Because several states, most major metropolitan area school districts, and many other school districts have banned the use of corporal punishment, teachers must determine if physical punishment is allowed before using it. Charges of intentional tort liability may be upheld in court when teachers do not follow policies.

Strict liability involves intentional behavior for which the tortfeasor is automatically liable if any damage or injury results. **Principle III**

The legal concept of strict liability arose when the courts recognized that persons could be injured by some unusual hazard even though the party responsible for the hazard was not directly responsible for the injury. The person who creates the potential for abnormal danger to others is held strictly liable for any injuries that occur, and almost no defenses are allowed in court to excuse the liability of the tortfeasor. However, strict liability is not lightly imposed. An activity or object must be classified as hazardous or even "ultrahazardous" to allow claims under strict liability. Some examples of actions or items that fall under strict liability are excavating, the keeping of wild and ferocious animals, and the keeping or using of explosives and inflammable liquids. The courts arė inclined to rule that persons who maintain dangerous apparatuses or undertake abnormally hazardous activities are aware of the risks and are much more able to shoulder the burden of loss than are innocent victims. Strict liability seldom arises in education cases, although attempts are sometimes made to classify some activities and equipment often found in schools as ultrahazardous.

Before equipment can be classified under strict liability, it must be inherently dangerous or hazardous to others. In 1983 a kindergarten teacher was teaching the letter *D* to her students by making doughnuts in a deep-fat fryer. In spite of the teacher's reasonable efforts to keep the students away from the fryer, one child pulled the fryer over and was burned. In first addressing a strict liability claim, the court ruled that "a deep-fat fryer does not fall under the [category] of inherently 'ultrahazardous,' as do wild animals or dynamite." The court noted that the teacher had provided appropriate supervision for the activity:

> The degree of supervision that is required by law over kindergarten students necessarily varies with the activities in which they are engaged, i.e., resting, drawing, playing, listening to stories or watching a cooking demonstration. The standard of care imposable upon school authorities does of necessity depend on the situational setting. (*Wetsel v. Independent School District I-1,* 1983).

Sports and athletic equipment have often been the subject of court cases, but only cases involving product liability have been upheld under strict liability, sometimes resulting in the manufacturer being held responsible for any damages. In 1981 a student was killed when a metal soccer goal fell and struck her as she knelt to tie her shoe during a physical education class. Her parents sued for punitive damages, claiming that the school district and physical education teacher maintained a nuisance (the soccer goal) on school property. The court did not rule that the soccer goal was an unusually dangerous type of equipment, and the district and teacher were protected by Georgia's sovereign immunity statute (*Truelove v. Wilson,* 1981).

Attempts have been made to rule trampolines as hazardous or dangerous equipment, but these cases have thus far failed. In 1983 a 15-year-old girl broke her wrist and arm when she and four friends were jumping on a trampoline during a free play period in a physical education class. The teacher had repeatedly told them that no more than two students were to use the trampoline at one time, and one student was watching for the return of the teacher at the time of the incident because they knew they were breaking the rule. The court ruled that the trampoline was not an inherently dangerous object and that the accident had not been foreseeable (*Smith v. Vernon Parish School Board,* 1983).

Many attempts have been made to categorize certain types of playground equipment as hazardous. These claims have generally not been upheld, and damage awards for injuries that have resulted from use of equipment in poor repair, misuse of equipment, or unsupervised use of equipment have been sustained on grounds of negligence, not strict liability (*Jackson v. Board of Education of City of Chicago,* 1982).

Although claims of strict liability are being brought more frequently against schools because of activities or equipment, few of these claims have succeeded because of the difficulty of meeting the legal requisites to establish a strict liability claim. Teachers must ensure that all equipment is approved for use in schools and not introduce activities or items that could make the teacher strictly liable for any injury. Field trips and extracurricular programs should not include activities that the courts have ruled are ultrahazardous. Even the most innovative teacher should use common sense and attempt to foresee the potential for injury in order to ensure that students are protected from harm inherent to certain activities and equipment.

Principle IV

An unintentional tort is a negligent action that a reasonable and prudent person would not have done, or the failure to do something that a reasonable and prudent person would have done in a similar situation. The negligent action becomes the proximate cause of an injury to a person to whom a duty of care is owed by the tortfeasor.

The most common type of tort involves the unintentional or negligent action by a tortfeasor that results in an injury to another person. In education, the greatest number of court cases arises from claims of negligence against teachers, administrators, and school districts. Of course, not all injuries result from negligent acts; accidents do occur. Yet, because teachers are generally held to a higher standard of care in the school setting than are laypersons, they are often expected to prevent some types of mishaps and may be found negligent for failing to do so. Reasonable and prudent teachers will usually be expected to conduct themselves in accordance with the specialized skills and knowledge indicated by their teaching certificates. A teacher must always take the actions (or avoid taking the actions) that a reasonable and prudent teacher would take (or avoid taking) in similar circumstances. The courts become involved when teachers are charged with unreasonable and imprudent actions.

An often-quoted case of teachers failing to act as reasonable and prudent teachers was heard in 1942. In this case, a grade school student's finger was infected but not so badly that the boy missed recess. In spite of having no evidence of a medical emergency, two teachers treated the boy's hand after school. After heating water to scalding, they immersed the boy's hand and held it in the water for 10 minutes, causing permanent disfigurement. The teachers were found liable for their inappropriate, negligent behavior (*Guerrieri v. Tyson,* 1942).

Parents sometimes bring suit when teachers do not act as the parents would prefer in regard to the welfare of their children. In 1951 a student broke his arm in a fall during gymnastics exercises. The physical education teacher had him walk the short distance to the school office from where he was taken to the hospital for treatment. The boy's father charged the teacher with negligence for having the boy walk after the injury instead of calling emergency services. The court ruled for the teacher:

> Common experience dictates that transportation to a hospital is the better choice of expedients under the circumstances rather than waiting to summon a physician who would be ready and able to come to the scene of the event. The conduct of the teacher was more in the nature of humanitarian interest rather than evocative of any negligence (*Sayers v. Ranger,* 1951).

In a similar case in California, a boy was injured during a touch football game. After being hit, the boy stayed in the game for two more plays and then sat on the sideline. He then went to the first aid room, where the principal had him lie down, and two hours later the physical education teacher took the boy home. Five hours later the boy had surgery to have his spleen and left kidney removed. The parents sued on the grounds that medical attention had been negligently applied and that the teachers had carelessly neglected to give prompt medical attention. However, the court ruled in favor of the teacher when medical experts testified that no additional injury had been done to the boy by the delay (*Pirkle v. Oakdale Union Grammar School District,* 1953).

However, if teachers do not conform to reasonable standards of behavior, they may be held liable for injuries. In 1970 a boy had been in a wrestling class for six weeks prior to his being injured in a match. The instructor, who had had little previous training in wrestling techniques, had taught the class a number of wrestling maneuvers that were potentially dangerous and were illegal in high school wrestling. The boy was consistently paired against boys heavier than himself, and, at the time of the incident, the instructor was attempting to supervise two matches at the same time. The United States Court of Appeals, Sixth Circuit, in ruling against the coach, stated the standard of care required of teachers:

> A . . . school's athletic instructors are required only to exercise that degree of care which a reasonably prudent man would exercise under the same or similar circumstances. . . . A teacher's superiority in knowledge and experience imposes responsibilities in his dealing with students which become an inherent element in measuring his compliance with the due care which is required of him (*Stehn v. Bernarr MacFadden Foundations, Inc.,* 1970).

An Oregon student injured her back in a physical education class, even though the teacher and principal were aware that she had a history of back problems and had been excused from physical education courses in the past. Her mother had asked the teacher on four occasions for the list of physical education activities so she could check with a doctor on the advisability of her daughter participating in them. The court ruled that "a physical education instructor is required to exercise reasonable care for the protection of the students under his supervision" (*Summers v. Milwaukie Union High School District No. 5, Clackamas County,* 1971).

Teachers are expected to use standard procedures in teaching their subject matter, and failure to use the methods that most teachers of that subject would use may result in a teacher being liable for damages if a student is injured. In 1982 a sixth grade student lost a front tooth when she hit the wall during a vertical jump exercise. In court another teacher testified that the correct way of performing the vertical jump is to stand parallel to a wall and jump from a standing position. The teacher charged with negligence had allowed students to run at the wall from six to eight feet away before jumping, and she admitted in court that she had not checked on the correct method of teaching the exercise. The appellate court ruled that the teacher had been negligent (*Dibortolo v. Metropolitan School District of Washington Township,* 1982).

Courts have occasionally used the *in loco parentis* standard to determine whether or not a teacher was negligent. In 1985 a student was hit in the eye with an eraser flipped by another student, and the parents sued the teacher. The court ruled that the teacher had exercised the same reasonable care that a parent of ordinary prudence would exercise under comparable circumstances (*Rock by Rock v. Central Square School District,* 1985). In an Arkansas case, a third grader intentionally hanged himself with a "bathroom pass" a teacher had made from plywood and a 20-inch nylon cord and was severely brain damaged as a result of the incident. Suit was brought, and the court ruled in favor of the school district, stating that the duty owed by the district was one of "ordinary care" and that that duty had been met because the cause of the accident was the intentional act of the child (*Gathright v. Lincoln Insurance Company,* 1985). In 1990 the Alabama Supreme Court ruled that the principal and physical education teacher were not responsible for the design or maintenance of the light fixtures and bulbs in the school gymnasium. Therefore, they could not be held liable for the eye injuries of a sixth grader who was cut by falling glass when a ball hit and broke a light bulb (*Beasley by and through Beasley v. Morton,* 1990).

Therefore, teachers may be held liable for acts of negligence if they do not conform to the standards expected of a reasonable and prudent teacher. Inexperienced teachers need to be aware that their teaching credentials indicate that they may be held to a higher standard than laypersons if a student in their charge is injured through a negligent action. All teachers must be constantly updating their skills and knowledge in order to act in the manner that an ordinary, reasonable, and prudent teacher would act. At the same time, they must avoid taking any actions that the courts would determine would not be taken by the ordinary, reasonable, and prudent teacher in a similar situation. School districts and administrators should assign teachers only to those curricular areas for which they are certificated and to those extracurricular activities for which they are qualified. Injuries to students resulting from negligent actions of teachers who are not professionally qualified for the supervising of the activity to which they are assigned may result in damage awards against school districts and administrators.

A public school teacher may be charged with negligence if he or she does not anticipate and take action to prevent an event that could reasonably have been foreseen as a potential threat to the safety or welfare of students. **Principle V**

The reasonable and prudent teacher is able to anticipate possible dangers and to take action to prevent injury to students. Therefore, "foreseeability" is a standard used by the courts to determine whether or not a teacher was negligent. No breach of the duty of care can occur when a teacher could not have reasonably foreseen the danger that led to an injury. Teachers of such courses as physical education, vocational education, and science, where some dangers may be encountered by inexperienced students, are expected to have learned to anticipate and to prevent potential injuries that other teachers and laypersons may not be able to foresee. All teachers are expected to have learned enough about student behavior to be able to foresee the potential for injury that is part of school experiences. The interrelationship between the reasonable person standard and foreseeability was explained by the Wisconsin Supreme Court:

> Every person is negligent when, without intending any wrong, he does such an act or omits to take such a precaution that under the circumstances present he, as an ordinarily prudent person, ought reasonably to foresee that he will thereby expose the interests of another to an unreasonable risk of harm. . . . A person is required to take into account such of the surrounding circumstances as would be taken into account by a reasonably prudent person and possess such knowledge as is possessed by an ordinarily reasonable person and to use such judgment and discretion as is exercised by persons of reasonable intelligence and judgment under the same or similar circumstance (*Osborne v. Montgomery,* 1931).

An extreme example of a teacher failing to foresee injury to students involved a teacher who participated in the administration of an electric shock to boys being initiated into a school club. The last boy to be shocked was killed, and the teacher was found guilty of negligence for failing to exercise the "highest degree of care that skill and vigilance can suggest" (*De Gooyer v. Harkness,* 1944). In 1965 a six-year-old child was injured on a school outing to the seacoast when a log on which he was standing was temporarily buoyed by a wave and then rolled over him. The school district claimed that a reasonably prudent teacher would not have been able to foresee the occurrence of unexpected wave action, but the court disagreed and ruled against the teacher:

> It is common knowledge that accidents substantially like the one that occurred in this case have occurred at beaches along the Oregon coast. Foreseeability of such harm is not so remote as to be ruled out as a matter of law. . . . Foreseeability of harm gives rise to a duty to take reasonable care to avoid the harm (*Morris v. Douglas County School District No. 9,* 1965).

Foreseeability was also an issue in a case where a physical education teacher left his class of 50 teenage boys unsupervised for 25 minutes after telling them to "shoot around" with basketballs. The boys became more and more rowdy, and one boy was finally injured. However, even while ruling against the teacher, the court stated that a teacher is not expected to remain in a classroom at all times regardless of circumstances that may compel occasional absences:

> This should not, of course, mean that a teacher who absents himself from a room is negligent as a matter of law. . . . What this means must depend upon the circumstances under which the teacher absented himself from the room. Perhaps relevant considerations would be the activity in which the students are engaged, the instrumentalities with which they are working (band saws, dangerous chemicals), the age and composition of the class, the teacher's past experience with the class and its propensities, and the reason for and duration of the teacher's absence (*Cirillo v. City of Milwaukee,* 1967).

Science teachers are generally expected to anticipate the types of experimenting that inexperienced students may do and to prevent injuries by supervising laboratory exercises and science projects. For example, a 13-year-old student was injured when he was building a model volcano at home. The teacher was found negligent for conducting a classroom volcano demonstration and then allowing the student to take his own volcano project home without determining exactly what chemical substances the student had used (*Simmons v. Beauregard Parish School Board,* 1975).

However, the courts have stated repeatedly that teachers cannot be in all places at one time and cannot be expected to foresee all possible dangers faced by students. In 1949 a teacher left the classroom for a few minutes to store some school supplies in a hall closet. During her absence, a pupil threw a pencil at a second student but missed, hitting a third student in the eye. The injured student claimed that if the teacher had been present, the injury would not have occurred. The court held for the teacher:

> It does not follow that such absence was the proximate producing cause of the injury, which was due, as we see it, to the tossed pencil. Whether it was done mischievously and heedlessly or wantonly and willfully, or with the serious purpose of returning the pencil to its owner, it was the act of an intervening third party which under the circumstances could hardly have been anticipated in the reasonable exercise of the teacher's legal duty toward the [student] (*Ohman v. Board of Education of City of New York,* 1949).

The Wisconsin Supreme Court ruled that a school personnel director could not have foreseen a student's suicide from information received in interviewing the student; the personnel director was not negligent for failing to refer the student to a psychiatrist (*Bogust v. Iversen,* 1960). Another teacher was not held liable for failure to foresee an injury to a child who was jumping rope when the rope was jerked from the teacher's hand and hit the child in the eye (*Wire v. Williams,* 1965). In a 1972 case, a teacher was sued for negligence after supervising a playground where a child threw a rock, which hit a larger rock and then hit another child in the eye. In ruling for the teacher, the Wyoming Supreme Court stated their view on the measure of foreseeability required of teachers:

> A teacher cannot anticipate the varied and unexpected acts which occur daily in and about the school premises. Where the time between an act of a student and injury to a fellow student is so short that the teacher has no opportunity to prevent injury, it cannot be said that negligence of the teacher is a proximate cause of the injury (*Fagan v. Summers,* 1972).

In 1972 two teachers took 50 students to a museum where the students were allowed to look at the exhibits without supervision. While at the museum, one boy was beaten by several boys not connected with the school, and the parents sued, charging that the teacher who had organized the trip should have foreseen the student's injury. The court discussed the likelihood of that type of injury, the magnitude of the burden of guarding against it, and the consequences of placing that burden on teachers, and it ruled in favor of the teacher (*Mancha v. Field Museum of Natural History,* 1972).

A Louisiana court ruled that a teacher could not be expected to foresee that a hidden can in an incinerator would explode and injure a child who was sent to empty wastebaskets (*Prier v. Horace Mann Insurance Company,* 1977). An Ohio teacher was not held liable when a student was injured by falling to the floor after another student kicked her stool from under her. The court ruled that the liability of a teacher cannot be predicated upon an unforeseeable assault in the classroom by one student upon another (*Boyer v. Jablonski,* 1980). A child was blinded in one eye after being stabbed twice with a pen by another child on a Louisiana playground. However, the teachers who were on duty were absolved of liability because the stabbing was not a foreseeable act that could have been prevented even with increased supervision (*Batiste v. Iberia Parish School Board,* 1981).

In another playground incident in 1988, a first grader's eye was permanently injured by a dirt ball thrown by a fourth grader. The Ohio appellate court noted that such an event cannot be foreseen:

> Recess is a physical outlet for young students who have spent a few hours in class. It is a time for play and the risk of injury is always present. This risk is partially minimized by the enforcement of rules, but it is unreasonable to expect that young children will behave during recess as the supervising adults and school officials hope (*Allison v. Field Local School District,* 1988).

In 1990 a teacher and school district were accused of negligence when a kindergarten child took a toothpick from her art project and stuck it into the ear of a younger child who was visiting in the first child's home. Entrusting a minor with a dangerous instrument is evidence of negligence, and the court, before ruling for the school personnel, had to determine if the teacher should have foreseen that the toothpick could be used as a dangerous instrument:

> An object such as a toothpick, not dangerous in itself, may be adjudged a dangerous instrument under certain factual circumstances. The key is foreseeability . . . To say that a toothpick was a dangerous instrument in the hands of [the kindergarten child] would mean that any number of objects commonly handled by kindergarten-age children would have to be judged dangerous. A sharpened pencil or a pen could cause serious injury if a child pokes another in the ear; so might a crayon if jabbed into an eye; a wire hanger, a ruler or paper clips may do damage if grossly mishandled . . . The toothpicks at issue were not sent home loose, but were glued to construction paper. Under these circumstances, the intended use of the toothpicks did not create a foreseeable danger (*Fuzie v. South Haven School District No. 30,* 1990).

Although foreseeability of potential injury is demanded of teachers in the fulfillment of their professional duties, the courts recognize that accidents happen and not every action by students can be foreseen by even the most astute teacher. Teachers must analyze situations for possible danger and take action to prevent harm or injury because they will usually be expected to foresee more potential problems than the layperson. Taking every reasonable preventive action shows foresight on the part of teachers and administrators, and evidence of that type of anticipatory action will help absolve educators of charges of negligence.

A public school teacher may be charged with negligence if he or she fails to fulfill assigned duties and that failure leads to the injury of a student.

Principle VI

The assignment of teachers to professional duties is generally the responsibility of building administrators, who are then responsible for ensuring that those duties are fulfilled. Teachers will be held responsible for being at their assigned places—classrooms during class time; hallways during passage of students between classes; playgrounds during recess, before and after school, and at noon; bus loading areas before and after school; and on playing fields, in gymnasiums, and at other assigned posts during student activities. The courts may hold administrators liable if they fail to assign teachers to supervise places of student activity and injuries occur. Similarly, teachers who are not at their assigned posts may be held liable if a student is injured and the teachers' presence could have prevented the injury. Being where they are supposed to be is the best way teachers can preclude being held liable for negligence.

The courts have ruled in many cases where teacher supervision has been the issue. In 1939 California teachers were instructed by the courts that they were responsible for preventing boys from riding their bikes on a playground where small children were playing (*Buzzard v. East Lake School District of Lake County, California,* 1939). The high court in New York ruled that the supervision of a playground must take place on the playground rather than from a window overlooking the playground (*Miller v. Board of Education, Union Free School, District No. 1, of Town of Albion,* 1943). A teacher was held liable for negligence when he failed to supervise the testing of a gun being repaired in a vocational education course and a student was shot (*Govel v. Board of Education of City of Albany,* 1944). A California teacher was held liable for injuries to a student who was struck in the eye by a knife used in a game of mumblety-peg when the game was conducted in full view of the teacher. The appellate court stated that teachers were responsible for maintaining adequate discipline and preventing students from engaging in potentially harmful acts such as fights, shuffling, or playing with dangerous objects such as knives (*Lilienthal v. San Leandro Unified School District of Alameda County,* 1956). In 1970 the California Supreme Court reminded teachers of their duties in supervision of students:

> The standard of care imposed upon school personnel in carrying out this duty to supervise is identical to that required in the performance of their other duties. This uniform standard to which they are held is that degree of care "which a person of ordinary prudence, charged with [comparable] duties, would exercise under the same circumstances" (*Dailey v. Los Angeles Unified School District,* 1970).

Yet, teachers cannot be held liable for every injury that occurs when they are supervising students. School districts are not the guarantors of student safety, and holding teachers liable for all injuries could be expected only if the schools could insure students from all injuries. A New York appellate court stated that if a teacher is liable for every tortious occurrence in the classroom, a teacher could never leave a classroom unattended. This expectation would "effectively impose on both a school board and teacher a standard of care akin to an insurer rather than the standard of a reasonable and prudent parent" (*Swaitkowski v. Board of Education of City of Buffalo,* 1971). In 1972 the concept of "unremitting scrutiny" was discussed by a court in regard to teachers' duties of supervision:

> There is no requirement for a teacher to have under constant and unremitting scrutiny all precise spots where every phase of play activities is being pursued; and there is no compulsion that general supervision be continuous and direct at all times and all places (*Fagan v. Summers,* 1972).

The question of whether or not a teacher's presence would have prevented an injury has been raised in several cases. The parents of an Hawaiian child, who was struck in the eye with a rock and lost her eye, sued the playground supervising teacher and school district for negligence. Although ruling in favor of the school personnel, the court reminded the school district of its responsibilities:

> The duty of reasonable supervision does not require the [school district] to provide personnel to supervise every portion of the school buildings and campus area. However if certain specific areas are known . . . as dangerous, or the [school district] should have known that a specific area is dangerous, or the [school district] knew or should have known that certain students would or may conduct themselves in a manner dangerous to the welfare of others, duty of reasonable supervision would require specific supervision of those situations (*Miller v. Yoshimoto,* 1975).

In 1982 a child was hit in the eye with a pencil thrown by a classmate, both boys having been kept in from recess for causing disciplinary problems earlier in the day. Their teacher was monitoring the return of the rest of the students from recess at the time of the incident and was sued for negligent supervision. In ruling for the teacher, the court made statements quoted in later cases:

> The teacher, it may confidently be observed, could not have been at two places at the same time. With equal confidence, it can be said that it was not negligence for the teacher to give priority to an entire class of approximately thirty students returning from recess rather than to remain in the classroom to supervise three students who had been required to stay in the classroom during the recess period.
>
> It is common knowledge that children may indulge in horseplay. They may throw a pencil, shoot a paper clip or snap a rubber band when a teacher is absent or turns his or her back. In the instant case, the teacher attempted to guard against any horseplay by instructing the three students who were in the classroom to return to their seats and remain there. While these students were capable of free spirits and were even being punished for unrelated misconduct at breakfast, there is no evidence that they were hellions who required constant custody.
>
> To require the teacher to anticipate the events which occurred while she was outside the classroom door would be to hold that a teacher is required to

> anticipate the myriad of unexpected acts which occur daily in classrooms in every school in the land (*Simonetti v. School District of Philadelphia,* 1982).

Teachers who are not at their assigned places of duty may be held liable if a student is injured. In Louisiana, a student who had stolen apples from the cafeteria threw one into the girls' rest room while another student held the door open. The girl who lost her eye after being hit by the apple was awarded $3,000 in general damages and $969.55 in special damages because the teacher assigned to patrol the area was not there when the incident occurred (*Carson v. Orleans Parish School Board,* 1983). In 1985 a shop instructor was found guilty of negligence when one student's improper operation of a drill press caused the drill bit to deflect and strike an assisting student in the temple, fracturing his skull. Although the student had been told to wait for the teacher's assistance, the court found the teacher negligent for giving the student the drill bit before he was ready to supervise him, for failing to warn the students of the dangers involved in assisting one another, and for leaving students unsupervised in a room of operational shop equipment. The student was awarded $25,000 (*Roberts v. Robertson County Board of Education,* 1985).

Some school activities naturally involve some risks to participants, and no school district can guarantee that no injury will occur during those activities. For example, a complaint against the coach of a soccer team was dismissed by the court in a 1985 case. A student on the opposing team had been injured during a game and then had alleged that the coach taught his players to compete in an aggressive and intense manner and that winning the game was all important. The court made several observations about the nature of coaching:

> No student or parent is blind to the realities of interscholastic athletics. The possibility of a serious injury exists regardless of the care exercised by schools and their personnel. Imposing liability upon schools and their coaches based on negligent or wrongful acts of players, committed during the course of play would have the practical effect of eventually eliminating interscholastic athletics. Interscholastic athletic activities have become an integral part of the intellectual, physical and social development of young people. No matter what the intentions or good purpose, a coach cannot insure or guarantee that each and every member of his team will not commit a foul or will not in the heat of the contest do an act beyond that which is acceptable. A coach cannot be held responsible for the wrongful acts of his players unless he teaches them to do the wrongful act or instructs them to commit the act (*Nydegger v. Don Bosco Preparatory High School,* 1985).

Supervision of athletics and sports events often gives rise to charges of liability for lack of supervision. An elementary school student's parents sued the teacher and school district after their child was killed when struck in the head by a softball bat during noon recess. The boy had gone behind the plate to recover his glove just as the batter swung at a pitched ball. The teacher on duty had 40 children in her charge, about half of whom were involved in the game. The court ruled for the teacher because "constant and undeviating supervision . . . is prohibitive and probably impossible" (*Ferguson v. DeSoto Parish School Board,* 1985).

In 1990 the Alabama Supreme Court noted that "a teacher cannot possibly be expected to personally supervise each student in his charge at every moment of the school day" (*Stevens v. Chesteen,* 1990). In another 1990 case, a five-year-old child broke her arm after being pushed or falling from a playground slide during recess. The parent sued, citing inadequate supervision as the cause of the injury. The 22-year veteran teacher was able to show that she had been in a position near the merry-go-round (where several injuries had occurred in the past) where she could watch the slides. The court ruled that there was no evidence of lack of supervision or negligent supervision:

> The school board is not the insurer of the safety of its pupils . . . Rather, the board and its supervising teachers are only required to follow a reasonable standard of care commensurate with the age of the children under the attendant circumstances. There is no requirement that the supervisor of a group of children have each child under constant scrutiny (*Brooks v. Orleans Parish School Board,* 1990).

Therefore, teachers who fulfill their assigned duties for supervising students are generally upheld in court when injured students or their parents file suit against them on grounds of negligence. Administrators must make every reasonable effort to ensure that all areas of the school or campus are under supervision when students are present, and then teachers must be at their assigned posts and aware of the activities in which students are engaged. All injuries will never be prevented, but teachers must realize that their being at their assigned places will prevent many injuries and will be a viable defense should claims of negligent supervision be raised.

Principle VII

Actions by the injured student may result in his or her being charged in a tort action with contributory negligence, which may decrease the teacher's liability. However, students are not expected to have the same degree of foresight, caution, or judgment as a teacher.

Oftentimes in schools, an injury results from actions taken by a student who knew that such conduct could lead to an injury. Teachers may be diligent in supervising the activities of their students; yet, students who deliberately do something that will injure themselves or others cannot always be stopped from engaging in those activities. To hold teachers liable for all actions of students who knew or reasonably should have known that injury would result would impose an unreasonable duty of care on teachers. The courts often must determine whether or not a student contributed to his or her own injury, and, if the student is found guilty of contributory negligence, the teacher may not be held liable. The age, maturity, and intelligence of students are considered in cases of contributory negligence, and younger students are not expected to be as aware of possible dangers or to take as many precautions for their own safety as are older students.

The courts began hearing cases where contributory negligence was used as a defense by teachers and school districts as early as the 1920s. In 1925 a boy who climbed on top of wire screening at the school and fell through a hole, injuring his leg, was held to be contributorily at fault because he did not exercise a reasonable degree of care for his own protection (*Basmajian v. Board of Education of City of New York,* 1925). In 1962 a boy who was "fooling around" with chemicals in a school laboratory and was injured in a resulting explosion was held contributorily negligent because he knew that mixing chemicals was dangerous (*Wilhelm v. Board of Education of City of New York,* 1962). In 1972 a 12-year-old girl severely injured her hand when it went through a glass panel in a door. The Louisiana Court of Appeals ruled that she should have been aware of the danger of rushing toward a glass paneled door with her hand reaching for the panic bar when she was looking in the opposite direction (*Tyler v. Jefferson Parish School Board,* 1972).

However, when a student cannot reasonably be expected to have adequate knowledge about a hazardous situation, a teacher may be held liable. For example, at the conclusion of a physical education class, several girls were told to put the springboard in a storage room. Instead, they set up the board in the smaller room and attempted to use it to propel themselves into the gym. One girl severely injured her head when she struck it on the low doorway beam; she brought suit against the teacher for negligence. The teacher claimed that the girl was contributorily negligent in jumping on the board without permission at a time when and a place where it was not supposed to be used, in using the springboard with too much force, and in failing to maintain a proper lookout. However, the court ruled that the student had had only one day of instruction on the use of a springboard and could not be expected to know of the dangers:

> There is no testimony to the effect that [the student] knowingly embarked on a course of dangerous conduct. Her contributory negligence, if any, was in her failure to appreciate the danger of her act, not in her failure to perceive the source of her danger. She knew the beam was there but jumped anyway, thinking she would miss it. If she should have known this was dangerous and did it anyway, then she would be guilty of negligence. . . . However, the question of what she should have known . . . is a question that depends upon what a hypothetical child of like age, intelligence, and experience should have known given similar circumstances (*Grant v. Lake Oswego School District No. 7, Clackamas County,* 1973).

In 1970 two 15-year-old boys made a cannon, which exploded when they lit it, severely injuring one boy's hand. They claimed the teacher had given them the chemical substance that caused the explosion, but two years later one boy admitted that they had taken the chemical without the teacher's knowledge. The court ruled that the injured boy was contributorily negligent because the boys had previously experimented with homemade gunpowder and knew of its dangers and because the teacher had given them many warnings about their cannon (*Hutchison v. Toews,* 1970). In another case involving high school chemistry, a beaker of burning alcohol spilled on a student after he and friends decided to light some heated alcohol during an experiment in spite of their having been warned not to place any flame near alcohol. The teacher was ruled negligent in the way he attempted to put out the fire, but the student's negligence was ruled the substantial factor contributing to his injury (*Rixmann v. Somerset Public Schools, St. Croix County,* 1978).

In a high school shop class, a student attempted to remove a piece of wood from a machine in operation and severed two fingers. The teacher had demonstrated the safe use of power tools, had assigned a safety booklet for students to read, had given a safety examination, and had watched the girl operate the machine safely. Therefore, the court ruled the student was negligent in failing to use the ordinary care that a student of her age and maturity would have used in like circumstances (*Miles v. School District No. 138 of Cheyenne County,* 1979). In another case involving a shop student, a 14-year-old severed fingers from his left hand while cutting a piece of wood with a power saw. The student had previously attended another school where he had learned to use an electric saw, had received instruction from the teacher in the use of the saw, and had been supervised in the correct operation of the saw on other occasions. The student's suit against the teacher for negligence in instructing and warning students about the use of the saw failed because the student was contributorily negligent (*Izard v. Hickory City Schools Board of Education,* 1984).

In 1990 a high school student stole an oxidizing agent from the science lab. That night a fire started in the boy's home, burning his leg and some property. The mother charged the school district with negligent supervision for allowing the boy access to the dangerous chemical. In court the boy admitted he had stolen the substance and that the teacher had told the students never to remove chemicals from class. The court dismissed the case, stating that the boy's conduct went beyond contributory negligence and rose to such a level of culpability as to replace any negligence on the part of the teacher or district (*Brazell v. Board of Education of Niskayuna Public Schools,* 1990).

Historically, a ruling of contributory negligence meant that the injured party received no compensation, regardless of the degree of negligence. The concept of comparative negligence arose to handle cases where the injured party was not more than 50 percent negligent in causing his or her own injury. Under comparative negligence, the court assigns the percentage of negligence to all involved parties, and damages are assessed accordingly. In a few recent education cases, the student, teacher, school district, and any other parties to the student's injuries have been assigned a degree of the fault for the injury.

In 1984 a van driven by a student cheerleader was involved in a car collision, and one of the 12 girls in the van was severely injured. The cheerleading squad was bannering the homes of the football players when the incident occurred, and the adviser was not with the girls even though she had known of the plans. The school year had not started yet, and the adviser was not directly responsible for sponsorship duties until school officially began. The trial court awarded damages on a comparative basis, and the Minnesota Supreme Court upheld them. The school district was held 35 percent liable, the driver of the other vehicle was held 26 percent liable, and the student driver was held 39 percent liable for payment of $200,000 in damages to the injured girl and $14,000 to her father. The adviser was not assigned any degree of negligence because of her not being required by the district to perform summer duties (*Verhel v. Independent School District No. 709,* 1984).

After a nine-year-old Louisiana girl broke her leg when she jumped off the merry-go-round, the playground supervisor carried her into the principal's office. According to district policy, the girl's parents had to be notified before medical aid could be given to her, but the parents could not be located. The principal finally reached the girl's grandparents, who lived in a town over an hour away. They took the girl to a hospital where she had to stay for five days to allow the swelling to go down prior to a cast being put on the break. When the parents brought suit, the court ruled that the girl was equally responsible for causing the injury and reduced the amount of compensation awarded to her by 50 percent (*Rollins v. Concordia Parish School Board,* 1985).

In summary, when students have contributed to their own injury through their own negligent actions, teachers may not be held liable. The courts will consider age and maturity of the students, the amount of knowledge the student should have about the activity or equipment, and the extent of instruction the student has received about the activity or equipment when determining if contributory negligence can be claimed against the student. Many courts will use the concept of comparative negligence to assign the degree of fault for an injury. The degree or percentage of fault will then be used to determine the amount of damages owed by each party contributing to the injury. Teachers should not rely on contributory negligence as a defense in all cases of tort liability because students are not expected to be able to foresee the potential for injury as well as teachers.

Principle VIII

A student assumes some risk when he or she knowingly participates in activities known to involve some inherent hazard. A teacher is responsible for instructing students about risks and in correct procedures to reduce the chance of injury, for ensuring that equipment and facilities are safe, and for maintaining a safe instructional environment.

Some classes and activities at a school involve certain risks that students accept as part of enrolling in the course or participating in the activity. The students (and their parents) who assume the reasonable risks inherent to some courses, such as chemistry, physical education, carpentry, and auto mechanics, and to some activities, such as athletics, science club, and rodeo, are generally unable to claim that teachers and school districts are liable for all injuries that may occur. The courts will usually rule that students assume the risk when they voluntarily place themselves in positions of danger with the knowledge that injuries might occur. Those risks must be reasonable for the educational setting.

Teachers are responsible for instructing their students about the risks and potential dangers involved in a course or activity. They must presume that students do not have knowledge about hazards, how to prevent injury, or how to foresee injury-causing situations. All policies for the safe operation of equipment, procedures for safe conduct in the class, laboratory, shop, or sports area, and rules for behavior during the activity must be clearly conveyed to the students and some assurance made that students understand the policies, procedures, and rules. Teachers are also responsible for maintaining a safe environment for learning, including keeping order, ensuring that equipment is in safe working condition, and providing safe facilities. The courts are called upon to determine when teachers have violated expectations of safety and injuries have resulted that a student did not assume as part of the risk of the course or activity.

When lack of instruction leads to injury, a teacher may be held liable. For example, in 1947 a teacher was held liable for negligent acts when he allowed two boys to box several rounds without prior instruction nor proper supervision, and one boy was killed (*LaValley v. Stanford,* 1947).

Student athletes assume the normal risks associated with the sports in which they participate. In 1952 a boy collided with a doorjamb in a brick wall while playing on an informal basketball team in the school gymnasium. In ruling that the boy assumed the risk of playing in a gym where he had played before and therefore was aware of the dangers, the court established some standards for assumption of risk cases involving school sports:

> "Assumption of risk consists in the actual doing of the deed with foresight of the consequences. The essential requisite to invocation of the application of the doctrine of assumption of risks embraces not only a knowledge of the physical defect but includes also an appreciation of the danger produced by the physical condition." . . . The [injured student] had played basketball on this court many times prior to the accident. The risk of the court and the door being open and the wall being near the end of the basketball court were risks that were obvious and necessary to the sport as played on this particular court. His prior experience made him aware of the very hazards and dangers of which he now complains. He was not only aware of these dangers but had experienced them before, and he voluntarily assumed them. He accepted them with foresight of the consequences. He not only knew of the existing conditions but had or should have had an appreciation of the danger produced by the physical conditions existing (*Maltz v. Board of Education of New York City,* 1952).

In a similar case in 1971, several boys went into the gym when the school was closed and played basketball. Two of them collided as they went after a loose ball, and one fell, fracturing his back. The school was not held liable for the boy's injuries:

> The record lacks any evidence as to how the presence of a coach or teacher would have prevented the collision of the boys chasing the rebounding basketball. . . . Physical contact in such a situation in an athletic contest is foreseeable and expected. The general rule is that participants in an athletic contest accept the normal physical contact of the particular sport (*Albers v. Independent School District No. 302 of Lewis County,* 1971).

In another case related to sports, the court ruled that a girl assumed the risk of sitting along the third base line, and the coach was not held liable for her injuries after she was struck in the mouth with a baseball bat during a game (*Brackman v. Adrian,* 1971). However, an 11-year-old who lost several teeth in a floor hockey game did not assume the risk of his injuries. The court held that the assumption of risk was not a viable defense when the student's lack of experience, lack of information, and tender age impaired his appreciation of the dangers involved in floor hockey. Also, the school district had refused to supply proper safety equipment, such as helmets and pads, and the school district, not the teacher, was held liable for $83,190 (*Berman by Berman v. Philadelphia Board of Education,* 1983). In 1983 a 17-year-old who challenged the basketball coach to a wrestling match was injured when his foot caught between the mats. He claimed he did not know that he could get hurt wrestling, but the court stated that a teenage boy should have known that he could be hurt from a fall while wrestling. The teacher was not held liable for the boy's injuries (*Kluka v. Livingston Parish Board,* 1983).

Maintaining a safe educational environment is a primary responsibility of teachers, and injuries that result from unsafe conditions may lead to liability for damages. Students cannot assume risk when dangerous conditions result in an injury. A teacher was ruled negligent for allowing the use of blowtorches in an automobile mechanics shop where there was an open gas tank, which exploded, injuring several students (*Dutcher v. City of Santa Rosa High School District,* 1955). Another teacher and the school district were held responsible for the injuries to a boy's arm when it went through the glass pane in a door behind the basketball backboard because the boy did not know the glass was not shatterproof (*Stevens v. Central School District No. 1 of Town of Ramapo,* 1966).

Keeping equipment in good repair and maintaining all safety devices are responsibilities of teachers. A ninth grader lost four fingers while working with a circular saw in an industrial arts class. Because one of the saw guards was broken and the teacher was supervising another class in an adjacent room, the school district and teacher were held liable for the student's injuries (*South Ripley Community School Corporation v. Peters,* 1979). In another case where a student amputated one finger in a circular saw, the teacher and principal were held liable for damages because the guard with which the saw had been equipped had been removed by the wood shop instructor earlier in the semester and had never been replaced (*McKnight v. City of Philadelphia,* 1982). In 1984 students in an industrial arts class were hammering pieces of scrap metal through a hole in an anvil when a metal chip flew into one student's eye, causing visual impairment. The teacher had told them to quit hammering but then had gone back into his office in another room, and they had continued. The court held that the teacher was guilty of willful and wanton misconduct for not knowing that the metal scraps, which had been donated to the class, were likely to splinter (*Hadley v. Witt Unit School District 66,* 1984).

Although students assume a certain amount of risk when they enroll in classes such as industrial arts, chemistry, and physical education, teachers are still responsible for the proper instruction and supervision of inexperienced students. Teachers must be diligent in instructing students about skills needed to prevent injuries and the hazards inherent to the activities. Similarly, coaches and other teachers who supervise extracurricular activities must take precautions to instruct students in proper techniques, skills, and behavior to avoid injuries. Teachers should document their teaching of safety procedures, the maintenance and repair of equipment, and inspection of equipment and facilities. The assumption of risk defense will be valid only when all reasonable efforts are made by teachers to inform students about the risk they are assuming and to decrease the risk as much as possible through maintenance of a safe setting.

Principle IX

Teachers and other school officials may be held personally liable under the federal tort law if they knew or should have known that they were violating a student's constitutional or civil rights.

Until recently, tort cases were brought exclusively before state civil courts, and the federal courts were never involved. However, with the interpretation of Section 1983 of the Civil Rights Act of 1871 (42 U.S.C.A. Section 1983) to allow damages for violation of an individual's constitutional or civil rights, a federal tort law has evolved. Section 1983 of the Civil Rights Act of 1871 reads as follows:

> Every person who, under color of any statute, ordinance, regulation, custom, or usage, of any State or Territory, subjects, or causes to be subjected, any citizen of the United States or other person within the jurisdiction thereof to the deprivation of any rights, privileges or immunities secured by the Constitution and laws, shall be liable to the party injured in an action at law, suit in equity, or other proper proceeding for redress.

School officials have attempted to shield themselves from tort liability under this federal law by claiming qualified immunity. However, in 1975 a case heard by the United States Supreme Court involved the allegation that school board members had violated the constitutional rights of students. The students in this case had "spiked" the punch at a school activity with malt liquor, an action that violated the school's rules against use of alcohol by students. Although the illicit punch was served at the meeting "without apparent effect," news of the girls' actions reached school officials, and the girls were expelled from school for the rest of the semester. The expulsion vote was taken at a meeting at which neither the girls nor their parents were present. In the court action, the girls claimed their constitutional rights to due process were violated under 42 U.S.C.A. Section 1983, while the school board claimed immunity from liability. The high court determined that the procedural due process issue had not been considered by the lower courts and remanded the case. However, in their decision the court warned school officials that they are not immune to liability for their actions under Section 1983:

> A school board member is not immune from liability for damages under Section 1983 if he knew or reasonably should have known that the action he took within his sphere of official responsibility would violate the constitutional rights of the student affected, or if he took the action with the malicious intention to cause a deprivation of constitutional rights or other injury to the student (*Wood v. Strickland,* 1975).

The *Wood* ruling was later amended by the high court when it declared that abrogation of all immunity was incompatible with the court's admonition that insubstantial claims should not proceed to trial. The refined ruling held that "government officials performing discretionary functions generally are shielded from liability for civil damages insofar as their conduct does not violate clearly established statutory or constitutional rights of which a reasonable person would have known" (*Harlow v. Fitzgerald,* 1982).

Recent court cases have begun to expand this developing area of the law further by imposing an affirmative duty upon school officials to protect certain persons, especially students, from harm caused by violation of constitutional rights. In 1989, the United States Court of Appeals, Third Circuit, found a high school principal and assistant principal both guilty of a constitutional tort under 42 U.S.C.A. Section 1983 because of the "deliberate indifference" they had shown to complaints by students regarding the sexual abuse to which they had been subjected by the school's band director. The court upheld the claim of a constitutional right to be free from sexual assault, noting "it [is] clearly established that it was impermissible for school teachers and staff to sexually molest students." Although the principal and assistant principal were not personally involved in the acts of sexual abuse, the Third Circuit Court concluded from the evidence that the administrators had failed to take sufficient action to protect students in their care from harm stemming from violation of the students' constitutionally protected right to be free from sexual abuse. In coming to that decision, the court noted that the action or policy guiding the school officials need not suggest that the school officials approved of the sexual abuse. It needed only to be shown that from among the choices of policy available to the officials, they chose a route that reflected a deliberate indifference to the constitutional rights of the students (*Stoneking v. Bradford Area School District,* 1989).

In another 1989 case, a New York federal district court refused to dismiss a constitutional tort action based upon the allegation that school officials had failed to take action to protect an elementary school student from verbal and physical abuse received from other students. Noting that the courts have recognized that government owes a duty to protect persons from harm if there exists a "special relationship," and that the student being subjected to the abuse had complained numerous times to school officials, the judge took the position that the failure to act or to take preventive steps could be considered indifference to an affirmative duty (*Pagano v. Massapequa Public Schools,* 1989).

In two 1990 cases of alleged sexual abuse by teachers, school boards were not found guilty of Section 1983 actions. In the Missouri case, six female students filed a 1983 action against the board for failing to protect them from sexual abuse at the hands of a teacher. The federal district court found that the board had not had sufficient knowledge of the alleged abuse to violate the students' civil rights when they failed to take action against the teacher (*Thelma D. v. Board of Education of City of St. Louis,* 1990). In the Oklahoma case, elementary school students were allegedly abused by a teacher when the boys stayed overnight at the teacher's home during a fund raising activity for a summer basketball camp. The school district was charged with negligent hiring but was able to show that a reasonable investigation of the teacher's background had been conducted during the hiring process. The United States Supreme Court denied review of *D.T. by M.T. v. Independent School District No. 16 of Pawnee County, Oklahoma* (1990).

Claims under the federal tort law are likely to increase, especially when teachers or administrators are accused of abuse of students or the violation of other civil or constitutional rights. Administrators and school board members will not be immune from liability if students can show that a school official had a duty to protect the rights of students and a breach of that duty led to the injury of the students.

Summary

Of all the issues in education law, tort liability results in the greatest number of cases coming before the courts. Although some charges of intentional tort and strict liability arise in educational settings, negligence is the most common tort claim against teachers, administrators, and school districts. To sustain a claim of negligence against a teacher, a student must show that the teacher owed a duty of care, that the teacher breached that duty of care, that the student sustained an actual injury, and that the negligent act was the proximate cause of the injury. Many more claims of tort liability are dismissed by the courts than are upheld because most teachers are able to show that they acted as a reasonable and prudent teacher would act in similar circumstances.

Because of a teacher's professional training and background, he or she is expected to be able to foresee potential injury-causing situations in educational settings and to take action to prevent them from happening. The teacher who is conscientious about fulfilling assigned duties, including being at the areas where students are likely to be and anticipating behavior that could jeopardize student safety and welfare, is acting as a reasonable and prudent teacher would act, and claims of negligence will be difficult to prove.

Students sometimes contribute to their own injuries by taking actions that reasonable and prudent students of their age, maturity, and knowledge or skill level would not take. When a student is shown to have been contributorily negligent, a teacher will not be held liable for the student's injuries or will be held liable only to the comparative degree determined by the court. The nature of some courses and activities results in students assuming some normal risks by enrolling or participating in those classes and activities, and teachers will usually not be held liable for injuries that result.

In addition to common law tort claims, teachers are also increasingly subject to federal tort claims under Section 1983 of the Civil Rights Act of 1871. This developing area of the law will demand close attention on the part of teachers and other school officials who may be accused of violating the constitutional or civil rights of students.

Questions and Responses

1. What is a tort?

A tort is a civil wrong other than breach of contract for which a court will award damages. When a person causes injury to another person through violation of some legal duty (the commitment of a tort), the tortfeasor is liable to the injured party for damages. A tort may also be a crime, but the remedy for a tort is damages for the victim rather than fines or prison sentences for the wrongdoer.

2. What are the various types of torts?

Three types of torts have been identified by the courts:

a. Intentional torts are those committed on purpose, with the intent to cause harm or injury, or in reckless disregard of whether or not injury will result. Examples of intentional torts are assault, battery, defamation, false imprisonment, and trespass. Some defenses against claims of intentional tort are prior consent by the injured party, self-defense, defense of property, and truth (in the case of defamation charges).
b. Strict liability arises when a danger is inherent to some activity or product. If an injury or damages occur in relation to the activity or product, the tortfeasor is automatically liable. Examples of strict liability are the keeping of ferocious animals, attractive nuisances, and activities such as parachuting and skydiving. Product liability is also strict, which is the reason for the immediate recall of items when an injury-causing defect is found. Almost no defenses are recognized in court in instances of strict liability. If a person alters or tampers with a product or has a unique reaction to a product, then some courts will vacate charges of strict liability. Occasionally, an injury may be held to be an act of God.
c. Unintentional torts are those that result from negligence. The tortfeasor did not mean to cause injury but should have foreseen that injury or harm would occur and taken action to prevent it. A tort cannot be claimed if the action can be shown to have been an accident not arising from negligence. Ignorance is not a defense for negligence, but other defenses have been allowed by the courts. For example, if the injured party can be shown to have assumed the risk of possible injury or contributed to the negligent action, then the liability of the tortfeasor may be lessened.

3. What criteria do the courts use to determine if an unintentional tort has occurred?

Before a claim of negligence will be sustained by the courts, the following elements of proof must be established by the party bringing suit in tort:

a. A legal duty of care was owed to the injured party.
b. That duty of care was breached by the perpetrator.
c. The negligent act was the proximate cause of the injury.
d. Real harm or an actual injury was suffered by the party bringing suit.

4. How do the courts determine if a teacher has been negligent?

Any person accused of a tort will be held to the standard of the "reasonable and prudent person." However, because of the professional qualifications and expectations of a teacher, generally he or she will be held to a higher standard, that of the "reasonable and prudent teacher," in cases that arise in school settings. In other words, the courts will determine if a reasonable and prudent teacher would have done, or failed to do, the same thing as the accused teacher if faced with the same situation. Using the elements of proof for negligence, the courts would then determine whether or not the teacher owed a duty of care to the injured party and what that duty of care was, according to the actions expected of the reasonable and prudent teacher. If a duty of care was owed, then the courts must decide if that duty was breached or if the teacher failed to conform to the expected behavior of a reasonable and prudent teacher. The court must also determine if actual harm or injury was suffered by the injured party, and, finally, if the alleged negligent act was the proximate cause of injury. If all of these elements of proof are upheld, then the teacher will likely be found guilty of negligence.

5. Why are torts almost always tried in state courts?

Tort law arises from the English common law and is not part of the federal Constitution. Therefore, torts have long been considered the exclusive domain of state courts because only state laws were involved. Because no federal issue was involved, the federal courts were not used to pursue claims in tort. However, some suits are being brought under Section 1983 of the federal Civil Rights Act of 1871 when the constitutional or civil rights of a person are violated.

6. When may a teacher be held personally liable for torts that occur when the teacher is acting as an agent of the school?

Teachers have always been held accountable for the safety and welfare of the children in their charge under the doctrine of *in loco parentis,* where teachers are expected to protect children as parents would. Under the host powers of the school district, teachers are also responsible for the well-being of students. A teacher has always been held liable for personal torts that were committed intentionally or through negligence. However, some states have enacted save harmless statutes that indemnify teachers against suits that may arise from negligent actions that may occur when the teachers are carrying out official duties. In addition, the United States Supreme Court in *Wood v. Strickland* (1975) ruled that school officials who knew or should have known that they were violating the rights of students may be held personally responsible for damages under Section 1983.

7. What can a teacher do to keep from being sued for negligence?

A teacher who follows all reasonable rules, regulations, policies, and directives of the administration and school board will be able to show in court that he or she was performing all required duties as a reasonable and prudent teacher would do. Being in assigned areas to supervise students and anticipating the dangers and hazards inherent to student play and activities will also show that a teacher took the necessary precautions to prevent injuries. Ensuring that adequate supervision is available for activities such as parties, field trips, and sports events shows preparation and foresight. Teachers of some classes, such as physical education, chemistry, industrial arts, and auto mechanics, must take extra efforts to ensure that students have been informed of the inherent risks involved in these classes, that students are obeying all rules, that equipment is in good repair, and that classes are not left unsupervised. Regardless of all reasonable precautions, accidents do happen and students are injured, but the teacher who is able to show that he or she did what any reasonable and prudent teacher would do in similar circumstances will likely be able to show that the injury did not result from negligence.

8. When may a teacher be liable for educational malpractice?

Malpractice cases based on tort theories have been introduced into the courts of several states. However, none has prevailed to date. The plaintiffs in these cases have attempted to convince the courts that students have a right to a certain level of academic achievement in return for their mandated attendance and a right to an expectation of functional literacy upon graduation from high school. Critical to the outcome of these decisions has been the magnitude of the public policy issues involved, including judicial concern over (a) the ability of educators to control and personally account for all the elements essential to learning, (b) the appropriateness or desirability of courts substituting their judgment for that of education professionals in matters of academic discretion, (c) the potential for excessive numbers of court cases, and (d) the possible adverse impact on the already publicly battered and underfunded educational enterprise.

Case References

Albers v. Independent School District No. 302 of Lewis County, 487 P.2d 936 (Idaho 1971).
Allison v. Field Local School District, 553 N.E.2d 1383 (Ohio App. 1988).
Basmajian v. Board of Education of City of New York, 207 N.Y.S. 298 (N.Y.A.D. 1925).
Batiste v. Iberia Parish School Board, 401 So.2d 1224 (La. App. 1981).
Beasley by and through Beasley v. Morton, 564 So.2d 45 (Ala. 1990).
Berman by Berman v. Philadelphia Board of Education, 456 A.2d 545 (Pa. Super. 1983).
Bogust v. Iverson, 102 N.W.2d 228 (Wis. 1960).
Boyd v. State, 7 So. 268 (Ala. 1890).
Boyer v. Jablonski, 435 N.E.2d 436 (Ohio App. 1980).
Brackman v. Adrian, 472 S.W.2d 735 (Tenn. App. 1971).
Brazell v. Board of Education of Niskayuna Public Schools, 557 N.Y.S.2d 645 (N.Y.A.D. 3 Dept. 1990).
Brooks v. Orleans Parish School Board, 560 So.2d 633 (La. App. 4 Cir. 1990).
Buzzard v. East Lake School District of Lake County, California, 93 P.2d 233 (Cal. App. 1939).
Calway v. Williamson, 36 A.2d 377 (Conn. 1944).
Carson v. Orleans Parish School Board, 432 So.2d 956 (La. App. 4 Cir. 1983).
Cirillo v. City of Milwaukee, 150 N.W.2d 460 (Wis. 1967).
Cooper v. McJunkin, 4 Ind. 290 (1853).
D.T. by M.T. v. Independent School District No. 16 of Pawnee County, Oklahoma, 894 F.2d 1176 (10th Cir. 1990), cert. denied, ____ U.S. ____ (1990).
Dailey v. Los Angeles Unified School District, 87 Cal.Rptr. 376 (Cal. 1970).
DeGooyer v. Harkness, 13 N.W.2d 815 (S.D. 1944).
Dibortolo v. Metropolitan School District of Washington Township, 440 N.E.2d 506 (Ind. App. 1982).
Dutcher v. City of Santa Rosa High School District, 290 P.2d 316 (Cal. App. 1955).
Eastman v. Williams, 207 A.2d 146 (Vt. 1965).
Fagan v. Summers, 498 P.2d 1227 (Wyo. 1972).
Ferguson v. DeSoto Parish School Board, 467 So.2d 1257 (La. App. 2 Cir. 1985).
Frank v. Orleans Parish School Board, 195 So.2d 451 (La. App. 1967).
Fuzie v. South Haven School District No. 30, 553 N.Y.S.2d 961 (Sup. 1990).
Gaincott v. Davis, 275 N.W. 229 (Mich. 1937).
Gardner v. State, 4 Ind. 632 (1853).
Gathright v. Lincoln Insurance Company, 688 S.W.2d 931 (Ark. 1985).

Govel v. Board of Education of City of Albany, 48 N.Y.S.2d 299 (N.Y.A.D. 1944).
Grant v. Lake Oswego School District No. 7, Clackamas County, 515 P.2d 947 (Or. 1973).
Guerrieri v. Tyson, 24 A.2d 468 (Pa. Super. 1942).
Hadley v. Witt Unit School District 66, 462 N.E.2d 877 (Ill. App. 5 Dist. 1984).
Harlow v. Fitzgerald, 457 U.S. 800 (1982).
Hutchison v. Toews, 476 P.2d 811 (Or. App. 1970).
Ingraham v. Wright, 430 U.S. 651 (1977).
Izard v. Hickory City Schools Board of Education, 315 S.E.2d 756 (N.C. App. 1984).
Jackson v. Board of Education of City of Chicago, 441 N.E.2d 120 (Ill. App. 1982).
Kain v. Rockridge Community Unit School District No. 300, 453 N.E.2d 118 (Ill. App. 3 Dist. 1983).
Klucka v. Livingston Parish Board, 433 So.2d 302 (La. App. 1 Cir. 1983).
Lander v. Seaver, 32 Vt. 114 (1859).
LaValley v. Stanford, 70 N.Y.S.2d 460 (N.Y.A.D. 1947).
Lilienthal v. San Leandro Unified School District of Alameda County, 293 P.2d 889 (Cal. App. 1956).
Maddox v. Boutwell, 336 S.E.2d 599 (Ga. App. 1985).
Maltz v. Board of Education of New York City, 114 N.Y.S.2d 856 (N.Y. 1952).
Mancha v. Field Museum of Natural History, 283 N.E.2d 899 (Ill. App. 1972).
McKnight v. City of Philadelphia, 445 A.2d 778 (Pa. Super. 1982).
Miles v. School District No. 138 of Cheyenne County, 281 N.W.2d 396 (Neb. 1979).
Miller v. Board of Education, Union Free School, District No. 1, of Town of Albion, 50 N.E.2d 529 (N.Y. App. 1943).
Miller v. Yoshimoto, 536 P.2d 1195 (Hawaii 1975).
Morris v. Douglas County School District No. 9, 403 P.2d 775 (Or. 1965).
Nydegger v. Don Bosco Preparatory High School, 495 A.2d 485 (N.J. Super. 1985).
Ohman v. Board of Education of City of New York, 90 N.E.2d 474 (N.Y. App. 1949).
Osborne v. Montgomery, 234 N.W. 372 (Wis. 1931).
Pagano v. Massapequa Public Schools, 714 F.Supp. 641 (E.D. N.Y. 1989).
Pirkle v. Oakdale Union Grammar School District, 253 P.2d 1 (Cal. 1953).
Prier v. Horace Mann Insurance Company, 351 So.2d 265 (La. App. 1977).
Rixmann v. Somerset Public Schools, St. Croix County, 266 N.W.2d 326 (Wis. 1978).
Roberts v. Robertson County Board of Education, 692 S.W.2d 863 (Tenn. App. 1985).
Rock by Rock v. Central Square School District, 494 N.Y.S.2d 579 (A.D. 4 Dept. 1985).
Rollins v. Concordia Parish School Board, 465 So.2d 213 (La. App. 3 Cir. 1985).
Sayers v. Ranger, 83 A.2d 775 (N.J. Super. A.D. 1951).
Simmons v. Beauregard Parish School Board, 315 So.2d 883 (La. App. 1975).
Simms v. School District No. 1, Multnomah County, 508 P.2d 236 (Or. App. 1973).
Simonetti v. School District of Philadelphia, 454 A.2d 1038 (Pa. Super. 1982).
Smith v. Vernon Parish School Board, 442 So.2d 1319 (La. App. 3 Cir. 1983).
South Ripley Community School Corporation v. Peters, 396 N.E.2d 144 (Ind. App. 1979).
State ex rel. Burpee v. Burton, 45 Wis. 150 (1878).
State of Ohio v. Hoover, 450 N.E.2d 710 (Ohio App. 1982).
Stehn v. Bernarr MacFadden Foundations, Inc., 434 F.2d 811 (6th Cir., 1970).
Stevens v. Central School District No. 1 of Town of Ramapo, 270 N.Y.S.2d 23 (N.Y.A.D. 1966).
Stevens v. Chesteen, 561 So.2d 1100 (Ala. 1990).
Stoneking v. Bradford Area School District, 882 F.2d 720 (3d Cir. 1989).
Suits v. Glover, 71 So.2d 49 (Ala. 1954).
Summers v. Milwaukie Union High School District No. 5, Clackamas County, 481 P.2d 369 (Or. App. 1971).
Swaitkowski v. Board of Education of City of Buffalo, 319 N.Y.S.2d 783 (N.Y. A.D. 1971).

Templar v. Decatur Public School District, 538 N.E.2d 195 (Ill. App. 4 Dist. 1989).
Thelma D. v. Board of Education of City of St. Louis, 737 F.Supp. 541 (E.D.Mo. 1990).
Truelove v. Wilson, 285 S.E.2d 556 (Ga. App. 1981).
Tyler v. Jefferson Parish School Board, 258 So.2d 206 (La. App. 1972).
Verhel v. Independent School District No. 709, 359 N.W.2d 579 (Minn. 1984).
Wetsel v. Independent School District I-1, 670 P.2d 986 (Okl. 1983).
Wilhelm v. Board of Education of City of New York, 227 N.Y.S.2d 791 (N.Y. A.D. 1962).
Wire v. Williams, 133 N.W.2d 840 (Minn. 1965).
Wood v. Strickland, 420 U.S. 308 (1975).

A Appendix

THE CONSTITUTION OF THE UNITED STATES

SELECTED CONSTITUTIONAL PROVISIONS

Amendment I

Congress shall make no law respecting an establishment of religion, or prohibiting the free exercise thereof; or abridging the freedom of speech, or of the press; or the right of the people peaceably to assemble, and to petition the Government for a redress of grievances.

Amendment IV

The right of the people to be secure in their persons, houses, papers, and effects, against unreasonable searches and seizures, shall not be violated, and no Warrants shall issue, but upon probable cause, supported by Oath or affirmation, and particularly describing the place to be searched, and the persons or things to be seized.

Amendment V

No person shall be held to answer for a capital or otherwise infamous crime, unless on a presentment of indictment of a Grand Jury, except in cases arising in the land or naval forces, or in the Militia, when in time of War or public danger; nor shall any person be subject to the same offense to be twice put in jeopardy of life or limb; nor shall be compelled in any criminal case to be a witness against himself, nor be deprived of life, liberty or property, without due process of law; nor shall private property be taken for public use, without just compensation.

Amendment VIII

Excessive bail shall not be required, nor excessive fines imposed, nor cruel and unusual punishments inflicted.

Amendment X

The powers not delegated to the United States by the Constitution, nor prohibited by it to the States, are reserved to the States respectively, or to the people.

Amendment XIV

Section 1. All persons born or naturalized in the United States, and subject to the jurisdiction thereof, are citizens of the United States and of the State wherein they reside. No state shall make or enforce any law which shall abridge the privileges or immunities of citizens of the United States; nor shall any State deprive any person of life, liberty, or property, without due process of law; nor deny to any person within its jurisdiction the equal protection of the laws.

Section 2. Representatives shall be apportioned among the several States according to their respective number, counting the whole number of persons in each state, excluding Indians not taxed. But when the right to vote at any election for the choice of electors for President and Vice President of the United States, Representatives in Congress, the Executive and Judicial officers of a State, or the members of the Legislature thereof, is denied any of the male inhabitants of such State, being twenty-one years of age, and citizens of the United States, or in any way abridged, except for participation in rebellion, or other crime, the basis of representation therein shall be reduced in the proportion which the number of such male citizens shall bear to the number of male citizens twenty-one years of age in such State.

Section 3 and 4. (Omitted)

Section 5. The Congress shall have power to enforce, by appropriate legislation, the provisions of the article.

B Appendix

SELECTED FEDERAL STATUTES

CIVIL RIGHTS ACT OF 1964

TITLE VI

(Selected Parts)

42 U.S.C.A. §§ 2000d—d-1

FEDERALLY ASSISTED PROGRAMS

§ 2000d. **Prohibition against exclusion from participation in, denial of benefits of, and discrimination under Federally assisted programs on ground of race, color, or national origin**

No person in the United States shall, on the ground of race, color, or national origin, be excluded from participation in, be denied the benefits of, or be subjected to discrimination under any program or activity receiving Federal financial assistance.

. . .

§ 2000d-1. **Federal authority and financial assistance to programs or activities by way of grant, loan, or contract other than contract of insurance or guaranty; rules and regulations; approval by President; compliance with requirements; reports to Congressional committees; effective date of administrative action**

Each Federal department and agency which is empowered to extend Federal financial assistance to any program or activity, by way of grant, loan, or contract other than a contract of insurance or guaranty, is authorized and directed to effectuate the provisions of section 2000d of this title with respect to such program or activity by issuing rules, regulations, or orders of general applicability which shall be consistent with achievement of the objectives of the statute authorizing the financial assistance in connection with which the action is taken. No such rule, regulation, or order shall become effective unless and until approved by the President. Compliance with any requirement adopted pursuant to this section may be effected (1) by the termination of or refusal to grant or to continue assistance under such program or activity to any recipient as to whom there has been an express finding on the record, after opportunity for hearing, of a failure to comply with such requirement, but such termination or refusal shall be limited to the particular political entity, or part thereof, or other recipient as to whom such a finding has been made and, shall be limited in its effect to the particular program, or part thereof, in which such noncompliance has been so found, or (2) by any other means authorized by law: *Provided, however,* That no such action shall be taken until the department or agency concerned has advised the appropriate person or persons of the failure to comply with the requirement and has determined that compliance cannot be secured by voluntary means. In the case of any action terminating, or refusing to grant or continue, assistance because of failure to comply with a requirement imposed pursuant to this section, the head of the Federal department or agency shall file with the committees of the House and Senate having legislative jurisdiction over the program or activity involved a full written report of the circumstances and the grounds for such action. No such action shall become effective until thirty days have elapsed after the filing of such report.

CIVIL RIGHTS ACT OF 1964

42 U.S.C.A. § 2000e—e-2

TITLE VII

(Selected Parts)

EQUAL EMPLOYMENT OPPORTUNITIES

Unlawful employment practices § 2000e-2.

Employer practices

(a) It shall be an unlawful employment practice for an employer—

(1) to fail or refuse to hire or to discharge any individual, or otherwise to discriminate against any individual with respect to his compensation, terms, conditions, or privileges of employment, because of such individual's race, color, religion, sex, or national origin; or

(2) to limit, segregate, or classify his employees or applicants for employment in any way which would deprive or tend to deprive any individual of employment opportunities or otherwise adversely affect his status as an employee, because of such individual's race, color, religion, sex, or national origin.

Employment agency practices

(b) It shall be an unlawful employment practice for an employment agency to fail or refuse to refer for employment, or otherwise to discriminate against, any individual because of his race, color, religion, sex, or national origin, or to classify or refer for employment any individual on the basis of his race, color, religion, sex, or national origin.

. . .

Training programs

(d) It shall be an unlawful employment practice for any employer, labor organization, or joint labor-management committee controlling apprenticeship or other training or retraining, including on-the-job training programs to discriminate against any individual because of his race, color, religion, sex, or national origin in admission to, or employment in, any program established to provide apprenticeship or other training.

Businesses or enterprises with personnel qualified on basis of religion, sex, or national origin; educational institutions with personnel of particular religion

(e) Notwithstanding any other provision of this subchapter, (1) it shall not be an unlawful employment practice for an employer to hire and employ employees, for an employment agency to classify, or refer for employment any individual, for a labor organization to classify its membership or to classify or refer for employment any individual, or for an employer, labor organization, or joint labor-management committee controlling apprenticeship or other training or retraining programs to admit or employ any individual in any such program, on the basis of his religion, sex, or national origin in those certain instances where religion, sex, or national origin is a bona fide occupational qualification reasonably necessary to the normal operation of that particular business or enterprise, and (2) it shall not be an unlawful employment practice for a school, college, university, or other educational institution or institution of learning to hire and employ employees of a particular religion if such school, college, university, or other educational institution or institution of learning is, in whole or in substantial part, owned, supported, controlled, or managed by a particular religion or by a particular religious corporation, association, or society, or if the curriculum of such school, college, university, or other educational institution or institution of learning is directed toward the propagation of a particular religion.

. . .

Seniority or merit system; quantity or quality of production; ability tests; compensation based on sex and authorized by minimum wage provisions

(h) Notwithstanding any other provision of this subchapter, it shall not be an unlawful employment practice for an employer to apply different standards of compensation, or different terms, conditions, or privileges of employment pursuant to a bona fide seniority or merit system, or a system which measures earnings by quantity or quality of production or to employees who work in different locations, provided that such differences are not the result of an intention to discriminate because of race, color, religion, sex, or national origin, nor shall it be an unlawful employment practice for an employer to give and to act upon the results of any professionally developed ability test provided that such test, its administration or action upon the results is not designed, intended or used to discriminate because of race, color, religion, sex or national origin. It shall not be an unlawful employment practice under this subchapter for any employer to differentiate upon the basis of sex in determining the amount of the wages or compensation paid or to be paid to employees of such employer if such differentiation is authorized by the provisions of section 206(d) of Title 29.

. . .

Preferential treatment not to be granted on account of existing number or percentage imbalance

(j) Nothing contained in this subchapter shall be interpreted to require any employer, employment agency, labor organization, or joint labor-management committee subject to this subchapter to grant preferential treatment to any individual or to any group because of the race, color, religion, sex, or national origin of such individual or group on account of an imbalance which may exist with respect to the total number or percentage of persons of any race, color, religion, sex, or national origin employed by any employer, referred or classified for employment by any employment agency or labor organization, admitted to membership or classified by any labor organization, or admitted to, or employed in, any apprenticeship or other training program, in comparison with the total number or percentage of persons of such race, color, religion, sex, or national origin in any community, State, section, or other area, or in the available work force in any community, State, section, or other area.

EDUCATION AMENDMENTS OF 1972

TITLE IX

(Selected Parts)

20 U.S.C.A. F 1681

DISCRIMINATION BASED ON SEX

Sex § 1681.

Prohibition against discrimination; exceptions

(a) No person in the United States shall, on the basis of sex, be excluded from participation in, be denied the benefits of, or be subjected to discrimination under any education program or activity receiving Federal financial assistance, except that:

Classes of educational institutions subject to prohibition

(1) in regard to admissions to educational institutions, this section shall apply only to institutions of vocational education, professional education, and graduate higher education, and to public institutions of undergraduate higher education;

Educational institutions commencing planned change in admissions

(2) in regard to admissions to educational institutions, this section shall not apply (A) for one year from June 23, 1972, nor for six years after June 23, 1972, in the case of an educational institution which has begun the process of changing from being an institution which admits only students of one sex to being an institution which admits students of both sexes, but only if it is carrying out a plan for such a change which is approved by the Commissioner of Education or (B) for seven years from the date an educational institution begins the process of changing from being an

institution which admits only students of only one sex to being an institution which admits students of both sexes, but only if it is carrying out a plan for such a change which is approved by the Commissioner of Education, whichever is the later;

Educational institutions of religious organizations with contrary religious tenets

(3) this section shall not apply to an educational institution which is controlled by a religious organization if the application of this subsection would not be consistent with the religious tenets of such organization;

Educational institutions training individuals for military services or merchant marine

(4) this section shall not apply to an educational institution whose primary purpose is the training of individuals for the military services of the United States, or the merchant marine;

Public educational institutions with traditional and continuing admissions policy

(5) in regard to admissions this section shall not apply to any public institution of undergraduate higher education which is an institution that traditionally and continually from its establishment has had a policy of admitting only students of one sex;

Social fraternities or sororities; voluntary youth service organizations

(6) this section shall not apply to membership practices—

(A) of a social fraternity or social sorority which is exempt from taxation under section 501(a) of Title 26, the active membership of which consists primarily of students in attendance at an institution of higher education, or

(B) of the Young Men's Christian Association, Young Women's Christian Association, Girl Scouts, Boy Scouts, Camp Fire Girls, and voluntary youth service organizations which are so exempt, the membership of which has traditionally been limited to persons of one sex and principally to persons of less than nineteen years of age;

Boy or Girl conferences

(7) this section shall not apply to—

(A) any program or activity of the American Legion undertaken in connection with the organization or operation of any Boys State conference, Boys Nation conference, Girls State conference, or Girls Nation conference; or

(B) any program or activity of any secondary school or educational institution specifically for—

(i) the promotion of any Boys State conference, Boys Nation conference, Girls State conference, or Girls Nation conference; or

(ii) the selection of students to attend any such conference;

Father-son or mother-daughter activities at educational institutions

(8) this section shall not preclude father-son or mother-daughter activities at an educational institution, but if such activities are provided for students of one sex, opportunities for reasonably comparable activities shall be provided for students of the other sex; and

Institution of higher education scholarship awards in "beauty" pageants

(9) this section shall not apply with respect to any scholarship or other financial assistance awarded by an institution of higher education to any individual because such individual has received such award in any pageant in which the attainment of such award is based upon a combination of factors related to the personal appearance, poise, and talent of such individual and in which participation is limited to individuals of one sex only, so long as such pageant is in compliance with other non-discrimination provisions of Federal law.

Preferential or disparate treatment because of imbalance in participation or receipt of Federal benefits; statistical evidence of imbalance

(b) Nothing contained in subsection (a) of this section shall be interpreted to require any educational institution to grant preferential or disparate treatment to the members of one sex on account of an imbalance which may exist with respect to the total number or percentage of persons of that sex participating in or receiving the benefits of any federally supported program or activity, in comparison with the total number or percentage of persons of that sex in any community, State, section, or other area: *Provided,* That this subsection shall not be construed to prevent the consideration in any hearing or proceeding under this chapter of statistical evidence tending to show that such an imbalance exists with respect to the participation in, or receipt of the benefits of, any such program or activity by the members of one sex.

Educational institution defined

(c) For purposes of this chapter an educational institution means any public or private preschool, elementary, or secondary school, or any institution of vocational, professional, or higher education, except that in the case of an educational institution composed of more than one school, college, or department which are administratively separate units, such term means each such school, college, or department.

EQUAL PAY ACT

(Selected Parts)

29 U.S.C.A. F 206

Minimum wage § 206.

Prohibition of sex discrimination

(d)(1) No employer having employees subject to any provisions of this section shall discriminate, within any establishment in which such employees are employed, between employees on the basis of sex by paying wages to employees in such establishment at a rate less than the rate at which he pays wages to employees of the opposite sex in such establishment for equal work on jobs the performance of which requires equal skill, effort, and responsibility, and which are preformed under similar working conditions, except where such payment is made pursuant to (i) a seniority system; (ii) a merit system; (iii) a system which measures earnings by quantity or quality of production; or (iv) a differential based on any other factor other than sex:

Provided, That an employer who is paying a wage rate differential in violation of this subsection shall not, in order to comply with the provisions of this subsection, reduce the wage rate of any employee.

(2) No labor organization, or its agents, representing employees of an employer having employees subject to any provisions of this section shall cause or attempt to cause such an employer to discriminate against an employee in violation of paragraph (1) of this subsection.

(3) For purposes of administration and enforcement, any amounts owing to any employee which have been withheld in violation of this subsection shall be deemed to be unpaid minimum wages or unpaid overtime compensation under this chapter.

(4) As used in this subsection, the term “”labor organization” means any organization of any kind, or any agency or employee representation committee or plan, in which employees participate and which exists for the purpose, in whole or in part, of dealing with employers concerning grievances, labor disputes, wages, rates of pay, hours of employment, or conditions of work.

FAMILY RIGHTS AND PRIVACY ACT (BUCKLEY AMENDMENT)

(Selected Parts)

20 U.S.C.A. F 1232g

§ 1232g. Family educational and privacy rights

Conditions for availability of funds to educational agencies or institutions; inspection and review of education records; specific information to be made available; procedure for access to education records; reasonableness of time for such access; hearings; written explanations by parents; definitions

(a)(1)(A) No funds shall be made available under any applicable program to any educational agency or institution which has a policy of denying, or which effectively prevents, the parents of students who are or have been in attendance at a school of such agency or at such institution, as the case may be, the right to inspect and review the education records of their children. If any material or document in the education record of a student includes information on more than one student, the parents of one of such students shall have the right to inspect and review only such part of such material or document as relates to such student or to be informed of the specific information contained in such part of such material. Each educational agency or institution shall establish appropriate procedures for the granting of a request by parents for access to the education records of their children within a reasonable period of time, but in no case more than forty-five days after the request has been made.

. . .

(2) No funds shall be made available under any applicable program to any educational agency or institution unless the parents of students who are or have been

in attendance at a school of such agency or at such institution are provided an opportunity for a hearing by such agency or institution, in accordance with regulations of the Secretary, to challenge the content of such student's education records, in order to insure that the records are not inaccurate, misleading, or otherwise in violation of the privacy or other rights of students, and to provide an opportunity for the correction or deletion of any such inaccurate, misleading, or otherwise inappropriate data contained therein and to insert into such records a written explanation of the parents respecting the content of such records.

. . .

Release of education records; parental consent requirement; exceptions; compliance with judicial orders and subpoenas; audit and evaluation of Federally-supported education programs; record-keeping

(b)(1) No funds shall be made available under any applicable program to any educational agency or institution which has a policy or practice of permitting the release of education records (or personally identifiable information contained therein other than directory information, as defined in paragraph (5) of subsection (a) of this section) of students without the written consent of their parents to any individual, agency, or organization, other than to the following—

(A) other school officials, including teachers within the educational institution or local educational agency who have been determined by such agency or institution to have legitimate educational interests;

(B) officials of other schools or school systems in which the student seeks or intends to enroll, upon condition that the student's parents be notified of the transfer, receive a copy of the record if desired, and have an opportunity for a hearing to challenge the content of the record;

(C) authorized representatives of (i) the Comptroller General of the United States, (ii) the Secretary, (iii) an administrative head of an education agency (as defined in section 1221e-3(c) of this title), or (iv) State educational authorities, under the conditions set forth in paragraph (3) of this subsection;

(D) in connection with a student's application for, or receipt of, financial aid;

(E) State and local officials or authorities to whom such information is specifically required to be reported or disclosed pursuant to State statute adopted prior to November 19, 1974;

(F) organizations conducting studies for, or on behalf of, educational agencies or institutions for the purpose of developing, validating, or administering predictive tests, administering student aid programs, and improving instruction, if such studies are conducted in such a manner as will not permit the personal identification of students and their parents by persons other than representatives of such organizations and such information will be destroyed when no longer needed for the purpose for which it is conducted;

(G) accrediting organizations in order to carry out their accrediting functions;

(H) parents of a dependent student of such parents, as defined in section 152 of Title 26; and

(I) subject to regulations of the Secretary, in connection with an emergency, appropriate persons if the knowledge of such information is necessary to protect the health or safety of the student or other persons.

Nothing in clause (E) of this paragraph shall prevent a State from further limiting the number or type of State or local officials who will continue to have access thereunder.

(2) No funds shall be made available under any applicable program to any educational agency or institution which has a policy or practice of releasing, or providing access to, any personally identifiable information in education records other than directory information, or as is permitted under paragraph (1) of this subsection unless—

(A) there is written consent from the student's parents specifying records to be released, the reasons for such release, and to whom, and with a copy of the records to be released to the student's parents and the student if desired by the parents, or

(B) such information is furnished in compliance with judicial order, or pursuant to any lawfully issued subpoena, upon condition that parents and the students are notified of all such orders or subpoenas in advance of the compliance therewith by the educational institution or agency.

. . .

(B) With respect to this subsection, personal information shall only be transferred to a third party on the condition that such party will not permit any other party to have access to such information without the written consent of the parents of the student.

. . .

Students' rather than parents' permission or consent

(d) For the purposes of this section, whenever a student has attained eighteen years of age, or is attending an institution of post-secondary education the permission or consent required of and the rights accorded to the parents of the student shall thereafter only be required of and accorded to the student.

. . .

§ F1232h. Protection of pupil rights

Inspection by parents or guardians of instructional material

(a) All instructional material, including teacher's manuals, films, tapes, or other supplementary instructional material which will be used in connection with any research or experimentation program or project shall be available for inspection by the parents or guardians of the children engaged in such program or project. For the purpose of this section “”research or experimentation program or project” means any program or project in any applicable program designed to explore or develop new or unproven teaching methods or techniques.

Psychiatric or psychological examinations, testing, or treatment

(b) No student shall be required, as part of any applicable program, to submit to psychiatric examination, testing, or treatment, or psychological examination, testing, or treatment, in which the primary purpose is to reveal information concerning:

(1) political affiliations;

(2) mental and psychological problems potentially embarrassing to the student or his family;

(3) sex behavior and attitudes;

(4) illegal, anti-social, self-incriminating and demeaning behavior;

(5) critical appraisals of other individuals with whom respondents have close family relationships;

(6) legally recognized privileged and analogous relationships, such as those of lawyers, physicians, and ministers; or

(7) income (other than that required by law to determine eligibility for participation in a program or for receiving financial assistance under such program), without the prior consent of the student (if the student is an adult or emancipated minor), or in the case of unemancipated minor, without the prior written consent of the parent.

EDUCATION OF HANDICAPPED CHILDREN

(Selected Parts)

20 U.S.C.A. FF 1400-1461

Congressional statements and declarations § 1400.

. . .

Definitions § 1401.

. . .

Purpose

(c) It is the purpose of this chapter to assure that all handicapped children have available to them, within the time periods specified in section 1412(2)(B) of this title, a free appropriate public education which emphasizes special education and related services designed to meet their unique needs, to assure that the rights of handicapped children and their parents or guardians are protected, to assist States and localities to provide for the education of all handicapped children, and to assess and assure the effectiveness of efforts to educate handicapped children.

As used in this chapter—

. . .

(15) The term "children with specific learning disabilities" means those children who have a disorder in one or more of the basic psychological processes involved in understanding or in using language, spoken or written, which disorder may man-

ifest itself in imperfect ability to listen, think, speak, read, write, spell, or do mathematical calculations. Such disorders include such conditions as perceptual handicaps, brain injury, minimal brain dysfunction, dyslexia, and developmental aphasia. Such term does not include children who have learning problems which are primarily the result of visual, hearing, or motor handicaps, of mental retardation, of emotional disturbance, or of environmental, cultural, or economic disadvantage.

(16) The term "special education" means specially designed instruction, at no cost to parents or guardians, to meet the unique needs of a handicapped child, including classroom instruction, instruction in physical education, home instruction, and instruction in hospitals and institutions.

(17) The term "related services" means transportation, and such developmental, corrective, and other supportive services (including speech pathology and audiology, psychological services, physical and occupational therapy, recreation, and medical and counseling services, except that such medical services shall be for diagnostic and evaluation purposes only) as may be required to assist a handicapped child to benefit from special education, and includes the early identification and assessment of handicapping conditions in children.

(18) The term "free appropriate public education" means special education and related services which (A) have been provided at public expense, under public supervision and direction, and without charge, (B) meet the standards of the State educational agency, (C) include an appropriate preschool, elementary, or secondary school education in the State involved, and (D) are provided in conformity with the individualized education program required under section 1414(a)(5) of this title.

(19) The term "individualized education program" means a written statement for each handicapped child developed in any meeting by a representative of the local educational agency or an intermediate educational unit who shall be qualified to provide, or supervise the provision of, specially designed instruction to meet the unique needs of handicapped children, the teacher, the parents or guardian of such child, and, whenever appropriate, such child, which statement shall include (A) a statement of the present levels of educational performance of such child, (B) a statement of annual goals, including short-term instructional objectives, (C) a statement of the specific educational services to be provided to such child, and the extent to which such child will be able to participate in regular educational programs, (D) the projected date for initiation and anticipated duration of such services, and (E) appropriate objective criteria and evaluation procedures and schedules for determining, on at least an annual basis, whether instructional objectives are being achieved.

(20) The term "excess costs" means those costs which are in excess of the average annual per student expenditure in a local educational agency during the preceding school year for an elementary or secondary school student, as may be appropriate, and which shall be computed after deducting (A) amounts received under this subchapter or under title I or title VII of the Elementary and Secondary Education Act of 1965, and (B) any State or local funds expended for programs which would qualify for assistance under this subchapter or under such titles.

(21) The term "native language" has the meaning given that term by section 703(a)(2) of the Bilingual Education Act.

(22) The term "intermediate educational unit" means any public authority, other than a local educational agency, which is under the general supervision of a State educational agency, which is established by State law for the purpose of providing free public education on a regional basis, and which provides special education and related services to handicapped children within that State.

Procedural safeguards § 1415.

Establishment and maintenance

(a) Any State educational agency, any local educational agency, and any intermediate educational unit which receives assistance under this subchapter shall establish and maintain procedures in accordance with subsection (b) through subsection (e) of this section to assure that handicapped children and their parents or guardians are guaranteed procedural safeguards with respect to the provision of free appropriate public education by such agencies and units.

Required procedures; hearing

(b)(1) The procedures required by this section shall include, but shall not be limited to—

(A) an opportunity for the parents or guardian of a handicapped child to examine all relevant records with respect to the identification, evaluation, and educational placement of the child, and the provision of a free appropriate public education to such child, and to obtain an independent educational evaluation of the child;

(B) procedures to protect the rights of the child whenever the parents or guardian of the child are not known, unavailable, or the child is a ward of the State, including the assignment of an individual (who shall not be an employee of the State educational agency, local educational agency, or intermediate educational unit involved in the education or care of the child) to act as a surrogate for the parents or guardian;

(C) written prior notice to the parents or guardian of the child whenever such agency or unit—

(i) proposes to initiate or change, or

(ii) refuses to initiate or change,

the identification, evaluation, or educational placement of the child or the provision of a free appropriate public education to the child;

(D) procedures designed to assure that the notice required by clause (C) fully inform the parents or guardian, in the parents' or guardian's native language, unless it clearly is not feasible to do so, of all procedures available pursuant to this section; and

(E) an opportunity to present complaints with respect to any matter relating to the identification, evaluation, or educational placement of the child, or the provision of a free appropriate public education to such child.

(2) Whenever a complaint has been received under paragraph (1) of this subsection, the parents or guardian shall have an opportunity for an impartial due process hearing which shall be conducted by the State educational agency or by the local educational agency or intermediate educational unit, as determined by State law or by the State educational agency. No hearing conducted pursuant to the requirements of this paragraph shall be conducted by an employee of such agency or unit involved in the education or care of the child.

Review of local decision by State educational agency

(c) If the hearing required in paragraph (2) of subsection (b) of this section is conducted by a local educational agency or an intermediate educational unit, any party aggrieved by the findings and decision rendered in such a hearing may appeal to the State educational agency which shall conduct an impartial review of such hearing. The officer conducting such review shall make an independent decision upon completion of such review.

Enumeration of rights accorded parties to hearings

(d) Any party to any hearing conducted pursuant to subsections (b) and (c) of this section shall be accorded (1) the right to be accompanied and advised by counsel and by individuals with special knowledge or training with respect to the problems of handicapped children, (2) the right to present evidence and confront, cross-examine, and compel the attendance of witnesses, (3) the right to a written or electronic verbatim record of such hearing, and (4) the right to written findings of fact and decisions (which findings and decisions shall also be transmitted to the advisory panel established pursuant to section 1413(a)(12) of this title).

Alphabetical List of Case References

Aberdeen Education Association v. Aberdeen Board of Education, Aberdeen Independent School District, 215 N.W.2d 837 (S.D. 1974).
Acanfora v. Board of Education, of Montgomery County, 359 F.Supp. 843, (D.Md. 1973), aff'd. on other grounds, 491 F.2d 498 (4th Cir., 1974), cert. denied, 419 U.S. 836 (1974).
Ackerman v. Board of Education of City of New York, 387 F.Supp. 76 (S.D.N.Y. 1974).
Adams v. Campbell County School District, Campbell County, Wyoming, 511 F.2d 1242 (10th Cir., 1975).
Adams v. State Professional Practices Council, 406 So.2d 1170 (Fla. App. 1981).
Adcock v. Board of Education of San Diego Unified School District, 513 P.2d 900 (Cal. 1973).
Adelt v. Richmond School District, 58 Cal.Rptr. 151 (Cal. App. 1967).
Adkins v. Children's Hospital of the District of Columbia, 261 U.S. 525 (1923).
Adler v. Board of Education of City of New York, 342 U.S. 485 (1952).
Ahern v. Board of Education of School District of Grand Island, 456 F.2d 399 (8th Cir., 1972).
Albers v. Independent School District No. 302 of Lewis County, 487 P.2d 936 (Idaho 1971).
Alexander v. Holmes County Board of Education, 396 U.S. 19 (1969).
Alexander v. Manton Joint Union School District in Tehama and Shasta Counties, 255 P. 516 (Cal. App. 1927).
Alford v. Department of Education, 91 Cal. Rptr. 843 (Cal. App. 1970).
Allen v. Autauga County Board of Education, 685 F.2d 1302 (11th Cir., 1982).
Allen v. Board of Education of Jefferson County, 584 S.W.2d 408 (Ky. App. 1979).
Allison v. Field Local School District, 553 N.E.2d 1383 (Ohio App. 1988).
Alvarado v. El Paso Independent School District, 426 F.Supp. 575 (W.D. Tex. 1976).
Amador v. New Mexico State Board of Education, 455 P.2d 840 (N.M. 1969).
American Communications Association v. Douds, 339 U.S. 382 (1950).
American Federation of State, County, and Municipal Employees, AFL-CIO v. Woodward, 406 F.2d 137 (8th Cir. 1969).
Anchorage Education Association v. Anchorage School District, 648 P.2d 993 (Alaska, 1982).
Anderson v. Evans, 660 F.2d 153 (6th Cir., 1981).
Anderson Federation of Teachers, Local 519 v. School City of Anderson, 251 N.E.2d 15 (Ind. 1969); cert. denied, 399 U.S. 928 (1970).
Andrews v. Union Parish School Board, 184 So. 574 (La. App. 1938).
Appeal of Dugan, 59 A.2d 888 (Pa. 1948).
Appeal of Ganaposki, 2 A.2d 742 (Pa. 1938).
Appeal of Mulhollen, 39 A.2d 283 (Pa. Super 1944).

Appeal of Ritzie, 94 A.2d 729 (Pa. 1953).
Appeal of Santee, 156 A.2d 830 (Pa. 1959).
Appeal of Schneider, 79 A.2d 865 (N.J. Super, 1951).
Appeal of School District of Pittsburgh, 52 A.2d 17 (Pa. 1947).
Armstrong Education Association v. Armstrong School District, 542 A.2d 1047 (Pa. Cmwlth., 1988).
Atkins v. City of Charlotte, 296 F.Supp. 1068 (W.D. N.C. 1969).
Averell v. City of Newburyport, 135 N.E. 463 (Mass. 1922).
Avery v. Homewood City Board of Education, 674 F.2d 337 (5th Cir., 1982).
Ayer v. Board of Education of Central School District No. 1, 330 N.Y.S.2d 465 (1972).
Baggett v. Bullitt, 377 U.S. 360 (1964).
Baker v. School Board of Marion County, 450 So.2d 1194 (Fla. App. 5 Dist. 1984).
Ballard v. Board of Education of Goshen Local School District, 469 N.E.2d 951 (Ohio App. 1984).
Balog v. McKeesport Area School District, 484 A.2d 198 (Pa. Cmwlth. 1984).
Barcheski v. Board of Education of Grand Rapids Public Schools, 412 N.W.2d 296 (Mich. App. 1987).
Barton v. Governing Board of Middletown Unified School District of Lake County, 131 Cal. Rptr. 455 (Cal. App. 1976).
Basmajian v. Board of Education of City of New York, 207 N.Y.S. 298 (1925).
Bates v. Dause, 502 F.2d 865 (6th Cir., 1974).
Batiste v. Iberia Parish School Board, 401 So.2d 1224 (La. App. 1981).
Bay v. State Board of Education, 378 P.2d 558 (Or. 1963).
Bay City Education Association v. Bay City Public Schools, 422 N.W.2d 504 (Mich. 1988).
Beasley by and through Beasley v. *Morton,* 564 So.2d 45 (Ala. 1990).
Beers v. Nyquist, 338 N.Y.S.2d 745 (1972).
Begich v. Jefferson, 441 P.2d 27 (Alaska 1968).
Bellevue School District No. 405 v. Bentley, 684 P.2d 793 (Wash. App. 1984).
Benson v. School District No. 1 of Silver Bow County, 344 P.2d 117 (Mont. 1959).
Berman by Berman v. Philadelphia Board of Education, 456 A.2d 545 (Pa. Super. 1983).
Bernasconi v. Tempe Elementary School District No. 3, 548 F.2d 857, (9th Cir., 1977) cert. denied, 434 U.S. 825 (1977).
Bethel Park School District v. Krall, 445 A.2d 1377 (Pa. Cmwlth. 1982).
Bettendorf Education Association v. Bettendorf Community School District, 262 N.W.2d 550 (Iowa 1978).
Bevsek v. Huerfano School District RE-1, 728 P.2d 325 (Colo. App. 1986).
Bickford v. Board of Education of School District No. 82 of Hall County, 336 N.W.2d 73 (Neb. 1983).
Big Sandy School District No. 100-J v. Carroll, 433 P.2d 325 (Colo. 1967).
Biggs v. School City of Mt. Vernon, 90 N.E. 105 (Ind. App. 1909).
Birdwell v. Hazelwood School District, 491 F.2d 490 (8th Cir., 1974).
Black v. School Committee of Malden, 341 N.E.2d 896 (Mass. 1976).
Black v. Wyalusing Area School District, 365 A.2d 1352 (Pa. Cmwlth. 1976).
Blaine v. Moffat County School District RE. No. 1, 709 P.2d 96 (Colo. App. 1985).
Blanchet v. Vermilion Parish School Board, 220 So.2d 534 (La. App. 1969).
Blunt v. Marion County School Board, 515 F.2d 951 (5th Cir., 1975).
Board of Directors of Sioux City Community School District v. Mroz, 295 N.W.2d 447 (Iowa 1980).
Board of Education Borough of Union Beach v. New Jersey Education Association, 247 A.2d 867 (N.J. 1968).
Board of Education, Island Trees Union Free School District No. 26 v. Pico, 457 U.S. 853 (1982).

Board of Education of Alamogordo Public Schools District No. 1 v. Jennings, 651 P.2d 1037 (N.M. App. 1982).
Board of Education of Argo-Summit School District No. 104, Cook County v. Hunt, 487 N.E.2d 24 (Ill. App. 1 Dist. 1985).
Board of Education of Berwyn School District No. 100, Cook County v. Metskas, 436 N.E.2d 587 (Ill. App. 1982).
Board of Education of City of Asbury Park v. Asbury Park Education Association, 368 A.2d 396 (N.J. Super. 1976).
Board of Education of City of Englewood v. Englewood Teachers Association, 311 A.2d 729 (N.J. 1973).
Board of Education of City of New York v. Shanker, 283 N.Y.S.2d 548 (N.Y., 1967).
Board of Education of District of Columbia v. Wilson, 290 A.2d 400 (D.C. App. 1972).
Board of Education of Hopkins County v. Wood, 717 S.W.2d 837 (Ky. 1986).
Board of Education of Laurel County v. McCollum, 721 S.W.2d 703 (Ky. 1986).
Board of Education of Long Beach Unified School District of Los Angeles County v. Jack M., 566 P.2d 602 (Cal. 1977).
Board of Education of Marshallton-McKean School District v. Sinclair, 373 A.2d 572 (Del. 1977).
Board of Education of New Concord School District v. Best, 39 N.E. 694 (Ohio 1894).
Board of Education of Rockford School District No. 205 v. Rockford Education Association, 501 N.E.2d 338 (Ill. App. 2 Dist. 1986).
Board of Education of Santa Fe Public Schools v. Sullivan, 740 P.2d 119 (N.M. 1987).
Board of Education of Taos Municipal Schools v. Singleton, 712 P.2d 1384 (N.M. App. 1985).
Board of Education of Township of North Bergen v. North Bergen Federation of Teachers, 357 A.2d 302 (N.J. Super. A.D. 1976).
Board of Education of Vocational School in County of Camden v. Cam/Voc Teachers Association, 443 A.2d 756 (N.J. Super. A.D. 1982).
Board of Education, Tucson High School District No. 1 v. Williams, 403 P.2d 324 (Ariz. App. 1965).
Board of Regents of State Colleges v. Roth, 408 U.S. 564 (1972).
Board of School Directors of the Abington School District v. Pittenger, 305 A.2d 382 (Pa. Cmwlth. 1973).
Board of School Trustees of South Vermillion School Corporation v. Benetti, 492 N.E.2d 1098 (Ind. App. 1 Dist. 1986).
Board of Trustees of Santa Maria Joint Union High School District v. Judge, 123 Cal.Rptr. 830 (Cal. App. 1975).
Bogust v. Iverson, 102 N.W.2d 228 (Wis. 1960).
Bolin v. San Bernardino City Unified School District, 202 Cal.Rptr. 416 (Cal. App. 1984).
Booth v. Argenbright, 731 P.2d 1318 (Mont. 1987).
Borman v. Gorham-Fayette Board of Education, 502 N.E.2d 1031 (Ohio 1986).
Boston Teachers Union, Local 66 v. School Committee of Boston, 434 N.E.2d 1258 (Mass. 1982).
Bovino v. Board of School Directors of Indiana Area School District, 377 A.2d 1284 (Pa. Cmwlth. 1977).
Bowbells Public School District No. 14 v. Walker, 231 N.W.2d 173 (N.D. 1975).
Bowman v. Pulaski County Special School District, 723 F.2d 640 (8th Cir., 1983).
Boyd v. State, 7 So. 268 (Ala. 1890).
Boyer v. Jablonski, 435 N.E.2d 436 (Ohio App. 1980).
Brackman v. Adrian, 472 S.W.2d 735 (Tenn. App. 1971).
Bradley v. Cothern, 384 F.Supp. 1216 (E.D. Tex. 1974).
Bradley v. School Board of City of Richmond, 382 U.S. 103 (1965).
Braun v. Glade Valley School, Inc., 334 S.E.2d 404 (N.C. App. 1985).

Braxton v. Board of Public Instruction of Duval County, Florida, 303 F.Supp. 958 (M.D. Fla. 1969).
Brazell v. Board of Education of Niskayuna Public Schools, 557 N.Y.S. 2d 645 (N.Y.A.D. 3 Dept. 1990).
Breen v. Runkel, 614 F.Supp. 355 (W.D. Mich. 1985).
Brinson v. School District No. 431, 576 P.2d 602 (Kan. 1978).
Bristol Township School District v. Karafin, 478 A.2d 539 (Pa. Cmwlth. 1984).
Brooks v. Orleans Parish School Board, 560 So.2d 633 (La. App 4, Cir. 1990).
Brough v. Board of Education of Millard County School District, 463 P.2d 567 (Utah 1970).
Brubaker v. Board of Education, School District 149, Cook County, Illinois, 502 F.2d 973 (7th Cir., 1974).
Buckley v. Coyle Public School System, 476 F.2d 92 (10th Cir., 1973).
Bullock v. Joint Class "A" School District No. 241, 272 P.2d 292 (Idaho 1954).
Bump v. Union High School District No. 3, 24 P.2d 330 (Or. 1933).
Burk v. Unified School District No. 329, Wabaunsee County, Kansas, 646 F.Supp. 1557 (D. Kan. 1986).
Burton v. Cascade School District Union High School No. 5, 353 F.Supp. 254 (D. Or. 1973).
Burton v. School Committee of Quaboag Regional School District, 432 N.E.2d 725 (Mass. App. 1982).
Buzzard v. East Lake School District of Lake County, California, 93 P.2d 233 (Cal. App. 1939).
Bye v. Special Intermediate School District No. 916, 379 N.W.2d 653 (Minn. App. 1986).
Cahill v. Board of Education of City of Stamford, 502 A.2d 410 (Conn. 1985).
Calhoun v. Cassady, 534 S.W.2d 806 (Ky. 1976).
California Teachers' Association v. Parlier Unified School District, 204 Cal.Rptr. 20 (Cal. App. 5 Dist. 1984).
Calway v. Williamson, 36 A.2d 377 (Conn. 1944).
Camden County Vocational Technical Association v. Board of Education of Camden County Vocational Technical Schools, Camden County, 503 A.2d 890 (N.J. Super. A.D. 1986).
Carangelo v. Ambach, 515 N.Y.S.2d 665 (N.Y.A.D. 3 Dept. 1987).
Carlan v. Board of Education of Lawrence Union Free School District, 513 N.Y.S.2d 202 (N.Y.A.D. 2 Dept. 1987).
Carson v. Orleans Parish School Board, 432 So.2d 956 (La. App. 4th Cir. 1983).
Cary v. Board of Education of Adams-Arapahoe School District 28-J, 598 F.2d 535 (10th Cir., 1979).
Casada v. Booneville School District No. 65, 686 F.Supp. 730 (W.D.Ark. 1988).
Cedar Rapids Community School District v. Parr, 227 N.W.2d 486 (Iowa 1975).
Celestine v. Lafayette Parish School Board, 284 So.2d 650 (La. App. 1973).
Chalk v. United States District Court Central District of California, 840 F.2d 701 (9th Cir., 1988).
Chambers v. Central School District School Board of Greene County, 514 N.E.2d 1294 (Ind. App. 1 Dist. 1987).
Chester Upland School District v. Brown, 447 A.2d 1068 (Pa. Cmwlth. 1982).
Chicago Board of Education v. Payne, 430 N.E.2d 310 (Ill. App. 1981).
Chicago Division of the Illinois Education Association v. Board of Education of City of Chicago, 222 N.E.2d 243 (Ill. App. 1966).
Childers v. Independent School District No. 1 of Bryan County, State of Oklahoma, 676 F.2d 1338 (10th Cir., 1982).
Cirillo v. City of Milwaukee, 150 N.W.2d 460 (Wis. 1967).
City of Beloit v. Wisconsin Employment Relations Commission, 242 N.W.2d 231 (Wis. 1976).
City School District of City of Elmira v. New York State Public Employment Relations Board, 536 N.Y.S.2d 214 (N.Y.A.D. 3 Dept. 1988).
Claiborne County Board of Education v. Martin, 500 So.2d 981 (Miss. 1986).

Clark v. Ann Arbor School District, 344 N.W.2d 48 (Mich. App. 1983).
Clark v. Mt. Greylock Regional School District, 336 N.E.2d 750 (Mass. App. 1975).
Clark County School District v. Local Government Employee Management Relations Board, 530 P.2d 114 (Nev. 1974).
Clarke v. Board of Education of School District of Omaha, 338 N.W.2d 272 (Neb. 1983).
Clarke v. Shoreline School District No. 412, King County, 720 P.2d 793 (Wash. 1986).
Cleveland Board of Education v. LaFleur, 414 U.S. 632 (1974).
Coats v. Board of Education Unified School District No. 353, Sumner County, 662 P.2d 1279 (Kan. 1983).
Cohen v. Chesterfield County School Board, 414 U.S. 632 (1974).
Cole v. Richardson, 405 U.S. 676 (1972).
Coles v. Glenburn Public School District No. 26, 436 N.W.2d 262 (N.D. 1989).
Collins v. Wakonda Independent School District No. 1, 252 N.W.2d 646 (S.D. 1977).
Comings v. State Board of Education, 100 Cal.Rptr. 73 (Cal. App. 1972).
Commonwealth v. County Board of Arlington County, 232 S.E.2d 30 (Va. 1977).
Commonwealth v. Herr, 78 A. 68 (Pa. 1910).
Commonwealth, Deptartment of Education v. Charleroi Area School District, 347 A.2d 736 (Pa. Cmwlth. 1975).
Commonwealth Department of Education v. Kauffman, 343 A.2d 391 (Pa. Cmwlth. 1975).
Commonwealth ex rel. Wesenberg v. School District of City of Bethlehem, 24 A.2d 673 (Pa. Super. 1942).
Conley v. Board of Education of City of New Britain, 123 A.2d 747 (Conn. 1956).
Connell v. Higginbotham, 403 U.S. 207 (1971).
Connick v. Myers, 461 U.S. 138 (1983).
Consolidated School District No. 4, Bryan County v. Millis, 139 P.2d 183 (Okl. 1943).
Cook v. Board of Education for County of Logan, 671 F.Supp. 1110 (S.D.W.Va. 1987).
Cooley v. Board of Education of Forrest City School District, 453 F.2d 282 (8th Cir., 1972).
Cooper v. Eugene School District No. 4J, 723 P.2d 298 (Or. 1986).
Cooper v. McJunkin, 4 Ind. 290 (1853).
Coriou v. Nyquist, 304 N.Y.S.2d 486 (N.Y. App. Div. 1969).
Coronway v. Lansdowne School District No. 785 (Ct.Com.Pl. of Delaware County, Pa. 1951).
Council of Directors and Supervisors of the Los Angeles City Schools v. Los Angeles Unified School District, 110 Cal. Rptr. 624 (Cal. App. 1973).
County Board of Education of Clarke County v. Oliver, 116 So.2d 566 (Ala. 1959).
Coupeville School District No. 204 v. Vivian, 677 P.2d 192 (Wash. App. 1984).
Covington v. Beaumont Independent School District, 714 F.Supp. 1402 (E.D. Tex. 1989).
Cox v. Dardanelle Public School District, 790 F.2d 668 (8th Cir., 1986).
Cramp v. Board of Public Instruction of Orange County, 368 U.S. 278 (1961).
Crockett v. Sorenson, 568 F.Supp. 1422 (W.D. Va. 1983).
Crutchfield v. Pulaski County Special School District, 647 F.Supp. 884 (E.D. Ark. 1986).
D. T. by M. T. v. Independent School District No. 16 of Pawnee County, Oklahoma, 894 F.2d 1176 (10th Cir. 1990), cert. denied. ___ U.S. ___ (1990).
Dailey v. Los Angeles Unified School District, 87 Cal.Rptr. 376 (Cal. App. 1970).
Dallastown Area School District v. Commonwealth, Pennsylvania Human Relations Commission, 460 A.2d 878 (Pa. Cmwlth. 1983).
Davis v. Board of Education of Aurora Public School District No. 131, 312 N.E.2d 335 (Ill. App. 1974).
Dayton Board of Education v. Brinkman, 443 U.S. 526 (1979).
Dean v. Timpson Independent School District, 486 F.Supp. 302 (E.D. Tex. 1979).
Decatur Board of Education, District No. 61 v. Illinois Educational Labor Relations Board, 536 N.E.2d 743 (Ill. App. 4 Dist. 1989).

DeGooyer v. Harkness, 13 N.W.2d 815 (S.D. 1944).
deLaurier v. San Diego Unified School District, 588 F.2d 674 (9th Cir., 1978).
Denton v. South Kitsap School District No. 402, 516 P.2d 1080 (Wash. App. 1973).
DeSoto County School Board v. Garrett, 508 So.2d 1091 (Miss. 1987).
DeVito v. Board of Education, 317 S.E.2d 159 (W.Va. 1984).
Dibortolo v. Metropolitan School District of Washington Township, 440 N.E.2d 506 (Ind. App. 1982).
Diehl v. Albany County School District No. 1, 694 F.Supp. 1534 (D.Wyo. 1988).
Dillon v. Board of Education of County of Wyoming, 351 S.E.2d 58 (W.Va. 1986).
DiPasquale v. Board of Education, Williamsville Central School District, 626 F.Supp. 457 (W.D.N.Y. 1985).
District 300 Education Association v. Board of Education of Dundee Community Unit School District No. 300, 334 N.E.2d 165 (Ill. App. 1975).
Doe v. Anker, 451 F.Supp. 241 (S.D.N.Y. 1978).
Domico v. Rapides Parish School Board, 675 F.2d 100 (5th Cir., 1982).
Dooley v. Fort Worth Independent School District, 686 F.Supp. 1194 (N.D.Tex. 1987).
Dore v. Board of Education of Township of Bedminster, Somerset County, 449 A.2d 547 (N.J. Super. A.D. 1982).
Dougherty County, Georgia, Board of Education v. White, 439 U.S. 32 (1978).
Downey v. School Committee of Lowell, 25 N.E.2d 738 (Mass. 1940).
Downs v. Board of Education of Hoboken District, 171 A. 528 (N.J. 1934).
Doyal v. School Board of Liberty County, 415 So.2d 791 (Fla. App. 1982).
Drinnin v. Heartland Area Education Agency 11, 332 N.W.2d 328 (Iowa 1983).
Dupree v. School Committee of Boston, 446 N.E.2d 1099 (Mass. App. 1983).
Dusanek v. Hannon, 677 F.2d 538 (7th Cir., 1982), cert. denied, 459 U.S. 1017 (1982).
Dutart v. Woodward, 279 P. 493 (Cal. App. 1929).
Dutcher v. City of Santa Rosa High School District, 290 P.2d 316 (Cal. App. 1955).
Earnest v. School Board of Independent District No. 16 of Stillwater, Oklahoma, 666 P.2d 1287 (Okl. 1983).
East County Bargaining Council v. Centennial School District No. 28JT, 685 P.2d 452 (Or. App. 1984).
East Hartford Education Association v. Board of Education of the Town of East Hartford, 562 F.2d 838 (2d Cir., 1977).
Eastbrook Community Schools Corporation v. Indiana Education Employment Relations Board, 446 N.E.2d 1007 (Ind. App. 1983).
Eastman v. Williams, 207 A.2d 146 (Vt. 1965).
Eckmann v. Board of Education of Hawthorn School District No. 17, 636 F.Supp. 1214 (N.D. Ill. 1986).
Edwards v. Aguillard, 482 U.S. 578 (1987).
Ehret v. School District of Borough of Kulpmont, 5 A.2d 188 (Pa. 1939).
Elfbrandt v. Russell, 384 U.S. 11 (1966).
Ellis-Adams v. Whitfield County Board of Education, 356 S.E.2d 219 (Ga. App. 1987).
Ellis v. Ambach, 508 N.Y.S.2d 624 (N.Y.A.D. 3 Dept. 1986).
Elrod v. Harrisonville Cass R-IX School District, 706 S.W.2d 465 (Mo. App. 1986).
Epperson v. Arkansas, 393 U.S. 97 (1968).
Fabian v. Independent School District No. 89 of Oklahoma County, Oklahoma, 409 F.Supp. 94 (W.D. Okl. 1976).
Fadler v. Illinois State Board of Education, 506 N.E.2d 640 (Ill. App. 5 Dist. 1987).
Fagan v. Summers, 498 F.2d 1227 (Wyo. 1972).
Fairplay School Township v. O'Neal, 26 N.E. 686 (Ind. 1891).
Faulkner v. New Bern-Craven County Board of Education, 316 S.E.2d 281 (N.C. 1984).

Fayette County Education Association v. Hardy, 626 S.W.2d 217 (Ky. App. 1980).
Ferguson v. DeSoto Parish School Board, 467 So.2d 1257 (La. App. 2 Cir. 1985).
Fernald v. City of Ellsworth Superintending School Committee, 342 A.2d 704 (Me. 1975).
Ferrara v. Mills, 781 F.2d 1508 (11th Cir., 1986).
Ferris v. Special School District No. 1, 367 F.Supp. 459 (D. Minn. 1973).
Fidler v. Board of Trustees of Roseville Union High School, 296 P. 912 (Cal. App. 1931).
Fink v. Board of Education of Warren County School District, 442 A.2d 837 (Pa.Cmwlth. 1982).
Finot v. Pasadena City Board of Education, 58 Cal.Rptr. 520 (Cal. App. 1967).
Firefighters Local Union No. 1784 v. Stotts, 467 U.S. 561 (1984).
Fischler v. Askew, 349 So.2d 227 (Fla. App. 1977).
Fiscus v. Board of School Trustees of Central School District of Greene County, 509 N.E. 2d 1137 (Ind. App. 1 Dist. 1987).
Fisher v. Fairbanks North Star Borough School District, 704 P.2d 213 (Alaska 1985).
Fisher v. Snyder, 476 F.2d 375 (8th Cir., 1973).
Florian v. Highland Local School District Board of Education, 493 N.E.2d 249 (Ohio App. 1983).
Forehand v. School Board of Washington County, 481 So.2d 953 (Fla. App. 1 Dist. 1986).
Foster v. Carson School District No. 301, Skamania County, 385 P.2d 367 (Wash. 1963).
Fowler v. Board of Education of Lincoln County, Kentucky, 819 F.2d 657 (6th Cir. 1987), cert. denied, 484 U.S. 986 (1987).
Fox v. Board of Education of Doddridge County, 236 S.E.2d 243 (W.Va. 1977).
Frank v. Orleans Parish School Board, 195 So.2d 451 (La. App. 1967).
Franklin v. Alabama State Tenure Commission, 482 So.2d 1214 (Ala. Civ. App. 1985).
Freeport Area School District v. Commonwealth, Human Relations Commission, 335 A.2d 873 (Pa. Cmwlth. 1975).
Fry v. Commonwealth, 485 A.2d 508 (Pa. Cmwlth. 1984).
Fuzie v. South Haven School District No. 30, 553 N.Y.S.2d 961 (Sup. 1990).
Gaincott v. Davis, 275 N.W. 229 (Mich. 1937).
Gamble v. Mills, 483 So.2d 826 (Fla. App. 4 Dist. 1986.
Gardner v. State, 4 Ind. 632 (1853).
Garner v. Stephens, 460 F.2d 1144 (6th Cir., 1972).
Gathright v. Lincoln Insurance Company, 688 S.W.2D 931 (Ark. 1985).
Gaylord v. Tacoma School District No. 10, 559 P.2d 1340 (Wash. 1977) cert. denied, 434 U.S. 879 (1977).
Geduldig v. Aiello, 417 U.S. 484 (1974).
General Electric Company v. Gilbert, 429 U.S. 125 (1976).
George v. School District No. 8R of Umatilla County, 490 P.2d 1009 (Or. App. 1971).
Georgia Association of Educators v. Gwinnett County School District, 856 F.2d 142 (11th Cir., 1988).
Gere v. Council Bluffs Community School District, 334 N.W.2d 307 (Iowa 1983).
Gerhardt v. Heid, 267 N.W. 127 (N.D. 1936).
Gibbons v. New Castle Area School District, 500 A.2d 922 (Pa.Cmwlth. 1985).
Gieringer v. Center School District No. 58, 477 F.2d 1164 (8th Cir., 1973), cert. denied, 414 U.S. 832 (1973).
Gilbertson v. McAlister, 403 F.Supp. 1 (D. Conn. 1975).
Gillett v. Unified School District No. 276, Jewell County, 605 P.2d 105 (Kan. 1980).
Gilliland v. Board of Education of Pleasant View Consolidated School District No. 622 of Tazewell County, 365 N.E.2d 322 (Ill. 1977).
Giordano v. Ambach, 509 N.Y.S.2d 203 (N.Y.A.D. 3 Dept. 1986).
Givhan v. Western Line Consolidated School District, 439 U.S. 410 (1979); on remand, *Ayers v. Western Line Consolidated School District,* 691 F.2d 766 (5th Cir., 1982).

Glanville v. Hickory County Reorganized School District No. 1, 6537 S.W.2d 328 (Mo. App. 1982).
Glendale School District v. Feigh, 513 A.2d 1093 (Pa. Cmwlth. 1986).
Glennon v. School Committee of Boston, 378 N.E.2d 1372 (Mass. 1978).
Goldberg v. Kelly, 397 U.S. 254 (1970).
Golden v. Board of Education of County of Harrison, 285 S.E.2d 665 (W.Va. 1981).
Goldsmith v. Board of Education of Sacramento City High School District, 225 P. 783 (Cal. App. 1924).
Goldwasser v. Brown, 417 F.2d 1169 (D.C. Cir., 1969), cert. denied, 397 U.S. 992 (1970).
Goose River Bank v. Willow Lake School Township, 44 N.W. 1002 (N.D. 1890).
Govel v. Board of Education of City of Albany, 48 N.Y.S.2d 299 (N.Y.A.D. 1944).
Governing Board of Nicasio School District of Marin County v. Brennan, 95 Cal.Rptr. 712 (Cal. App. 1971).
Grant v. Lake Oswego School District No. 7, Clackamas County, 515 P.2d 947 (Or. 1973).
Gray v. Union County Intermediate Education District, 520 F.2d 803 (9th Cir., 1975).
Greater Clark County School Corporation v. Myers, 493 N.E.2d 1267 (Ind. App. 4 Dist. 1986).
Green v. Fairfield City Board of Education, 365 So.2d 1217 (Ala. Civ. App. 1978).
Green v. Jenkintown School District, 441 A.2d 816 (Pa. Cmwlth. 1982).
Green v. Waterford Board of Education, 473 F.2d 629 (2d Cir., 1973).
Greene v. County Board of Education of Calhoun County, 197 So.2d 771 (Ala. 1967).
Greene v. School Board of Hamilton County, 501 So.2d 50 (Fla. App. 1 Dist. 1987).
Greminger v. Seaborne, 584 F.2d 275 (8th Cir., 1978).
Grim v. West Chester Area School District, 529 A.2d 71 (Pa. Cmwlth. 1987).
Grissom v. Board of Education of Buckley-Loda Community School District No. 8, 388 N.E.2d 398 (Ill. 1979).
Griswold v. Connecticut, 381 U.S. 479 (1965).
Grounds v. Tolar Independent School District, 707 S.W.2d 889 (Tex. 1986).
Guerra v. Roma Independent School District, 444 F.Supp. 812 (S.D. Tex. 1977).
Guerrieri v. Tyson, 24 A.2d 468 (Pa. Super. 1942).
Guthrie v. Board of Education of Jefferson County, 298 S.W.2d 691 (Ky. App. 1957).
Hachiya v. Board of Education, Unified School District No. 307, Saline County, 750 P.2d 383 (Kan. 1988).
Hadley v. Witt Unit School District 66, 462 N.E.2d 877 (Ill. App. 5 Dist. 1984).
Hale v. Board of Education, City of Lancaster, 234 N.E.2d 583 (Ohio 1968).
Hall v. Board of School Commissioners of Mobile County, Alabama, 681 F.2d 965 (5th Cir., 1982).
Halley v. Board of School Trustees of Blackford County School Corporation, 531 N.E.2d 1182 (Ind. App. 4 Dist. 1988).
Hanlon v. Board of Education of Parkway School District, 695 S.W.2d 930 (Mo. App. 1985).
Harlow v. Fitzgerald, 457 U.S. 800 (1982).
Harrah Independent School District v. Martin, 440 U.S. 194 (1979).
Harris v. Mechanicville Central School District, 382 N.Y.S.2d 251 (1976).
Harrisburg R-VIII School District v. O'Brian, 540 S.W.2d 945 (Mo. App. 1976).
Harvey v. Jefferson County School District No. R-1, 710 P.2d 1103 (Colo. 1985).
Hawkins v. Linn County School District No. 14, 517 P.2d 330 (Or. App. 1973).
Hentschke v. Sink, 109 Cal.Rptr. 549 (Cal. App. 1973).
Herfindahl v. Independent School District No. 126, Clara City, 325 N.W.2d 36 (Minn. 1982).
Hesse v. Board of Education of Township High School District No. 211, Cook County, Illinois, 848 F.2d 748 (7th Cir., 1988).
Holley v. Seminole County School District, 755 F.2d 1492 (11th Cir., 1985).
Hood v. Alabama State Tenure Commission, 418 So.2d 131 (Ala. Civ. App. 1982).

Horosko v. Mt. Pleasant Township School District, 6 A.2d 866 (Pa. 1939).
Horton v. Lawrence County Board of Education, 449 F.2d 793 (5th Cir., 1971).
Hortonville Joint School District No. 1 v. Hortonville Education Association, 426 U.S. 482 (1976).
Hosack v. Smiley, 276 F.Supp. 876 (D. Colo. 1967), aff'd. 390 U.S. 744 (1968).
Hoskins v. Walker, 315 N.E.2d 25 (Ill. 1974).
Hovland v. School District No. 52, 278 P.2d 211 (Mont. 1954).
Hutchison v. Toews, 476 P.2d 811 (Or. App. 1970).
Hyde v. Wellpinit School District No. 49, 648 P.2d 892 (Wash. App. 1982).
Hysong v. School District of Gallitzin Borough, 30 A. 482 (Pa. 1894).
In re Block, 236 A.2d 589 (N.J. 1967).
In re Dowden, 446 So.2d 853 (La. App. 2 Cir. 1984).
In re Grossman, 316 A.2d 39 (N.J. Super. 1974).
In re Swink, 200 A. 200 (Pa. Super. 1938).
In re Womer, 11 A.2d 146 (Pa. 1940).
Ingraham v. Wright, 430 U.S. 651 (1977).
Izard v. Hickory City Schools Board of Education, 315 S.E.2d 756 (N.C. App. 1984).
Jackson v. Board of Education of City of Chicago, 441 N.E.2d 120 (Ill. App. 1982).
Jacksonville v. Akers, 11 Ill. App. 393 (1880).
James v. Board of Education of Central District No. 1, 461 F.2d 566 (2d Cir., 1972).
James v. Hitchcock Independent School District, 742 S.W.2d 701 (Tex. App.-Houston [1st Dist.] 1987).
Jantzen v. School Committee of Chelmsford, 124 N.E.2d 534 (Mass. 1955).
Jarvella v. Willoughby-Eastlake City School District Board of Education, 233 N.E.2d 143 (Ohio 1967).
Jefferson Classroom Teachers Association v. Jefferson Elementary School District, 187 Cal.Rptr. 542 (Cal. App. 1982).
Jefferson School Township of Miami County v. Graves, 150 N.E. 61 (Ind. App. 1926).
Jefferson Union High School District v. Jones, 100 Cal.Rptr. 73 (Cal. App. 1972).
Jersey Shore Education Association v. Jersey Shore Area School District, 512 A.2d 805 (Pa. Cmwlth. 1986).
Jinks v. Mays, 332 F.Supp. 254 (N.D. Ga. 1971).
Johnson v. United School District Joint School Board, 191 A.2d 897 (Pa. Super. 1963).
Joint School District No. 8, City of Madison v. Wisconsin Employment Relations Board, 155 N.W.2d 78 (Wis. 1967).
Jones v. Alabama State Tenure Commission, 408 So.2d 145 (Ala. Civ. App. 1981).
Jones v. Battles, 315 F.Supp. 601 (D. Conn. 1970).
Jones v. Birdsong, 530 F.Supp. 221 (N.D. Miss. 1980).
Jones v. Holes, 6 A.2d 102 (Pa. 1939).
Jones v. Wrangell School District, 696 P.2d 677 (Alaska 1985).
Jordahl v. Independent School District No. 129, 225 N.W.2d 224 (Minn. 1974).
Kain v. Rockridge Community Unit School District No. 300, 453 N.E.2d 118 (Ill. App. 3 Dist. 1983).
Kaplan v. School Committee of Melrose, 294 N.E.2d 209 (Mass. 1973).
Karbach v. Board of Education of Lawndale School District, 114 Cal. Rptr. 84 (Cal. App. 1974).
Katz v. Ambach, 472 N.Y.S.2d 492 (N.Y.A.D. 3 Dept. 1984).
Kaufman v. School Committee of Boston, 463 N.E.2d 1195 (Mass. App. 1984).
Keefe v. Geanakos, 418 F.2d 359 (1st Cir., 1969).
Kelso Education Association v. Kelso School District No. 453, 740 P.2d 889 (Wash. App. 1987).
Kenai Peninsula Borough Board of Education v. Brown, 691 P.2d 1034 (Alaska 1984).
Kenai Peninsula Borough School District v. Kenai Peninsula Education Association, 572 P.2d 416 (Alaska 1977).

Kenaston v. School Administrative District No. 40, 317 A.2d 7 (Me. 1974).
Kennedy v. Board of Education, 22 P. 1042 (Cal. 1890).
Kersey v. Maine Consolidated School District No. 10, 394 P.2d 201 (Ariz. 1964).
Keyishian v. Board of Regents of the University of the State of New York, 385 U.S. 589 (1967).
Kimble v. Worth County R-III Board of Education, 669 S.W.2d 949 (Mo. App. 1984).
King v. Iowa Civil Rights Commission, 334 N.W.2d 598 (Iowa 1983).
Kingsville Independent School District v. Cooper, 611 F.2d 1109 (5th Cir., 1980).
Kinsella v. Board of Education of Central School District No. 7 of Towns of Amherst and Tonawanda, Erie County, 407 N.Y.S.2d 78 (1978).
Kirk v. Miller, 522 P.2d 843 (Wash. 1974).
Kizer v. Dorchester County Vocational Educational Board of Trustees, 340 S.E.2d 144 (S.C. 1986).
Klucka v. Livingston Parish Board, 433 So.2d 302 (La. App. 1 Cir. 1983).
Knapp v. Whitaker, 757 F.2d 827 (7th Cir., 1985).
Knight v. Board of Regents of University of State of New York, 269 F.Supp. 339 (S.D.N.Y. 1967), aff'd, 390 U.S. 36 (1968).
Knipmeyer v. Diocese of Alexandria, 492 So.2d 550 (La. App. 3 Cir. 1986).
Kornblum v. Newark Unified School District, 112 Cal.Rptr. 457 (Cal. App. 1974).
Krizek v. Board of Education of Cicero-Stickney Township High School District No. 201, Cook County, Illinois, 713 F.Supp. 1131 (N.D. Ill. 1989).
Kurlander v. School Committee of Williamstown, 451 N.E.2d 138 (Mass. App. 1983).
LaBelle v. San Francisco Unified School District, 189 Cal.Rptr. 530 (Cal. App. 1983).
Lagos v. Modesto City School District, 843 F.2d 347 (9th Cir., 1988).
Laird v. Independent School District No. 317, Deer River, Minnesota, 346 N.W.2d 153 (Minn. 1984).
Lake Park Education Association v. Board of Education of Lake Park High School District No. 108, DuPage County, Illinois, 526 F.Supp. 710 (N.D. Ill. 1981).
Lake Washington School District No. 414 v. Lake Washington Education Association/Washington Education Association, 745 P.2d 504 (Wash. 1987).
Lander v. Seaver, 32 Vt. 114 (1859).
Lang v. Great Falls School District No. 1 and A, 842 F.2d 1046 (9th Cir., 1988).
LaRocca v. Board of Education of Rye City School District, 406 N.Y.S.2d 348 (App. Div. 1978).
Last v. Board of Education of Community Unit School District No. 321, 185 N.E.2d 282 (Ill. App. 1962).
LaValley v. Stanford, 70 N.Y.S.2d 460 (N.Y.A.D. 1947).
Lee v. Pickens County School System, 563 F.2d 143 (5th Cir., 1977).
LeGalley v. Bronson Community Schools, 339 N.W.2d 223 (Mich. App. 1983).
Lenox Education Association v. Labor Relations Commission, 471 N.E.2d 81 (Mass. 1984).
Lesley v. Oxford Area School District, 420 A.2d 764 (Pa. Cmwlth. 1980).
Lewis v. Board of Education of North Clay Community Unit School District No. 25, Clay County, 537 N.E.2d 435 (Ill.App. 5 Dist. 1989).
Lewis v. East Feliciana Parish School Board, 452 So.2d 1275 (La. App. 1 Cir. 1984).
Lewis v. Harrison School District No. 1, 805 F.2d 310 (8th Cir., 1986).
Lewis v. Los Angeles City Unified School District, 429 F.Supp. 935 (C.D. Cal. 1977).
Lexington County School District One Board of Trustees v. Bost, 316 S.E.2d 677 (S.C. 1984).
Libe v. Board of Education of Twin Cedars Community School District, 350 N.W.2d 748 (Iowa App. 1984).
Lile v. Hancock Place School District, 701 S.W.2d 500 (Mo. App. 1985).
Lilienthal v. San Leandro Unified School District of Alameda County, 293 P.2d 889 (Cal. App. 1956).
Lindgren v. Board of Trustees High School District No. 1, 558 P.2d 468 (Mont. 1976).

Lockhart v. Board of Education of Arapahoe County School District No. 6, 735 P.2d 913 (Colo. App. 1986).
Loehr v. Board of Education, 108 P. 325 (Cal. App. 1910).
Logan v. Warren County Board of Education, 549 F.Supp. 145 (S.D. Ga. 1982).
Lomas v. Board of School Directors of Northwestern Lehigh School District, 444 A.2d 1319 (Pa. Cmwlth. 1982).
Los Angeles Teachers Union Local 1021, American Federation of Teachers v. Los Angeles City Board of Education, 455 P.2d 827 (Cal. 1969).
Louthan v. Commonwealth, 79 Va. 196 (1884).
Lucia v. Duggan, 303 F.Supp. 112 (D. Mass. 1969).
Lusk v. Estes, 361 F.Supp. 653 (N.D. Texas 1973).
Lyznicki v. Board of Education, School District 167, Cook County, Illinois, 707 F.2d 949 (7th Cir., 1983).
MacDonald v. Ferguson Reorganized School District R-2, 530 F.Supp. 469 (E.D. Mo. 1981).
Maddox v. Boutwell, 336 S.E.2d 599 (Ga. App. 1985).
Maddox v. St. Paul School District, 697 S.W.2d 130 (Ark. App. 1985).
Mailloux v. Kiley, 323 F.Supp. 1387 (D. Mass. 1971), aff'd., 448 F.2d 1242 (1st Cir., 1971).
Malcolm v. City of Boston, 53 N.E. 812 (Mass. 1899).
Maltz v. Board of Education of New York City, 114 N.Y.S.2d 856 (N.Y. 1952).
Mancha v. Field Museum of Natural History, 283 N.E.2d 899 (Ill. App. 1972).
Mandan Education Association v. Mandan Public School District No. 1, 425 N.W.2d 917 (N.D. 1988).
Marsh v. Board of Education of City of Flint, 581 F.Supp. 614 (E.D. Mich. 1984).
Mass v. Board of Education of San Francisco Unified School District, 394 P.2d 579 (Cal. 1964).
Matter of Shelton, 408 N.W.2d 594 (Minn. App. 1987).
Matter of Tanelli, 477 A.2d 394 (N.J. Super. A.D. 1984).
Matters of Hackensack Board of Education, 446 A.2d 170 (N.J. Super. A.D. 1982).
McAndrew v. School Committee of Cambridge, 480 N.E.2d 327 (Mass. App. 1985).
McAuliffe v. Mayor of City of New Bedford, 29 N.E. 517 (Mass. 1892).
McBeth v. Board of Education of DeVall's Bluff School District No. 1, Arkansas, 300 F.Supp. 1270 (E.D. Ark. 1969).
McBroom v. Board of Education, District No. 205, 494 N.E.2d 1191 (Ill. App. 2 Dist. 1986).
McCutcheon v. Chicago Principals Association, 513 N.E.2d 55 (Ill. App. 1 Dist. 1987).
McGrath v. Burkhard, 280 P.2d 864 (Cal. App. 1955).
McKnight v. City of Philadelphia, 445 A.2d 778 (Pa. Super. 1982).
McLaughlin v. Board of Education, 659 S.W.2d 249 (Mo.App. 1983).
McLaughlin v. Tilendis, 398 F.2d 287 (7th Cir., 1968).
McPherson v. School District No. 186, 426 F.Supp. 173 (S.D. Ill. 1976).
Memphis Community School District v. Stachura, 477 U.S. 299 (1986).
Merchant v. Board of Trustees of Pearl Municipal Separate School District, 492 So.2d 959 (Miss. 1986).
Meyer v. Nebraska, 262 U.S. 390 (1923).
Miles v. School District No. 138 of Cheyenne County, 281 N.W.2d 396 (Neb. 1979).
Millar v. Joint School District No. 2, Village of Wild Rose, 86 N.W.2d 455 (Wis. 1957).
Miller v. Board of Education of the County of Lincoln, 450 F.Supp. 106 (S.D. W.Va. 1978).
Miller v. Board of Education Union Free School, District No. 1, of Town of Albion, 50 N.E.2d 529 (N.Y. App. 1943).
Miller v. Grand Haven Board of Education, 390 N.W.2d 255 (Mich. App. 1986).
Miller v. School District No. 167, Cook County, Illinois, 495 F.2d 658 (7th Cir., 1974).
Miller v. South Bend Special School District No. 1, McHenry County, 124 N.W.2d 475 (N.D. 1963).

Miller v. Yoshimoto, 536 P.2d 1195 (Hawaii 1975).
Millikan v. Board of Directors of Everett School District No. 2, 611 P.2d 414 (Wash. 1980).
Mindemann v. Independent School District No. 6 of Caddo County, 771 P.2d 996 (Okl. 1989).
Minneapolis Federation of Teachers Local 59, AFL-CIO v. Obermeyer, 147 N.W.2d 358 (Minn. 1966).
Minor v. Sully Buttes School District No. 58-2, 345 N.W.2d 48 (S.D. 1984).
Mission Independent School District v. Diserens, 188 S.W.2d 568 (Tex. 1945).
Mitchell v. Board of Trustees of Visalia Union High School District, 42 P.2d 397 (Cal. App. 1935).
Mitchell v. Caddo Parish School Board, 415 So.2d 227 (La. App. Cir., 1982).
Mitchell v. Garrett, 510 S.W.2d 894 (Tenn. 1974).
Mohr v. Dade County School Board, 287 So.2d 337 (Fla. App. 1973).
Monaghan v. School District No. 1 Clackamas County, 315 P.2d 797 (Or. 1957).
Montgomery v. Starkville Municipal Separate School District, 665 F.Supp. 487 (N.D. Miss. 1987).
Montgomery County Education Association, Inc. v. Board of Education of Montgomery County, 534 A.2d 980 (Md. 1987).
Moore v. Board of Education, 212 N.E.2d 833 (Ohio 1965).
Moore v. School Board of Gulf County, Florida, 364 F.Supp. 355 (N.D. Fla. 1973).
Moran v. Board of School Trustees of Mt. Pleasant Township Community Schools, Delaware County, 501 N.E.2d 472 (Ind. App. 2 Dist. 1986).
Morgan v. Huntsville City Board of Education, 510 So.2d 260 (Ala. Civ. App. 1987).
Morris v. Douglas County School District No. 9, 403 P.2d 775 (Or. 1965).
Morrison v. Hamilton County Board of Education, 494 S.W.2d 770 (Tenn. 1973).
Morrison v. State Board of Education, 82 Cal.Rptr. 175 (1969).
Morton v. Hampton School District No. 1, 700 S.W.2d 373 (Ark. App. 1985).
Mott v. Endicott School District No. 308, 713 P.2d 98 (Wash. 1986).
Mt. Healthy City School District Board of Education v. Doyle, 429 U.S. 274 (1977).
Mouras v. Jefferson Parish School Board, 300 So.2d 540 (La. App. 1974).
Mozert v. Hawkins County Board of Education, 827 F.2d 1058 (6th Cir., 1987).
Myers v. Greater Clark County School Corporation, 464 N.E.2d 1323 (Ind. App. 1984).
Myrtle Springs Reverted Independent School District v. Hogan, 705 S.W.2d 707 (Tex. App. 6 Dist. 1985) cert. denied, 480 U.S. 906 (1987).
N.A.A.C.P. v. Lansing Board of Education, 429 F.Supp. 583 (W.D. Mich. 1976).
Narragansett Electric Company v. Rhode Island Commission for Human Rights, 374 A.2d 1022 (R.I. 1977).
Nashville Gas Company v. Satty, 434 U.S. 136 (1977).
National Gay Task Force v. Board of Education of City of Oklahoma City, 729 F.2d 1270 (10th Cir., 1984).
NEA-Goodland v. Board of Education, Unified School District No. 352, Sherman County, 775 P.2d 675 (Kan. App. 1989).
Negrich v. Dade County Board of Public Instruction, 143 So.2d 498 (Fla. App. 1962).
Nelson v. Doland Board of Education of Doland School District No. 56-2, 380 N.W.2d 665 (S.D. 1986).
Nelson v. Western Beaver County School District, 491 A.2d 964 (Pa. Cmwlth. 1985).
New Haven v. Torrington, 43 A.2d 455 (Conn. 1945).
New Mexico State Board of Education v. Stoudt, 571 P.2d 1186 (N.M. 1977).
Newell v. Orleans Parish School Board, 370 So.2d 655 (La. App. 1979).
Newman v. Board of Education of City School District of New York, 594 F.2d 299 (2d Cir., 1979).
New York City Board of Education v. New York State Human Rights Appeal Board, 387 N.Y.S.2d 873 (App. Div. 1976).
New York Times Company v. Sullivan, 376 U.S. 254 (1964).

Niedbalski v. Board of Education of School District No. 24 of Platte Center, 418 N.W.2d 565 (Neb. 1988).
Niederhuber v. Camden County Vocational and Technical School District Board of Education, 495 F.Supp. 273 (D.N.J. 1980).
Noel v. Andrus, 810 F.2d 1388 (5th Cir., 1987).
Nordlund v. School District No. 14, 738 P.2d 1299 (Mont. 1987).
North Haven Board of Education v. Bell, 456 U.S. 512 (1982).
Northeast Community Education Association v. Northeast Community School District, 402 N.W.2d 765 (Iowa 1987).
Norwalk Teachers' Association v. Board of Education of City of Norwalk, 83 A.2d 482 (Supreme Court of Errors of Conn., 1951).
Nydegger v. Don Bosco Preparatory High School, 495 A.2d 485 (N.J. Super. 1985).
O'Connor v. Hendrick, 77 N.E. 612 (N.Y. 1906).
Ohlson v. Phillips, 304 F.Supp. 1152 (D. Colo. 1969), aff'd. 397 U.S. 317 (1970).
Ohman v. Board of Education of City of New York, 90 N.E.2d 474 (N.Y. App. 1949).
Oneal v. Colton Consolidated School District No. 306, 557 P.2d 11 (Wash. App. 1976).
Osborne v. Bullitt County Board of Education, 415 S.W.2d 607 (1967).
Osborne v. Montgomery, 234 N.W. 372 (Wis. 1931).
O'Toole v. Forestal, 511 A.2d 1236 (N.J. Super. A.D. 1986).
Pagano v. Massapequa Public Schools, 714 F.Supp. 641 (E.D. N.Y. 1989).
Palone v. Jefferson Parish School Board, 306 So.2d 679 (La. 1975).
Parducci v. Rutland, 316 F.Supp. 352 (M.D. Ala. 1970).
Parker v. Board of Education of Prince George's County, Maryland, 237 F.Supp. 222 (D. Md.), aff'd. 348 F.2d 464 (4th Cir., 1965).
Parrish v. Moss, 106 N.Y.S.2d 577 (1951).
Passaic Township Board of Education v. Passaic Township Education Association, 536 A.2d 1276 (N.J. Super. A.D. 1987).
Paxman v. Wilkerson, 390 F.Supp. 442 (E.D.Va. 1975).
Pearson v. School Board of Independent School District No. 381, 356 N.W.2d 438 (Minn. App. 1984).
Pease v. Millcreek Township School District, 195 A.2d 104 (Pa. 1963).
Pegues v. Morehouse Parish School Board, 706 F.2d 735 (5th Cir., 1983).
Pennell v. Board of Education of Equality Community Unit School District No. 4, Gallatin County, 484 N.E.2d 445 (Ill. App. 5 Dist. 1985).
Pennsbury School District v. Walker, 447 A.2d 1089 (Pa. Cmwlth. 1982).
Pennsylvania Labor Relations Board v. State College Area School District, 337 A.2d 262 (Pa. 1975).
People ex rel. Callahan v. Board of Education of City of New York, 66 N.E. 674 (N.Y. 1903).
People ex rel. Fursman v. City of Chicago, 116 N.E. 158 (Ill. 1917).
Perry v. Milwaukee Board of School Directors, 388 N.W.2d 638 (Wis. App. 1986).
Perry v. Sindermann, 408 U.S. 593 (1972).
Perryman v. School Committee of Boston, 458 N.E.2d 748 (Mass. App. 1983).
Petrie v. Forest Hills School District Board of Education, 449 N.E.2d 786 (Ohio App. 1982).
Pettit v. State Board of Education, 513 P.2d 889 (Cal. 1973).
Philadelphia Association of School Administrators v. School District of Philadelphia, 471 A.2d 581 (Pa. Cmwlth. 1984).
Pickering v. Board of Education, 391 U.S. 563 (1968).
Pierce v. Douglas School District No. 4, 686 P.2d 332 (Or. 1984).
Pinsker v. Joint District No. 28J of Adams and Arapahoe Counties, 554 F.Supp. 1049 (D. Colo. 1983).
Pirkle v. Oakdale Union Grammar School District, 253 P.2d 1 (Cal. 1953).

Pizzolato v. State Board of Elementary and Secondary Education, 452 So.2d 264 (La. App. 1984).
Pocahontas Community School District v. Levene, 409 N.W.2d 698 (Iowa App. 1987).
Ponton v. Newport News School Board, 632 F.Supp. 1056 (E.D. Va. 1986).
Portage Area School District v. Portgage Area Education Association, 368 A.2d 864 (Pa. Cmwlth. 1977).
Potter v. Kalama Public School District No. 402, 644 P.2d 1229 (Wash. App. 1982).
Potts v. Gibson, 469 S.W.2d 130 (Tenn. 1971).
Powell v. Board of Trustees of Crook County School District No. 1, 550 P.2d 1112 (Wyo. 1976).
Powers v. Freetown-Lakeville Regional School District Committee, 467 N.E.2d 203 (Mass. 1984).
Prier v. Horace Mann Insurance Company, 351 So.2d 265 (La. App. 1977).
Proviso Council of West Suburban Teachers Union, Local 571 v. Board of Education, Proviso Township High Schools, District 109, Cook County, 513 N.E.2d 996 (Ill. App. 1 Dist. 1987).
Public Employee Relations Board v. Washington Teachers' Union Local 6, AFT, 556 A.2d 206 (D.C. App. 1989).
Rankin v. Independent School District No. I-3, Noble County, Oklahoma, 876 F.2d 838 (10th Cir. 1989).
Rawlings v. Butler, 290 S.W.2d 801 (Ky. 1956).
Ray v. Minneapolis Board of Education Special School District No. 1, 202 N.W.2d 375 (Minn. 1972).
Retzlaff v. Grand Forks Public School District No. 1, 424 N.W.2d 637 (N.D. 1988).
Rhodes v. Laurel Highlands School District, 544 A.2d 562 (Pa.Cmwlth. 1988).
Rible v. Hughes, 150 P.2d 455 (Cal. 1944).
Richards v. Omaha Public Schools, 232 N.W.2d 29 (Neb. 1975).
Ridgefield Park Education Association v. Ridgefield Park Board of Education, 393 A.2d 278 (N.J. 1978).
Riforgiato v. Board of Education of City of Buffalo, 448 N.Y.S.2d 74 (N.Y.A.D. 1982).
Rinaldo v. Dreyer, 1 N.E.2d 37 (Mass. 1936).
Riverhead Central School District v. Riverhead Central Faculty Association, 528 N.Y.S.2d 611 (N.Y.A.D. 2 Dept. 1988).
Rixmann v. Somerset Public Schools, St. Croix County, 266 N.W.2d 326 (Wis. 1978).
Robbins v. Board of Education of Argo Community High School District 217, 313 F.Supp. 642 (N.D. Ill. 1970).
Roberts v. Robertson County Board of Education, 692 S.W.2d 863 (Tenn. App. 1985).
Robinson v. Jefferson County Board of Education, 485 F.2d 1381 (5th Cir., 1973).
Rochester Education Association v. Independent School District No. 535, 271 N.W.2d 311 (Minn. 1978).
Rock by Rock v. Central Square School District, 494 N.Y.S.2d 579 (A.D. 4 Dept. 1985).
Rockwell v. Board of Education of the School District of Crestwood, 227 N.W.2d 736 (Mich. 1975).
Rodgers v. Berger, 438 F.Supp. 713 (D. Mass. 1977).
Rogers v. Paul, 382 U.S. 198 (1965).
Rogliano v. Fayette County Board of Education, 347 S.E.2d 220 (W.Va. 1986).
Rollins v. Concordia Parish School Board, 465 So.2d 213 (La. App. 3 Cir. 1985).
Romeike v. Houston Independent School District, 368 S.W.2d 895 (Tex. Civ. App. 1963).
Rosenthal v. Orleans Parish School Board, 214 So.2d 203 (La. App. 1968).
Roseville Education Association v. Independent School District No. 623, 380 N.W.2d 512 (Minn. App. 1986).
Ross v. Springfield School District No. 19, 716 P.2d 724 (Or. 1986).
Rush-Henrietta Central School District v. Newman, 542 N.Y.S.2d 440 (N.Y.A.D. 4 Dept. 1989).
Russo v. Central School District No. 1, 469 F.2d 623 (2d Cir., 1972).

Ryan v. Aurora City Board of Education, 540 F.2d 222 (6th Cir., 1976).
St. Louis Teachers Union Local 420 v. Board of Education of the City of St. Louis, 666 S.W.2d 25 (Mo. App. 1984).
Sams v. Board of Commissioners of Creek County, 178 P. 668 (Okl. 1919).
San Dieguito Union High School District v. Commission on Professional Competence, 185 Cal.Rptr. 203 (Cal. App. 1982).
San Mateo City School District v. Public Employment Relations Board, 663 P.2d 523 (Cal. 1983).
Sayers v. Ranger, 83 A.2d 775 (N.J. Super. A.D. 1951).
Schmid v. Lovette, 201 Cal.Rptr. 424 (Cal. App. 1 Dist. 1984).
Schneiderman v. United States, 320 U.S. 118 (1943).
School Board of the City of Richmond v. Parham, 243 S.E.2d 468 (Va. 1978).
School Board of Nassau County, Florida v. Arline, 480 U.S. 273 (1987).
School City of East Chicago v. Sigler, 36 N.E.2d 760 (Ind. 1941).
School District of Abington Township, Pennsylvania v. Schempp, 374 U.S. 203 (1963).
School District of City of Duquesne v. Duquesne Education Association PSEA/NEA, 512 A.2d 103 (Pa. Cmwlth. 1986).
School District of Philadelphia v. Brockington, 511 A.2d 944 (Pa.Cmwlth. 1986).
School District of Philadelphia v. Twer, 447 A.2d 222 (Pa. 1982).
School District No. 8, Pinal County v. Superior Court of Pinal County, 433 P.2d 28 (Ariz. 1967).
School District No. 21 v. Hudson, 277 S.W. 18 (Ark. 1925).
Schwabenbauer v. Board of Education of City School District of City of Olean, 777 F.2d 837 (2d Cir., 1985).
Scopes v. State, 289 S.W. 363 (Tenn. 1927).
Scott v. Board of Education of Alton, Community Unit School District #11, 156 N.E.2d 1 (Ill. App. 1959).
Scranton School District v. Weiss, 537 A.2d 910 (Pa.Cmwlth. 1988).
Seattle High School Chapter No. 200 of the AFT v. Sharples, 293 P. 994 (Wash. 1930).
Seemuller v. Fairfax County School Board, 878 F.2d 1578 (4th Cir. 1989).
Sells v. Unified School District No. 429, Doniphan County, 644 P.2d 379 (Kan. 1982).
Shelton v. Tucker, 364 U.S. 479 (1960).
Sherburne v. School Board of Suwannee County, 455 So.2d 1057 (Fla. App. 1984).
Shipley v. Salem School District 24J, Marion County, 669 P.2d 1172 (Or. App. 1983).
Shirck v. Thomas, 486 F.2d 691 (7th Cir., 1973).
Shirer v. Anderson, 88 F.Supp. 858 (E.D.S.C. 1950).
Shockley v. Board of Education Laurel Special School District, 149 A.2d 331 (Del. 1959).
Shurgin v. Ambach, 436 N.E.2d 1324 (N.Y. App. 1982).
Silver, Burdett and Company v. Indiana State Board of Education, 72 N.E. 829 (Ind. App. 1904).
Simard v. Board of Education of Town of Groton, 473 F.2d 988 (2d Cir., 1973).
Simmons v. Beauregard Parish School Board, 315 So.2d 883 (La. App. 1975).
Simms v. School District No. 1, Multnomah County, 508 P.2d 236 (Or. App. 1973).
Simonetti v. School District of Philadelphia, 454 A.2d 1038 (Pa. Super. 1982).
Singleton v. Iberville Parish School Board, 136 So.2d 809 (La. App. 1961).
Singleton v. Jackson Municipal Separate School District, 419 F.2d 1211 (5th Cir., 1970), cert. denied, 402 U.S. 944 (1971).
Skinner v. Oklahoma ex rel. Williamson, Attorney General, 316 U.S. 535 (1942).
Skripchuk v. Austin, 379 A.2d 1142 (Del. Super. 1977).
Slaughter v. East Baton Rouge Parish School Board, 432 So.2d 905 (La. App. 1983).
Slockett v. Iowa Valley Community School District, 359 N.W.2d 446 (Iowa 1984).
Smith v. Board of Education of County of Logan, 341 S.E.2d 685 (W.Va. 1985).

Smith v. Board of Education of Fort Madison Community School District, 293 N.W.2d 221 (Iowa 1980).
Smith v. Board of Education of Urbana School District No. 116 of Champaign County, Illinois, 708 F.2d 258 (7th Cir., 1983).
Smith v. Board of School Commissioners of Mobile County, 827 F.2d 684 (11th Cir., 1987).
Smith v. Fort Madison Community School District, 334 N.W.2d 701 (Iowa 1983).
Smith v. School District of Township of Darby, 130 A.2d 661 (Pa. 1957).
Smith v. School District of Philadelphia, 5 A.2d 535 (Pa. 1939).
Smith v. School District No. 18, Pondera County, 139 P.2d 518 (Mont. 1943).
Smith v. Vernon Parish School Board, 442 So.2d 1319 (La. App. 3 Cir. 1983).
Snider v. Kit Carson School District R-1, 442 P.2d 429 (Colo. 1968).
Sorlie v. School District No. 2, 667 P.2d 400 (Mont. 1983).
South Ripley Community School Corporation v. Peters, 396 N.E.2d 144 (Ind. App. 1979).
Southside Public Schools v. Hill, 827 F.2d 270 (8th Cir., 1987).
Sparks v. Board of Education of Ashland Independent School District, 549 S.W.2d 323 (Ky. App. 1977).
Special School District of Fort Smith v. Lynch, 413 S.W.2d 880 (Ark. 1967).
Spiewak v. Board of Education of Rutherford, 447 A.2d 140 (N.J. 1982).
Stachura v. Memphis Community School District, 763 F.2d 211 (6th Cir., 1985).
Stafford v. Board of Education of Casey County, 642 S.W.2d 596 (Ky. App. 1982).
Stamper v. Board of Education of Elementary School District No. 143, 491 N.E.2d 36 (Ill. App. 1 Dist. 1986).
State v. Lillard, 521 A.2d 1110 (Del. Super. 1986).
State ex rel. Burpee v. Burton, 45 Wis. 150 (1878).
State ex rel. Board of Education of County of Kanawha v. Casey, 349 S.E.2d 436 (W. Va. 1986).
State ex rel. Charbonnet v. Jefferson Parish School Board, 188 So.2d 143 (La. App. 1966).
State ex rel. Ging v. Board of Education of City of Duluth, 7 N.W.2d 544 (Minn. 1942).
State ex rel. Frank v. Meigs County Board of Education, 44 N.E.2d 455 (Ohio 1942).
State ex rel. Johnson v. Boyd, 28 N.E.2d 256 (Ind. 1940).
State ex rel. McNeal v. Avoyelles Parish School Board, 7 So.2d 165 (La. 1942).
State ex rel. Melvin v. Board of Education of City of St. Bernard, 34 N.E.2d 285 (Ohio App. 1940).
State ex rel. Pemberton v. Wilson, 481 S.W.2d 760 (Tenn. 1972).
State ex rel. Richardson v. Board of Regents of University of Nevada, 261 P.2d 515 (Nev. 1953).
State ex rel. Scoggins v. Vernon Parish School Board, 44 So.2d 385 (La. App. 1950).
State ex rel. Sepulvado v. Rapides Parish School Board, 108 So.2d 96 (La. 1959).
State ex rel. Williams v. Avoyelles Parish School Board, 147 So.2d 729 (La. App. 1962).
State ex rel. Withers v. Board of Education of Mason County, 172 S.E.2d 796 (W. Va. 1970).
State of Indiana ex rel. Anderson v. Brand, 303 U.S. 95 (1938).
State of New Mexico ex rel. State Board of Education v. Montoya, 386 P.2d 252 (N.M. 1963).
State of Ohio v. Hoover, 450 N.E.2d 710 (Ohio App. 1982).
Stehn v. Bernarr MacFadden Foundations, Inc., 434 F.2d 811 (6th Cir., 1970).
Stellmaker v. DePetrillo, 710 F.Supp. 891 (D.Conn. 1989).
Sterzing v. Ft. Bend Independent School District, 376 F.Supp. 657 (S.D. Tex. 1972).
Stevens v. Central School District No. 1 of Town of Ramapo, 270 N.Y.S.2d 23 (N.Y.A.D. 1966).
Stevens v. Chesteen, 561 So.2d 1100 (Ala. 1990).
Stiver v. State ex rel. Kent, 1 N.E.2d 1006 (Ind. 1936).
Sto-Rox School District v. Horgan, 449 A.2d 796 (Pa. Cmwlth. 1982).
Stoddard v. School District No. 1, Lincoln County, Wyoming, 590 F.2d 829 (10th Cir., 1979).
Stoneking v. Bradford Area School District, 882 F.2d 720 (3d Cir. 1989).

Street v. Board of Education of School District of City of Ferndale, Oakland County, 104 N.W.2d 748 (Mich. 1960).
Suits v. Glover, 71 So.2d 49 (Ala. 1954).
Summers v. Milwaukie Union High School District No. 5, Clackamas County, 481 P.2d 369 (Or. App. 1971).
Summers v. Vermilion Parish School Board, 493 So.2d 1258 (La. App. 3 Cir., 1986).
Swab v. Cedar Rapids Community School District, 494 F.2d 353 (8th Cir., 1974).
Swager v. Board of Education, Unified School District No. 412, Sheridan County, Kansas, 688 P.2d 270 (Kan. App. 1984).
Swaitkowski v. Board of Education of City of Buffalo, 319 N.Y.S.2d 783 (N.Y. A.D. 1971).
Swayne v. Board of Education of Rock Island School District No. 41, 494 N.E.2d 906 (Ill. App. 3 Dist. 1986).
Sweet Home Central School District v. Sweet Home Education Association, 455 N.Y.S.2d 685 (N.Y.A.D. 1982).
Sweezy v. New Hampshire, 354 U.S. 234 (1957).
Swilley v. Alexander, 448 F.Supp. 702 (S.D. Ala. 1978).
Szabo v. Board of Education of Community Consolidated School District 54, 454 N.E.2d 39 (Ill. App. 1 Dist. 1983).
Szumigala v. Hicksville Union Free School District Board of Education, 539 N.Y.S.2d 83 (N.Y.A.D. 2 Dept. 1989).
Tardif v. Quinn, 545 F.2d 761 (1st Cir., 1976).
Tate v. Board of Education of Kent County, 485 A.2d 688 (Md. App. 1985).
Tawney v. Board of Education of County of Boone, 426 F.Supp. 528 (S.D. W.Va. 1977).
Templar v. Decatur Public School District, 538 N.E.2d 195 (Ill. App. 4 Dist. 1989).
Terry v. Houston County Board of Education, 342 S.E.2d 774 (Ga. App. 1986).
Thelma D. v. Board of Education of City of St. Louis, 737 F.Supp. 541 (E.D.Mo. 1990).
Thomas v. Board of Education of Community Unit School District No. 1, 453 N.E.2d 150 (Ill. App. 5 Dist. 1983).
Thompkins v. Stuttgart School District No. 22, 858 F.2d 1317 (8th Cir. 1988).
Thompson v. Board of Education of Romeo Community Schools, 526 F.Supp. 1035 (W.D. Mich. 1981).
Thompson v. Board of Education of the City of Chicago, 711 F.Supp. 394 (N.D.Ill. 1989).
Thompson v. Modesto City High School District, 566 P.2d 237 (Cal. 1977).
Thompson v. Southwest School District, 483 F.Supp. 1170 (W.D. Mo. 1980).
Thrash v. Board of Education, School District No. 189, 435 N.E.2d 866 (Ill. App. 1982).
Tichenor v. Orleans Parish School Board, 144 So.2d 603 (La. App. 1962).
Tingey v. Vaughn, 17 Ill. App. 347 (1885).
Tinker v. Des Moines Independent Community School District, 393 U.S. 503 (1969).
Tressler v. Upper Dublin School District, 373 A.2d 755 (Pa. Cmwlth. 1977).
Truelove v. Wilson, 285 S.E.2d 556 (Ga. App. 1981).
Trumansburg Central School District v. Chalone, 449 N.Y.S.2d 92 (N.Y.A.D. 1982).
Turk v. Franklin Special School District, 640 S.W.2d 218 (Tenn. 1982).
Tyler v. Jefferson Parish School Board, 258 So.2d 206 (La. App. 1972).
Unified School District No. 241, Wallace County v. Swanson, 717 P.2d 526 (Kan. App. 1986).
Union County School Corporation Board of School Trustees v. Indiana Education Employment Relations Board, 471 N.E.2d 1191 (Ind. App. 4 Dist. 1984).
United States v. DeSoto Parish School Board, 574 F.2d 804 (5th Cir., 1978).
United States v. Lawrence County School District, 799 F.2d 1031 (5th Cir., 1986).
United States v. School District 151 of Cook County, Illinois 404 F.2d 1125 (7th Cir., 1968).
United States v. Tolla, 781 F.2d 29 (2d Cir., 1986).

Vail v. Board of Education of Paris Union School District No. 95, 706 F.2d 1435 (7th Cir., 1983); aff'd., 466 U.S. 377 (1984).
Valley National Bank of Phoenix v. Glover, 159 P.2d 292 (Ariz. 1945).
Verhel v. Independent School District No. 709, 359 N.W.2d 579 (Minn. 1984).
Verret v. Calcasieu Parish School Board, 103 So.2d 560 (La. App. 1958).
Viemeister v. Board of Education of Borough of Prospect Park, Passaic County, 68 A.2d 768 (N.J. Super. 1949).
Vukadinovich v. Bartels, 853 F.2d 1387 (7th Cir., 1988).
Wagner v. West Perry School District, 480 A.2d 1336 (Pa. Cmwlth. 1984).
Walter v. Board of Education of Quincy School District No. 172, 442 N.E.2d 870 (Ill. 1982).
Walter v. Independent School District No. 457, Trimont, 323 N.W.2d 37 (Minn. 1982).
Warren Education Association v. Adams, 226 N.W.2d 536 (Mich. App. 1975).
Warwick Board of School Directors v. Theros, 430 A.2d 268 (Pa. 1981).
Wasilewski v. Board of School Directors of the City of Milwaukee, 111 N.W.2d 198 (Wis. 1961).
Watkins v. Oldham, 731 S.W.2d 829 (Ky. App. 1987).
Watson v. Burnett, 23 N.E.2d 420 (Ind. 1939).
Weaver v. Board of Education of Pine Plains Central School District, 514 N.Y.S.2d 473 (N.Y.A.D. 2 Dept. 1987).
Weissman v. Board of Education of Jefferson County School District No. R-1, 547 P.2d 1267 (Colo. 1976).
Welch v. Board of Education of Chandler Unified School District No. 80 of Maricopa County, 667 P.2d 746 (Ariz. App. 1983).
Wertz v. Southern Cloud Unified School District No. 334, 542 P.2d 339 (Kan. 1975).
West Bend Education Association v. Wisconsin Employment Relations Commission, 357 N.W.2d 534 (Wis. 1984).
West Hartford Education Association v. DeCourcy, 295 A.2d 526 (Conn. 1972).
West Hempstead Union Free School District v. State Division of Human Rights, 497 N.Y.S.2d 721 (N.Y.A.D. 2 Dept. 1986).
Western Grove School District v. Strain, 707 S.W.2d 306 (Ark. 1986).
Wetsel v. Independent School District I-1, 670 P.2d 986 (Okl. 1983).
White v. South Park Independent School District, 693 F.2d 1163 (5th Cir., 1982).
Whitsel v. Southeast Local School District, 484 F.2d 1222 (6th Cir., 1973).
Whittaker v. City of Salem, 104 N.E. 359 (Mass. 1914).
Wichita Public Schools Employees Union, Local No. 513 v. Smith, 397 P.2d 357 (Kan. 1964).
Wieder v. Board of Education of Borough of High Bridge, 170 A.631 (N.J. 1934).
Wieman v. Updegraff, 344 U.S. 183 (1952).
Wilhelm v. Board of Education of City of New York, 227 N.Y.S.2d 791 (N.Y.A.D. 1962).
Williams v. Albemarle City Board of Education, 508 F.2d 1242 (4th Cir., 1974).
Williams v. School District No. 40 of Gila County, 417 P.2d 376 (Ariz. App. 1966).
Williams v. Southfield School, Inc., 494 So.2d 1339 (La. App. 2 Cir. 1986).
Winston-Salem/Forsyth County Unit of the North Carolina Association of Educators v. Phillips, 381 F.Supp. 644 (M.D.N.C. 1974).
Wire v. Williams, 133 N.W.2d 840 (Minn. 1965).
Wood v. City of Haverhill, 55 N.E. 381 (Mass. 1899).
Wood v. Strickland, 420 U.S. 308 (1975).
Wright v. State Commission on Ethics, 389 So.2d 662 (Fla. App. 1980).
Wyatt v. School District No. 104, Fergus County, 417 P.2d 221 (Mont. 1966).
Wygant v. Jackson Board of Education, 476 U.S. 267 (1986).
Yanzick v. School District No. 23, Lake County, Montana, 641 P.2d 431 (Mont. 1982).
Yielding v. Crockett Independent School District, 707 F.2d 196 (5th Cir., 1983).

Young v. Board of Education of Central School District No. 6, Town of Huntington, 315 N.E.2d 768 (N.Y. App. 1974).

Yuen v. Board of Education of School District No. U-46, 222 N.E.2d 570 (Ill. App. 1966).

Zaslawsky v. Board of Education of Los Angeles City Unified School District, 610 F.2d 661 (9th Cir., 1979).

Zellers v. Huff, 236 P.2d 949 (N.M. 1951).

Zeluck v. Board of Education of City School District of City of New Rochelle, 307 N.Y.S.2d 329 (N.Y. 1970).

Zoll v. Eastern Allamakee Community School District, 588 F.2d 246 (8th Cir., 1978).

Bibliography

Alexander, K., & Alexander, M. D. (1985). *American public school law.* 2d ed. St. Paul, MN: West Publishing Company.

Anderson, C. C., & McKinney-Browning, M. C. (1982). What principals should know about law-related education. *Principal,* 61(3): 42–46.

Anderson, P., & Wetzel, K. L. (1982). A survey of legal knowledge of high school principals on censorship issues. *English Journal,* 71(2): 34–39.

Armstrong, D. G. (1986). School reform: Looking backward at looking forward. *The High School Journal,* 70(1): 1–6.

Atkin, J. M. (1981). The government in the classroom. *Educational Horizons,* 59(2): 59–66.

Bailey, M. A., & Sindelar, N. W. (1987). Freedom of speech and the incompetent/competent teacher. *Education Law Reporter,* 38: 1151.

Bailey, M. A. & Sindelar, N. W. (1987). Teacher competence and employer discrimination. *Education Law Reporter,* 41: 1199.

Bailey, S. K. (1980). Education in the eighties: The case for optimism. *The National Elementary Principal,* 59(2): 14–16.

Beckham, J. (1985). Legally sound criteria, processes and procedures for the evaluation of public school professional employees. *Journal of Law and Education,* 14: 529–51.

Beckham, J. C. (1986). *Arline v. School Board of Nassau County:* Contagious disease as a "handicap" within the meaning of Section 504 of Rehabiliation Act. *Education Law Reporter,* 28: 325.

Beckham, J. C. (1986). Standardized examinations as a measure of teacher competence. *Education Law Reporter,* 30: 995.

Beezer, B. (1990). School district liability for negligent hiring and retention of unfit employees. *Education Law Reporter,* 56: 1117.

Beezer, B. (1990). Teacher dismissal: Indictment or conviction for nonsexual-related behavior. *Education Law Reporter,* 58: 1085.

Beezer, B. (1984). Teacher removal for physical or mental incapacity. A legal perspective. *Education Law Reporter,* 16: 689.

Beezer, B., & Goldberg, R. (1989). Employment status of a teacher-coach. *Education Law Reporter,* 49: 835.

Beezer, B., & McKnight, J. (1989). Assigning teachers extracurricular duties. *Education Law Reporter,* 48: 737.

Bell, T. H. (1982). The federal role in education. *Harvard Educational Review,* 52: 375–80.

Berger, S. D. (1985). Don't let legal threats paralyze your board. *The American School Board Journal,* 172(10): 32, 47.

Bernheim, E. (1986). Free speech for public employees: The Supreme Court strikes a new balance. *Education Law Reporter:* 31, 7.

Bierman, L. (1983). The scope of collective bargaining in public education. *Education Law Reporter,* 9: 823.

Bjorklun, E. C. (1990). Assumption of risk and its effect on school liability for athletic injuries. *Education Law Reporter,* 55: 349.

Bogert, E. (1985). Censorship and "The Lottery." *English Journal,* 74(1): 45–47.

Bredeson, P. V., & Caldwell, W. E. (1988). Personnel screening and selection: An analysis of legal compliance of schools. *The High School Journal,* 71(2): 81–87.

Bright, M. H. (1979). The constitution, the judges, and the school administrator. *NASSP Bulletin,* 63(424): 74–83.

Brodinsky, B. (1979). Something happened: Education in the seventies. *Phi Delta Kappan,* 61: 238–41.

Broido, L. (1979). Update looks back: Life in the fishbowl. *Update on Law-Related Education,* 3(3): 20–23.

Butts, R. F. (1960). Search for freedom: The story of American education. [Special issue]. *NEA Journal,* 33–48.

Citron, C. H. (1985). An overview of legal issues in teacher quality. *Journal of Law and Education,* 14(3): 277–307.

Clark, T. (1975). Editorial reflections: Freedom to teach and to learn: Our responsibility. *Social Education,* 39: 202–3.

Clay, G. V. (1984). Maintaining order and discipline: A duty requiring knowledge of the law. *The High School Journal,* 67(3): 178–83.

Clayton, E. M., & Jacobsen, G. S. (1974). An analysis of court cases concerned with student rights 1960–1971. *NASSP Bulletin,* 58(379): 49–53.

Cohen, D. K. (1987). Schooling more and liking it less: Puzzles of educational improvement. *Harvard Educational Review,* 57(2): 174–77.

Collins, P., & Nelson, D. Q. (1983). Reducing the teacher workforce: A management perspective. *Journal of Law and Education,* 12(2): 249–72.

Considine, D. M. (1985). Censorship, the classroom, and the electronic environment. *English Journal,* 74(1): 38–41.

Cooper, E. L., & Westerberg, S. G. (1981). Teacher can protect themselves against tort and liability. *The Agricultural Education Magazine,* 54(4): 14–16.

Daniel, G. H. (1985). Excessive emphasis on the law: When 'legalism' gains a foothold in schools, leadership takes a hike. *The American School Board Journal,* 172(10): 28–29.

Delon, F. G. (1983). Is a teacher's pregnancy out of wedlock constitutionally protected conduct? *Education Law Reporter,* 7: 9.

Delon, F. G. (1985). A teacher's sexual involvement with pupils: "Reasonable cause" for dismissal. *Education Law Reporter,* 22: 1085.

Delon, F. G., & Van Zandt, M. A. (1984). Statutory grounds for teacher dismissal survive vagueness challenges. *Education Law Reporter,* 17: 313.

Denoyer, R. A., & White, M. (1987). Legislating school reform: Denigrating educators. *The High School Journal,* 70(2): 69–71.

Dietrich, C. R. (1988). H.C.P.A. spells higher legal costs for schools. *The American School Board Journal,* 175(1): 32, 39.

Donelson, K. (1987). Censorship: Heading off the attack. *Educational Horizons,* 65(4): 167–70.

Donley, M. O., Jr. (1976). The American schoolteacher: From obedient servant to militant professional. *Phi Delta Kappan,* 58: 112–17.

Drowatzky, J. N. (1977). On the firing line: Negligence in physical education. *Journal of Law and Education,* 6(4): 481–90.

Drummond, W. H., & Andrews, T. E. (1980). The influence of federal and state governments on teacher education. *Phi Delta Kappan,* 62: 97–100.

Duckworth, E. (1984). "... What teachers know: The best knowledge base ..." *Harvard Educational Review,* 54(1): 15–20.

Duke, D. L., Donmoyer, R., & Farman, G. (1978). Emerging legal issues related to classroom management. *Phi Delta Kappan,* 60: 305–9.

Dunklee, D., & Shoop, R. (1986). Potpourri: Teacher preparation in a litigious society: Implications in times of reform. *Journal of Teacher Education,* 37(5): 57–60.

DuVall, C. R., & Krepel, W. J. (1972). Teacher liability during field trips. *Journal of Law and Education,* 1: 637–48.

Egner, J. T. (1989). Teachers' discretion in selecting instructional materials and methods. *Education Law Reporter,* 53: 365.

Emans, R. L. (1987). Abuse in the name of protecting children. *Phi Delta Kappan,* 68: 740–43.

Epley, B. G. (1985). Teachers and torts: Avoiding litigation. *Kappa Delta Pi Record,* 22(1): 4–7.

Erickson, R. (1981). How firm are teacher tenure laws? *Kappa Delta Pi Record,* 17(4): 114–16.

Essex, N. L. (1987). Mandating safe schools: This stunning legal decision might lead to increased board liability. *The American School Board Journal,* 174(3): 32–33.

Essex, N. L. (1986). The teacher and malpractice—Is there a lawsuit in your future? *American Secondary Education,* 15(3): 2–5.

Fillichio, S. (1988). Legal literacy: Legal literacy for laypeople. *Update on Law-Related Education,* 12(1): 35–38, 64–65.

Fischer, L. (1978). The civil rights of teachers in post-industrial society. *The High School Journal,* 61(8): 380–91.

Fischer, L., Schimmel, D., & Kelly, C. (1991). *Teachers and the Law.* 3rd ed. New York: Longman.

Fischer, L. (1989). When courts play school boards: Judicial activism in education. *Education Law Reporter,* 51: 693.

Fleshman, R. C. (1972). Extra duties without extra pay? Not if teachers can help it. *The American School Board Journal,* 159(7): 32–33.

Flygare, T. J. (1986). DeJure: Courts foil schools' efforts to detect drugs. *Phi Delta Kappan,* 68: 329–30.

Flygare, T. J. (1985). DeJure: The hundredth column: Looking back/looking forward. *Phi Delta Kappan,* 67: 229–30.

Flygare, T. J. (1987). Kentucky teacher hits the wall with Pink Floyd. *Phi Delta Kappan,* 69: 237–38.

Flygare, T. J. (1987). DeJure: Some thoughts on the Tennessee textbook case. *Phi Delta Kappan,* 68: 474–75.

Flygare, T. J. (1987). DeJure: Supreme Court holds that contagious diseases are handicaps. *Phi Delta Kappan,* 68: 705–6.

Flygare, T. J. (1983). The future of law in educational reform. *Phi Delta Kappan,* 64: 416.

Flygare, T. J. (1979). Schools and the law: John Tinker: Still an idealist. *Phi Delta Kappan,* 60: 210–12.

Flygare, T. J. (1981). Schools and the law: Some jubilee year observations. *Phi Delta Kappan,* 62: 390–91.

Flygare, T. J. (1976). Schools and the law: Teaching law in elementary and secondary school: A growing trend. *Phi Delta Kappan,* 57: 617.

Forsythe, J. L., & Jellison, J. A. (1977). It's the law. *Music Educators Journal,* 64(3): 30–35.

Furlong, M. S., & Arbetman, L. (1980). Learning about law: Law-related education is creating a renaissance in civic education. *Educational Leadership,* 38(1): 41–43.

Garrison, X. L., & Hardin, E. (1973). The principal and school law. *NASSP Bulletin,* 57(376): 48–54.

Gee, E. G., & Sperry, D. J. (1978). *Educational law and the public schools: A compendium.* Boston: Allyn and Bacon.

George, T. W. (1973). Upheaval in school law. *NASSP Bulletin,* 57(373): 118–26.

Gertsman, L. (1985). Minimal procedural safeguards for dismissal of tenured public employees: *Cleveland Board of Education v. Loudermill. Education Law Reporter,* 24: 695.

Glenn, C. L. (1987). Textbook controversies: A 'disaster for public schools'? *Phi Delta Kappan,* 68: 451–55.

Goldhammer, K. (1983). Evolution in the profession. *Educational Administration Quarterly,* 19: 249–72.

Goldsmith, A. H. (March 1981). Student discipline codes: Developments, dimensions, directons. *A Legal Memorandum of the National Association of Secondary School Principals,* 1–8.

Goldstein, A. (1974). Students and the law: A changing relationship. *NASSP Bulletin,* 58: 50–53.

Goodlad, J. I. (1984). *A place called school: Prospects for the future.* New York: McGraw-Hill.

Gordon, R. M. (1984). Freedom of expression and values inculcation in the public school curriculum. *Journal of Law and Education,* 13: 523–79.

Gottesman, R. (1974). The principal, the student, and the law. *NASSP Bulletin,* 58: 177–81.

Guilinger, J. (1981). How quality vo-ag programs impact liability. *The Agricultural Education Magazine,* 54(4): 6.

Harrington-Lueker, D. (1991). Book battles. *The American School Board Journal,* 178(2): 18–21, 37.

Hayman, R., & Kassouf, G. (1985). Court briefs: The high court goes to school. *Update on Law-Related Education,* 9(1): 3–5, 29–32.

Hazard, W. R. (1974). Courts in the saddle: School boards out. *Phi Delta Kappan,* 52: 259–61.

Hazard, W. R. (1976). Schooling and the law: Reflections on social change. *Education and Urban Society,* 8: 307–31.

Hazard, W. R. (1979). A tort is not a piece of cake: Teachers' legal responsibility. *Music Education Journal,* 65(8): 26–33, 62–65.

Henderson, D. H. (1987). Negligent liability suits emanating from the failure to provide adequate supervision: A critical issue for teachers and school boards. *Journal of Law and Education,* 16: 435–51.

Henderson, D. H., Golanda, E. L., & Johnson, N. C. (1989). The use of force by public school teachers as a defense against threatened physical harm. *Education Law Reporter,* 54: 773.

Henson, K. T. (1979). Emerging student rights. *Journal of Teacher Education,* 30(4): 33–34.

Hill, H. W. (1973). Curriculum legislation and instructional decision-makers. *The Elementary School Journal,* 73: 407–11.

Hoffmann, E. (1972). School law: Do districts have the right to transfer teachers involuntarily? *School Management,* 16(8): 9.

Hoffman, E. E. (1979). Legally speaking, which way do they run? *Illinois School Research and Development,* 15(2): 67–70.

Hoffman, E. E. (1984). Negligence in the science department. *Education Law Reporter,* 16: 365.

Hollister, C. A. (1969). The rights of children: The 'authority' school boards thought they had: Where did it all go? *The American School Board Journal,* 156(12): 8–12.

Hooker, C. P. (1984). Balancing free expression and government interests: *Connick v. Myers. Education Law Reporter,* 15: 633.

Hooker, C. P. (1985). *Connick* and beyond. *Education Law Reporter,* 20: 1.

Hooker, C. P. (1983). Seniority v. race: A case for both sides in school layoffs. *Education Law Reporter,* 12: 617.

Hooker, C. P. (1987). Teacher dismissal for improper touching or sexual contact with students. *Education Law Reporter,* 39: 941.

Hooker, C. P. (1988). Teachers and the courts, 1965–1986. *Education Law Reporter,* 48: 7–18.

Hopkins, W. W. (1988). Teachers as public officials in libel actions. *Education Law Reporter,* 47: 353.

Horner, J. J., & Frels, K. (1986). The death knell to the negligence cause of action under 42 U.S.C. Section 1983. *Education Law Reporter,* 31: 1.

Howard, S. S. (1989). Negligent hiring and employer liability in the selection of employees. *Education Law Reporter,* 49: 1.

Hoy, A. K. (1977). Controversial English lessons and the law. *English Journal,* 66(2): 21–25.

Hudson, M. (1987). Censorship threatens education. *Kappa Delta Pi Record,* 23(3): 67–71.

Hulsizer, D. (1987). Public education on trial. *Educational Leadership,* 44(8): 12–16.

Imber, M., & Gayler, D. E. (1988). A statistical analysis of trends in education-related litigation since 1960. *Educational Administration Quarterly,* 24: 55–78.

Jacobsen, G. S., Sperry, D. J., & Jensen, B. F. (1972). The dismissal and non-reemployment of teachers. *Journal of Law and Education,* 1: 435–48.

Jenkinson, E. (1985). Preparing for a winter of challenges to school books and courses. *Educational Horizons,* 64(1): 48–52.

Jenkinson, E. B. (1985). Protecting Holden Caulfield and his friends from censors. *English Journal,* 74(1): 26–33.

Jenkinson, E. B. (1987). Selected responses to *Mozert. Phi Delta Kappan,* 68: 447.

Jenkinson, E. B. (1987). The significance of the decision in 'Scopes II.' *Phi Delta Kappan,* 68: 445–50.

Journal after the fact: Holding the line against anarchy. (1987). *The American School Board Journal,* 174(4): 16.

Joyce, R. P. (February 1986). Constitutional protections of teachers and other public employees. *A Legal Memorandum of the National Association of Secondary School Principals,* 1–8.

Joye, E. M. (1978). Law and the laboratory. *The Science Teacher,* 45(6): 23–25.

Jurenas, A. C. (1989). "Instant tenure" or "fair treatment" for probationary teachers? *Education Law Reporter,* 54: 1099.

Kaestle, C. F., & Smith, M. S. (1982). The federal role in elementary and secondary education, 1940–1980. *Harvard Educational Review,* 52: 384–408.

Kamhi, M. M. (1981). Censorship vs. selection—choosing the books our children shall read. *Educational Leadership,* 39(3): 211–15.

Katzenmeyer, W. G., & Surratt, J. E. (1975). Police at the school house. *Phi Delta Kappan,* 57: 206–7.

Kelley, C., & McCarthy, B. (1980). Law in the 80's: Educationel [*sic*] malpractice worying [*sic*] you? *Update on Law-Related Education,* 4(1): 16–20.

Kemerer, F. R. (1984). The legal record: Censorship, academic freedom, and the right to know. *Kappa Delta Pi Record,* 20(3): 73–76.

Kemerer, F. R. (1983). The legal record: Classroom academic freedom: Is it a right? *Kappa Delta Pi Record,* 19(4): 101–4.

Kemerer, F. R. (1983). The legal record: How much education law do you know? *Kappa Delta Pi Record,* 19(3): 76–79.

Keough, K. E., & Seaton, G. (1988). Superintendent's views on AIDS: A national survey. *Phi Delta Kappan,* 69: 358–61.

Keppel, F. (1980). Education in the eighties. *Harvard Educational Review,* 50(2): 149–53.

Kirp, D. L. (1977). Law, politics, and equal educational opportunity: The limits of judicial involvement. *Harvard Educational Review,* 47(2): 117–37.

Kopecky, F. J., & Wilken, R. S. (1980). It all started with ordeals, oaths, and battles. *Update on Law-Related Education,* 4(3): 20–21.

Kraus, L. L. (1984). Dealing constructively with censorship. *Kappa Delta Pi Record,* 20(3): 77–79.

LaMorte, M. W. (1976). What is your school law IQ? *Phi Delta Kappan,* 57: 679–681.

Larke, P. J. (1987). Criminal conduct: A cause for discipline of teachers. *Journal of Law and Education,* 16(1): 63–70.

Larson, D. H. (1983). Firm but fair: Dismissing incompetent staff. *The School Administrator,* 40(2): 28, 35–36.

Larson, D. H. (1983). A model for dismissal of personnel. *The School Administrator,* 40(2): 37.

Leary, J. (1981). *Educators on trial.* Farmington: Action Inservice.

Leary, J. L. (1987). But these six factors have reduced the threat of education malpractice. *The American School Board Journal,* 174(3): 33–34.

Lehr, F. (1985). Academic freedom: A guide to major court cases. *English Journal,* 74(1): 42–44.

Lenich, J. P. (1987). One strike and you're out: An overview of negligence and high school athletics. *Education Law Reporter,* 41: 1.

Lescault, P. R. (1988). Guidelines for developing a discipline code for an effective learning environment. *NASSP Bulletin,* 72(504): 45–46, 48–49.

Lines, P. M. (1985). Teacher competency testing: A review of legal considerations. *Education Law Reporter,* 23: 811.

Mallios, H. C. (1971). Freedom of expression in the public schools and the law. *Journal of Secondary Education,* 46(3): 109–16.

Mazzarella, J. (1982). Self-defense for principals: On staying out of court. *Principal,* 62(2): 22–26.

Mazzarella, J. (1983). Self-defense for principals: On staying out of court (part two). *Principal,* 62(3): 10–15.

McCarthy, M. M. (1985). Legal update: Curriculum controversies and the law. *Educational Horizons,* 64(1): 53–55.

McCarthy, M. M., & Cambron-McCabe, N. H. (1987). *Public school law: Teachers' and students' rights.* (2d ed. Needham Heights, MA: Allyn and Bacon.

McCormick, K. (1986). One-in-a-million odds: Sound policies and expert advice are your best protection against AIDS. *The American School Board Journal,* 173(5): 36–37.

McDaniel, T. R. (1982). The principal's school law quiz. *American Secondary Education,* 12(2): 29–30, 32.

McDaniel, T. R. (1977). Special creation and evolution in the classroom: Old wine in new wineskins? *School Science and Mathematics,* 77(1): 47–52.

McDaniel, T. R. (1979). The teacher's ten commandments: School law in the classroom. *Phi Delta Kappan,* 60: 703–8.

McMahon, J. (1982). Learning or lawsuits: The principal interest: The contract between secondary and elementary administrators' continuing education interests. *American Secondary Education,* 12(2): 7–8.

Meade, E. J., Jr. (1979). Opposing views: Is law polluting the schools? *Update on Law-Related Education,* 3(3): 24–25.

Menacker, J. (1987). *School law: Theoretical and case perspective.* Englewood Cliffs, NJ: Prentice-Hall.

Menacker, J., & Pascarella, E. (1983). How aware are educators of Supreme Court decisions that affect them? *Phi Delta Kappan,* 64: 424–26.

Michel, G. J. (1988–89). Teaching law to school administrators—What should be taught. *National Forum of Educational Administration and Supervision Journal,* 5(2): 108–16.

Morris, A. A. (1986). Affirmative action and "quota" systems. *Education Law Reporter,* 28: 1203.

Morris, A. A. (1980). *The Constitution and American education.* 2d ed. St. Paul, MN: West Publishing.

Morris, A. A. (1985). Seniority, tenure and affirmative action layoffs under Title VII. *Education Law Reporter,* 19: 459.

National Commission on Excellence in Education. (1983). *A nation at risk: The imperative for educational reform.* Washington, D.C.: Department of Education.

Naylor, D. (1979). Classroom strategies: Teaching about students rights and responsibilities. *Update on Law-Related Education,* 3(3): 14–16, 43–47.

Nelson, F. H. (1982). Educators, illegal behavior, and deterrence: A resource allocation approach to malpractice in education. *Educational Administration Quarterly,* 18: 81–94.

Nelson, J. L., & Crum, L. R. (1983). Forum: The power and challenges of local school boards. *American Education,* 19(10): 10–16.

Nolte, M. C. (1974). Brush up in one short sitting: Ten years of tumult in school law, and their lessons. *The American School Board Journal,* 161(1): 48–51.

Nolte, M. C. (1973, September). Concerning the legal status of the principal. *A legal Memorandum of the National Association of Secondary School Principals,* 1–4.

Nolte, M. C. (1984). Crosses teachers bear: The parental right to criticize. *Education Law Reporter,* 18: 1–8.

Nolte, M. C. (1987). Establishing the nexus: A school board primer. *Education Law Reporter,* 38: 1–11.

Nolte, M. C. (1975). How to survive the Supreme Court's momentous new strictures on school people. *The American School Board Journal,* 162(5): 50–53.

Nolte, M. C. (1975). School boards: Your authority has just been restricted; School board members: Your security has just been threatened. *The American School Board Journal,* 162(4): 33–35.

Nolte, M. C. (1983). Teacher dismissal for drug abuse: The legal dilemma. *Education Law Reporter,* 6: 1.

Nolte, M. C. (1986). Teachers may communicate directly with school boards on matters of public concern. *Education Law Reporter,* 27: 443.

Nolte, M. C. (1975). Use and misuse of tests in education: Legal implications. *Educational Horizons,* 54(1): 11–16.

Ornstein, A. C. (1985). The changing federal role in education. *Kappa Delta Pi Record,* 21(3): 85–88.

Orenstein, A. C. (1981). Improving the quality of teachers. *Educational Horizons,* 59(4): 168–72.

Peach, L. J. (1988). Legal literacy: Why do I have to go to school? *Update on Law-Related Education,* 12(1): 23–29, 65.

Pepe, T. J., & Tufts, A. L. (1987). So you want to be a yearbook advisor! *Education Law Reporter,* 37: 1013–27.

Pharis, B. (1980). Personal opinion: Judges are apt to be naif. *The National Elementary Principal,* 59(2): 112.

Phay, R. (1982). Seeking excellence: Not reappointing an "average" teacher in order to employ a better teacher. *Education Law Reporter,* 4: 357.

Phay, R. (1985). What constitutes arbitrary nonrenewal of teachers? *Education Law Reporter,* 21: 773.

Popovich, P. S., & Niles, D. W. (1986). A new court looks at school law. *Education Law Reporter,* 27: 1.

Potter, C. A. (1982). Precautions teachers should take to avoid professional liability. *Kappa Delta Pi Record,* 19(1): 23–24.

Quarles, T. A. (1981). Tort liability and the vo-ag teacher. *The Agricultural Education Magazine,* 54(4): 9–11.

Reed, S. (1986). AIDS in the schools: A special report. *Phi Delta Kappan,* 66: 494–98.

Remley, T. P., Jr., & MacReynolds, V. B. (1988). Due process in dismissals: A reflection of our values. *NASSP Bulletin,* 72(504): 41–44.

Rhode, D. B. (1984). Conflicts of interest in educational reform litigation. *American Journal of Education,* 92(4): 440–72.

Rice, D. R., Strope, J. L., & Brown, C. L. (1981). Test your legal liability IQ. *The Science Teacher,* 48(5): 42–45.

Rodriguez, R. C. (1986). Rules of evidence for due process hearing: Administrative responsibilities. *American Secondary Education,* 15(2): 24–26.

Roos, P. D. (1983). Litigation: A necessary tool for educational reform. *Phi Delta Kappan,* 64: 417–19.

Rosenthal, A., & Fuhrman, S. (1982). State legislatures and education policy: An overview. *Educational Horizons,* 61(1): 4–9, 49.

Rowell, C. G. (1987). Implications of the Tennessee textbook controversy for public education. *Educational Leadership,* 44(8): 14–15.

Russo, C. J. (1987). Drug testing of teachers and the Fourth Amendment. *Education Law Reporter,* 35: 899.

Russo, C. J. (1987). Drug testing of teachers: *Patchogue-Medford Congress of Teachers* revisited. *Education Law Reporter,* 40: 607.

Russo, C. J. (1987). Maternity leave: A working mother's right. *Education Law Reporter,* 39: 7.

Sacken, D. M. (1986). Against the grain: School abuses often are what cause outside intervention in education. *The American School Board Journal,* 173(11): 40–41.

Sacken, D. M. (1988). The limits to a teacher's privacy rights: *Ponton v. Newport News School Board. Education Law Reporter,* 42: 19.

Sametz, L. (1981). The educator's role in the juvenile justice system. *Adolescence,* 16(61): 101–9.

Sametz, L. (1983). Teacher certification programs should require knowledge of children and the law. *Contemporary Education,* 54: 263–66.

Sametz, L., & Mcloughlin, C. S. (1984). Curriculum innovation: Legal education. *Educational Horizons,* 62(3): 113–15.

Sametz, L., Mcloughlin, C., & Streib, V. (1983). Legal education for preservice teachers: Basics or remediation? *Journal of Teacher Education,* 34(2): 10–12.

Savage, D. G. (1987). Watching a changing court: Will the center hold? *Phi Delta Kappan,* 69: 135–37.

Schimmel, D. (1975). The question of academic freedom: The Bill of Rights and the public schools: Change and challenge. *Social Education,* 39: 206–13.

Schimmel, D., & Williams, R. (1984–85). Does due process interfere with school discipline? *The High School Principal,* 68(2): 47–50.

Schuster, J. H. (1982). Out of the frying pan: The politics of education in a new era. *Phi Delta Kappan,* 63: 583–91.

Scott, M. F., & Zirkel, P. A. (1987). The legality of prayer in the public schools: Teachers' knowledge, attitude, and practice. *Education Law Reporter,* 36: 533–44.

Sendor, B. (1987). School law: If you think mass drug tests are dandy for teachers and students, think again. *The American School Board Journal,* 174(4): 26–27.

Sharp, R. E. (1985). Accommodating school employees' religious practices and observances under Title VII. *Education Law Reporter,* 21: 1.

Sharp, R. E. (1987). Title VII's prohibition against retaliation. *Education Law Reporter,* 38: 13.

Shaw, F. W., II (1985). A summary of legal implications of teacher evaluations for merit pay and a model plan. *Educational Administration Quarterly,* 21: 51–69.

Sheffield, W. R. (1978). In defense of principals. *NASSP Bulletin,* 62(421): 16–19.

Siegel, R. V. (1987). Requisites for affirmative action: What do *Wygant; Sheetmetal Workers;* and *Firefighters* mean? *Education Law Reporter,* 38: 399.

Simpson, M. (1988). You and the law: Caveat slaptor—let the paddler beware. *NEA Today,* 6(7): 27.

Simpson, M. (1988). You and the law: Teachers fight right-wing attacks. *NEA Today,* 6(9): 21.

Smalls, O. (1983). A legal framework for academic freedom in public secondary schools. *Journal of Law and Education,* 12(4): 529–59.

Smith, B. O. (1980). Pedagogical education: How about reform? *Phi Delta Kappan,* 62: 87–91.

Spare the rod sparingly? (1970). *The American School Board Journal,* 158(4): 31.

Starr, I. (1988). Legal literacy: Lawyers and the quest for justice. *Update on Law-Related Education,* 12(1): 3–5, 63.

Stelzer, L., & Banthin, J. (1982). Practical law: Teachers do have rights. *Update on Law-Related Education,* 6(2): 41–46.

Strauss, S. (1988). Sexual harassment in the school: Legal implications for principals. *NASSP Bulletin,* 72(506): 93–97.

Strope, J. L. (1988). Teachers with AIDS. *Education Law Reporter,* 47: 827.

Tatel, D. S., & Mincberg, E. M. (1988). Affirmative action decisions in the lower courts: Implications for school boards and educators. *Education Law Reporter,* 42: 705.

Tulloch, R. W. (1981). Could you be found guilty? *The Agricultural Education Magazine,* 54(4): 17.

Tyack, D. (1987). An American tradition: The changing role of schooling and teaching: Was there ever a golden age in teaching? *Harvard Educational Review,* 57(2): 171–77.

Tyack, D., & Hansot, E. (1984). Hard times, then and now: Public schools in the 1930's and 1980's. *Harvard Educational Review,* 54(1): 33–66.

Tyack, D., & Hansot, E. (1982). *Managers of virtue: Public school leadership in America, 1829–1980.* New York: Basic Books.

Ullman, J. A. (1983). Upon the advent of *Perry:* A review and analysis of the constitutional challenges to the use of school mail facilities by minority representatives. *Education Law Reporter,* 7: 475.

Underwood, J. (1987). End sexual harassment of employes, or your board could be held liable. *The American School Board Journal,* 174(4): 43–44.

United States Supreme Court Education Cases. (1990). Rosemount, MN: Data Research, Inc.

Valente, W. D. (1987). *Bowers v. Hardwick* and the homosexual teacher. *Education Law Reporter,* 35: 1.

Valente, W. D. (1982). Federal tort liability for civil rights deprivations in public schools. *Education Law Reporter,* 5: 701.

Valente, W. D. (1987). *Law in the schools,* 2d ed. Columbus, OH: Merrill Publishing Company.

Valente, W. D. (1990). School district and official liability for teacher sexual abuse of students under 42 U.S.C. 1983. *Education Law Reporter,* 57: 645.

Valente, W. D. (1987). Searches of teachers' offices, desks, and files in public schools. *Education Law Reporter,* 39: 931.

Violas, P. (1971). Fear and the constraints on academic freedom of public school teachers. *Educational Theory,* 21(1): 70–80.

Walden, J. C. (1989). Sex discrimination in small school district. *Education Law Reporter,* 49: 1115.

Walden J. C., & Culverhouse, R. (1990). Homosexuality and public education. *Education Law Reporter,* 55: 7.

Walden, J. C., & Deaton, W. L. (1988). Alabama teacher certification test fails. *Education Law Reporter,* 42: 1.

Wasden, F. D., & Thomas, G. J. (1987). *Supreme Court rulings in education: A compendium.* Provo, UT: Brigham Young University.

Washburn, J. W., Jr. (1988). An open letter to my colleagues. *Phi Delta Kappan,* 69: 357.

Welch, I. D., Medeiros, D. C., & Tate, G. A. (1981). Censorship, criticism, creationism: Education, religion, and the new right. *Educational Leadership,* 39(3): 203–8.

Wise, A. E. (1988). The two conflicting trends in school reform: Legislated learning revisited. *Phi Delta Kappan,* 69: 328–33.

The year in review. (1987). *School Law News,* 15(1): 8–10.

Zirkel, P. A. (1988). DeJure: Wrong by Wright: Liability for sexual abuse. *Phi Delta Kappan,* 69: 451–52.

Zirkel, P. A. (1987). The maturing relationship of courts and schools. *Education Law Reporter,* 35: 905–7.

Zirkel, P. A. (1983). The Supreme Court's Perry Education Association decision: Underestimating the importance of the exclusivity principle. *Education Law Reporter,* 11: 1.

Zirkel, P. A. (1978). A test on Supreme Court decisions affecting education. *Phi Delta Kappan,* 59: 521–22, 555.

Zirkel, P. A., & Gluckman, I. B. (1985). It's the law: Dismissal of principals. *Principal,* 65(2): 54–56.

Zirkel, P. A., & Gluckman, I. B. (1986). It's the law: Teacher grievances and the first amendment. *Principal,* 65(5): 47–49.

Zirkel, P. A., & Gluckman, I. B. (1987). A legal brief: Drug testing in public schools. *NASSP Bulletin* (and *National Elementary Principal*), 71(497): 138–41.

Zirkel, P. A., & Gluckman, I. B. (1988). A legal brief: Unfulfilled hiring promises. *NASSP Bulletin,* 72(504): 125–29.

Zirkel, P. A., & Katz, E. H. (1985). The law on agency shop for school district. *Education Law Reporter,* 26: 567.

Zirkel, P. A., & MacMurtrie, F. (1988). A quick quiz on Supreme Court decisions affecting public schools. *Kappa Delta Pi Record,* 24(3): 92–96.

Zirkel, P. A., & Moore, J. T. (1986). Playground accidents: When are you liable? *Principal,* 65(4): 43–46.

Zirkel, P. A., & Reichner, H. F. (1987). Is *in loco parentis* dead? *Phi Delta Kappan*, 68: 466–69.

Zirkel, P. A., & Reichner, H. F. (1986). Is the *in loco parentis* doctrine dead? *Journal of Law and Education,* 15(3): 271–83.

Zirkel, P. A., & Richardson, S. N. (1988). *A Digest of Supreme Court Decisions Affecting Education.* 2d ed. Bloomington, IN: Phi Delta Kappa Educational Foundation.

Zirkel, P. A., & Richardson, S. N. (1989). The "explosion" in education litigation. *Education Law Reporter,* 53: 767.

Zirkel, P. A., & Shulman, B. (1984). Before stepping up to the witness stand, examine these 22 tips on testifying. *The American School Board Journal,* 171(4): 46.

Glossary of Legal Terms

Allegation: A statement of fact made in a legal proceeding.

Appeal: An application by an appellant to a higher court to rectify the order of the court below.

Appellant: One who appeals from a judicial decision.

Appellate court: A court that reviews the decisions of lower courts upon request of losing parties.

Appellee: The person against whom an appeal is taken.

Arbitrary: Not founded in the nature of things; nonrational; not done or acting according to reason or judgment; depending on the will alone.

Breach: A breaking; either the invasion of a right or the violation of a duty.

Capricious: Fickle; characterized by sudden changes or whims.

Cause of action: Basis for a legal claim or lawsuit.

Civil action: An action that has for its object the recovery of private or civil rights or compensation for their infraction.

Collective bargaining: Process of negotiating a labor contract by representatives of labor and management.

Common law: Legal principles derived from usage and custom or from court decisions affirming such usages and custom.

Complaint: The pleading by the party initiating a lawsuit that alleges the grievance and request for relief.

Damages: A pecuniary compensation that may be recovered in the courts by any person who has suffered loss, detriment, or injury, whether to his or her person, property, or rights through the unlawful act or omission or negligence of another.

De facto: In fact; as exists in practice; derived from practice, not created by law.

Defendant: One required to make answer in a lawsuit; the one against whom the suit is brought.

De jure: By right; as exists by law; derived from law.

Due process: Law in the regular course of administration through courts; rules and forms that have been established for the protection of private rights.

Ex rel: At the instance of; on behalf of; on relation of information.

Grievance: Formal complaint, usually in regard to alleged breach of negotiated contract.

Host power: Inherent power to care for the welfare and safety of others.

Immunity: Exemption from legal obligations or liability.

Injunction: A writ to force a party to refrain from doing something.

In loco parentis: In place of the parent; charged with some of the parents' rights, duties, and responsibilities.

In re: In the affair of; in the matter of; concerning.

Malice: Hatred, ill will.

Mandamus: A writ to force a party to carry out a duty it is under legal obligation to perform.

Mandate: A legal command.

Motion: A request for a court ruling.

Opinion: A court's explanation of its decision.

Original jurisdiction: The jurisdiction of a court to entertain a case in its inception.

Per se: By itself, alone.

Petition: Written application to the court for the redress of a wrong or the grant of a privilege or license.

Plaintiff: Person who brings an action; the one who sues by filing a complaint.

Police power: Inherent power to enact laws for the comfort, health, and prosperity of the state; the right to modify for the common good.

Precedent: A decision considered as furnishing an example or authority for an identical or similar case arising afterward on a similar question of law.

Prima facie: At first view; taken as is if not disproved.

Remand: An action by an appellate court to send the case back to the court from which it came for further proceedings there.

Review: Judicial reconsideration of a decision by an administrative agency or a lower court.

School code: A compilation of statutes, divided into chapters, subheadings, and sections, with a table of contents and an index, that concerns schools; a collection of the laws dealing with the schools.

Stare decisis: Adherence to precedent.

Statute: Law enacted by the legislative power of a country or state.

Summary judgment: A decision made by a court in response to one party that believes there is no genuine issue of material fact and that he or she is entitled to prevail as a matter of law.

Tort: Legal injury or wrong committed upon the person or property of another independent of contract.

Trespass: The unauthorized entry upon, taking, or interfering with the property of another.

Trial court: Court of original jurisdiction, which hears the evidence and rules on a case the first time it comes before the court system.

Ultra vires: Beyond the power.

Void: Null; ineffectual; having no legal force or binding effect.

Index*

*Bold-faced terms and pages refer to chapter by same title. Subentries under bold-faced chapter titles refer exclusively to references in that chapter.